Dangerous Dreamers

T0369058

Dangerous Dreamers

✦

The Australian Anti-Democratic Left and Czechoslovak Agents

Peter Hruby

iUniverse, Inc.
New York   Bloomington

iUniverse books may be ordered through booksellers or by contacting:

iUniverse
1663 Liberty Drive
Bloomington, IN 47403
www.iuniverse.com
1-800-Authors (1-800-288-4677)

ISBN: 978-1-4401-7499-5 (pbk)
ISBN: 978-1-4401-7501-5 (cloth)
ISBN: 978-1-4401-7500-8 (ebk)

Printed in the United States of America

iUniverse rev. date: 12/31/2009

To Milena, Jeffrey, Nathaniel, and Caleb

Contents

Preface

Peter Hruby's valuable book, highlighting the successful efforts by the Soviet and Czechoslovak foreign intelligence services to recruit and suborn left-wing intellectuals and journalists in Australia, sheds important and disturbing light on an underexplored aspect of the Cold War. Even though the large majority of leftist intellectuals in the West were not traitors to their countries, far too many were remarkably complacent about the minority of leftists in their midst who actively colluded with Communist governments and worked to subvert democratic freedoms. Hruby's book shows that this effort was not a trivial dimension of the "active measures" adopted by the Soviet and Czechoslovak state security organs. On the contrary, the Soviet-bloc countries pursued an aggressive program of subversion and propaganda in the West, using leftists as their agents and intermediaries. What Hruby shows about Australia is also true of Western Europe and even North America.

Hruby's book is important not only because of the evidence it meticulously presents and the fascinating analyses it provides of numerous Australian leftists, but also because it has a direct bearing on political debates today. Almost all of the individuals discussed by Hruby are still held in high regard both in Australia and outside. Even a notorious Communist propagandist like Wilfred Burchett, whose work in favor of totalitarian regimes deserve eternal condemnation, has undergone a partial rehabilitation in Australia in recent years, thanks to the determined efforts of his son and the naïveté of the Australian media and intellectual circles. No one would ever think of granting such leniency to an agent of the Nazis, but Burchett is treated with relative indulgence. Hruby's book will make this double standard more difficult to sustain

Finally, Hruby's book is important because it shows the immense value of the huge repositories on which he relies. Although Hruby has done extensive archival work in the United States and Australia as well as the Czech Republic, the heart of his book is what he found in the former Czechoslovak State Security archives. Some former Communist countries, notably Russia, have kept their Communist-era state security archives tightly sealed, but the Czech Republic, to its great credit, has decided that a full reckoning with the past is essential in a democratic society. For researchers, this is a valuable boon. I serve on the advisory board of the Czech government's Institute for the Study of Totalitarian Regimes, which oversees the repository now known as Archiv bezpečnostních složek (ABS). The ABS houses all the Czechoslovak state security documents from 1945 through early 1990, covering the entire Communist period. These files are now completely open, and I have been strongly encouraging researchers to make use of them, knowing that they contain an enormous amount of evidence about key topics in the Cold War. Hruby began his work even before the files were completely open, but the opening of the archives has enabled him to gather a vast amount of evidence about left-wing intellectuals in Australia and their connections with Communist dictatorships. He has produced what is by far the most authoritative book on the subject, and I hope that the example of this book will encourage other researchers to travel to Prague to work in the ABS.

Mark Kramer
Harvard University

Acknowlegments

One day in 1996 in Perth, Western Australia, a colleague of mine, Patrick O'Brien, came to see me together with Peter Kelly, who was for the occasion coming from the other side of the continent. They came with the news that in Prague, Czech Republic, the until then secret files of the political police, StB, were opened and available to researchers. They asked me if I would be willing to fly to Prague and investigate if anything could be found concerning Australia. Another democratic Australian who was worried about the prevalent anti-British, anti-American, but pro-Soviet attitude among the academics and journalists, Chris Mitchell, then editor-in-chief of the Queensland paper published in Brisbane, *Courier Mail*, was willing to sponsor my investigation. It was my duty to help. I also wanted to know more about the secret history of the modern world that I only had glimpses of from books.

I was myself surprised by my findings in Prague. Important Australians, like naïve historian Manning Clark, and others, among them Wilfred Burchett and Ian Milner, acted as Communist agents or advocates of Communism. The Brisbane paper then published two articles of mine based on these discoveries. It created a panic among pro-Soviet intellectuals.

My second flight to Prague was not so successful, althouth I discovered some complementary facts. Peter Kelly since then regularly has been informing me about new developments in Australia in relation to the topic of this book. I am very grateful to these three gentlemen for their iniciative and support, since it led me into a new and fascinating path of following the very important world of secret deals.

On my own I then explored the very rich files lodged in Canberra. Kind archivists kept sending me thousands of photocopies of documents from files that I have selected from the lists I was supplied with. It was costly but very rich and enjoyable. I also owe a debt of gratitude to

Patrik Virkner whe kept sending me from Prague to Perth detailed information about his findings in the police archives. Then I traveled to the United States. From my stay at the Hoover Institution I especially like to remember friendly and efficient Blanka Pasternak. I am grateful to Barry W. Mawn and Michael J. Armes from the U.S. Department of Justice. Thanks to them, my request under the Freedom of Information Act to have access to the until then secret file on Ian Milner was made available to me. In the East I am very grateful to Dr Zdenek David, who led me to a few specialized archives I did not know about. I am also obliged to several universities' librarians and archivists all over the United States and Canada whose names remained unknown to me.

When teaching at Charles University in the Czech Republic, I did not know how to proceed with the publication of the result of more than ten years of research and work on the manuscript, Pavel Palecek helped with a Czech translation and publication of a different and shorter version in Brno, and arranged its public introduction in Prague. I owe him gratitude for such an encouragement.

Last but not least, my wife Shirley, before her untimely death, helped me in many different ways, especially by her native American English.

Out of the named representatives of my publisher iUniverse I am thankful to kind and professional help by consultants Kyle Randolph, Cathy Raymond, and Lacy Perry. I appreciate the professional way my editor Laura McGin improved the style and appearance of the book. No one, of course, is responsible for eventual mistakes or errors but the author.

Glossary

AA: Australian Archives
A.C.T.U.: Australian Council of Trade Unions
AMFA: Archive of the Ministry of Foreign Affairs in Prague
AMI: Archive ot the Ministry of the Interior
AMO: Archiv Ministerstva Obchodu [Archive of theTrade Ministry]
AMV: Archiv Ministerstva vnitra [Archive of the Ministry of the Interior]
ASIO: Australian Security Intelligence Organization
CC: Central Committee
CHEKA: All-Russian Extraordinary Commission for Combatting Counter-Revolution and Sabotage
CIA: Central Intelligence Agency
CPA: Communist Party of Australia
CPCZ: Communist Party of Czechoslovakia
CPSU: Communist Party of the Soviet Union
CR: Czech Republic
CSR: Czechoslovak Republic
CSSR: Czechoslovak Socialist Republic
CUZ: Ceskoslovensky ústav zahranicní [Czechoslovak Foreign Institute]
CZMFA: Czechoslovak Ministry of Foreign Affairs
FBI: Federal Bureau of Investigation
Kc: Koruna ceska [Czech crown]
KGB: Komitet Gosudarstvennoy Bezopasnosti [Committee of State Security]
Ksc: Koruna ceskoslovenská [Czechoslovak crown]
MZV: Ministerstvo zahranicních vecí [Ministry of Foreign Affairs]
SCA: State Central Archive in Prague

SSR: Svaz sovetskych socialistickych republik [Union of Soviet Socialist Republics]
USSR: Union of Soviet Socialist Republics
UV: Ustredni vybor [Central Committee]

Introduction

This is a book about dreams and illusions that were truly dangerous because the dreamers sought to destroy Australian democracy and in its place install a Stalinist dictatorship of the type found in Central and Eastern Europe and other regions. In these countries, similar dreamers helped ruthless dictators achieve power; dictators who killed, imprisoned, put people into concentration camps, or exiled millions of democrats, all because, according to Marxist-Leninist tenets, they were obstructing the way to the happy Communist future that never came.

It will be shown how the Australian dreamers were being manipulated by Soviet and Czechoslovak secret agents, among others, who on their march to global expansion also targeted Australia. Documentation found in Czech, Australian, American, and Soviet secret archives will be used to demonstrate the often successful methods foreign agents used to persuade prominent Australians to cooperate and commit treasonable deeds. It will be revealed how naïve the illusions were that drove these Australians. The pro-Soviet or pro-Chinese dreamers had blind faith in a murderous conspiracy that they did not bother to truly understand. It led some of them to treason, collaboration with totalitarian regimes, and betrayal of the very ideals that motivated them.

The distaste they felt for the wars, poverty, unemployment, and the imperfections of democracy was justified. Their hope to improve the lot of their compatriots and other people around the world was genuine. However, their understanding of the societies that they believed had reached a higher stage of development was negligible and—more often than not—incorrect. They believed what they wanted to believe and generally refused to learn the truth. They were supported by their certainty that Marxism-Leninism, or Maoism, gave them the proper understanding of historical development. They trusted the dictates of their ideology and did not acknowledge its limitations or fallacy. Their utopianism became a substitute for religion. Socialism was supposed to solve all human problems and even help people achieve universal personal happiness. Dreams of a violent revolution appealed to intellectuals, professors of history, and other self-professed lovers of humanity whose hate of their own bourgeois class was stronger than their desire to learn about the existing "socialist" countries that were in fact much worse than their own capitalist societies.

Only rarely has there appeared a study of this strange phenomenon in Australia, and to this day misguided believers in Marxist-Leninist utopia are able to keep their influential positions. In other countries, many books analyzing this ideological mythology appeared. For instance, in 1981, Paul Hollander published a book entitled *Political Pilgrims: Travels of Western Intellectuals to the Soviet Union, China, and Cuba 1928–1978*[1]. It is an incredible collection of accounts by Western travelers of their journeys to police states in which they were enchanted by many things in spite of the fact that they were visiting the harshest enslavers in the world. Such was the power of their wishful thinking and their hosts' effective propaganda that they came back home persuaded that they had witnessed realized utopias. Hollander came to the conclusion that the concept of "the intellectual" needs revision: "The capacity to cast aside critical faculties in exchange for credulity and unrestrained admiration is not the only trait that has to be entered into the revised conception of the intellectual."[2] Other traits he mentioned include the lack of commitment to freedom, the propensity to disclaim information contrary to illusions, the depersonalizing of victims, double standards, and selective moral indignation.[3] The author feared that "Western intellectuals will contribute to the destruction of their relatively free societies, in part because of their illusions about other societies and their recurrent fantasies of new forms of liberation and collective gratification."[4]

---

1   New York: Oxford University Press, 1981.
2   Ibid., p. 419.
3   Ibid., pp. 416–428.
4   Ibid., p. 435.

My Personal Experience, Study, and Teaching

Refugees who migrated to Australia from Central and East European countries that had become victims of the Soviet expansion had the advantage of knowledge of Communist methods of infiltration, subversion, and domination. Their reports were not trusted by Australian intellectuals who believed they were biased because they had been hurt personally. In the same way, decades before, Czechoslovakia accepted hundreds of thousands of refugees from the Soviet Union, but Czechs did not learn from them the nature of Russian Communism. The Czechs considered themselves more intelligent and civilized than the Russians. In the fifties, the French were telling refugees coming from the East that what happened there could not happen in France, because the French were more advanced and their Communists much more decent and democratic than the Russian, Czech, and other Communists. This was another unfortunate example of "he who does not learn from the past is doomed to repeat it."

Between 1945 and 1948, I saw the looming disaster that was to befall Czechoslovakia at the hands of the Soviet Union. I also saw how eagerly the Soviets were being aided by Czech and Slovak Communists and their fellow-travelers. I left the country in August 1948 and for the next fifty years attempted to study the whole question. Since 1965, I have warned my students against the danger of naïve illusions about the real enemies of progress. From 1951 to 1964, I spent thirteen years closely following daily developments in the Soviet empire while working for Radio Free Europe in Munich and New York City broadcasting to Czechoslovakia.

I published two books about the dreams and illusions of Czech and Slovak intellectuals and about their gradual disappointments once the anticipated "just society" turned out to be much more cruel and unjust than the democratic one they helped to destroy.[5] When I came to Australia to teach in 1971, my university colleagues, whose sentiments were mostly pro-Soviet and anti-American, thought that I did not support Communism like they did because of my personal hurts. Full of misconceptions, they could not understand that although I was not personally harmed by the Communists, I spoke out against the Soviet Union because of the terrible damage it was causing to hundreds of millions of people.

One student called my attention to a publication entitled *Soviet Society: A Study in Communism*. In 1971, the Education Department of Western Australia distributed it to its high schools for the enlightenment of students. I could not believe my eyes. The Soviet Embassy would not have dared to publish the propaganda that the West Australian Ministry for Education put out. (Although the Soviet Embassy's input was acknowledged.) The eighty-two-page booklet has a statue of Lenin being revered by children on its cover. In a crossword puzzle, Lenin and Stalin are identified as "strong leaders."[6] Marx's ideas are misrepresented, since the booklet claims that according to Marx, "the workers ... will need a strong leader."[7] That contradicts the *Communist Manifesto*'s assertion that there is no need for a Communist Party and ignores Marx's concern about "strong leaders." Introductory pages five and six demonstrate to West Australian students Marx's ideas about capitalism and Communism. Cartoons accompany the propaganda text: fat capitalists with big bags of money marked with dollar signs face hungry-looking workers carrying heavily loaded sacks. The text is explicit: "Capitalists exploit labor.... Capitalists accumulate more and more wealth. Workers always suffer."

On the next page, smiling workers with bags of money are joyfully marching toward the future, and the text stresses the happiness of people under Communism: "The majority (workers) rule, all are

---

5   *Fools and Heroes: The Changing Role of Communist Intellectuals in Czechoslovakia* [Oxford: Pergamon, Press, 1980] and *Daydreams and Nightmares: Czech Communist and Ex-Communist Literature 1917– 1987* [East European Monographs, distributed by Columbia University Press, New York, 1990].

6   *Soviet Society,* p. 10.

7   Ibid., p. 7.

equal. Workers work harmoniously together. Profits are shared among workers. The state (meaning all the people) own and control means of production.... Free education is available for all children. One political party—the workers' party—will rule the country." The last sentence was allegedly taken from the *Communist Manifesto*. Go and look for it; you will not find it. In Perth, even Marx was adapted to Stalinism. Several pages are devoted to questions that students have to answer by repeating Communist slogans so they can be gently brainwashed. Many pages were devoted to useless descriptions of the Soviet government, falsely claiming that the Soviet Union is governed according to its constitution. Elections are described as free and democratic! "The First Secretary Leonard Ilyich Brezhnev ... is good looking and seems straight forward. He moves like an ex-athlete with a 'middle age spread'."[8]

Reading about Soviet agriculture, students were taught that "small farms were grouped together to make larger units." The "collectives ... belonged to the farmers who worked them."[9] It says nothing about the horrors of the collectivization and the ten million peasants who were massacred on their farms, died of starvation, or in concentration camps.

In a chapter devoted to "Work," the Ministry for Education of Western Australia demonstrates the Soviet love for work by reproducing parts of the trial of the world-famous poet, "Parasite Brodsky." The judge is repeatedly quoted denouncing his poetry as "your so-called poems." He is asked why he changed jobs thirteen times since 1956. When Brodsky answers, "I began to work at the age of fifteen; I found everything interesting; I changed jobs because I wanted to find out as much as possible about life and people," it is not good enough for the judge. He asks, "And what good have you done for your country?" Writing poetry and translations was considered anti-Soviet.[10]

All over the world, the sham trial and mistreatment of Iosif Alexandrovich Brodsky—known as Joseph Brodsky since his emigration to the US, Nobel Prize winner for literature in 1977—was considered a major totalitarian scandal, but not in Western Australia, where he was

---

8   Ibid., p. 29.
9   Ibid., p. 47.
10   Ibid, pp. 64–66.

shamed and Soviet unjust "justice" celebrated as a good example to students. They were even asked to playact the court case in class!

Teachers were issued an additional booklet of thirty-one pages with suggestions on how they should use *Soviet Society* for proper indoctrination into Communism. For instance, students should be asked: "Write a letter to your local Communist Party branch applying for Membership. Outline why you wish to become a member and why you think you should be accepted."[11]

Many class exercises are suggested, such as to play as the politburo, electoral officers, and select "enemies of the people" and "find out what can be done about them."[12] Great stress is put on identifying "what were Karl Marx's ideas concerning social class."[13] How are the students to be marked? Simple. "Allocate marks for students' reports which test the hypothesis: Soviet society is a classless society." [14] In the book for students, there are no doubts expressed about the validity of this ridiculously false claim.

The supplemental booklet advises teachers that they must properly use the trial of poet Brodsky. As a quiz, students are to answer true or false: "The Communist Party encourages its members to be hardworking."[15] Based on the book's material, the only non-failing answer is affirmative. Students playing part in the Brodsky trial are to pronounce a verdict. "Caution students that they are trying Brodsky according to Soviet law and that *they must think within the framework of Communism.*"[16]

Several additional pages instruct teachers about Marxism and the Soviet official claim that the dictatorship was a democratic government. Very rarely is there a hint of criticism, and when there is, it is circumscribed as in the following false statement: "Despite any social differentiation [based on education level and subsequent occupation] which may exist in the U.S.S.R., Soviet society still appears more flexible than many modern Western societies. There is more opportunity for and more evidence of 'social mobility' in the U.S.S.R.

---

11   *Teacher's Notes*, pp.10 and 33.
12   Ibid., p. 10.
13   Ibid., p. 15.
14   Ibid., p. 17.
15   Ibid., p. 18.
16   Ibid. My italics.

than in the U.S.A. or the U.K."[17] (Mobility to where? Concentration camps?)

High school students in Western Australia were thus properly indoctrinated into Communism. Once when I talked in Perth about Stalin's crimes in my class on Soviet history, a girl started to cry and vehemently protested that I was lying; she thought Stalin was a great humanitarian and a strong leader of a happy society.

When I wrote a long scholarly critique of the booklets and sent it to the premier and the minister for education of Western Australia, I was assured that they did not find any bias in the publications. No journal wanted to publish any criticism. A TV channel put on a panel of high school kids who liked the book. The dean of our school saved me from disciplinary action when to an inquiry by university authorities he said that I had the right to voice academic criticism. Another inquiry, this time into my grading, failed when my colleagues wanted to chase me out claiming that my unusually high number of students was due to my giving them better marks than average. The difference proved to be negligible. At the same time, under different pretexts, a colleague who taught the facts about Soviet history at the University of Western Australia was threatened with expulsion. Only one legislator and one teacher objected to the falsifications of the *Soviet Society*, but also without success.

During the controversy over *Soviet Society*, I met some of the key players. The person responsible for secondary education in Western Australia seemed like a nice man, totally innocent of any suspicion that students were being manipulated. Meeting the author of the book was interesting. He was a Greek, one of thousands that Soviet secret services kidnapped during the civil war in Greece in order to indoctrinate them for future use. This practice was similar to what Lenin did with Russian children who lost parents during the war following his coup d'état, the so-called *bezprizorni*. They were prepared for their service in prisons and concentration camps, since their hate for the class enemy was genuine. The Greek author told me that he was grateful to the Communists for everything they had done for him.[18]

---

17   Ibid., p. 28.

18   For years, Australian officials tried to help Czechoslovak immigrants to get passports and exit visas for their relatives, mainly their children, to be able to join them in their new home. The "Operation Reunion"

To my surprise, I realized rather soon that I had come to a country that was being systematically conditioned for a future takeover by Communist conspirators and their fellow-travelers. Once when replacing a colleague who happened to be unavailable, I took part in a committee session selecting books for courses on China. I objected to the biased selection. All proposed sources were Communist or pro-Communist and pro-Mao. The other members looked at me askance. *How did he get here?* Nothing was changed. Indoctrination was to go on, systematically.

Several generations of Australian students were educated by teachers and professors who believed in the Soviet Union and Mao's China. They were brainwashed into disliking Australian democracy and its American and British allies. That is one of the reasons much attention will be paid in this book to Professor Manning Clark. He and other educators like him bear a great responsibility for the damage done. Their influence was great, and judging by library books I have checked, they were read and believed much more than members of the Communist Party. It is just anecdotal evidence but surprisingly extensive; books by Australian Communists or by Marx and Lenin were rarely borrowed from the libraries and looked untouched. On the other hand, books by Manning Clark, Humphrey McQueen, and Wilfred Burchett circulated often and were heavily underlined on many pages.

Reader Frank Knopfelmacher, maligned as a Cold War anti-Communist warrior, and I had a modest advantage against our pro-Communist colleagues in that they dreamed about the benefits of Communism, but we knew its horrors from our own experiences as well as from our study. We could recognize Communist methods, strategies, and even the types of people serving the cause, their lack of moral scruples and intentional propaganda lies. We could see behind the facade that our colleagues often did not even dare to suspect it was a facade. They believed that anti-Communism was wrong, part

---

did not have much success. When in 1962 the situation improved, four exit visas were issued in Prague to Czechs but nineteen to Greek nationals leaving Czechoslovakia [Australian Archives, Canberra A1838/2, Item 1531/17 PT1, Department of Immigration in a letter to the Secretary, Department of External Affairs, 2.18.1964]. Were the Czechs getting rid of the Greeks or rather were they sending their agents to Australia?

and parcel of Fascist or extremely conservative hatred of peace and of everything progressive. Communist propaganda quite successfully established such a distrust of anti-Communism.

WHY PRAGUE?

Czechoslovak Communists were heavily engaged in targeting Australia as a future satellite of the Soviet Union. Until 1996, however, in spite of a far-reaching study of world Communism, I did not have any idea of the scope of their activities. Communist actions in Australia were mentioned rarely and briefly in books devoted to the history of the Soviet Union, its satellites, and other Communist countries; almost all such references were included in memoirs or monographs written by Czech Communists who left Czechoslovakia after the Soviet invasion in 1968. Research in Czech secret archives in Prague since 1996 exposed the serious role Soviet secret services assigned to their Czech and Slovak collaborators.

They were engaged in penetration of several countries, not only Australia; they had noteworthy success in controlling the French Communist Party,[19] several important members of the British Parliament, and trade unionists. Here we will concentrate only on their activities in Australia. To a certain degree, it would help to make a comparative study of the Australian and Czechoslovak situations.

After the Communist coup in February 1948, the capital city of Czechoslovakia began to play a major role in the Soviet conspiracy to prepare future takeovers in other countries, Australia among them. A whole group of world organizations led by trusted Communist operatives existed in Prague. Some of these organizations started to be built soon after the end of World War II, showing Stalin's long-term planning once it was clear that the war would be won. However, after the coup, their activities could no longer be hampered by members of Czech democratic parties whose "moral prejudices"—according to the

---

19   Eugen Fried, born in 1900 in Eastern Slovakia, translator of Karel Capek into Hungarian, who helped to Stalinize the CPCz in 1928, as a Comintern agent Stalinized the French Communist Party in 1930 and was in charge of it behind the scene until WWII. See Annie Kriegel and Stephane Courtois, *Eugen Fried, Le Grand Secret du PCF* [Paris: Seuil, 1997].

Stalinist jargon—were preventing them from mercilessly pursuing the aims and orders of Moscow's directorate.

Several Australian Communists and fellow-travelers worked in Prague from around 1948 on. This is only a partial list: Dave Bearlin, Robert Noel Ebbels, Helen Ginty, Ken and Beth Gott, Jack Hutson, Stephen and Nita Murray-Smith, Arthur and Kath Pike, Jack Redouf, Ken and Moira Tolhurst, Ian Turner, and Bert Williams. They worked for the International Union of Students (IUS) in its Secretariat or in its Press and Information Service, for World Students News, and for Telepress. They came from Melbourne and Sydney universities and most of them were members of the Australian Union of Students (AUS) and of the Communist Party of Australia (CPA). Besides the IUS, there were other important Soviet front organizations operating from Prague: the World Federation of Trade Unions, the World Council of Churches, the World Peace Council, the World Association of Journalists, Telepress, the Communist Party Training School, the Revolutionary Institute of Linguistics, and others. Also many Australian Communists, trade unionists, and fellow-travelers came to Prague on the way to Moscow and Peking.

Why were Czechoslovak Communists entrusted with such an important part in Soviet attempts to infiltrate and use world organizations for preparation for future takeovers? First, Czech and Slovak agents were much more well-liked and much less suspect than Soviet citizens. They were rarely thought to have ulterior motives. Many foreigners believed that Czechoslovakia continued to be a democracy and that the February coup was a genuine people's revolution. They were also fooled by election results showing 99 percent support for the Communist government, masked as the National Front, composed of several Czech and Slovak parties (led by Communist agents). Foreign sympathizers did not know, or did not want to know, that election results were always decided before election day by the politburo of the Communist Party. Compared with Soviet agents, Czechs and Slovaks knew foreign languages and had a general cultural knowledge which had yet to be taught to Soviet agents. In many international organizations outside of Czechoslovakia, and in the United Nations and its agencies, Czechs were in leading positions, having been installed there by the Soviets with other nations' consent. After the Soviet Invasion in 1968, they had to be replaced, mainly by Romanians who also seemed to be more neutral than the Russians.

The second reason Czechs served Soviet endeavors so well was that between the two world wars, Czechoslovakia was the only state in Central Europe with a democratic government. The Communist Party could exist legally until the end of the thirties. In the highly industrialized state, the party was well supported in free elections. Large parts of the Czech and Slovak intelligentsia, especially writers, were members of the party or were at least pro-Soviet and left-leaning. Therefore, after the end of World War II, the Communist Party of Czechoslovakia (CPCZ) had at its disposal many willing supporters, especially among prominent writers, journalists, professors, teachers, and artists. Between 1945 and 1948, almost all my professors at Charles University in Prague were Communists or pro-Soviet, pro-Russian dreamers. Deceived by Western allies in the Munich Agreement of 1938, the political orientation of large segments of the population and even of non-Communist politicians was more pro-Russian than pro-Western.

Finally, the Communist takeover of 1948 was carefully and capably prepared by Czechoslovak Communists during World War II in Moscow who planned the strategy of a united front with a limited number of political parties dominated by Communists and their agents in the other parties. The largest pre-war Czech agriculture party was banned, accused of collaboration with the Germans. Since May 1945, the Communists took over all important positions of power and influence in such institutions as the army, police, trade unions, media, and associations of students, women, writers, artists, and journalists. The total takeover was just a question of timing once the propaganda role of the so-called Czechoslovak bridge between the West and the East, demonstrating Soviet willingness to cooperate with the West, exhausted its usefulness.

SOVIET ARCHIVES DEMYTHOLOGIZE THE PEOPLE'S REVOLUTION

The myths of the Czechoslovak independent path to socialism without Soviet interference and the spontaneous revolution by Czechoslovak people in February 1948 were both proved false by the recent publication of Soviet documents from the period. On the basis of Russian archives, Valentina V. Maryna, senior researcher at the Institute of Slavonic and Balcan Studies, Academy of Sciences of the Russian Federation, Moscow, wrote: "Let us stress the word declaration [of Soviet foreign policy in relation to Czechoslovakia] because in fact it did not concern the substance of executed policy but its wrapping up into verbally appropriate proclamations that were supposed to create the impression that the principle on non-interference into internal affairs of the CSR is being maintained."[20]

In a special report to the Soviet foreign minister, Vyacheslav M. Molotov, from the Soviet ambassador in London, Ivan M. Majskij, dated January 11, 1944, a special role was assigned to Czechoslovakia: "SSSR is intent on advantageously creating a strong Czechoslovakia ... to become our front bastion of influence."[21]

According to Valentyna V. Maryna, Stalin changed his original policy of a parliamentary way to socialism in Czechoslovakia. Now he requested a revolutionary seizure of power by the Communist Party and blamed it for its previous implementation. At the founding meeting of Cominform, the secretary general of the CPC, Rudolf Slánský, bending to Soviet pressure, denounced Edvard Beneš and Jan Masaryk as agents of Anglo-American imperialism and announced the forthcoming crushing of the "reaction" with the support of "wide masses." Maryna wrote, "The plan of an attack against the 'reaction' was discussed at a meeting of the CPCZ Central Committee on 2 October 1947, and we have to admit that it was executed as quick as by lightning: begun by the 'discovery' of a so-called anti-State conspiracy in Slovakia and culminating in the February victory of the CPC."[22]

20   "Od důvěry k podezíravosti: Sovětští a českoslovenští komunisté v létech 1945–48" [From Trust to Distrust: Soviet and Czechoslovak Communists in 1945–48] *Soudobé dějiny* [Contemporary History] (Prague), Vol. IV, Nos. 3-4, 1997, p. 453. Her Soviet source is *Rossijskij centr chranenia i izucenia dokumentov neovejsej istorii*, 17-126-1083, 256, 258.

21   Maryna, op.cit., p. 452? quoting from *SSSR i germanskij vopros: 1941-1949 gg.* Dokumenty z Archiva vnesnej politiky Rossijskoj federacii, Vol. 1, Moscow 1996, pp. 342 and 353.

22   *The Cominform:* The Minutes of Three Conferences: 1947/1948/1949. *Annali* (Milan), pp. 146 and 282. Quoted by Maryna, op. cit., p. 466.

Another Russian author, Galina P. Murashko, head researcher at the Institute of Slavonic and Balcan Studies in Moscow, whose contribution to the second session of the Commission of Historians and Archivists of the Czech Republic and the Russian Federation of April 28–29, 1997 appeared in the Czech journal *Contemporary History*, wrote in detail about Soviet systematic pressure on Prague Communists to seize total power: "Moscow evidently was greatly interested in solving the question of power in Czechoslovakia and in bringing an end to the coalition government before the spring elections of 1948."[23] Murashko summarized her study:

> The foreign policy department of the CC CPSU … at that time was working intensively on justification of the need for changing the leadership of Communist parties of Eastern Europe in order to introduce in the political arena functionaries who are willing to unconditionally accept the Soviet model of society's development.… The Communist victory in February 1948 was a prologue to complete subordination of all public life in Czechoslovakia to total control by the CC CPSU.[24]

What a coincidence that so many people's democracies leaders were soon executed or died "of natural causes."

After the coup that was successfully masked as constitutional, thanks to the strength and guile of the Communists and the weakness and illusions of their democratic opponents, much was written in Marxist journals about the so-called Prague model of transition to a Communist dictatorship by peaceful means of "people's democracy." This model was recommended in Moscow as suitable for developed democratic countries, such as Australia, that were not yet ripe

---

23   "Únorová politická krize roku 1948 v československu a 'sovětský faktor': Z materiálů ruských archivů [February Poltical Crisis in Czechoslovakia and the 'Soviet Factor': Materials from Russian Archives], *Soudobé dějiny*, IV, 3-4/97, p. 272.

24   Ibid., p. 475.

for a violent seizure of power by the Lenin-Trotsky method. It is understandable that Czech and Slovak Communists who had personal experience with its implementation were highly regarded as useful for its application in Australia.

The future developments did show, however, that there was a problem with this model if applied to a country without the Red Army on its borders as it was in Poland, Hungary, and Czechoslovakia. In Australia, there were no Soviet armed forces present nor any immediate threat of them. The model advocated a gradual, parliamentary approach to socialism, but when Gough Whitlam introduced gradual reforms in Australia that by some could be interpreted as a proper way to the final socialist takeover, more radical Communists or fellow-travelers accused him of collaboration with democratic-bourgeois forces, thus disarming the nascent revolution.

THE PROBLEM OF PERSONAL RESPONSIBILITY

The millennial hope encouraged by Hegel, Marx, and Lenin with their scenario of overcoming the shortcomings of modern capitalist society was so strong that it took a long time to grasp its falsity. Similarly, we can observe how other messianic hopes of a final solution to human problems only very slowly lose their attraction, undermined by reason and science.

Marxism and Leninism grew out of the weaknesses of capitalism and poorly realized democracies. Idealistic dreamers hoped to create a better and more just order. The trouble with their efforts was that by attaching their dream to a system of states with police dictatorships, they lost any real chance of improving their societies and, on the contrary, threatened their survival. However, the dream was so strong, so obsessive, that many believers only very slowly—and some never—admitted that they were wrong.

In all countries that realized the promise, intellectuals gradually came to the conclusion that they had helped bring into power not idealists like themselves, but cruel and cynical dictators bent on killing and suppressing anybody who dared to oppose their tyranny and exploitation. When some of the dreamers complained that what they got was not what they fought for, they were victimized too. That would have been their fate even in Australia had they succeeded in their effort to replace the bourgeois leaders with the proletarians who usually came from the strata of the lumpen-proletariat and lumpen-intelligentsia.

In a review of Stuart Macintire's book *The Reds: The Communist Party of Australia from its Origins to Illegality* (1998), Peter Coleman quoted the former Communist author's implicit self-criticism. He cast a cool but fresh eye over pre-war Communist leaders. Lance Sharkey was an "uncouth, scruffy" lift-driver whose "binges in Moscow were notorious." J. B. Miles was a hypocrite of "libidinous sanctimony." Jock Garden was a "plausible rogue." Bert Moxon was a "blustering con-man," always able to open any lock. Bill Earsman, "secretive and self-serving," took to bouts of heavy drinking in Moscow, interspersed with casual "knee-tremblers" in the foreign quarter.[25]

Stalin could be counted as belonging to the strata of the lumpen-proletariat, so much hated and feared by Karl Marx. Among other dictators ruling over Communist societies, the first two Czechoslovak "workers presidents" were also suspect "workers": Antonín Zápotocký used to play accordion in taverns before he embarked on a career of organizing workers for the Communist Party, and Klement Gottwald also very quickly preferred party agitation to manual work.

Intellectuals who have access to universities, media, and publications bear great responsibility for what they teach and preach. They are responsible for the consequences of their messages. Therefore, this book—like my previous publications—concentrates on a few selected individuals representing different aspects of the dangerous dream. Influential public personalities should know the facts and reality of politics, not just their fanciful ideas about it. Because they have the power to affect history, they should carefully study what is available in books and testimonies of live witnesses.

All the radical idealists presented in this volume often let slip the mask of self-denying altruism and occasionally show a malicious nasty streak in their character. It is part of the Marxist-Leninist proposal that hate is a necessary part of the movement; that the so-called enemies of the beneficial revolution must be suppressed and eliminated one way

---

25 "Sunk by Stalinism," *Weekend Australian Review,* May 9–10, 1998, p. 11.

or another; that for ultimate success, it is necessary to misrepresent, lie, and pretend. Cruelty is acceptable when used against class enemies.

The basically bourgeois revolutionary preachers enjoy the feeling of superiority to those who do not share the dream. They rarely give up the advantages of their bourgeois positions, but also flatter themselves by feeling elevated to a higher class of honorary proletarians and saviors of humanity.

Chapters will be devoted to Ian Milner, Wilfred Burchett, Humphrey McQueen, and Manning Clark in order to explore the lives, the works and characters of the revolutionary messengers.

In the second part of the book, using documents found in the archives of Prague and Canberra, I will describe the rather unusual activities of Czechoslovak general consuls in Sydney and Melbourne, their influencing of local politicians, trade unionists, and fellow-travelers as well as their use of willing informers in order to prepare the groundwork for an eventual Communist takeover.

The third part of the book is dedicated to comparing the facts of history with the illusions of Manning Clark,[26] such an eloquent interpreter of some of the basic tenets of the Marxist-Leninist vision that he and others adopted. Across the globe, such revolutionary dreamers prepared or were busy preparing the way for political criminals to come to power. An essay on political criminality concludes the third part of the book.

The conclusion will explore Australian Communist or ex-Communist books on the chances and difficulties of their envisioned revolution.

---

26 A noted Australian journalist and previous member of the CPA, Philip
    Adams, described Manning Clark as "our most admired and revered
    scholar." See his feature "A Prophet's Dividends," *The Weekend Austra-
    lian,* Review, February 6–7, 1999, p. 32.

PART I
Four Different Dreamers

1

The Secret Life Of Ian Milner,
Agent No. 9006

After the Communist coup in February 1948, many Czechs and Slovaks fled the country in desperation, risking their lives to cross a frontier that was fiercely defended by border guards and large dogs, watchtowers, electrical wires, and minefields. Many of my compatriots lost their lives trying to escape this supposed paradise. Between eleven and twelve thousand of these lucky escapees managed to reach Australian shores.

Incredibly, at the same time, several Australians were settling in Prague, the capital of Czechoslovakia (ČSR), intending to help deliver the blessings of Communism to their countrymen. In an interview with Professor Patrick O'Brien, one of them, the poet Stephen Murray-Smith, talked about "an Australian colony in Prague, largely built around the International Union of Students [IUS]. We were impressed with the young revolution."[27]

This reverse parallel fascinated me. In 1996, traveling from Australia to Prague when I had a chance to spend two weeks exploring Czech archives, I tried to look up the activities of these Australian expatriates. It was not easy. I found very helpful people in the Institute of Contemporary History in Prague. Its then director, Vilém Prečan, and a few of his selected colleagues facilitated my access to some of the main archives.

Most friendly and helpful were the archivists at the Ministry of Foreign Affairs, World Federation of Trade Unions, and their colleagues at the State Central Archives that houses many of the documents of the

---

27   Transcription of an interview taped in 1975, p. 11.

Communist Party of Czechoslovakia. I brought back documentation of how Australian Communists and some labor leaders, in cooperation with agents of the Communist regime in Prague, worked to undermine and eventually destroy Australian democracy. At the same time, they requested and often obtained various favors from their contacts in Moscow and Prague.

Although I attempted to gain access to the archives of the International Union of Students, all my efforts were in vain. Its general secretary starting in 1953 and its president since 1955, Jiří Pelikán, led this important Soviet front organization. For at least ten years, he traveled widely over all continents bolshevising student unions. After the Soviet invasion in 1968, Jiří Pelikán moved to Rome, and later as ‚Giorgio Pelicano' was active for years as deputy of the European Parliament for the Italian Socialist Party. Either he took the documents with him or destroyed them. I was repeatedly told in Prague that they were not there. That is a pity. Pelikán published a book about his life, including his years as the head of the IUS,[28] but on forty pages devoted to this part of his life, the reader does not find anything about the real, secret work of this front, only platitudes about meetings, toasts to liberty in colonial countries, speeches, and resolutions. Useless. Just the misleading surface.

For two weeks in Prague, I tried to meet Mr. Oberman, who, I was told, might have some of the documents or know about their fate, but it was again in vain; he was always not there or unavailable. He was busy, attending meetings, the usual.

I hoped to gain access to even more revealing secret files of the Ministry of the Interior, which in this part of the world means the Ministry of Police and Secret Services. A few months before, its archives were declared open to researchers and to citizens interested in their own police files. But its two main representatives proved to be most reluctant. One of them said, "We do not want a lot of suicides." I submitted a list of ten world organizations working for Moscow from Prague and about sixty names of possible agents I would have liked to explore. In spite of many telephone calls, interventions from the Institute of Contemporary History, and repeated visits, I did not get far. Only on my last working day in Prague was I promised a copy of

---

28   *S'ils me tuent... (Paris, 1975).*

the file of one Australian agent, and that might have been due to a mistake on their part.

I was assured repeatedly that they have nothing in their files on the institutions or Australians I was interested in. I was also told that much was destroyed when the police lost interest in such subjects as the Council of Free Czechoslovakia in the USA. Finally, to stop my constant pestering, the director of the archives took me to one of their many computers to show me that there was nothing that I wanted on file.

From my list, he selected the name of Ian F. Milner. Apparently, to his surprise, the name appeared on the screen in company with a few other Milners. I was then blamed for not supplying them with dates of birth for all the people I suggested and for the confusion about Milner's first name. In his native New Zealand, Australia, and England it was spelled "Ian." In Czechoslovakia, even in the Prague telephone book in the sixties, he became "Jan" which translates as "John."

I think that only thanks to this incident, after a few more calls, I was asked to come to the archives again. However, there is another "but" to this story. I was not allowed to take copies of the fifteen pages of Milner's file with me, but only to take notes by hand. In a few hours I copied the whole file. In 1985, as is mentioned in the last entry of the file under the code "S FMV-SEO STRICTLY SECRET! Order 4/1978," out of the original 164 pages, 149 were destroyed. I bet these were the most interesting, but even those that survived could be of some interest to my Australian compatriots or other readers.

Very much like in a proper spy story—one thinks of Agent 007— the anti-democratic and anti-Australian spy was given a number and a pseudonym as well as code words: Ian F. Milner became A. Jánský, agent No. 9006. For Czech agents meeting him, the code name was Dvořák and the code phrase was "greetings from comrade Kořínek." He was identified as a non-legal member of the Communist Party of Australia.

The first secret document on Milner I was allowed to see was dated November 29, 1960. It narrated the history of Milner's involvement with the spy network: "During his employment in the Ministry of Foreign Affairs in Australia between 1944 and 1947, Ian Milner transferred to us through third persons valuable materials on political questions. From 1947 to 1950 he worked in the political department of the Security Council of the United Nations as a senior official for the Far East and South Asia. On March 6, 1949, J. [sic] Milner was won over for cooperation. As a basis for that served Milner's progressive assurances that he often showed in conversations with our representatives. After we had won his cooperation, Milner spent quite some time representing the UN in Korea, Palestine and other countries. He kept sending us reports on the activities of individual minor sections of UN and about some leading officials."

As is known from the Petrov affair and as was documented by Venona transcripts of Canberra-Moscow coded messages, Milner was then working as a spy for the Soviet Union. He was a busy man, serving at least two new masters at the same time: the Soviets and Czechoslovakia. Did he just send two copies of the same material? Was he paid twice as a spy? That was of course in addition to his rich UN salary.

Milner was subsequently warned that his spying had been detected. Here is the story as written by the Czechoslovak secret service:

> In 1950 we received information from the American counterespionage [Philby?] agency about a possible repression against Milner working for us as an agent. Therefore, a decision was made to relocate Milner to one of the people's democracies. In connection with it, under the pretext of his wife's medical treatment and his leave of absence, Milner left for Czechoslovakia where he is now working as a lecturer at Prague university.

The choice of phrase is significant: "A decision was made," not "We have decided." The decision was made in Moscow, and the Czechs were ordered to arrange for the spy to be moved to Prague. The document completes the saga of Milner's United Nations employment: "In 1951, on our recommendation, Milner requested the secretariat of the UN to release him from his contract; he then obtained the official UN notification."

Take notice: Australia sent Milner as its representative to the United Nations, but he was recalled by Czechoslovakia. From then on, he would take orders from his new, more implacable masters.

His paychecks would come from the secret police. "On the basis of the services that he provided us with and also because he came to Czechoslovakia on our order, we are supporting him financially since his arrival to the ČSR with 25,000 Czech crowns monthly. If he were to get 7,000 crowns from the university, our support would be lowered by this amount."

From the next statement, it seems that Milner was not too happy in Prague at a time when a Stalinist purge was going on against many of the top echelon of Czech and Slovak Communist leaders. Eleven of them would be hanged in the infamous Slánský process and many others tortured, shot, or beaten to death. He was looking for an escape: "Milner underestimates the danger of possible repression against himself, and he attempted to visit New York in order to work in the UN Secretariat or to return to his fatherland." The police report becomes ominous: "It is necessary to persuade him by all means that he should not travel to countries of the Anglo-American bloc." In the original Czech language, the expression "všemi prostředky" has a much uglier implication than the English "by all means," especially considering common Soviet methods of persuasion. It meant at least forcible detention if not death. And, of course, he must work for his upkeep: "In the ČSR, Milner can be utilized for work among Anglo-American representatives as well as among other foreigners who either permanently or temporarily happen to be in our country. For contacts use the codename 'Dvořák' and 'greetings from comrade Kořínek'." There ends the first preserved secret report on agent No. 9006, written toward the end of November 1960.

According to Richard Hall,[29] Milner was teaching at the Revolutionary Institute of Linguistics, instructing future spies in his mother tongue. However, Hall did not have any idea of Milner's spying for the Czechs: "Not one of the people I spoke to believe he was an informer."[30] He clearly was a capable spy. Now the book on Milner has to be rewritten as does so much else in the history of the Communist Party of Australia.

On November 27, 1958, a three-men Australian cultural delegation arrived in Prague from Moscow. At its head was Professor Manning

---

29   *The Rhodes Scholar Spy* (Melbourne: Random House, 1991) , pp. 174 on.

30   Ibid., p. 177.

Clark. According to a secret internal report of the week-long visit,[31] on the first day, "in the evening the delegation met specialist lecturer Ian Milner." And again on their last night in Prague: "Evening: Czech Trio concert. Dinner at Milner's." Foreign visitors in Communist Czechoslovakia could not meet whoever they wished. All contacts had to have the special permission of the secret police, or, in Milner's case, its order. Did Professor Manning Clark know what kind of the specialist his old friend was, that he was a Soviet and also a Czechoslovak spy? Did he care? Did Milner tell him? On such occasions, rooms are bugged. What did Milner write to his masters about the two visits?

The tense atmosphere in the country and the demanding job of dissimulation and of spying on his colleagues and students as well as on English-speaking diplomats were exacting a price and badly strained Milner's mental and physical health.

According to the second secret report by the district office of the Ministry of the Interior, Prague, MKO, 6th Department, on March 3, 1964, Milner complained of "nervous exhaustion." During the Christmas reception at the British Embassy in December 1963 [which, of course, for Milner was a working assignment], he fainted. He was transported to the hospital near Petřín, a Prague hilly park.... It was a nervous breakdown. The undersigned chief of the 6th department, Captain Hradil, and the spy's handler, Lieutenant Kořínek, recommended that Milner should still fulfill his duty to meet an official of the British Embassy, Bohacek [a Czech name; was he also a spy?]], but afterward „his work should be interrupted for three months except in case of some pressing need."

The secret police decided to prepare an "Evaluation of the Collaborator." First Lieutenant (promoted!) Kořínek filed his report on September 9, 1966. On Milner's family life, Kořínek observed that Milner divorced his wife, Margot, who "did not feel well in Prague." In 1953, he married his New York mistress and close friend of his ex-wife, Jarmila Frühauf, born Mařanová, "and also accepted in his home her daughter Linda." It worried the police that his first wife, living in London, knew about his "contact with organs of the Ministry of the Interior."

---

31   Archive of the Ministry of Foreign Affairs (AMFA), four unclassified
      pages, copies in my archive.

Milner was a diligent spy. "During his stay in the ČSR, our collaborator was used for reporting on university personnel who had contacts with the USA and Great Britain. Until 1960, his collaboration was valued positively: he submitted a great amount of information on individuals [perhaps on Manning Clark's visit?].... The collaborator fulfills his imposed tasks very well. He submits reports on people from the circle of university staff and on his contacts abroad.... He traveled to England in 1959 and 1960."

Milner's bank accounts in Switzerland, New York, and London were checked; for instance, in Switzerland he had twenty thousand Swiss franks, but transferred them to London. For his close contacts, the police mentioned two officials of the Communist Party of Australia: Noel Ebbels, highly praised by Professor Manning Clark until his death in 1952, and Rolf Gibson.

At the end of his report, First Lieutenant Kořínek wrote, "I will arrange censorship of his correspondence and bugging of his telephone; from P. K. [?] following movements of his London account." The secret police clearly started to have some doubts about their agent.

The last major report on Agent No. 9006 I was allowed to peruse was marked "STRICTLY SECRET!" and was prepared on March 18, 1968 (the year of Dubček and the Prague Spring) by the Second Lieutenant Beneš. It proposed to store the personal file of No. 9006, A. Jánský, for five years (later extended to the year 2000) in the archives of the Ministry of the Interior along with "the working file of the collaborator," which I did not see. It might be even more interesting than the personal file. I will quote the evaluation of our spy, admired and beloved by some Australians: "The collaborator Jánský during his cooperation was valued as willing, with his own initiative and exact in fulfilling his assigned tasks. During his collaboration with inimical objects [sic] at universities, he submitted 110 reports. He was targeted mainly for contacts with the staff of institutions of higher learning who visit England and the USA and who lived in these countries during the war."

The report continues, "Our collaborator Jánský claimed that due to poor health and lack of free time, he does not have a chance to engage in further interesting contacts." These weak excuses make one wonder about Milner's real feelings. The strictly secret report then enumerates "seven organs [who] were in contact with him" from February 31,

1953 to March 18, 1968: "Captain Bartoš, comrade Drápalík, Captain Arazim [not a Czech name], First Lieutenant Spěvák Boh., Lieutenant Kořínek, and Second Lieutenant Beneš Josef." The report concludes, "Recently, our meetings took place in coffeehouses."

Between March 1956 and 1984, Milner repeatedly denied to officials in Australia and to his friends that he was spying for the Communists. Melbourne professor Boyce Gibson called him "a rigidly honorable man." So much for Milner's honor.

SECOND REPORT AGENT NO. 9006

One year after discovering the secret family file in the Czech Ministry of the Interior concerning Ian Milner, I returned to Prague hoping to get access to his working file. I was disappointed, but also found additional sources for understanding his life.

A. A new law strictly limits access to personal files to close relatives of deceased persons. After many requests, I was finally given, as I was repeatedly told, the same Milner file that I had already received last year. However, to my surprise, this time the file contained twenty-eight pages instead of fifteen. The cover page was new to me and the second page carefully described the contents of 149 pages destroyed on January 16, 1985. Additional pages included more detailed reports on Milner's spying activities. Other previously seen pages obviously had parts of pages given to me last year deleted by covering them during copying. In this second review devoted to Milner's double life, I was able to significantly complement facts that were revealed in my report in the *Courier Mail* (Brisbane, Australia) on November 30, 1996.

B. In addition, Milner's personal file kept at Charles University, the place of his other more official occupation, lecturer in the field of Anglo-American literature, helps me to understand a little more than just his professional career.

C. Telephone conversations with his close friend at the University and with the daughter of his Czech second wife who died the same year as Milner (1991), add interesting revelations to the story of treason.

D. Milner's uncompleted memoirs, *Intersecting Lines*, published posthumously in New Zealand in 1993, and his many translations of

Czech poetry printed in the West individually in scholarly journals and together in a few books, allow us to see the personal, to some degree tragic, history of the successful Soviet spy and Czech undercover agent.

E. Recently revealed ASIO files also shed some light on a secret agent who obviously did not manage to completely conceal his treason from agencies working for countries he was betraying.

A. CZECH SECRET POLICE FILES

The more extensive copy of the Strictly Secret report by his sixth handler, First Lieutenant Kořínek, from the KS SNB (State Security) Prague, II/A, seventh section, dated November 9, 1966, File No. 621743, specifies that agent 9006 "while working in the Australian Ministry of Foreign Affairs between 1944 and 1947, transferred through third persons valuable material on political questions to the Soviet espionage agency and later to ours.... March 6, 1949, he agreed to work for us." That is a concrete confirmation of the Venona decrypts about Milner's supplying the Soviet Union with detailed planning by the British and American governments for post-war strategy in the Mediterranean, Indian, and Pacific seas. Milner always denied it and claimed to be upset even by suspicion.

One and a half years later, Milner's last handler until Dubček's year of reforming Communism, Second Lieutenant Josef Beneš, reported to the same office as mentioned above (KS SNB Prague, II/A, seventh section) on March 18, 1968, Strictly Secret, that "Milner John (sic) Frank, born 6.6.1911 in New Zealand, employed as lecturer at the department of anglistics of the Faculty of Philosophy at Charles University in Prague on March 6, 1949 started to work with agents of the 1st Administration of the Ministry of the Interior."

From this brief I will further quote only sentences that provide additional information to what was already known from the previous report: "Between 1947 and 1950 [Milner] worked in the political section of the Security Council of the United Nations' Far East Department. Most of his time he spent on official assignments to Korea, Palestine and elsewhere. He supplied us with news of activities of individual countries."

This Strictly Secret report then repeats the previously divulged story of how Milner was ordered to come to Czechoslovakia under the pretext of his wife's medical treatment and how he was advised by the secret police to request a release from his United Nations contract. For a police stipend of twenty-five thousand Czech crowns, he was "asked to report on foreigners, especially Englishmen who visited Czechoslovakia. He also reported on what occurred in the British Embassy. On May 11, 1954 he was re-assigned for further operations to the third section of the Ministry of the Interior where he reported on university professors and scientific workers, especially concerning their contacts with foreigners.... He submitted 110 reports."

The brief then states, "In 1964 it was proposed to interrupt the cooperation with our collaborator for medical reasons. From that time the number of meetings and consequently the number of submitted reports diminished."

Let us now go back to the much more substantial intelligence review of September 9, 1966. First Lieutenant Kořínek related to his superiors Milner's travels, his and his wife's money, friends, and relatives. Parts of the report are new to us: "Until 1959, the collaborator did not leave the country because of concerns of possible repression against him. In 1959, he had a short study trip in England, again in 1960, this time with his second wife. According to the brief he submitted, no foreign secret service showed interest in him, and he did not experience any unpleasantness."

Milner was evidently trusted enough to be accompanied by his second wife. Now appears the question of money invested abroad: "In 1962, it was discovered that his second wife had a Swiss account of 20,000 *francs*. By questioning the collaborator, it was ascertained that the account came from the time when she was employed by the UN. They draw from the account when shopping at Tuzex [special shops in Communist Czechoslovakia for holders of US dollars providing goods otherwise not available]. They also pay their foreign trips from this account. Later our collaborator told us that he transferred his wife's account to his London bank. He also deposited a smaller amount in a bank in New York; it is money from his work at the United Nations. In London he also deposits his royalties from various literary translations into English and articles published in British journals."

After praising Milner's fulfillment of his assignments to report on university employees and his contacts abroad—"These revelations are very good"—First Lieutenant Kořínek mentions some warning signs:

> Lately, diverse persons manifested interest in our collaborator, during their visits to Czechoslovakia or directly in England when he was there. For instance, New Zealander O'Connor, who spent half a year in Prague on a fellowship, and a journalist, Mr. Thomas. Both took a detailed interest in the life of our collaborator: how he is living here, if he has a chance to travel abroad, etc. In 1964, when he visited Leeds, England, he met Mrs. Morrish from the British Council who also in great detail enquired about his life and opinions.

Milner's handler then mentions that several times he was investigated but never "in depth." For the purpose of "deconspiration," his first wife could have mentioned his involvement with the secret police to somebody in London. "His second wife also knows about his contact with the Ministry of the Interior. He was advised to say that due to his sickness, he interrupted his contacts with the Ministry of the Interior and that for a long time no one met him."

The following part of Kořínek's report discusses agent 9006 and his value for secret services. "The collaborator has a good chance to penetrate the university staff who are teaching foreign languages, mainly English. Concerning our enemy, he can infiltrate hostile persons and provide us with their 'typification' and possibility of 'exploitation.' Because of his nervous disorder, however, this potential is limited." After that comes a fascinating disclosure about Milner's twisted and tortured mind: "He shows fears of being branded for the second time as a spy."

This part of Kořínek's long "Evaluation of the Collaborator" stresses the need to scrutinize Milner again: "Because it is possible that a foreign agency is interested in him and it is impossible to exclude the chance that he was already contacted, before further operational use, an examination in depth will be carried out."

Out of the long list of Milner's "contacts and their character" in Kořínek's review, I was only allowed to see two names the previous year: Noel Ebbels and Rolf Gibbson. Here are the others, some with police comments:

> MILNER(ová), Jarmila, previously Fryhauf(ová), born Mařan(ová), [the Czechs here Czechisize the German 'ü' after 'Fr' into 'y'] born 8-18-1913, a Czechoslovak citizen. Second wife of the collaborator. She studied at the Faculty of philosophy in Prague until 1937. Then she studied in the USA, stayed there during the war and married Fryhauf, US citizen. Since 1948, she has worked in the UN library. She divorced in 1949 and requested transfer to the information center of the UN in Prague. Here she promised to cooperate with the Ministry of the Interior, but the result of her cooperation was feeble; she was not interested. She confided her contact with the Ministry of the Interior to her new husband. Her file was deposited in the archives.

> FRÜHAUF Bedřich—living in Washington, DC, USA, US citizen, works as engineer, building highways and airports for the military. Lately, he worked in Taiwan. A few times he visited Prague where he met Mrs. Milner(ová) and his daughter Linda. We suspect him of spying. Our collaborator feels antipathy toward him, met him only once, socially.

> MILNER John Keith, born 2-5-1917 in New Zealand, British citizen, collaborator's brother. He works as general business representative of a New Zealand cotton company in London. He often visits socialist states, including ČSSR. Our collaborator had many disagreements with him, mainly about his staying in ČSSR and about some political opinions. For a few years they did not talk to each other. Recently, they met in Prague and keep more amicable contacts. John knows his first wife and met her in

London. It is possible that she told him about her ex-husband's contacts with the Czech Security.

BERTRAM James Munto, born 8-11-1910, Auckland, British citizen—a close and long time friend of our collaborator. In 1953, through him he sent a letter to Mr. R. Tomes in New Zealand.

MILNER Margaret, born 12-15-1911, British citizen, his ex-wife. She divorced him, left for the USA, later England, now lives in the neighborhood of London.

EBBELS Noel—member of the CPA, died in February 1952. The collaborator was in close contact with him while in Australia.

GIBBSON Rolf—CPA functionary; our collaborator entertained close contacts with him. These contacts were interrupted.

BRASS Douglas—British citizen, Australian journalist. They have close friendly relations. He was interested in collaborator's position in the CSSR.

Dr FRIED Vilém, born 4-15-1915, Czech nationality, Czechoslovak citizenship, living in Prague, Betlémská 7 – amicable contacts. FRIED spent the whole war in England, has frequent contacts with British citizens and often leaves for NSR [German Bundesrepublik].

Several of these contacts that very much interested Czech secret police will reappear when we come to Milner's memoirs. I have no idea why this list was shown to me in what is probably its complete form this year, but not last year. The lack of caution (or graceful offering in spite of imposition of stricter conditions for access to police files?) extended even to the following chapter of Milner's handler's "Evaluation of the Collaborator," namely his conclusions:

Because in our collaborator's materials there are some uncleared points and some uncleared contacts, *checking measures* will be adopted:

A) During meetings with the collaborator I will gradually go through his life and the way he cooperated with the organs of espionage between 1944 and 1949. I will compare information gained that way with our files. As far as possible, I will identify his contacts from these years and will investigate the files of the first section of the Ministry of the Interior. [This is another confirmation of Milner's pro-Soviet spying between 1944 and 1949.]

B) Step by step I will evaluate his contacts during his stay in the ČSSR and will check them. I will target especially these persons: Dr O'CONNOR – British professor; Dr THOMAS – British journalist whom he kept meeting in Prague; GIBIÁN Jiří, US citizen with whom he arranged a meeting in Prague in 1960. [Author's comment: Gibián, George Jiří was an eminent professor of Russian and Comparative Literature at Cornell University in Ithaca, New York; he was born in Prague in 1924, completed his BA at Pittsburgh University in 1943, MA in Comparative Literature at Harvard in 1951, and his PhD in International Relations in in Washington DC in 1977. Professor Gibián was an accomplished scholar; he published and edited several books on Czech and Russian history and literature.]

C) I will interrogate the collaborator about contacts with his brother and his ex-wife; when his brother comes to Prague a decision will be made to check both of them together.

D) I will begin to read his correspondence and arrange bugging of his telephone. His London account will be followed from PK. [?]

E) I will find out his contemporary contacts in order to ascertain if there is a collaborator among them who could be used for spying on him.

The concluding sentence of Milner's evaluation by his secret service employers reads as follows: "Until the check of our collaborator is carried out, he will spy on the staff of the Department of Philosophy and he will be used for contacting individual foreigners the same way as up to the present time."

If compared with the same "Evaluation of the Collaborator" on which I reported in the *Courier-Mail*, November 30, 1996, it is clear that much more detail was revealed on the second occasion. However, out of the section entitled "Family Life," only a few sentences quoted above remained in the file that I was allowed to see. Therefore, I think I should repeat at least two crucial sentences from the original report: "Until 1960, his collaboration was valued positively; he submitted much information on individuals.... The collaborator fulfills his tasks very well."

In spite of some divergence of material from secret files of the Czech Ministry of the Interior, I have no doubts about their authenticity. They never contradict but do complement each other. Several different copies might exist in the files or the officials in charge vary their opinion about what should be revealed at different times, or, quite simply, forget from one year to the next how much they allowed me to inspect the last time. It is possible to verify where a part of the same document is unveiled or suppressed dependent on the occasion. The omissions are compensated for by permission to read what previously was considered too revealing. Together, my two visits to the archives of the Ministry of the Interior allow us to study if not the whole, probably almost the whole report on Ian Milner's activities as an agent of the Czechoslovak secret police, but only as far as it is revealed in his family file. It is substantial, with one very important and regrettable exception.

This time I requested access to Milner's working (operative) file, but without success. As will be seen in the last document of the family file—again giving away to me more than a year ago—the working file supposedly does not exist anymore. I will quote some of the new passages from pages 26 and 27 of the file from the 24 of January 1985, marked "S FMV-SEO, STRICTLY SECRET!"

DECISION. In agreement with the article 31 of the service rules A-oper-II-1 and with reference to methodical orders of the chief SEO FMV concerning, this article, the commission established by the chief S Stb Prague by the order of No. 4/1978 thoroughly

studied documents filed in the archives SEU (SEO
FMV) in 1968 under the archival number 621743
MV on MILNER John (sic) Frank, born 6-6-1911,
New Zealand, British citizen, IS-A cover name
Jánský, problems VC, universities, and decided to
extend the time of keeping the file No. 621743 till
the year 2000.

The decision then repeats details of his collaboration with Soviet
and Czech secret services from 1944 and 1949 respectively and who
was in charge of handling him (seven specialists altogether). The next
part should be quoted: "TS was valued very positively, he was willingly
fulfilling his tasks, he took the initiative, his reports were written by
hand or typed.... In 1964 the number of meetings was limited due
to illness. After his transfer to the ČSSR he was receiving 25,000
Czech crowns; there is no mention of how long payment continued.
The cooperation was ended in March 1968 for health reasons.... The
commission decided to remove from the file unimportant materials
and cancel them. Pages 4-136, 138-148, 154-158 and the working
file TS, whose time for deposit passed, are to be destroyed. Number of
pages 164, destroyed 149. Prepared by Hošek."

Accordingly, the working file that I requested this time was
destroyed. Yet, number 2 of the sheets I was able to see on my second
visit carefully enumerates the destroyed pages and briefly identifies
their content. In spite of such bureaucratic precision, there is no similar
exactitude about the supposedly destroyed working file! Thus we can see,
for instance, that pages 4–8 described "the situation of the collaborator
in Australia," and pages 9–13 his "personal situation." His contacts
were checked on pages 18–33. The next page was devoted to the cost of
his initial stay in the ČSSR. Seven pages accounted for "arrangements
of his employment." Evidently, the official cover-up of his stay in the
country had to be secured with the university. Pages 39–41 contained
an "operational plan for collaboration" and page 45 evaluated it and
suggested his transfer. Three pages described his separation from his
first wife and eighteen investigated his second wife and her contacts.
Later, three additional pages checked her. Three pages studied his funds
abroad and two pages evidenced expenses. Dr. Gibián was investigated
on one destroyed page; a few pages included proposals and *assigned*

targets for Milner's trips to England, Yugoslavia, Austria, England again, and Greece. The collaborator obviously traveled abroad, conducting espionage. The remaining pages listed the detectives surveying their own devoted and paid agent 9006.

B. Milner's Personal File at Charles University in Prague

I was lucky to be acquainted with the chief archivist of Charles University where I studied from its opening after WWII in May of 1945 until my departure from the Stalinized country in August 1948. Milner's file was available to me the day after my request together with a desk and chair in a private office.

Although the Ministry of the Interior is mentioned only once, there are a few interesting points to be made. From 1951 to 1954, Milner worked as a specialist lecturer, and from 1955 to 1963 as an expert assistant lecturer. On November 1, 1964, he obtained the title of lecturer of contemporary English literature.

In order to get favorable points in the cadre personal files, during the period of "revolutionary building of socialism" in the fifties and sixties, everybody who wanted to advance his studies or career had to take part in unpaid "voluntary" brigades. According to his file, Milner took part in a brigade in 1952 to create (against fierce opposition by the peasants) and improve (failing) collective farms in Volary; in 1953 he helped to construct some buildings in the mining area of Most (now the most devastated area of the Czech Republic); in the sixties, he regularly took part in the so-called "Action 2" of "voluntary" work.

Professor Dr. R. Foustka, vice-chancellor of the university, signed a letter addressed to the dean of the philosophy department: "By a decree No. 52916/54, dated 7.5.1954, the Ministry of Education informed us that the Ministry of the Interior does not have any objection to the continuing employment of Ian F. G. Milner at Charles University as a specialist lecturer." What a surprise! They arranged the cover employment from the beginning. It was probably their idea to invite applications for the post of lecturer of contemporary English literature. Milner was the only candidate and dutifully received the nomination.

Professor Zdeněk Vančura, head of the department of English and Germanic literature and languages, praised the appointee on March 7, 1958: "During thirteen semesters of his work in this faculty he showed diligence, consciousness, and initiative.... He led his students to a correct ideological and artistic understanding of literary works and realism. He was helping to recognize the progressive line of English literature.... Politically, it is possible to value especially his cooperation with English Marxists on a new interpretation of the progressive traditions of English literature with the publications of essays in the London Marxist journal *Marxist Quarterly.*" Professor Vančura was an eminent and democratic representative of scholarship, but after the Communist coup d'état in 1948, in order to keep his chair, he learned how to collaborate at least by using the prescribed clichés about the progression of Marxism. He wrote an addition to the letter by hand: "During his stay here he learned fairly good Czech."

During January 1961, Milner was allowed to go to England to work on his dissertation, and on February 11, 1971, he obtained the degree of doctor of sciences and arts for successfully defending his dissertation on the topic of "Form and the Expression of Values in the Nineteenth and Twentieth Century English Novel."

Milner's habilitation thesis was entitled *The Heroic Pattern in George Elliot*, his favorite author. The Charles University file contains a synopsis:

I. Analysis of the aesthetic and moral role of the hero in George Elliot's novel points to her high esteem for characters drawn from the working people whom she presents as the bearers of positive moral and social values.
II. The dynamic principle of George Elliot's art is the counterpoint of contrasting planes of moral and social values.
III. George Elliot has as yet been neglected, misrepresented, and underestimated in Marxist literary criticism, though her contribution to English critical realism ranks among the greatest.

On the November 12, 1973, Milner took the "Vow of a University Teacher." Naturally, the same or similar socialist clichés abound in the text. However, it is remarkable to follow the transformation of a humanist British scholar into an agent of the police and also an agent of political brainwashing:

> I promise that I will be faithful to the Czechoslovak Socialist Republic and will always observe its constitution and legal system and will actively work and act in order to consolidate and promote its socialist regime.
>
> I promise that I will consciously fulfill all the duties of a university teacher and that I will conduct the education and upbringing of students in the spirit of Marxist-Leninist scientific concepts. I bind myself by the oath to deepen young people's socialist patriotism and lead them to friendship and cooperation with the people of the Soviet Union and socialist countries as well as with progressive members of all other nations in the spirit of proletarian internationalism. In my own political, educational, and scientific pedagogical activity, I will work to prepare politically and professionally highly mature workers capable of fulfilling demanding tasks during the building of socialism in our fatherland. By my own scientific work I will contribute towards fulfillment of these tasks.

What a solemn vow to make for a New Zealander, Australian historian, poet, and writer, lecturer, and foreign ministry planning specialist, as well as a United Nations Australian representative! How many loyalties this "subject of the British and Australian Queen" betrayed while traveling with a British passport!

Interestingly, he regularly omitted his employment by the Australian Ministry of Foreign Affairs on his curriculum vitae when his career as a Soviet spy began, as in his vita of July 19, 1955.

A few more details registered in the archives of the University of Prague complement the picture. In 1956, his car had license plate number RUU 231. Although his university salary was high with regular raises and he kept receiving the pay of an undercover agent, in the seventies he had a debt of seventy thousand Czech crowns and was repaying three hundred crowns monthly. Was it just pro forma in order to better hide his other job?

I was impressed when on a document from January 9, 1976, I could see that he was paying his first wife alimony. However, my admiration disappeared when I discovered that he was forced to by a Czech court decision in 1962 granting his ex-wife a court order.

On June 2, 1976, Milner requested his university contract be terminated because he had reached the age of sixty-five and completed twenty-five years of teaching at Charles University. His position was terminated September 30, 1976, and from October 1, 1976 he was given full retirement pension of 62 percent of his salary between 1971 and 1975; that is 2,334 Kč. (The Czech crown was devalued ten times in 1953 which provoked widespread workers' riots since they lost almost all of their savings.) It was based on the inclusion into his years of service of two years as specialist in Wellingtoh, five years at Melbourne University, one year (sic) in the Ministry of Foreign Affairs, five years at the United Nations, and twenty-five in Prague.

C. Telephone Conversations

Encouraged by my recent reading of Ian Milner's memoirs and poetry, both his translations and his own (remember Manning Clark always stressing that he preferred the *poet* in his close friend and spy Milner?), I tried to reach his second wife Jarmila while I was in Prague. After a few unanswered telephone calls, I wrote her a letter. I suggested that I would like to hear her own—and Milner's—side of the story of a tragic and very gifted man who found himself trapped in the net of the secret police due to his youthful idealism and enthusiasm.

Instead of Jarmila Milner(ová), her daughter Linda called me in my hotel. The Ministry of the Interior archives revealed only that Milner took Linda in when he married her mother in Prague. Linda was enraged. She warned me repeatedly to immediately stop my inquiries. She said that the false allegations against Ian Milner were already refuted several times, that it is now fashionable to throw as much dirt at people as possible, and that she knew her mother and Milner only as old people (nonsense, when she started to live in Milner's household she was only in her teens or twenties and they in their forties). She threatened me at least twice with a lawsuit if I persisted in spreading lies about her stepfather. She said it made no sense to believe such fantasies. She informed me that her mother died the same year as Milner in 1991. She absolutely refused to meet me. The chapter was closed for her. There was no need to reopen it. Anyway, all of us are trapped in one way or another. (I wonder if she read Milan Kundera. He likes to claim that all of us are trapped by History with capital "H.")

My second telephone interview on the same day was much more pleasant. The editor of Milner's memoirs mentions two of his friends at Charles University. I found one of them. When I reached professor Zdeněk Stříbrný at his home he was recovering from a serious illness. He was supposed to avoid any excitement. Yet, he was willing to tell me all that he could about his friend Milner. They were very happy to have Milner on the faculty since he was a dependable lecturer and spoke English beautifully. He did not know about his undercover activities. Milner sincerely liked Dubček and was shocked by the Soviet invasion in August 1968. After that time Milner called him from time to time and they met for a few glasses of beer. When I mentioned Milner's mother and sister's problems with schizophrenia and their nervous breakdowns (which Milner experienced too in Prague in the sixties), Dr Stříbrný acknowledged that Milner's spying combined with a successful career as an Anglicist could have been helped by something like a split personality. He also told me that Dr. Frank Cain from the University of New South Wales and the Australian Defense Force Academy wrote to him mentioning my name and asking him to help Cain to get access to the archives of the Ministry of the Interior. Dr. Cain defended Milner a few years ago as a victim of the Cold War spy mania in the journal *Overland*,[32] and in 1994, wrote about him in his book devoted to ASIO: "ASIO was eager to cast [Milner] as a Soviet spy. Petrov semi-fictional evidence helped sustain the ASIO fabrication before the Royal Commission on Espionage."[33] Cain agreed with a Swedish ambassador

32   "The Making of a Cold War Victim," *Overland*, No. 134, 1994, pp. 60–66.

33   *The Australian Security Intelligence Organizations: An Unofficial History* (Ilford, Essex: Frank Cass & Co, 1994,) pp. 138 and 193. The major spreader of the false claim that the Soviet spy Vladimir Petrov was manipulated into delayed defection by the Prime Minister R.G. Menzies in order to win the 1954 elections was Dr. H.V Ewatt, leader of

who said, "Petrov, of course, was a liar." Cain also claimed that "it is possible that Petrov could have been 'planted' on ASIO as a defector by the MVD."[34] Dr. Stříbrný suggested that Dr. Cain should turn to the Czech embassy in Canberra. He invited me to meet him when I come to Prague again. Professor Stříbrný has read everything available about Milner. Next time I would like to ask him, among other things, if he was approached by the secret police to spy on his friend when they were looking for someone among Milner's acquaintances as mentioned above. He was Milner's closest friend.

Maybe it is time to look at what Milner had to say about himself and his life. He was working on his memoirs when he died one week short of his eightieth birthday in Prague in 1991.

D. Milner as a Memoirist, Poet, and Liar

In 1993, Victoria University Press in Wellington published Milner's memoirs entitled *Intersecting Lines*. They were edited and introduced by Vincent O'Sullivan who chose the title of the book by selecting words from a poem Milner liked and commented on:

> John Cornford, the Cambridge student leader, Communist and occasional poet one of the finest minds of his generation—addressed the Labour Club. He had fought in Spain ... his death gripped me deeply. As Cornford put it in his fine but little-known poem "The Full Moon at Tierz: Before the Storming of Huesna" ... "The intersecting lines that cross both ways, / Time future, has no image in space, Crooked as the road that we must tread, / Straight as our bullets fly ahead. / We are the future, the last fight let us face."

---

the opposition Labor Party. For a detailed account see Robert Mann, *The Petrov Affair: Politics and Espionage* [Sydney: Pergamon, 1987], *passim*.

34   Ibid., p. 127.

As the editor informs us in his introduction, Milner managed to complete only twenty-three years of his life's reminiscences. His writings on his time in Oxford, Wellington, and Canberra were put together by the editor from Milner's drafts and notes. There is not much on New York or Prague.

Milner writes so beautifully and poetically that it seems almost inconceivable that he could be a spy, false propagandist, undercover agent, threat to other people's liberty and life by his denunciations, and systematic liar. But then in the text one finds obvious lies and the mask of an honest author slips from his face, revealing a typical Communist agent who from the beginning viscerally accepted the Leninist tenet that a good conspirator must use lies when fighting the hostile bourgeois system. The life of a spy is, of course, impossible without systematized disingenuousness and lying.

The book of Milner's memoirs was published by Vincent O'Sullivan with the intention of whitewashing the Rhodes scholar and defending him against what Frank Cain in his Autumn 1994 *Overland* article called "The Making of a Cold War Victim," or what Gregory Pemberton in *Canberra Times* (6-19-1991) attacked as a "spy mystery that will not die." As *A Suspect History*, a recent extremely venomous booklet produced by Humphrey McQueen, demonstrated, the local branch of the international club of disappointed Leftist dreamers is growing more vociferous in trying to defend its history of naïve hopes and serious political blunders.

In his long introduction to *Intersecting Lines*, O'Sullivan wrote, "It is also the account of a man whose decency and charm equaled that commitment (to socialism)."[35] Commenting on Milner's praise of Katherine Mansfield in 1932, he emphasized that Milner was "drawn by her moral quality" and "he quoted her conviction ... that it's only by being true to life that I can be true to art. And to be true to life is to be good, sincere, simple, honest!"[36]

Disapprovingly, O'Sullivan quotes Richard Hall's conviction that "Milner was nothing if not the honorable spy." Since so many authors keep stressing honesty, sincerity, and honor in connection with the question of Milner's spying, clearly they consider it possible to combine honor with spying and lying; Milner also tried to unite

35   Ibid., p. 8.
36   Ibid., p. 13.

the two contradictory traits. Can you have a single person with such split features? Obviously you can, but doesn't that indicate a "split personality"? Adjectives one can use describing a spy—on either side—could be successful, capable, shrewd, even heroic or tragic, but honorable, honest, or sincere? I doubt their appropriateness.

Although Milner does not complain about his childhood, it was miserable. His father was an authoritarian father and teacher. His mother and sister were sick with mental disorders. A "stiff nurse" stood between him "and the milk of human kindness." Duty was stressed by everybody, and Christian images were full of hell and flesh burning for ever and ever (Saint Augustine!). He rebelled against his father's provincial British patriotism and soon was called a Bolshie.

Substantial parts of Milner's memoirs are devoted to his friendships with Communists enumerated in the Prague archives of the secret police. James Bertram, his childhood friend, also attended the same college at Oxford. Together with another longtime friend, Charles Brash, they went to the Soviet Union in 1934 and came back charmed. Bertram, a Chinese specialist, became acquainted with Mao Tse-tung, Chou En-lai, and other Chinese Communist leaders and supported their cause in his writings.

Denis Glover, Milner's "Bolshie friend" since 1934, remained close to him until 1980, when Milner came to Wellington in New Zealand. In Sydney he met and enjoyed Rupert Lockwood, "a well-known journalist on the *Sydney Morning Herald*,"[37] whom Soviet spies appreciated for his long and cynical description of Australian internal affairs.. Lockwood introduced him to Ernie Thornton, "the resolute, able Communist leader of the powerful Ironworkers' Union which in those days, together with the Watersiders, could make or break the war effort of any government.... 'Ernie's a tough man,' said Rupert. 'When he hits you, the skin comes off.'"[38]

---

37   Ibid., p. 167. "Rupert Lockwood was a prominent Communist Party activist and journalist." In May 1953 in the Soviet Embassy in Canberra, he composed "a long, thirty-seven page typescript analysing the American and Japanese penetration of Australia ... under the supervision of Antonov," a Soviet spy. See Robert Manne, *The Petrov Affair: Politics and Espionage*, pp. 120, 68 and 99.

38   Ibid.

Admiring paragraphs are devoted to Milner's lifelong friend, the historian Manning Clark, who supposedly "concerned himself more and more with the fundamental problem of discovering a just moral and social order in the ideologically divided modern world" (pp. 174–75).

Milner recalls Manning Clark's visit to Prague in 1964: "More than anything else, he wanted to talk about Dostoyevsky as his 'model' for the troubled times."[39] Six years later in Moscow, Clark pointed out in an abject way, humbling himself, that Lenin did not consider Dostoyevsky a great writer. Lenin was a greater "model."[40]

His lasting friendship with Noel Counihan and Judah Waten is extolled, too. He values painter Counihan for his "volcanic energy, massive power of line, and surging protest of the great Mexican revolutionary artists, especially Sequiros."[41] (Sequiros was involved in Trotsky's murder.) "Like his friend Waten, Counihan knew a great deal about Australian politics, State and Federal—and politicians, including their private lives." About Waten he writes, "It is true that his exuberance often turned dialogue into monologue. And Judah never tired of monologue. He would repeat himself.… Others thought him dogmatic. To him the basic premises and tenets, political and aesthetic, were self-evident—or demonstrable from the Marxist classics wherein his faith lay."[42] Very lyrically, Milner evoked his first love when he was almost nineteen, "well laden with puritan restraints."[43]

Convincingly, he describes his unhappiness with social conditions in New Zealand, Australia, and Great Britain; he took part in demonstrations, strikes, and wanted to lose his upper-class bourgeois status as much as possible by joining the struggling working class. Reading Marx and Engels gave direction to his acceptance of the slogan that the world must be changed through solidarity and fighting. His travel to Germany, observing Hitler and his influence, as well as the Spanish civil war and the Munich Treaty's gift of Czechoslovakia to Nazism strengthened his belief that only the Soviet Union was able

---

39   Ibid., p. 175.
40   "He wanted a good life for everyone," *The Australian*, June 16, 1997, p. 11.
41   *Intersecting Liness,* pp. 176–77.
42   Ibid., p. 177.
43   Ibid., p. 80.

and willing to defeat fascism and militarism: "The phoenix of a new socialist order would soon be rising from the flames of capitalism in collapse."[44]

All this makes his attachment to Communism understandable. However, he never admits spying for the Soviet Union between 1944 and 1950 and for the Czechs since then. In his introduction, O'Sullivan, like Dr. Cain, accepts as true all the repeated lies about Milner's moving to Czechoslovakia with the sole intention of helping his wife's arthritis and the cover story of his employment at Charles University. At the end of Milner's memoirs he reprints the text of Milner's "Personal Statement" concerning his innocence that he sent to the Petrov Royal Commission.

Since Milner's transfer to Prague on the orders of his Soviet and Czech secret police handlers, his masters apparently would have liked to place such a successful agent in New Zealand. The Soviets made inquiries in 1953 in Canberra about how much was really known about his spying career. Milner attempted to settle in New Zealand several times. In 1971, he stayed for a year in Otago as a visiting professor in English at the university. In 1967, he managed to obtain invitations from the universities in Canterbury and Auckland to come as a visiting lecturer, but when the New Zealand weekly, *Truth*, denounced him as an ex-spy for the Russians, nothing came out of it. In 1980, he used the pretext of working on the biography of his father to return to Wellington.

Since the fifties and sixties, according to the material found in the Prague archives of the Ministry of the Interior, Milner was always assigned tasks as an undercover agent during his trips abroad. I would not be surprised if in the seventies and eighties he had resumed his collaboration with the secret police and worked for them while in New Zealand.

Milner's memoirs, *The Intersecting Lines*, contain a substantial bibliography of twenty-three pages. Seven pages are taken by his pre-war poetry and articles for New Zealand journals, usually only two or three pages long. Yet, the remaining entries testify to the fact that Milner took his teaching and scholarly career seriously. There is a large number of contributions to various encyclopedias on English and Australian literature, literary essays, and reviews often devoted to his

44   Ibid., p. 106.

favorite author George Elliot. Australian authors who are represented in his writing are Patrick White and Henry Lawson (not Manning Clark). In spite of sympathizers who claimed that in Prague Milner devoted himself to translations of Australian literature, the opposite is true; Milner spent a lot of time and energy translating Czech poetry into English and publishing it in British and American literary magazines, as well as in books. His favored poets were Petr Bezruč and the contemporary poets, J. Hanzlík, Vladimír Holan, and Miroslav Holub. The help of his wife was substantial; sometimes it was acknowledged, often not. The translations are good, even the translations of one of the most difficult Czech poets, Vladimír Holan. Milner himself admits, "Holan's verse is often difficult to understand at a first reading and sometimes remains obscure."[45]

The publication of this 126 page booklet is remarkable not only for the quality of the translation but also for the openness with which Milner characterized Holan as a victim of the Communist regime. The year of publication was ominous. Three years after the Soviet invasion, some 150,000 Czech and Slovak Communists lost their party cards and jobs when they refused to say to party screening officials that the friendly armies offered fraternal help to save socialism from its enemies. (In his memoirs, Milner refers to fraternal tanks on page sixty-nine.) One would think Milner would face consequences for his portrayal of the regime, but he got away with it. (Of course, secret police agents were sometimes encouraged to make a few otherwise outrageous remarks in order to strengthen their claim to objectivity or even dissidence.)

Nevertheless, let us examine some of these daring passages. "After 1948, by one of the absurd yet tragic ironies in which recent Czechoslovak history abounds, Holan, the author of postwar tributes to the Soviet Union and the nation-stirring anti-fascist poems of 1938–40, was accused by party dogmatists of decadent 'formalism' and was abused, or ignored, in the press. Until 1963, no further volume of his poetry was accepted for publication.... From this long vigil comes his finest poetry, a poetry which fuses, with compelling force, personal feelings of bitterness, scorn, anxiety, despair, mystification with social moods of oppression and fear."[46]

45   Vladimir Holan, *Selected Poems* (Penguin, 1971), p. 13.
46   Ibid., p. 10.

In 1976, ABC radio aired Milner's translation of Holan's long (forty-two pages in transcript) poem, *A Night with Hamlet*. Milner commented that it "was written during 1949–56, the grim years of isolation, and was finished in 1962," and quoted Holan's remark from an interview in a literary journal: "The years of writing *A Night with Hamlet* were the cruelest of my life. In my desperate loneliness I was well 'earthed' to receive, and survive, all the horrors of that time."[47] Approvingly, Milner quotes from Holan verses concerning years when Agent 9006 diligently worked for the secret police that was responsible for all the horrors: "To live is terrible since you have to stay/with the appalling reality of these years ... In me the heart of poetry bleeds"[48] and "Fraud alone is certainty here.... The brute is always with us."[49] It is hard to imagine Milner's state of mind when he was further describing Holan's—and his own—years in Prague: "Man was driven out of Paradise and is doomed to suffer his exile. The suffering is in the remembering: he strives to recover his lost innocence."[50]

Another verse from Milner's translation of Miroslav Holub, *Notes of a Clay Pigeon*, reminds us of the poetic and human side of the undercover agent: "And searching we lose, finding we conceal./For in essence we are looking for childhood."[51]

A Personal Tragedy or a Major Blunder?

There can be no doubt that Milner realized what was going on but persisted in working for the system responsible for murders, concentration camps, and lies. We know that right after his displacement to Prague in 1951, he would have liked to return to New York but was not allowed to by the secret police. We do not know what he told his lifelong friend Manning Clark in 1958, 1960, and 1964. Without access to Clark's diary, we can only speculate what was on his mind when he talked with him in Prague and in London.

---

47   Ibid., p. 11.
48   Ibid., p. 12.
49   Ibid., p. 64.
50   Ibid., p. 12.
51   London, 1977, p. 8.

We can only guess why he wanted to see comrade E. F. Hill in 1956. Documents discovered in the Prague Ministry of Foreign Affairs do not tell us. They just reveal that on May 28, 1958, Hill, accompanied by a member of the Central Committee of the Communist Party of the Soviet Union, comrade Michailov, requested help from the Czechoslovak ambassador in Moscow in the following urgent matter reported to Prague by the ambassador:

> In Czechoslovakia, Ian Milner lives as a political emigrant from Australia. He works as a lecturer at Charles University. In connection with the case of former Soviet diplomat Petrov, Milner was forced to go into emigration (more exactly could not return to Australia). Comrade Hill, at the beginning of this year, when he was traveling through Czechoslovakia on his way to the Soviet Union to attend the 20th Congress of the Communist Party of the Soviet Union, met Milner's wife in Prague (Milner was then not in Prague). She told him that her husband very much would like to meet him. Comrade Hill did not know what it was all about and was not interested in such a meeting. He did not object to Milner's coming to see him in Moscow. If that was not possible, he would, although not gladly, come to Prague to see Milner. Hill entreated that this question of his meeting with Milner were cleared up in Prague and remarked that the Czechoslovak government knows about Milner's case.... Comrade Hill told me that he would stay two more months in the Soviet Union and then depart to China.

This urgent request was sent May 29, 1956 marked strictly secret. On the twenty-fourth of July, "a coded message arrived from Moscow. They push this affair. The Ministry of Foreign Affairs requests a statement by comrade Souček." Signed comrade Moravec.

For the moment, the important affair between Hill, Prague, Moscow, and Milner remains a mystery. Milner initiated the process; the Australian CP was very much involved (Hill arrived in Prague with an introduction requesting help, signed by General Secretary of the CPA, L.L. Sharkey); Moscow was very much interested, and Prague was asked at least twice to expedite the whole thing. Hill, strangely enough, strongly tried to distance himself from Milner, reluctant to offer any help. So far, neither Ministry of the Interior nor ASIO archives tell us what was then on the mind of agent No. 9006. Did he want to leave Prague? Maybe. Yet, there is a more plausible explanation. Milner wanted to reply to the Petrov Royal Commission that implicated him in the Soviet spy network in Canberra from 1944 on. He needed a skilled lawyer for creating a believable text of defense against the defamation as he denounced it in his Personal Statement later sent to Australia. A secret ASIO report form May 18, 1956 written by C. C. F. Spry documents his good sense of observation. On the basis of proofs available to us only recently, we can vouchsafe for the valuable work of this often maligned agency.

Colonel Spry then wrote to the Prime Minister R.G. Menzies: "It is my belief that the preparation of this statement and his submission are part of a preconceived plan in which others could be concerned. Indeed, by examining this statement, I think Milner has been assisted in its composition. It is of interest that Edward Fowler Hill, who represented Communist Party of Australia's interests during the Royal Commission proceedings, departed from Australia by air for the U.S.S.R. on 26 January, 1956, and has not returned. It is quite possible that he has already visited Prague, since Czechoslovakia was listed as a country of destination in his official notification of travel."

From the available documents it is not certain that E. F. Hill actually helped Milner in the formulation of his statement, although it is possible, even probable. Milner evidently wanted to see him for that exact purpose. He was an experienced lawyer, well versed in the intricacies of the Petrov affair. The statement was definitely aided by an expert and a shrewd legal specialist.

Colonel Spry suspected even more, and from evidence available now, rightly so: "It is also significant that Rex Chiplin, Communist journalist, who was described in the Royal Commission as being asked to execute certain enquiries in connection with the possible return of Milner to Australia, has made official travel application to visit Czechoslovakia, departing Sydney, 24 May 1956, for a period of three weeks. This country appears to be the sole one of destination."

(Chiplin flew into Prague on May 29 and was put up in the hotel Praha until the eighth or ninth of June. He asked the Central Committee of the Czechoslovak Communist Party to help him with a following trip to the USSR.)

Colonel's letter continued: "We have now received advice that Dr. and Mrs. H. V. Evatt have been invited by the Czechoslovakian Ministry of Foreign Affairs to visit that country for two weeks.... I feel that this visit could also be connected with the activities of Milner, if not the primary reason." So concluded the letter to Prime Minister Menzies of May 18, 1956.

In his introduction to Milner's memoirs, Vincent O'Sullivan, quoting from this document on page thirty, sarcastically wrote, "I Spy with my little eye, indeed. There is not a flicker of evidence to support the Colonel's scenario of intrigue." Fortunately, there is a lot of evidence, although historians have an urgent task to discover in Prague or in Moscow what really did take place in Prague during the year 1956 that was considered of such crucial importance to the CPA that they had to arrange a meeting in Prague to discuss it and settle on a defensive strategy to fight against the revelations of the Petrov Royal Commission. We know, for instance, that Dr. Evatt's visit cost Czech Communist authorities thirty thousand Czech crowns, that Milner's statement was given professional legalistic form, and that other Australian Communist sympathizers came to Prague at that time, including Allan Dalziel (Soviet code name DENIS).

Milner's movements were followed by ASIO, or its predecessor from the forties, and in New York the FBI surveyed his supposedly secret activities. All considered, although Milner produced some translations of Czech poetry and to a certain degree managed to pursue his career as a literary historian and teacher of English (often to future agents abroad), he descended into the abyss of a spying traitor to several countries and an undercover agent well paid for his denunciations of friends, colleagues, and students. The cause he was serving on the basis of his youthful idealism and middle-aged pragmatism was doomed to failure. His life and work can be judged as a minor personal tragedy but a major blunder. However, his friends still remember him fondly (with the exception of the next one).

MILNER'S REPORTS ON HIS FRIEND

Secret files of the Prague Ministry of the Interior revealed that since 1950, the Australian Ian Milner was a well-paid agent of the political police, and up until 1963 submitted 110 highly praised reports on his university colleagues, students, and contacts with the British embassy that represented Australian interests. However, we had no idea what kind of reports he actually wrote. One would assume that caught in the tentacles of the dangerous secret police while the top Communist leaders of Czechoslovakia were being tortured, condemned on trumped up charges in spectacular show trials, and hanged, he was frightened and sent reports that would be not too damaging to the victims. We did not know with any certainty, because his active file (yet not his family file) was *skartován*—destroyed in 1985.

Now that some of his observations meant for secret police eyes have been recently revealed, we know the truth. It is only a fraction of Milner's communications with the Prague police, but it is a good sample. They were found in a file devoted to Dr. Vilém Fried, personal friend and superior of Milner in the philosophy faculty of Charles University. And they are very nasty and intentionally damaging indeed.[52]

Dr. Fried served as assistant dean of the School of Non-Slavonic Languages at the University in Prague. Milner was his subordinate as a lecturer in English language and literature. They were close friends.

On March 29, 1956, Milner wrote to the secret police that he became acquainted with Dr. Fried at the beginning of 1951: "Fried was friendly and talked freely; after the Slánský process he was tense, reserved, distrustful, even hostile." At a time when the official party line was that everybody was happy that a dangerous imperialist group of traitors was unmasked and crushed, such improper behavior was, of course, suspect. Milner added that Dr. Fried was inquisitive about what was going on and was chasing information about people—hinting that Dr. Fried might also be a foreign agent.

Furthermore, Milner suggested that although Fried professed a Marxist and party standpoint, "in fact, he remains a Social Democrat with a leftist tendency." At the time the regime was organizing a witch hunt of former Social Democrats. Then he stressed: "His manners are

52   AMI, V – 24 597.

authoritarian and he is very ambitious—he wants to make a successful career. That is for him decisive also in political and ideological questions.... He is envious of other people's successes and slanders them, mostly younger people. He has wide contacts in cultural circles and even in the State apparatus."

Milner concluded his secret report by what he, in a collectivist regime, must have considered a knock-out blow: "His way of solving problems shows that he is an individualist left Social Democrat. From time to time, he has critical comments to Soviet politics, especially in relation to the Czechoslovak Republic."

Fried was watched by two other agents with code names LUBOŠ and OPOČENSKÝ. The first considered him to be "a good pedagogue," but the other denounced him as "sly as a fox, insincere, eloquent, and dexterous." He also reported that after the twentieth congress of the CPSU, at a meeting of the Communist Party branch at the philosophy faculty, Fried publicly said that "it's time to be finally paid by the USSR for our uranium ore and mines in Jáchymov." This police agent also blamed Fried for lowering the importance of Russian language classes compared with other lectures at the universities.[53] (Since it is not clear if OPOČENSKÝ was not just a code name for Milner's handler, the information might have come from Milner. At that time, children in schools had more instruction in the Russian language than in the Czech or Slovak mother tongue.)

In spite of some of these damning reports, in 1958 the secret police tried to recruit Fried as its agent. When the English professor Robert Auty planned to visit Prague, the police wanted to use Fried's previous acquaintance with Auty. "Fried said about him that he is a person worthy of the attention of the Ministry of the Interior." Auty served at the Czechoslovak embassy in London as a translator during WWII. He had many contacts in the ČSR.

Another reason for Fried's recruitment was that British consul Lawrence sent greetings to him several times and invited him to a party. Fried did not want to accept the invitation, but the police requested that he go since they suspected that the British intelligence service wanted to hire him as their agent. Dr. Fried did not want to work for the Czech secret police. He found an original excuse. He claimed that it was not in his character and that "it perturbs him so much that it

---

53   AMI, T 514.

harms his potency and his wife then quarrels with him." The police persuaded him to go and gave him instructions on what to do. He later reported that he met both Lawrence and Auty. They talked just about work. Again, he repeated that he did not want to be an StB (Státní Bezpecnost [State Security]) agent. However, he criticized Milner: "He wants to be invited everywhere and intrudes on everybody. Universally it is known about him that he contacts every Anglo-Saxon." Then Fried added significantly, "You know more about Milner than I do." He refused to discuss it further. Still it was hard and dangerous not to cooperate with the secret police. Several doctors, for instance, had their careers curtailed for refusing to report on their colleagues. The police ordered him to contact Auty again and get his opinions about the international situation. A few days later Fried reported that Auty told him the international situation was good and there was no threat of a war.

Dr. Fried was caught in the police net. He was given the title candidate of cooperation, a code name DOCENT and further duties. He had to report on visiting Evans Garner, a friend of Prime Minister Harold Macmillan. When Garner questioned why Czech guides made no mention of former presidents Thomas Masaryk and Eduard Beneš, Auty, who was present, "explained it to him in the proper Marxist way."

Milner also reported that Fried said it was time to get rid of the (huge) Stalin monument (over Prague) and settle the question of Gottwald's remains. (They were displayed, like Lenin's, in a pompous mausoleum high above Prague.)[54]

On May 1, 1962, students demonstrated in Prague. Major Bartoš, code name NECHLEBA, reported that Dr. Fried did not condemn the students as the regime did, but, on the contrary, claimed that "the danger of the students was exaggerated and artificially inflated; there was a tendency to denounce students and the intelligentsia as subversive." (Bartoš belonged to Milner's group of police handlers.)

The report stressed that during WWII, Fried taught at the Czechoslovak school in England; it was an institute for the sons of officers and diplomats. It was alleged that Fried mishandled progressive

---

54   AMI, V – 24 597.

students and supported President Beneš and his government in exile.[55]

The situation of František Sosna, another police agent who supervised Fried, was complicated. According to a report from October 1962 by Milner's handler at the time, Lieutenant Jiří Kořínek, Sosna lectured on the Czech language at the school of non-Slavonic languages. In 1961, he spent a year at the University of Göttingen. Acting as agent of the police, "he became a victim of a provocation." An assistant flirted with him, but when he wanted to kiss her, she created a scandal. At a party trial at the Prague philosophy faculty, he was reprimanded and banned from foreign travel for six years. Privately, however, he was praised as a firm Communist while all the other faculty members opposed him because they would have liked to change the party policies. Dr. Fried would have liked to get rid of Sosna since Sosna criticized him a few times and called attention to political weaknesses in his lecture notes. It was also claimed that a British spy was among Fried's contacts with British reactionary professors and the British embassy in Prague.[56]

In October 1962, Ian Milner told his police handler that Fried went to a cocktail party where the British chargé d'affaires, Hunter, and the American military attaché, a Czech by origin, showed great interest in him. The next month Milner revealed that Fried was having constant conflicts with Sosna and was interfering with other people's work. In December, Milner again denounced his boss and friend: "Fried listens to radio broadcasts from Vienna. They announced that the Chinese CP Central Committee sent our CP a letter about their standpoint and opinions on the USSR–China conflict. This letter was not published in our country. He is very much interested in the views of Chinese Communists."

Such disagreements with the party leadership and their policies might seem to be minor, but often they led to punishment of those who were denounced. They could lose their jobs, be demoted, sent to prison or concentration camps, or be beaten to death when they could not disprove suspicions that they were masked imperialist agents.

In January 1963, Milner sent at least three reports of a university bulletin board poster in which students of English studies criticized the

55   AMI, 4 – 410.
56   AMI, V – 24 597.

twelfth congress of the CPCZ and requested answers to their questions about the difficult economic and political situation. Somebody took the poster down. "A likely author of these questions seems to be Mary Wheeler (the family requested asylum in the ČSR where her father works as an economist[57])."

When Khrushchev made a speech criticizing Yevtuchenko's poem Babi Yar, which evoked the suffering of Jews in the Ukraine during the war, and averred that not only Jews suffered, according to Milner's report to the police, Fried claimed that anti-Jewish tendencies were again appearing.

In November 1963, the agent code named D-FRANTA told the political police that Fried came from an old orthodox Jewish family and he was educating his adopted son in the same spirit (thus not the proper Communist way). Lieutenant Kořínek, Milner's handler, suggested using JÁNSKÝ to further investigate Fried.[58]

Although Milner complained about the state of his health at the beginning of 1964, and his work for the police was temporarily suspended, he obviously continued his good work, because he submitted another note concerning Fried in December. He reported that in November 1964, Fried took part in a linguistic congress in Sonnenberg: "He conducted himself as a great Czech patriot and in principle talked about socialist Czechoslovakia." Czech representatives wanted to prevent the departure of all participants to the border of Communist East Germany where a wreath was supposed to be laid honoring the memory of a refugee shot while trying to flee the German Democratic Republic. At the conference, Fried allegedly became acquainted with Professor Carsten. There, Fried praised him very much, but back in Prague he did the opposite. So two-faced and untrustworthy was Milner's boss!

---

57   Mary's father, George Wheeler, "a secret Communist, worked for the [US] Foreign Economic Administration and had come under Civil Service Commission suspicion" when his brother, Donald Wheeler, started to have problems as a very productive Soviet spy. That might have been the reason for his transfer to Prague. See John Earl Haynes, Harvey Klehr, and Alexander Vassiliev, *Spies: The Rise and Fall of the KGB in America* [Yale University Press, 2009, pp. 308 and 305-312.
58   AMI,V-24597.

Finally, in May 1965, D-SOSNA reported that during discussions about interviews of new students, Fried demanded that class origin and political membership of parents not be considered anymore. He lost.

Lieutenant Kořínek designated Dr. Fried to be "followed by D-SOSNA and A JÁNSKÝ," and "evaluated by all our confidants and collaborators as a schemer and careerist; he has many contacts with foreign, mainly British, university professors." He was often invited to British embassy receptions, especially by consul Fry who was expelled. In the spring, he was conspiratorially contacted by the secretary of the School of Slavonic Studies in London, Miss Lloyd, who had been suspected of being a spy trying to enlist Czech university professors visiting London. Fried was too well informed about political events at home and abroad. According to agent Milner, although in discussions Fried was cautious himself, he spurred others to speak for him.[59]

It is not surprising that Fried, who was so much watched by the political police, used the first opportunity after the August 1968 invasion by Soviet forces to leave the country of bureaucratic nightmares. In December 1968, he was sent by the Ministry of Education to Los Angeles. He was allowed to take his wife and thirteen-year-old son. When they did not return in January 1973, they were put on trial for the crime of desertion. The dean and the secretary of the philosophy faculty denounced him as an adherent to elitist theories. However, court proceedings were interrupted when the president declared an amnesty for refugees who would return home. When he did not come back in 1974, he was condemned to three years of prison and his wife to eighteen months. All their property was confiscated. They lived in exile.

Ian Milner stayed in Prague until his death in 1991.

HIS TWO WIVES AND THE SECRET POLICE

Ian

Additional material obtained by e-mail from the Office for Documentation and Investigation of Communist Crimes at the Prague Ministry of the Interior confirms from a new source facts that I

---

59   Ibid.

uncovered in 1996 and 1997. It also proves the authenticity of things that until now could have only been suspected.

For instance, the Czech political police knew about Milner's "non-legal membership in the Communist Party of Australia (CPA)" in the forties and later. The first written report in the police archive dated October 25, 1957 (unseen until now) mentions that "during his employment at the ministry of Foreign Affair in Canberra (1944–1947) he handed over to our Friends through third persons valuable materials on political questions." The documents explicitly state that Milner was already spying in Canberra, not only for the Soviet Union but that "he handed over important materials also to us."

When Milner worked for the United Nations in New York, "on the sixth of March 1949, he was won over by our Friends for cooperation." In the Czech Communist parlance, "our Friends" always means Soviet Russians.

A police document confirms our suspicion that the police "obtained a teaching position for him at the Charles University" when he was ordered by the Soviet spy network to transfer from New York to Prague when his cover was blown. He was told to move under the pretext of his wife's need for medical treatment. Milner's police agent's salary was twenty-five thousand Czech crowns (Kčs) when compared with his monthly paycheck as a lecturer of seven thousand Kčs.[60]

We now know that in Prague Milner often met members of the revolutionary Australian colony, Ken Gott, Stephen Murray-Smith, and Noel Ebbels, whose police file disappeared but who was supplying his revolutionary compatriots (probably through the Czechoslovak consulate in Sydney) with blank Australian passports.

What is more, we now also know that both of Milner's wives had close contacts with the Prague secret police. They had their own files and code names.

Margot

Milner's first wife, Margaret (Margot), was born with the name Treffort in New Zealand (like Milner) in 1911. In the police file of October 25, 1957, she was identified as "external translator and private teacher

60   AMI, file 620016.

of English." At the end of this (Milner's) file, we can read: "Enlisting the cooperation of Mrs. Milner can be valuable since she has contacts with foreigners and our artistic circles. Her family breakdown could be used by a foreign intelligence agency to harm her husband a the society they are trying to represent. Against recruitment is the fact that she is talkative."

It was decided to check her contacts by reading her correspondence and searching her apartment for compromising material. Her husband (code named JÁNSKÝ), would be asked to reveal all that he knew about her. Also, her attitude toward Soviet and Czech espionage had to be investigated. Informant MINAŘÍKOVÁ was commissioned to follow her.[61]

A secret police contact was made with Mrs. Milner on 10 October 1958. An agent pretending to be named KUBÍČEK explained to her that the police were interested in the foreigners living in the country, how were they satisfied, etc. Her visa was expiring; it was thought that that should encourage her to help. Mrs. Milner, speaking Czech poorly, told the agent that she was considering returning home to England. During her last visit to London, she and Milner's brother were invited to meet a man from the secret service who questioned her about the affair in Australia in which her husband was implicated as a spy.

Lieutenant Koška, who prepared this report, proposed that several meetings be arranged to check her relation to the Czech police and possibly to recruit her.

Eight days later, Koška wrote that Mrs. Milner told him that she was in Australia at the end of 1957. There she heard rumors that she was a Czechoslovak agent. She complained to the foreign office and was visited by secret agents who questioned her about the Petrov case. She referred them to her husband; she did not know a thing about it.

Koška remarked that it was known that she was looking for a job, but when she was offered help, she refused, claiming to be lazy and not liking to write—while her busy correspondence was known. She tried to avoid talking about her contacts and kept turning the conversation to the writer Jiří Mucha (an excellent Czech writer; it was rumored that after his imprisonment he acted as police informer). It was intimated to

---

61   AMI, T 773, 4/III/MI/341.

her that she knew many interesting people but not everyone was what he pretended to be. She retorted that all of them were clean.[62]

Mrs. Milner obviously attempted to stay clear of the police in spite of their constant courting of her. She told Ian Milner about these meetings with the police. At this time she had been separated from her husband for about two years. He told his handler OSPĚVÁK what she told him. Unfortunately, we have no idea what else Milner reported about his first wife, although they requested he tell them everything he knew.

At the end of 1958, police agents Jiří Čermák and Jan Koška recorded their interview with Mrs. Milner. Since her arrival in the ČSR, she had traveled several times to the West. Six times she was contacted by foreign intelligence: four times in Australia, once in England, and once in New Zealand. She was questioned about the circumstances of her stay in the ČSR and about the spy affair of her husband. English diplomats never showed any interest in her husband. She asserted that when questioned, she reacted shrewdly and vaguely. She was sure that she was believed. In June 1959, she wanted to settle in England. Did the Czech agents conclude that she treated them the same way: shrewdly and vaguely?

When she was asked if the British intelligence service offered cooperation, she answered no; anyway, she would not accept it. "Cursorily" she was offered cooperation by the Czech agents; "she neither refused nor accepted."[63]

From a notation found in the international department of the central committee of the Communist Party of Czechoslovakia, it is clear that when political worker McArra, a New Zealander, visited Milner and his wife in Prague, they informed him that during her stays in Australia, England, and New Zealand, she was investigated by secret services and that the Czechoslovak intelligence offered her cooperation.

The CPA was very interested in Margot and concerned that she could harm it. On March 23, 1959, E. F. (Ted) Hill, member of the politburo of the CPA, visited Rudolf Barák, Minister of the Interior (police). Hill told him that the so-called Petrov affair of 1954 was used for a pretext for breaking off diplomatic relations between Australia

---

62   AMI, file 620016.
63   Ibid.

and the USSR. A royal commission prepared a report in which it was asserted that J. (sic) F. Milner had contacts with a certain Clayton who served as his intermediary. "Hill revealed that Milner actually transferred some information to our Friends, but there was no proof that could have been used against him in a trial."

Hill further mentioned that Margaret Milner, during her visit to Australia, was interrogated by the Australian, British, and New Zealand police, even by deputy director Richardson. The leadership of the CPA was worried that the intelligence service would use her in a new campaign against the USSR and CPA. Mrs. Milner knew a great deal about the activities of her husband. Comrade Hill requested that by some nonviolent way she should not be allowed to resettle in England and be kept in Prague. He characterized her as honest, but careless and fickle. She could be made to disclose secrets to an experienced agent. He did not exclude the possibility that British intelligence could win her over.

The same day as Margot's interrogation, a member of the Ministry of the Interior prepared a brief for Minister Barák to give the following day to Comrade Hill. It said that the cultivation of Mrs. Milner began in the fall of 1958. She was considered to be a suitable agent for contacting Englishmen living in the ČSR. Since she had many contacts with Czechs, mainly in cultural circles, it was thought that she could be valuable in this area, too. She taught English, and all her pupils had significant social positions. She was also meeting the first secretary and the consul of the British embassy and was openly contacted by them. There were contradictions in her statements: she said that she wanted to stay in the ČSR if she could find a partner and a job, but she refused any help offered. She introduced the secretary of the British embassy, Lawrence, to our artists and cultural officials, but the Czech police determined that it was not a part of an intelligence service operation.[64]

It is not known if Comrade Hill was satisfied with this answer to his urgent inquiry. Maybe because of his intervention, Margot was not allowed to leave for England when she tried to in 1959 and 1960. The decision was later changed, and she left for London. She was given the code name INES and kept returning to Prague, mainly for the Prague spring music festival. However, there is only one report available that

---

64   AMFA, part 1/1, pp. 121–22.

she really worked for the Czech secret service. Thanks to her close friendship with Jiří Bartoš (code name VIKTOR), the police gained one of their important agents (we will hear about him later).

In the last memorandum concerning Margot Milner, written in May 1965, we read that in 1961, she enticed Czechoslovak employees of the embassy in London to private apartments and that she was in touch with a certain Dobson "who was exposed as a spy." Major Hampl concluded that Mrs. Milner could be an intelligence agent working for the British.[65] That would be a decisive change from a young radical Communist to an anti-Communist—due to her experience with real life in a Soviet satellite!

The cat and mouse game so unsuccessfully played with the shrewd first wife of Ian Milner, Margaret, was tried before with his second wife. It met with better, though limited, success.

Jarmila

Jarmila Frühaufová, Ian Milner's second wife, became a special agent of the Prague secret police while she was helping to destroy his marriage to Margot by being his mistress. She was born Jarmila Mařanová in 1913 in Prague. While studying in the USA, beginning in 1937, and then working at the United Nations Organization (UNO), she married a refugee and naturalized American builder and engineer named Bedřich Frühauf. She divorced him in 1947 and returned to Prague.

Miloslav Macháček, who worked in the American counterespionage section of theCzechoslovak State Security department, proposed on January 15, 1951 to engage her as an agent. The reason he gave was that she was employed "in the object of our StB interest, the United Nations Information Center in Prague." She worked there as a secretary, taking care of mutual contacts between the center and the American secretariat of the UN, making translations, and acting as an accountant. While all other employees of the center were reactionaries,

---

65   AMI, file 620016. According to Desmond Ball and David Horner, *Breaking the Codes: Australia's KGB Network* (St Leonards, NSW, Australia, p. 326), in London Margot organized "splendid parties, propagated Czech musical culture, and died on 11 August 1995."

her orientation was progressive. "We intend to use her to get general news from the center– she can do that."[66]

Macháček reviewed her background: In 1947, she returned to the ČSR. Her husband refused to come with her. They divorced with a proviso that their daughter (later to be adopted by Ian Milner) would be educated as a non-Communist. In Prague, Jarmila Frühaufová worked for the Information Center of the UNO. On the advice of the secret police, their agent and her lover, Josef Vinš (born 1906), persuaded her to supply him with information about her workplace. In July 1950, she gave the police the keys to the center so that they could copy them and gain an easy access. She was invited to the police station where she was told that it would be faster and thus aid socialism if she delivered her information directly to it. She was enlisted by referents Nos. 22 and 29 as an agent on February 7, 1951, and received the cover name HALBICH and number 7045. (Milner was 7006.) All her expenses were paid.[67]

There was an unusual level of interest in her. On May 19, 1952, the special department for preparation of agents in the UNO registered her under a second cover name, JULIE. Seargent Tomeš complained in his report on her that the other police department refused to transfer her to them, except in the event that she traveled abroad. On June 24, 1952, he also expressed the opinion that she was not compromised enough. It was barely sufficient for work on a domestic basis. In order to compromise her further, their agent CLAUS was assigned to get close to her. She seemed to be very intelligent, sociable, and a good type for a useful agent. The police officer mentioned that in 1951, she visited the USA and reported on it. However, she carefully hid her own opinions and kept her US citizenship as insurance. She stayed in contact with the Milners.[68] On May 5, 1953, a member of the other police agency, identified only as "referent 1011," reported that although she was gained as a police agent "on ideological grounds," some agencies suspected her of being a provocateur in service of Jiří Janeček from the secretariat of the New York office of the UNO. Her contacts were carefully examined. She was supposed to inform the secret police not only about the correspondence and activities of the Prague Center, but

66   AMI, file 336087.
67   Ibid.
68   AMI, file 10001/303.

especially watch all her colleagues, mainly the director Olaf Ritter and his deputy Arnošt Bareš. She became more dutiful "under the influence of O." (Who was O? A new lover supplied by the police?) When she was offered Czechoslovak citizenship, she equivocated.[69]

After several further documents testifying to her rather complicated life with several suspicious acquaintances and lovers (some of whom were assigned to supervise her by the police), her work for the secret police came to an end on November 20, 1956. This "special agent" was "unfortunately not motivated enough." Other agents at her workplace were delivering better and more important information, so the collaboration was terminated after five years. HALBICH's file was deposited in the archive.[70] Ten years later, the same thing happened to the second file on her with the cover name JULIE.[71]

Having read these two files on Mrs. Frühauf(ová)-Milner(ová), I understand better why when I telephoned while in Prague 1996, Linda, her daughter from her first marriage adopted by Ian Milner, was not at all cooperative and very angrily threatened me with court proceedings if I continued my inquiries in the archives.

A SOCIAL [SEXUAL] AGENT

Police files on Milner's wife Margot often mention Jiří Bartoš (b. 1932) and his close friendship with Milner's first wife. They say she used to teach Bartoš English and allowed him to use her car. She introduced him to the secret police who liked and trusted him because he "gave them many reports on her."[72] On March 7, 1959, Captain Bořivoj Kalandra, head of the first section of the second department, proposed to recruit Jiří Bartoš. At that time Bartoš worked at the ethnographical museum Náprstek where he was considered lazy. He was a chemist and before that worked as a laboratory technician in the chemical industry. He belonged to all the proper Communist organizations. However, his other non-proletarian characteristics pleased the police more: "He comes from a white-collar family, makes friends with people who like

---

69   Ibid.
70   Ibid.
71   AMI, file 336087.
72   AMI, file 620016 on code name of Margot, INES.

Western culture and often visits winerooms.... He seems to be a good type." Bartoš was recruited on March 27, 1959. His first assignment was to befriend the first secretary of the British embassy, Lawrence, since he was a good friend of Margot and could be an economic spy. He was also to try to seduce women working at the embassy. His cover name was VICTOR, agent No. 10005. He was twenty-six years old.[73]

The police arranged a better job for him, more suitable for his new career. He became an employee of Interhotel and quickly rose to chief of economic publicity at the headquarters of Prague Interhotels by 1966. He was valued as a man with a good work ethic. (More on the question of ethics later.)

Margot introduced him to several members of the British embassy, among whom he befriended especially first secretary Lawrence, third secretary Ratford, and clerk Robertson. He also entertained friendly relations with official representatives of Arabian states, most of all with the military attaché of Saudi Arabia, Said. In a police document we can read, "He was used mainly as a social agent and his task was to become friendly on amorous grounds with women employed by the British Embassy. Thus he was being used until 1962, the year of his marriage.... Three years later, divorced, he is again able to fulfill the duties of a special agent. But he performs his tasks only adequately; he hesitates."

Police criticism of Bartoš (VICTOR) mounted. It did not matter that he "was a close friend of our collaborator at the British embassy, Ms Veselá," but when in 1965 he accompanied a group of students to Western Germany and was targeted by the police on another police agent, Melichar, he told Melichar about it. Even worse was when he was assigned by the secret police to Dr. Ursula Korman, press leader of the travel agency Neckerman in West Germany. He continued sleeping with her beyond police duties. She liked him so much that she invited him abroad to accompany her on a month-long journey with Neckerman. That was too much, and Bartoš was not granted permission. When Margot invited him to London, he was not allowed to go there either.

A document appears in the police archive in which Major Emil Glogar complains about his amorous police agent: "He proved to be completely untrustworthy and therefore one cannot trust him." What

---

73   AMI, file 620303/10005.

else can one expect from an agent who was employed to pretend to be in love in order to spy from bed?

Another of Bartoš's mistresses, Milena Geisler(ová), was jealous of Miss Korman and made a drunken call to the police. She said that her intuition was telling her that Bartoš might escape during his planned trip to Germany. Major Glogar realized too late that, after all, the proletarian police could not trust such bourgeois people.

The last document in this file is short. Major Marcel Šimon, cover name JAROSLAV, noted, "Jiří Bartoš, departure into a foreign country. He had a lax attitude to work, was insincere." Among the directive organs of the police is mentioned the late comrade Grebeníček, who in this case acted as an institutional pimp. He was the father of the longtime leader of the Communist Party of the Czech Republic after the Velvet Revolution of 1989. [74]

Conclusion

Ian Milner began his espionage as an idealistic Marxist toward the end of WWII in an atmosphere of friendship with the victorious power that was secretly preparing for the next confrontation with its allies. Once he committed himself to work as an undercover agent for the Soviet Union and for its satellite Czechoslovakia, he became entrapped and as their valued tool could not escape their clutches. After he had committed treason against his adopted homeland of Australia at its Department of Foreign Affairs, compromising mainly British post-war planning, he served his hidden masters in United Nations' attempts to deal with crises in Greece and the Middle and Far East.

When his espionage was detected, he was transferred to Prague in 1950. In this important center of Soviet imperialist endeavors, he met many compatriots eager to learn how to Stalinize Australia from the successfully dictatorial Czech Communists. He became worried during the liquidation of many leading Communists, but his spy masters did not allow him to leave. He continued serving them while teaching at the university, dutifully reporting on his meetings with Anglo-Saxon and Czech colleagues, and fulfilling police assignments abroad. His two

74   Ibid.

wives also had contacts with the efficient Czechoslovak secret police who used false love and sexual seduction in their methods. Milner's sad disillusionment can be seen projected in his translations of Czech poetry.

2

A Devoted Scribe For Hire: Wilfred Burchett

Credibility is one of the major assets of a successful journalist; if he is not trusted, he will not be read. That Wilfred Burchett for decades was the most widely read and influential Australian reporter and writer on international affairs was facilitated by his claim that although he sometimes sympathized with Communist causes, he did not belong to any Communist party. He repeatedly denied that he was a member of the Communist Party of Australia (CPA). He lied, even under oath, to the New South Wales Supreme Court in 1974 when he categorically denied he had ever been a member of the CPA. Many people believed him; those who did not had no proof of his deception.

PRAGUE DOCUMENTS

Research in October 1996 in the State Central Archive of the Czech Republic, then on Karmelitská ulice (a street) in Prague, put an end to the late Burchett's credibility and to his defenders' claims that he was an honorable man and victim of Cold War fabrications.

In the archive that houses documents from the history of the Communist Party of Czechoslovakia (CPCZ), I found five documentations of Burchett's systematic lying. The oldest is from Decenber 27, 1950. Secretary H. Glaserová sent a "Note for Comrade Geminder." Geminder was her boss, the head of the International Department of the Central Committee of the CPCZ, and allegedly the most important Soviet agent in Prague. Comrade Glaserová reported

on the visit of Comrade Jack Hughes, Chairman of the Control
Commission of the CPA:

> Comrade Hughes talked about the case of the
> Australian journalist, Comrade Burchett, who after the
> war worked as a journalist in some countries of people's
> democracy; also for a short time in Czechoslovakia.
> Recently, he was expelled and returned to Australia.
> The Australian Party is content with his work and
> is certain he is a good comrade. The Party would be
> glad if his name was cleared, as well as his wife's whose
> nationality is of another people's democracy, maybe
> Bulgaria.[75]

The second document is even more important since it was written
and signed by G. W. Burchett himself on July 13, 1951 in room 314
in the Peking Hotel in China. It was addressed to Ernie Thornton,
former general secretary of the Federated Ironworkers Association and
prominent member of the CPA, who was on his way from China to
Czechoslovakia. In a very long letter, Burchett pleaded his innocence
as a member of the CPA. He blamed two other comrades for his
expulsion from Prague: Comrade Jakš, a former chief of Telepress who
supposedly owed him some money for work done, and Dr. Popper of
the Press Department of the Ministry of Information; they denounced
him as a British and American agent respectively. As a result, his
wife, whom he married in Sofia, was "suspended from the Bulgarian
Communist Party." In his letter, Burchett also claimed that "a number
of Telepress agents protected by Jakš were later proved to be Titoists
and Trotskyites."

The early fifties were very dangerous times for members of
Communist parties in Central and Eastern Europe. Stalin was purging
his own and his satellite empire of alleged foreign spies. The era typified
Lenin's slogan "Kto Kogo" ("Who Whom": who kills whom first).
Those who wanted to survive kept denouncing their colleagues before
their colleagues could denounce them.

Burchett seemed to be a good target because of his contacts with
the British and American officials that he was working against, mainly

---

75   State Central Archive (SCA), Fond 100/3, file 25, item 91; I/6-66.

in Berlin. In his defence, Burchett wrote, "Dear Comrade Thornton: I have never been expelled nor even disciplined by the CPA." He then stressed: "I was not, nor could have been, expelled by the Russians from Berlin.... I had the closest relations with Soviet colleagues in the Sovinform Buro. It was the latter who arranged the publication of my book Sonnenaufgang über Asien in the Soviet Sector of Berlin, *after* the time I was supposed to have been expelled. "

Burchett supported his good credentials with Russian, Hungarian, and Bulgarian regimes by enumerating his long stays in Berlin, Budapest, and Bulgaria. "Only in Prague ... did these most harmful rumours originate." He then showed that cunning agents can also be extremely naïve. He made an almost suicidal proposition: "I can be dealt with, extradited to Prague and charged." Later we will look at parts of his autobiography which demonstrate what kind of harm could have been done to him in Prague, which was then in the maelstrom of a vicious witch hunt of Communists by Soviet executioners.

The letter to Thornton ended in a touching, comradely note: "My wife has been a loyal worker in the Bulgarian C. P. or in the illegal Youth League since the age of 16. Needless to say our only wish on getting married was to serve the party together by combining our talents and using them wherever they were needed. With comradely greetings, W. G. Burchett."[76]

The last paragraph of the letter shows how well its author absorbed the Stalinist attitudes of the times: Soviet and people's democracies' textbooks, newspapers, and journals were full of stories about girls falling in love with tractor drivers just because they managed to surpass the norm for deep plowing, and men being enraptured by milkmaids who doubled the amount of milk from their collectively owned cows. Eros was acceptable only in the service to the party. Dating was sanctioned only if it was to attend party meetings.

Ernie Thornton delivered Burchett's letter as he was asked. He obviously kept the original letter and in Prague left a copy of it. We are able to read it thanks to its preservation in the State Central Archive in Prague. As a good comrade, Thornton did even more. On August 6, 1951, from the Czech hotel Paříž (Paris) in Prague, he forwarded to the International Department of the CPCZ a confirmation of Burchett's good standing in the party: "It might interest Comrade Geminder

---

76   Ibid., I/6-8651.

because some time ago I talked with him about it." He requested that a copy of the reference be sent to the Central Committee of the CP of Bulgaria, Sofia. It was sent on August 20, 1951, written in Russian.[77]

Finally, the fifth document should be reproduced in full:

> The Communist Party of Australia Central Committee, 40 Market Street, Sydney,
>
> 18.6.1951
>
> Dear Comrade,
> We obtained a request to confirm the status of comrade Wilfred Burchett. The Party does not issue recommendations except in extraordinary circumstances and does not possess any form of recommendation nor a seal that could be used to documents of that kind. In the case in question, Comrade Burchett has the trust of the Australian Party. His work is considered to be satisfactory and we have no reason to doubt his loyalty. The situation of his wife is known to us and we would be grateful for any help that would be offered to him. Since the entry into the Party, he has been its member without interruption.
>
> R. Dixon, Chairman
> L. L. Sharkey
> Secretary General[78]

Some Australians, trying to save the reputation of Burchett, claimed that these documents have been forged and therefore do not prove anything. I have no doubt that all five documents are genuine. At that time, Soviet and Czechoslovak secret services kept looking for comrades that they could use in staged trials, most murderous of them being the Slánsky trial. Burchett was obviously considered for such a role, but was not selected, just thrown out of the country. There

---

77 Ibid., I/6-8651.
78 Ibid.

does not seem to exist any possible reason for anybody forging these documents then. Later, there was no motivation for their forgery either. Who and why in Prague could have been interested in proving that an Australian journalist was a secret member of the CPA?[79]

Wilfred Burchett was not a pathological liar, but a Leninist-Stalinist operative who as such was convinced that in the war against bourgeois capitalism, in order to achieve the hoped-for Communist future, he

79   Mark Aarons, the son of the last leader of the CPA, Laurie Aarons, and himself a previous Communist, found further confirmation about their genuine origin in the Australian archives: "In late 1949 Burchett married a Bulgarian communist *Vessa Ossikovska* ... When his Bulgarian visa expired it was not extended, but Ossikovska was refused permission to leave ... Head of the CPA control commission (responsible for security), Hughes sought assistance to clear Burchett and Ossikovska, stating that the CPA was content with Burchett's work 'and is certain that he is a good comrade'. This intervention could not have occurred without Burchett enlisting the CPA's support ... Hruby also located a letter dated July 13. 1951, from Burchett to CPA leader and ex-Federated Ironworkers Association national secretary Ernie Thornton ... Burchett was leaving that day for Korea, but knew that Thornton would soon travel to Europe so he asked him to clear thing up to enable Ossikovska to leave Bulgaria ... ASIO located Thornton in Beijing at this time and soon after in Prague. ASIO determined that a senior Chinese unionist telegrammed Thornton from Prague on July 10, 1951 (three days before Burchett's letter), directing him to join him in Prague at the conclusion of a conference then under way in Beijing. ASIO also confirmed Thornton's arrival in Czechoslovakia nine days later. In Prague Thornton received a letter dated June 18, 1951, signed by CPA leaders Richard Dixon and Lance Sharkey that confirmed Burchett 'has the trust of the Australian Party', which considered his work satisfactory and did not doubt his loyalty. They specifically asked for assistance in resolving Ossikovska's problem. Thornton dispatched their letter to the Czechs on August 6, 1951, who sent it to Bulgaria a fortnight later. By April 1952, Ossikovska had her exit visa. These documents fit the known facts of Burchett's and Ossikovska's histories; forging them would have involved an improbable conspiracy. The pattern of contact between the CPA and Burchett has been confirmed by one of the younger generation of leaders, who recalled carrying a secret envelope to Burchett in Moscow from Dixon and Hughes in 1958." Mark Aarons, "Cut to size by the force of history," *The Australian,* June 04, 2008.

had the right, even the duty, to deceive the enemy. In Burchett's mind, there was no doubt that for achieving the ideal result, he had to use less than ideal methods, because the bourgeois enemy also lied.

Nevertheless, his books are always less than truthful, even when the bourgeois enemy is hard to see. For instance, in his autobiography published in 1981, he alleged that he had learned about the suspicion of his being a British intelligence agent "only ten years later," even though he obviously defended himself against such an accusation in 1951.[80] Therefore, it is difficult to believe his statement in the same memoir that early in his adult life he filled an application to join the CPA, but "there was no follow up to my application."[81]

FROM AUSTRALIA TO BERLIN AND BUDAPEST

Burchett became a Communist fighter for the usual reasons: he grew up during the Depression and shared the assumption that the class war and its injustices, the crises of capitalism, international wars, and colonialism could only be abolished by revolution and the establishment of Communism. His view of the world was Manichean; he hated the enemy, and he believed, or sometimes pretended to believe, that everything was great on his side of the barricades. The fact that for thirty years he was well paid and provided for by Communist regimes was probably also a factor.

Burchett's books are painful to read. They are loathsome and full of propaganda clichés that are all too familiar to someone who for long years had to read Soviet prose whose tactics and techniques Burchett adopted 100 percent. Although he obviously kept distorting the truth, it is surprising how many people believed his slanted reportage. One finds believable what one wants to believe.

He himself had to admit that he often falsified the truth with the excuse that at the time he believed it. After articles and books about his daring and adventurous trips to New Caledonia, China, Burma, and the Pacific during World War II, he established his popularity with the anti-American Left when in 1945 he managed to get to Hiroshima soon

---

80   W|ilfred Burchett, *At the Barricades* (Macmillan, Australia, 1981), p. 153.

81   Ibid., pp. 47–48.

after the atomic bomb devastated the city. Allegedly against American wishes, he reported on the damage done to people by the radiation. However, according to Pat Burgess, this fame was unearned, since the report was actually written by Henry Keyes who used "a mass of information from the Domei files and had interviewed a lot of people including some eye witnesses." Out of some two or three thousand words that Burchett wrote on the subject, the press agency released only two hundred, and even those were not used. Some Americans who came back from Hiroshima were surprised that Burchett had not asked them to take back his report, which they would have gladly done. Keyes sent the copy under the Burchett byline to the *Express*. "When Wilfred got back he said, 'Oh no! Don't tell me!'"[82]

From 1946 to 1949, Burchett continued to send his reports to the British press from Berlin. According to his book *Cold War in Germany*, the Americans were then planning a third world war and were provoking the Cold War against the peaceful Soviet Union that was interested only in safeguarding its own security. The creation of the Soviet satellite empire and brutal suppression of democracy and freedom in Central Europe was therefore good. He even blamed the Western allies for slow denazification in Germany and the Swiss for hoarding Nazi gold. He weakened his case with hateful exaggerations.

In his "Report of the Committee of the Judiciary, United States Senate" of the sixth and tenth of November, 1969, Soviet defector and former NKVD-KGB operative Yuri Krotkov testified that he cooperated with Burchett in Berlin from 1947 to 1949. The Australian journalist had access to Soviet funds and worked as a typical Soviet propagandist.

According to Burchett, "The Western Powers acted as did Hitler and Mussolini, using the same language as Goebbels."[83] East Germany remained occupied by Soviet armed forces until 1989; in spite of this fact, Burchett claimed that "the republic was given real powers immediately after it was founded, in contrast to the illusory powers

---

82   Pat Burgess, *WARCO: Australian Reporters at War* (Hawthorn, Vic.: William Heinemann Australia, 1986), pp. 182–83.

83   Wilfred Burchett, *Cold War in Germany* (Melbourne: World Unity Publications, 1950), p. 7.

vested in the Bonn regime ... the republic started life politically and economically independent."[84]

Soviet soldiers in Central and Eastern Europe committed many violent crimes. Historian John Lewis Gaddiss emphasized "the mass rape of some two million German women by Soviet soldiers as the war ended."[85] They were feared not only in Germany but also in countries supposedly liberated by them, such as Czechoslovakia. They raped women and used trucks for stealing all that could be removed from private, including workers', homes. Burchett found a way to exculpate them: "Many crimes of violence were being committed by criminals in Soviet uniforms."[86]

According to Burchett, there was a basic difference between puppets installed in East Germany by Soviet authorities and democratically elected West German politicians:

> Prime Minister Grotewohl is a clear-thinking, highly intelligent man who has won the confidence of the workers, farmers and lower middle-class in the Soviet Zone, and his influence extends far into the Western Zone as well. His speeches are models of clarity, and like those of Pieck, devoid of any trace of demagogy. His quiet demeanor is in sharp contrast to the antics of the West German politicians, especially the Social Democrat leaders, who have copied emotional ranting and shouting of the Nazis.[87]

Burchett's readers were not told about East German or Hungarian elections in which the Communists were so badly beaten that no free elections were ever allowed again.

On the last page of his book *Cold War in Germany*, published in 1950, Burchett wrote prophetically: "History will one day pass its verdict on who best served the interests of world peace and human

---

84   Ibid., p. 257.
85   See Neal Ascherson's review of Gaddis' *We Now Know: Rethinking Cold War History* (Oxford, 1997), entitled "Khrushchev's Secret," *London Review of Books*, October 16, 1997, p. 26.
86   Burchett, *Cold War in Germany*, p. 109.
87   Ibid., p. 254.

happiness, the Allies who built in the West or the Soviet Union who built in the East."[88]

The prophesy was as wrong as can be. East German workers attempted a revolution in 1953; millions of East Germans fled to the West before the Berlin Wall was erected, to be finally destroyed by rebelling East Germans in 1989.

Burchett's *Cold War in Germany* became popular in Australia. The year of its publication, a second printing was issued. To achieve even wider distribution, World Unity Publications began a series of pamphlets based on the book by editing sixty-four out of its 258 pages as *Warmongers Unmasked*.

Even more disgraceful than canvassed false propaganda from Berlin was Burchett's reporting from his next place of residence, Budapest. He was completely fooled by Stalinist show trials in Hungary and Bulgaria. In his book *Peoples' Democracies*, issued in 1951,[89] he reproduced pages of the official Hungarian proceedings of Cardinal Mindszenty and praised the organizers of the infamous show trial: "There is a quality of brilliance and imagination (sic!) in the leadership in Hungary today."[90]

The imaginary plot of one of the top Hungarian Communists, László Rajk, invented and staged by secret services, was described by Burchett as a carefully prepared conspiracy by Yugoslav and former fascist Horthy officers. Burchett embroidered Soviet secret police fabrications into his account: "Rajk and his gang were disclosed as miserable bloodthirsty adventurers."[91] Burchett thus helped to prepare the public for the intended Soviet invasion into Yugoslavia. The Hungarian general Kiraly later disclosed that he was in charge of Hungarian troops that were ready to put down Tito's insubordination to Stalin in Yugoslavia. "What stopped the attack was America's unexpectedly strong stand in Korea."[92]

---

88   Ibid., p. 258.
89   Burchett, *Peoples' Democracies* (Melbourne: World Unity Publications, 1951).
90   Ibid., p. 149.
91   Ibid., p. 253.
92   Richard Krygier, "Yalta and Its Aftermath," *Quadrant*, September 1985, p. 31.

Similarly, the judicial murder of the Bulgarian Communist leader Traicho Kostov inspired Burchett to colorful reporting on "a Yugoslav plan for Bulgaria every whit as diabolical and bloodthirsty as that for Hungary." Kostov "was a Bulgarian Trotsky."[93] It is worth noting that Burchett fully adopted the Stalinist vocabulary and sloganeering that was obligatory for all Central and East European Communist scribblers. He was one of them.

In a chapter of his book *Peoples' Democracies,* entitled "Liberty in Eastern Europe," he revealed the vicious side of the revolutionary idealists when he compared Stalinist show trials with events after the French Revolution in 1789: "The French revolutionaries certainly had no intention to grant 'liberty, equality and fraternity' to the Royalists. They quite properly chopped their heads off."[94]

He followed the official Stalinist line that liberty in people's democracies existed for 90 percent of the population and only "money-changers," bankers, and kulaks had their liberty curtailed. In fact, liberty did not exist at all; nobody could enjoy it; even the bosses could not feel safe. Burchett extolled the liberty of "hundreds of thousands of youths" since "each of these youths can look forward to a full and creative life."[95] That was written only five years before the Hungarian revolution, started by young people. Thousands of them disappeared in Siberian concentration camps. Tens of thousands ran away from their country into exile. Many of them emigrated to Australia.

In his autobiography, *At the Barricades* (1981), Burchett admitted that he was completely wrong: "In Belgrade [1956] ... I apologized for some of my own confused writings during the period immediately after Tito's expulsion."[96]

He also made a reversal concerning Bulgarian show trials: "[Traicho] Kostov had done what his old comrade Giorgi Dimitrov had done sixteen years earlier at the Reichstag Fire Trial. He had knocked the stuffing out of the prosecution [by publicly denying his guilt]. I was considerably shaken by the Kostov trial." [97]

---

93   *People's Democracies*, op. cit., p. 254.
94   Ibid., p. 278.
95   Ibid., p. 281.
96   *At the Barricades*, op. cit., p. 191.
97   Ibid., p. 146.

Burchett did not mention this at the time in his book devoted to these trials, of course. That means that he consciously lied at one time or the other. In 1981, he added a new twist to his false propagandizing: "Stalin was a dupe of [Allen] Dulles" who supposedly plotted the whole thing![98] Burchett's readers were asked to believe that Stalin's murderous show trials of his own agents were not meticulously planned for years and executed by his own secret services, but by the CIA!

Similarly, in 1981, he still blamed the Americans for the spontaneous nationwide Hungarian revolution of 1956, because, as he wrote: "Hungarian fascists expected Americans in June 1951. That was the state of mind induced by Radio Free Europe which hammered away implicitly on the theme 'get the fighting started—anywhere—and the Free World forces will be at your side.'"[99]

Burchett's analysis is a lie. Radio Free Europe began broadcasting in May 1951 to Czechoslovakia only, and much later to Hungary and other Soviet satellites. I worked for Radio Free Europe as an editor and writer for thirteen years starting before it began broadcasting; it never encouraged Eastern Europeans to start a revolution. Its American supervisors were very strict and cautious about that, and its Eastern European employees were responsible people who did not feel that from their relatively safe position they had any right to risk their compatriots' lives.

Notwithstanding his last assertion of CIA provocation of the revolting Hungarian fascists, Burchett expressly admitted in 1981 that "Hungarian workers at the time had good reasons to be in a rebellious mood."[100]

Although Burchett was obviously spreading false propaganda in the fifties, many people in England and Australia believed him. Goff McDonald pointed to that trust when he wrote:

> The main authority in such cases [the treachery of Tito] was the Australian journalist Wilfred Burchett, whose books such as *Peoples' Democracy* – together with his pamphlets and articles—echoed the voice of Stalin.... The Communist press, in Australia and

---

98   Ibid., p. 147.
99   Ibid.
100   Ibid., p. 192.

elsewhere, repeated the words of *Pravda* and material from Wilfred Burchett which explained the trial [of Rajk] was further proof of the plans of the Yugoslav Fascist clique of Tito.[101]

In spite of the fact that Burchett lied about events in Central and Eastern Europe, those who did not mind being deceived, or rather preferred to be told what would confirm their prejudices, went on trusting his judgment. And Burchett was able to go on fooling his readers about what was really happening and further spread biased propaganda.

ROLE MODEL

In his previous review of his life, *Passport: An Autobiography* (1969),[102] Burchett was not yet ready to admit his mistakes. However, in both books he revealed that throughout his political life, Egon Erwin Kisch (with his name often misspelled) served as his model. He led his readers to believe that Kisch was not a Communist in spite of the well-established fact that Kisch was not only a Communist but also one of the most important Soviet agents of the Comintern.

Kisch was a Czechoslovak citizen and an operative who was prominent in Stalin's propaganda campaign against "war and Fascism" that helped to attract many people to Communist causes. (An excellent source, explaining and tracing the seduction of the Innocents—as they called them—is Stephen Koch's book *Double Lives: Spies and Writers in the Secret Soviet War of Ideas Against the West*.[103])

In 1934, Kisch was invited to the all-Australian Congress Against War and Fascism in Melbourne. When he was not allowed by the authorities to disembark, he jumped the ship and broke his leg. Although relevant documents in the Australian archives were not yet available for scrutiny, the American ones were not so reluctant to

---

101   Geoff McDonald, *Australia at Stake* (North Melbourne: Peelprint, 1977), pp. 14 and 39.

102   Wilfred Burchett, *Passport: An Autobiography* (Melbourne: Nelson, 1969).

103   New York: Free Press, 1994, pp. 75–76.

reveal the reasons for Kisch's problems with landing in the land of the antipodes: „When he was enroute to Australia in 1936 (sic), Hitler declared that he would stop all German imports of Australian wool if Kisch were allowed to land in Australia. The Australian authorities forbade Kisch to land ... He is clever, courageous, and a very able writer ... In ordinary conversation, however, he does not flaut his political views, but is much more interested in obtaining those of others."[104] In the continuing scandal in which the government proved to be quite incapable to handle the situation, the CPA managed to stage large demonstrations for this "victim of the Australian Right." Burchett took part and decided to become an international journalist (and Communist agent) like his role model Kisch, who was a master of pro-Soviet propaganda carefully masked as one serving noble ideals.

---

104   FBI report from the American Embassy in Mexico, November 4, 1943, file 800.00B, Kisch, Egon Erwin/11. For Kisch's Melbourne adventure see Egon Erwin Kisch, *Landung in Australien* (Berlin, 1973); Robin Golan, *Communism and the Australian Labour Movement 1920–1955* (Canberra: Australian National University Press,1975), pp.44–48; and Josef Polacek, "Zu Egon Erwin Kischs Sprung nach Australien," Exil: Forschung, Erkenntnisse, Ergebnisse (Frankfurt, Vol. VII, 1987, No. 2), pp. 17–33; also *Julian Smith, On the Pacific Front: The Adventures of Egon Kisch in Australia* (Sydney, 1936). Australian documentation, the basis of Polacek's study written in German, is available in the State Central Archive in Prague. It was sent there in April 1962 by the Czechoslovak Consul in Sydney, Jaroslav Kafka. A. Keasing, the director of the publishing house Current Books which distributed books and journals sent in by Communist states, gave Kafka the complete archive, including the judicial protocol, worried that it could be seized by his own country's authorities. Proofs were found in the archive of the Czech Ministry of Foreign Affairs in Prague. The file also contains two interviews with Kisch in Fremantle and Melbourne, as well as clippings from the Australian press. Polacek's study concludes with them in English. According to Arthur Koestler, "in his attitude to politics, Kisch was a complete cynic. He always avoided getting involved in argument with the stock phrase 'I don't think; Stalin thinks for me' delivered with a straight face.... Hidden behind the mask of the humorous cynic was a tired, disenchanted man, who had no illusions about the Party, but even fewer about the world outside the Party." *The Invisible Writing* (New York: Stein and Day, 1984), p. 284.

Both duped many people not acquainted with modern totalitarian underhanded methods.[105]

In his first autobiography, *Passport*, Burchett wrote: "The whole Kisch incident had a profound effect on me in many ways. I was impressed by the quality of the man himself, his physical and moral courage, and also the way in which he used his pen to uncover injustice and fight for life's good causes. Subconsciously, I accepted him as the model of a progressive journalist."[106]

It is often interesting to compare Burchett's two autobiographical books. In his *Passport*, he recalls: "Years after the Sydney Domain meeting I met Ergon (sic) Irwin (sic) Kisch in his own beloved Prague, a few months after the liberation of Czechoslovakia from the Nazis. Because I was Australian, and he had fallen completely in love with Australia, he escorted me for days on end to show me Prague."[107]

The same visit to the Czech capital city plays a different role in Burchett's second autobiography, published twelve years later: "I had driven through Czechoslovakia from Vienna to Prague on the beautiful spring Sunday of May 26, 1946, when voters were going to the polls in the first general elections since 1935."

Kisch's time with him shrank from several days to a single day: "Just because I was an Australian, Kisch devoted the entire second day of my visit to escorting me around the marvels of his beloved Prague."[108] Although he wrote, "There must have been lots of Soviet troops around," in fact there were none. However, much more truthfully he wrote:

> I was approached by a compatriot and fellow journalist, John Fischer.... He insisted on dragging me off to a house party where I would meet some "interesting blokes." First was my idol of ten years earlier, Egon Irwin (sic) Kisch, who had survived Spain and French concentration camps.... With him were another well-known Czech writer, André Simone [alias Otto Katz], the future Foreign Minister

---

105   New York, Free Press, op.cit., Ibid.

106   *Passport*, op. cit., p. 83.

107   Ibid., pp. 83–84.

108   *At the Barricades*, op. cit., p. 133.

Vladimír Clementis, and the brother of Rudolf
Slánsky, general secretary of the Czechoslovakian
Communist Party ... almost all those in that room
were later executed as "spies" and "traitors."[109]

As far as I know, that is the only time Burchett, the biased specialist
on show trials in Central and Eastern Europe, wrote about the worst of
them which ended with eleven top Communist leaders of the CPCZ
being hanged. In his autobiography, he added: "Mutual friends later
commented that it was as well that he [Kisch] died a natural death
rather than see—and probably share—the humiliation and destruction
of some of his closest comrades."[110]

Burchett did not mention what must have been on his mind: he
himself might have shared the months-long tortures and humiliations
suffered by Kisch's closest friends had the Soviet specialists in scientific
torture (as they themselves proudly boasted) accepted his offer—
quoted from his letter to Thornton above—to be extradited to Prague
and put on trial in the years of judicial murders. As an Australian,
he might have escaped hanging, but as with the similarly committed
Communist agents, brothers Herman and Noel Field, who were used
in the Prague and Budapest trials as star witnesses, he would have
experienced some prolonged distress. He clearly was considered by the
organizers of the murderous circus and was proposed for such a role
by comrades Jakš and Popper. Burchett played with fire. Luckily for
him, the script writers of the show trials preferred the Fields because
as Hungarian American Jews they could better serve the dual purpose
of Stalin's campaign against the alleged American and Jewish Zionist
conspiracy.

After his close call, Burchett went to Australia to lecture on the
benefits that Communist regimes provided to citizens of Stalinized
countries. In his excellent study of Burchett, "He Chose Stalin," Rober
Manne described Burchett's four month tour, from September 1950
to February 1951: "Burchett assured his Australian audiences that
conditions in the people's democracies were 'paradise' in comparison to
those prevailing before the coming of Communist rule.... The peoples

109 Ibid.
110 Ibid., p. 134.

and governments of the Soviet block were peace-loving; to return from there to the west was 'like entering into a mad-house.'"[111]

During his Australian lecture tour, Burchett obviously did not reveal the whole ugly truth as he knew it to be, which he later admitted.

CHINA AND KOREA

Burchett found the next attraction for his Communist enthusiasm, and upkeep, in China. He essentially became employed by the Chinese Communist Party to serve as its propagandist. He was enchanted by the results of the revolution as shown in his book, published in Melbourne in 1952, *China's Feet Unbound*. By then he was already engaged in Korea as more than just a paid political propagandist. He took part in the brainwashing of the English-speaking captives. His contribution to the Soviet campaign, blaming the Americans for spreading germs over Korea in order to destroy crops, was far-reaching. By writing articles on the invented germ warfare and actively persuading American pilots to sign false confessions that he himself often wrote for them, Burchett descended into the depths of an agent-torturer.[112]

In *Passport*, Burchett claimed that "in exposing American experiments in germ warfare, I was doing my duty as a journalist and a responsible member of human society."[113] Compare this with the testimony of a member of the Czechoslovak Department for Active Measures, Ladislav Bittman, who revealed the truth in his 1985 book *The KGB and Soviet Disinformation*. "During the Korean War (1950–1953), the KGB conducted a worldwide disinformation campaign accusing the United States of using bacteriological warfare. With the

---

111 *The Shadow of 1917: Cold war Conflict in Australia* (Melbourne: Text, 1991), p. 38.

112 For details see Manne's book *Cold War...*, p. 39–66. Peter Kelly, in his unpublished study, "Burchett—Last Time," reveals how Burchett perjured himself at least three times in the New South Wales Supreme Court in 1974 and how he himself helped to search for witnesses of Burchett's brainwashing and participation in tortures in Korean prisoners' Communist camps for the trial of Burchett in New South Wales.

113 Burchett, *Passport*, op. cit., p. 285.

help of Western journalists like Wilfred Burchett, the Soviets publicized the forged evidence in Communist as well as Western newspapers."[114]

From documents recently published from Soviet archives, it is well established that Stalin resisted North Korean requests for an attack on South Korea for an entire year before he finally agreed and took part with large combat units of his own.[115] He even suggested a provocation from the south by sending North Korean troops across the border in order to be pursued back, exactly the same way Hitler had responded to the Polish invasion simulated by his own soldiers in Polish uniforms. Burchett always lied about the supposed South Korean attack on the North, thus beginning the war. Even as late as March 25, 1974, in a Stockholm lecture, he claimed: "According to my own, still incomplete investigation, the war started in fact in August-September, 1949, and not in June, 1950. Repeated attacks were made along key sections of the 38th parallel throughout the summer of 1949, by Rhee's forces, aiming at securing jump-off positions for a full-scale invasion of the North."[116]

Apparently Nikita Khrushchev was not so well informed as Burchett. At the July 1955 CPSU Plenum, he declared, turning to Molotov, "We started the Korean War," and repeated, "We started the war."[117]

While working for the Chinese, Soviet, and North Korean Communists, Burchett "told Reuters that in 1952 he was offered $100,000 by the CIA 'to come to the other side and write a few articles.' He said he declined the offer." Again, the truth is the other way around. As Manne learned from ASIO archives, Burchett himself approached the American military command in Korea in the first week of September 1953, "and let it be known that, in return for being offered an amnesty from the Australian government, he would be willing to give useful information to American military intelligence."

---

114 Washington, DC: Pergamon-Brassey's, 1985 p. 38. See also Laurence Jolidon, "Soviet Interrogation of US POWs in the Korean War," Washinton, DC: *Cold War International History Project BULLETIN*, Nos. 6–7, Winter 1995/1996, pp. 123–25.

115 Ibidem, pp. 4–122.

116 Pyongyang: Foreign Languages Publishing House, 1974, p. 11.

117 Quoted in *Cold War International History Project Bulletin*, Issue 10, March 1998, p. 6.

The Australians refused to accept such an offer when asked by the Americans and considered putting him on trial.[118]

Four nations were neutral members of the repatriation commission in Korea. However, the neutrality of the Czechoslovak and Polish group was very doubtful, as the other two, the Swiss and the Swedes, soon discovered. The two people's democratic representatives consulted each other before departure from Central Europe. They reached Keson in Korea in the second half of 1953.

According to documents found in the Czech Republic's Foreign Ministry archive, the Czechoslovak delegation numbered 365, although the ministry acknowledged that only 250 were requested. It was led by Colonel Vrba. Minutes of a meeting on 26 June 1954, marked "Strictly Secret!" reveal that Chu En-lai addressed them. The Polish delegate Krzemiew declared, "Our job is to fulfill the instructions of the Chinese and Korean governments." Li San-Cho said that "the speech of the Swiss delegate on the 23rd of June was unfavorable, equally the Swedish declaration; it would be difficult to reach any agreement with them." A Czech delegate commented, "The Swedes and the Swiss, we know what they are: svolotch." The Russian word used can be translated as "scoundrels,"[119] but its meaning is worse.

For his services to North Korean Communists, Burchett received a medal from Kill Il Sung, but he knew that in Australia he would have been put on trial. In 1955, in order to avoid flying to Hanoi through Singapore or Hong Kong where he could have been arrested, his friend (as he often claimed) Chu En-Lai transported Burchett in his own plane.[120]

The question of Burchett's treachery or innocence provoked a long and heated debate in Australia. His harshest critic was the Australian reader and refugee from Communist Czechoslovakia, Frank Knopfelmacher, who wrote: "The ancient Common Law definition of high treason – giving aid and comfort to Sovereign enemies; or Australia's enemies ... clearly applied to Burchett, and he ought to have

---

118 *The Shadow of 1917*, op. Cit., pp. 6–66.
119 CzMFA Archive, No 424-801/55.
120 Manne, op. cit., pp. 64–65; and Burchett, *At the Barricades*, op. cit., p. 281.

been tried, sentenced and executed, if found guilty of the felony of high treason."[121]

The severest punishment the Australian authorities bestowed on Burchett was their refusal to grant him a new passport when his old one was lost. That made him a victim in the eyes of the international brigade of anti-American and anti-capitalist stars such as Jane Fonda and Graham Greene.

VIETNAM BETWEEN MOSCOW AND PEKING

After his Chinese employers, the Vietnamese Communists took over Burchett's upkeep between 1954 and 1957. They provided him with money, a house, a car, a cook, a secretary, and military bodyguards whenever he visited the front of the war to take over the whole of Vietnam.

However, Burchett wanted to move to Moscow. In 1956, he again contacted KGB agent Yuri Krotkov. Burchett told Krotkov that he was an illegal, underground member of the CPA and "asked for money from the Soviet Communist Party."[122] He was hired and in 1957 settled in Moscow with his family. He wrote in his autobiography: "Suddenly space was available in the posh Vissotni Dom ('skyscraper') overlooking the Moscow river, half a mile downstream from the Kremlin.... Stalin himself, it was said, had chosen the original list of occupants."[123]

Burchett stayed there with the highest Soviet elite in the luxury apartment for more than five years, writing for the London conservative *Daily Express* under a pseudonym.

During Burchett's employment by the Soviet secret service, his shifting alliances became gradually more pronounced. In the developing conflict between the Soviet and Chinese Communist parties, he moved almost completely to Mao's side (and with him most of the Australian Communist apparatchiks).

Several times during the early sixties he went to see the former states of Indochina and began to prefer Vietnam, which had closer ties

---

121 "Wilfred Burchett's Treason," *Quadrant*, Vol. XXIX, No. 215(9), September 1985, p. 32.

122 Manne, op. cit., p. 68; and Santamaria, *Australia at the Crossroads: Reflections of an Outsider* (Melbourne University Press, 1987), p. 159.

123 *At the Barricades*, op. cit., p. 197.

with Moscow than with Peking. Although he publicly supported Mao Tse-tung's cultural revolution, he later admitted that he was nonplussed by it. In April 1967, he saw in Peking the violent infighting between various Communist groups denouncing each other. He was told, as he wrote, by the stauch supporter of revolutionary struggles, Anna Louise Strong [a Soviet agent]: "Mao has let the genie out of the bottle, and I'm not sure he's going to be able to get it back in!" She also told him that Chou En-lai, who was then "stamping out fires," was more important than Mao.[124]

For years, in his press reports and books on the Vietnamese conflict, Burchett claimed that there was *no* coordination between the North Vietnamese government and revolutionaries in the South. There would be *no* reunification. His autobiography confirms that he was systematically lying: "In truth, there was one single revolutionary strategy for the military, political, and diplomatic fronts of Vietnam and one united leadership of that strategy, but it was still secret."[125]

He was thus far receiving his stipend from Moscow as was witnessed in 1969 at the Phnom Penh airport by his filmmaker friend Edwin Morrisby and reported in Morrisby's *Memoir* in 1985. Morrisby also revealed that the large amount of money in American Express Travelers checks was delivered to him by a North Vietnamese man. Morrisby claimed that Burchett was a KGB agent and that his wife worked for the Bulgarian branch of the KGB.[126]

Since his close connection with Asian Communist parties was well known, he was often asked for inside information by journalists in Korea, and later even by Averell Harriman at the Paris peace talks, and in Washington DC by Henry Kissinger, as he proudly reported in his autobiography.[127] They knew that he could speak for the Communists.

Burchett's work for the Vietnamese Communist Party was probably the most sincere and closest to his heart, as well as most successful at obtaining results. As usual, he exaggerated, pretended, lied, but

---

124 Ibid., pp. 241–42.
125 Ibid., p. 242.
126 "Wilfred Burchett of the KGB?," *Quadrant*, October 1985, pp. 28–32. Other authors suggest that Burchett probably was not a KGB agent but rather a well paid agent of influence.
127 *At the Barricades*, op. cit., pp. 255 and 278.

the American capitalists and militarists were obviously involved in a controversial war. Viet Minh fighter Hinh Truong testified to Burchett's importance to the cause: "Mr Burchett was a Communist, an international Communist soldier."[128] Burchett's friend Morrisby wrote: "Wilfred proudly told me that the Vietnamese High command did not think that the war could be won on the ground and had to be won at the public relations level."[129]

Santamaria concluded his chapter devoted to him: "Burchett was a paid Soviet agent, who operated as a 'combattant' in support of forces fighting Australian soldiers in the field."[130]

IMITATING KISCH

In 1970, Burchett followed the example of his model Kisch, and flew to Australia without a passport or visa in a private plane provided by the millionaire Gordon Barton.[131] Once again, Australian authorities did not know how to handle him without making an even bigger martyr out of him. Burchett was able to entitle a chapter of his second memoir *Prodigal's Return.*"[132] In spite of a long history of lying and working actively for enemies of Australia and world democracies, he was still very popular with Leftist and liberal people.

Kisch's legend was still very much on Burchett's mind: "Telegrams started pouring in from trade unions, student organizations, personalities, some of them known to me, others not, pledging support and urging me to continue the Fight. My mind could not but go back to Egon Erwin Kisch and his fight thirty-six years earlier. But travel methods had changed. I could not jump out of a plane somewhere in Australia."

Burchett felt great that he could imitate—minus the jumping— the other Soviet agent, but in his biography, as we will see, only forty pages separate this triumph from expressions of desperation from the movement whose cause he served for decades.

---

128 Santamaria, op. cit., pp. 166–67.
129 Morrisby, op. cit., p. 29.
130 Santamaria, op. cit., p. 169.
131 David McKnight, *Australia's Spies and Their Secrets* (Sydney: Allen & Unwin, 1994), p. 263.
132 *At the Barricades*, op. cit., pp. 259–71.

CHINESE MIRACLES

Burchett managed to praise Mao Tse-tung's disastrous experimentation with huge anthill human communes. His book *China: The Quality of Life* (1976) was based on his visit in the summer of 1973. According to Burchett, "Mao's Gratest Leap," as he called the first chapter, did not produce a famine costing millions of Chinese lives, as was later admitted by the Chinese Communist Party, but was an enormous success: "Within four months ... China's more than a billion farmers were reorganized without any interruption in production."[133]

The communization was not ordered from above, not at all: "As the initiative for forming the communes came from the grassroots, there was no standard set of rules. Members made their own."[134] The Marxist spirit so moved peasants that—miracle of miracles—all made their own rules *exactly the same way*, as if ordered and enforced militarily from above: "A striking aspect was the general uniformity of the way things worked."[135] The credulity of intellectuals in the new *Holy Spirit* who wanted to be fooled is almost unbelievable. (I myself witnessed a colleague of mine in Perth extolling the virtues of the communes. He was believed by many. My objections were ignored.)

In the second chapter, "Fifty Thousand Police-less States," Burchett admired the decentralization of the strictly centralized police dictatorship: "The communes have
a certain degree of autonomy.... They represent almost
the ultimate of decentralization of state power - short
of the actual withering away of the state – which is
essential to Mao Tse-tung's philosophy."[136]

In the slaughterhouse that China was becoming, almost everything was ideal:

"Although there is a People's Militia, there is no army [only four or five million soldiers!], no police and no courts or gaols.... [137] Crime?... It's practically non-existent."[138]

133 Penguin Books, 1976, p. 16.
134 Ibid., p. 23.
135 Ibid., p. 29.
136 Ibid., p. 33.
137 Ibid., p. 34.
138 Ibid., p. 47.

In this Marxist paradise, "wherever we looked the picture was the same—of people running their own lives ... without interference from the outside and progressing steadily towards prosperity."[139] [All while millions of Chinese were dying of starvation!] Here Burchett surely reaches the apogee of his deception.

Another disaster, the closing of all universities and colleges, depriving a whole generation of Chinese students of higher education, was celebrated by Burchett: "Since the Cultural Revolution, everyone in China from kindergarten onwards has studied Marxist theory at some level or another.... [140] The achievements of the Great Leap Forward were consolidated during the Cultural Revolution."[141]

Burchett was enthusiastic about the alleged privileges obtained by ethnic minorities, especially the Tibetans: "The national minority peoples have been helped in every imaginable way to ... run their own affairs."[142] Why then did so many try to run away? Why were so many massacred?

It took years before the rest of the world was allowed to hear from Chinese Communists themselves about Mao's catastrophic policies and the incredible suffering imposed on the Chinese people, so several books devoted to Vietnam by the professional Communist enthusiast Burchett were avidly read and trusted. A copy of *Grasshopers and Elephants: Why Viet Nam Fell* that I saw in a university library was so heavily underlined by students on every page that I wondered how much damage such reckless readers could do in the guerrilla war for which many students in Australia were then being trained.

THE GODOT THAT FAILED[143]

Burchett's career of highly compensated admiration for everything done by Communist regimes was coming to an end. His only reward was to live in a private hell, as he truthfully—finally telling the truth—admitted in his memoirs:

---

139 Ibid.
140 Ibid., p. 99.
141 Ibid., p. 172.
142 Ibid., p. 302.
143 Allusion to Samuel Beckett's *Waiting for Godot* and Richard Crossman's *The God That Failed*

> Regardless of rights or wrongs in the China-Vietnam-Kampuchea confrontation, the main part of "my" world, in terms of reporting and engagement, was falling about my ears.... Now my Asian friends were at each other's throats—each waving the banner of socialism and revolution—and I was again in the thick of it. It was a shattering blow to a vision of things acquired during the previous, four decades, including my certainty as to the superior wisdom and morality of Asian revolutionaries.[144]

Burchett planned to write a book of praise for Pol Pot's Red revolution, imitating Mao's cultural revolution, when he himself joined the invasion of his Vietnamese friends into Kampuchea. He finally became disgusted by the butchery that was just a little faster and more brutal than usual. He wrote: "How to explain to my left-wing readers and supporters all over the world ... that the foulest barbarities were being committed in the name of 'socialism' and 'revolution'?... How this oasis of peace has been transformed into a slave-labor concentration camp and slaughterhouse?"[145] Didn't he ever see, or at least know of, concentration camps in all the Communist countries he ever lived in and celebrated?

Burchett's left-wing friends must have been shocked indeed—if they believed him—reading his report on Pol Pot's and Teng Sary's massacres. These two Kampuchean dictators were, as he now wrote, "passionate advocates of the Great proletarian Cultural Revolution," just as Burchett was. They just went a little too far. He felt their extremism justified his Vietnamese friends' invasion into Kampuchea: "Who but madmen would have uprooted an entire people. ... Who but homicidal maniacs could have massacred 40 percent—up to 3 million—of their compatriots and deliberately conditioned a whole generation of children to the most barbarous forms of torture and murder as a great joke?"[146]

Two years after the publication of his memoirs, Burchett, a heavy drinker, died in Bulgaria of liver failure.

---

144   *At the Barricades*, op. cit., p. 12.
145   Ibid.
146   Ibid., p. 307.

Attempts At Burgett's Resurrection In 2005–2008

The nostalgia of incorrigible and dangerous dreamers is so great in Australia that at the end of 2005 they tried to raise from the dead the journalist who was the most successful at preaching the gospel of their political messiahs. Wilfred Burchett's son, George Burchett, together with his friend, Nick Shimmin, published in 2005 a luxurious, 785-page edition of *Memoirs of a Rebel Journalist: The Autobiography of Wilfred Burchett,*[147] The editors claim that it is an unabridged version of his memoirs originally published in 1981. Nick Shimmin wrote that W. Burchett was "the greatest journalist Australia has ever produced, and one of the best foreign correspondents the world has ever seen." Such unmerited praise for a vicious traitor to Australia naturally provoked a lively exchange of opinions. Under the title "Comrade Burchett was a party hack," Peter Kelly wrote in the main Australian newspaper:

> Burchett was not a rebel journalist—he was a faithful, conformist Communist who never went against the party line despite claiming to be independent.... During two wars in which Australian troops fought and were killed—Korea and Vietnam – Burchett worked on the other side and reported from behind the enemy's lines with its support and agreement. In both of these wars he was paid by those enemies, China and North Vietnam respectively.

---

147   Sydney: University of New South Wales Press, 2005. Distinguished University of Melbourne historian, Stuart McIntire [who was appointed to the Chair of Australian Studies at Harvard University for 2007–08] launched the book with a speech in which he stressed that like Kisch, Burchett "was also the victim of official surveillance and vilification." According to him, the "remarkable Australian ... championed noble causes and also incurred victimization." However, "he praised the achievements of Stalinism and downplayed its repression." All that, because "he was no analyst." Also, "he insisted that he was not a member of the Communist Party, and none of his critics have ever shown that he was." By *Newmatilda.com*, "Remembering Burchett, 16 November 1965, pp. 1–3.

Kelly then reminded his readers of a story published by Pat Burgess who described the recollections of captured UN soldier Derek Kinne, veteran of the Korean war, of his captivity:

> We'd been in the Chongsam South camp, and were
> told Wilfred Burchett was going to give us a lecture
> in the football field. We all marched up, the British
> in front and the Americans behind. There were about
> 600 Brits and 800 Americans. A lot of the British
> carried little nooses and about 60 called out when
> he started his lecture, "You'll hang, you bastard" and
> others took up the chorus and were hundreds singing
> out, "You'll hang, you bastard" ... Burchett said the
> peace talks had broken down and we were just the
> lackeys of the Wall Street warmongers.

When Burchett was about to leave, Kinne asked Burchett if he was biased. He told him that "the POWs are dying like flies. The first day I was in this camp 39 men went to Boot Hill." Because he was hostile to Burchett, he was later beaten and tortured.[148]

Reviewing the new edition of Wilfred Burchett's *Memoirs*, Brigadier General Greville wrote:

> During the Korean War, Burchett worked directly
> for the Chinese Army, which clothed, fed and
> housed him, in addition to paying him. Throughout
> this period he was under the control of a Chinese
> press officer, Shen Chen-tu, who edited every item
> Burchett wrote and instructed him on what to reveal
> to Western journalists during the Truce negotiations
> and what information he should try to exact from
> them. Working alongside were two other journalists,

---

148 Peter Kelly, "Comrade Burchett was a party hack," *The Australian,*
     January 7, 2006.

Tibor Meray[149] from Hungary and Lucien Prachi from Poland.[150]

Since in his article Peter Kelly also repeated my own discovery in 1996 in the Prague archives of five documents testifying to Wilfred Burchett's admission that he was a secret member of the Communist Party of Australia, but the admirers of the treasonable journalist claimed that they were fabrications by the Czechoslovak secret service, I had to supply my testimony that I considered them to be genuine. My letter was published in the *Weekend Australian*.[151]

Such a nostalgia, however, is not limited to family members and close friends of the lying reporter Burchett.[152] A thesis accepted in 2007 and rewarded by a medal, unfortunately, proves that at least part of the University of Sydney is still suffering from the contagious malady of Marxism-Leninism-Stalinism-Maoism.

Jamie Miller entitled his thesis "Without Raising Problems of Proof or Refutation: Wilfred Burchett and Australian Anti-Communism." He succeeds in his detailed documentation of the problem the Australian government was facing when it would have liked, repeatedly, to put Burchett on trial for treason: "The Government had promoted the image of the treacherous Burchett, while simultaneously refusing to publicly substantiate any charges."[153] The government faced legal

---

149 We will soon hear what this important wittness has to say.

150 See Phil Greville, "Gold Coast Bullet: The Sedicious Activities of Wilfred Burchett," *Defender,* Autumn 2006, pp. 23–26.

151 *The Weekend Australian,* February 11, 2006.

152 Paul Hollander in his book devoted to *The End of Commitment: Intellectuals, Revolutionaries, and Political Morality* [Chicago: Ivan R. Dee, 2006] came to this conclusion: ". . . human beings have an apparently limitless capacity for wishful thinking and self-deception in order to preserve mistaken commitments and beliefs, and tirelessly cling to noxious illusions. Further evidence has been provided of the human capacity to venerate destructive causes, irrational beliefs, and brutal, inhuman leaders, and that the highly committed may altogether obscure or efface reality by their longings and hopes" [p. 365].

153 Jamie Miller, *Without Raising Problems of Proof or Refutation: Wilfred Burchett and Australian Anti-Communism,* thesis, University of Sydney, 2007, p. 42. I am quoting from an e-mail attachment of the thesis sent

difficulties, as Miller himself admits.[154] Also it was extremely difficult to prove Burchett's treason due to Communist secret services' well-hidden agenda. It was hard to find solid proofs that would not expose those who managed to infiltrate them. Miller is therefore able to criticize at length the government's refusal to renew Burchett's passport. In support of his arguments, Miller very often quotes Burchett himself.

However, Miller in his thesis attempts to do much more. He tries to condemn everybody who dared to point out Burchett's treasonable activities and his systematic lying. He defends him as a "victim" of an anti-Communist "obsession."[155] Although he had access not only to Burchett's books ("some thirty-five books translated into myriad {!} languages"[156]) and autobiographies (he never quotes from them their author's admissions of lying), as well as to books and articles criticizing his services to his Communist employees, but also to voluminous reports in Australian archives, including ASIO's, he uses all this material for the almost exclusive purpose of defending Burchett as a victim of the Cold War.

In order to achieve that he invents a "pervasive and unquestionned ideology" of "anti-Communism ... adhered to zealously ... founded on suspect premises..." by the "Establishment political and ideological circles in Australia ... his ideological enemies."[157] Contrasting with it was allegedly Burchett's "unquestionably a unique professional ethos."[158]

While authors critical of Burchett's systematic lies and treasonable activities were decent and honest people who could not stand Communist regimes that were murdering millions of their own people, Miller is able to see in them only "red-baiters," "a cabal of anti-Communist intellectuals," their "hysteria and intellectual dishonesty ... fused with a smear campaign."[159] According to Miller, Burchett's "ideological enemies" acted as a "lynch mob."[160] He writes about

to me from Australia. The copy looks as if the pages could correspond to the actual thesis format and pages.

154 Ibid., p.2.
155 Ibid., pp. 15 and 49.
156 Ibid., p.9.
157 Ibid., pp. 12, 17, and 47.
158 Ibid., p. 14.
159 Ibid., pp. 12, 77, 73, and 23.
160 Ibid., p. 50.

"the institutionalisation of anti-Communism," "a personal fixation masqueraded as detailed knowledge," "extraneous slurs" concerning his love of liquor, "partisan scholarship at its worst" by the "vicious anti-Communism ... distinctively Australian."[161]

Interestingly, only five pages before the end of his thesis, Miller only in a footnote [!] No. 449 admits that he knows about documentary proofs of Burchett's secret membership of the Communist Party of Australia, found in the Prague archives, but dismisses the evidence because he was not send photocopies.[162] I have sent only a report with quotations on five documents proving that Burchett was a secret member of the CPA. He trusts Burchett but he does not trust anybody else. Anyway, just a few lines later, in footnote No. 450, he even claims that "whether Burchett was or was not a member is beside the point!" And that concerns the vital fact that Burchett throughout his whole life as a Communist propagandist kept claiming that he was not a Communist and therefore he could be believed as a neutral reporter! At least in this footnote, and not in the main text, Miller admits about Burchett that "he was a biased source."[163]

And this propagandistic pamphlet submitted by Jamie Miller could win a medal at the Sydney University in the year 2007!

TESTIMONY OF A WITNESS

The Hungarian writer Tibor Méray, who spent fourteen months in Korea during the armistice talks in 1951–53 together with Burchett in Kaesong and Panmunjom, wrote an important book on his experiences.[164] He was sent there by the Communist newspaper *Szabad Nép*, where he worked as cultural editor. First, he liked Burchett and like him kept sending reports completely in agreement with Chinese and Korean propaganda. However, after the Soviet suppression of the Hungarian revolution in 1956, he fled and settled in Paris where he tried to come to terms with his foolish, youthful beliefs in Communism.

---

161   Ibid., pp., 60, 61, 65, 68, and 76.
162   Ibid., p. 123.
163   Ibid.
164   Tibor Méray, *On Burchett* [Kallista, Victoria, Australia: Callistemon, 2008].

Among other publications, this is his attempt to understand Burchett, but at the same time to rebuff him as a systematic liar.

He writes: "For me two things were never in doubt. First of all, I always knew that Burchett was a Communist. *He told me so without delay, right after we first met.* He added that this was a secret as far as non-Communists were concerned and the outside world should know him as an independent."[165] Another thing was clear to Méray: "Now to the second point ... Burchett—like Winnington—was '*attached to the Chinese'*".[166] Allan Winnington represented the British Communist Party; both of them were used by the Chinese for spreading their propaganda to Western journalists, but Burchett was trusted much more for his supposed independence: "The most regularly occurring scene taking place on the Panmunjom road was Burchett and Winnington, together or separately, in the centre of circle of eight or ten American or Western pressmen, carrying on lively discussion, providing them with information, talking over controversial issues.... He found many old friends among the American pressmen.... This, of course, increased his trustworthiness."[167]

Burchett was also screening Western journalists for the Chinese, supplying them with their personal data, always valued by secret services, informing them about positions of the other side. He was also used for testing new proposals that the Chinese intended to submit.[168] Burchett was not an independent non-Communist journalist. Méray testifies:

> He told me that he and Winnington were employed by the Chinese state. They recieved their pay not from *Ce Soir* and the *Daily Worker* but from the Chinese. He told me that he and Winnington worked as "propaganda advisers" to the Chinese delegation at Kaesong.... The Chinese described Burchett and Winnington as parts of their army.... Burchett and Winnington had their lodgings and full board. For more than two years they had no need to draw their

---

165 Ibid., p. 89. Méray's emphasis.
166 Ibid., p. 90. Méray's emphasis.
167 Ibid., pp.45–46.
168 Ibid., pp. 46–48.

actual pay. How much money awaited them in Peking, after the Korean war ended, as their undrawn salaries, only the Chinese government could tell.[169]

Burchett's reports on the Korean War and on the armistice talks had benefitted only from his English language, style and trustworthiness: "Every single report by Burchett on the armistice talks were instigated by Shen Chen-tu and he was Burchett's censor.... Chen was appointed by the Chinese government."[170]

On Burchett's crucial participation in the false Korean and Chinese accusations of American bacteriological warfare, Méray has this to say: "When he visited the camps he went there for no other reaon but to serve the *germ warfare campaign....* It was the Chinese who sent Burchett to the camps.... Burchett toured the camps between April and June 1952 and it was *immediately after* his visits that the confessions made by the American pilots were published."[171]

When a war correspondent and his old friend, Marguerite Higgins, met him in Panmunjom and called his attention to „mass executions currently conducted by the Chinese Communists ... Burchett replied with some contempt: ‚Well, Marguerite, you seem to have forgotten an elementary fact: that the purpose of terror is to terrorise.' "[172]

On Burchett's reporting on Cardinal Midszenty's trial, Méray, after careful analysis, comes to this conclusion: "*Burchett knew very well that he was not telling the truth.*"[173] Essentially, everything Burchett had reported from the Communist countries in Eastern Europe to the leading British papers was a lie, from the Midszenty trial and the Rajk trial to the Kostov trial.[174]

Méray was appalled by Burchett's eulogies of the chief public prosecutor during the Stalinist show trials, Andrei Vyshinsky, and most of all "the most hard-handed dictators of the second half of the twentieth century," Kim Il Sung, Mao Tse-tung, Castro, and, at the beginning, even Pol Pot: "His concern became to serve his bosses as

---

169 Ibid., pp. 93 and 97.
170 Ibid., pp. 99–100.
171 Ibid., p. 81. Italics in the original.
172 Ibid., p. 54.
173 Ibid., p. 145. Italics in the original.
174 Ibid., p. 159.

well as he could, and to sing their praises, in order to earn his keep. There is no other journalist, not even in the Eastern camp, who can match Burchett being a servant of the cult of the personality on such a wide scale.... He remained constantly in the service of any one of the various Communist governments and parties."[175]

"Cut To Size By The Force Of History"

That is the way a previous Communist Mark Aarons, son of the last leader of the CPA, Laurie Aarons, entitled his review of Méray's book. His subtitle expresses how at least some of the Communists and ex-Communists, with the mounting evidence of his systematic lying, now view Burchett: "The truth is undeniable: Much of Wilfred Burchett's journalism is explicable only as unalloyed Communist propaganda." I will further quote only the first sentence of his substantial review, since it mentions the vital discussion that the book once more provoked: "Wilfred Burchett died 25 years ago this September but the fierce debate about his life's work continues unabated."[176]

James Jeffrey in his *Weekend Australian's* review, under the title "Red between the lines," especially stressed Burchett's "icy ruthlessness" and that he "as an energetic servant of totalitarian regimes ... betrayed himself and his own ideals."[177]

Bob Gould, though praising Mark Aarons's review, still defends Burchett: "During the Vietnam antiwar agitation, as an ostensibly independent journalist, Burchett captured the imagination of antiwar activists throughout the world." For seven years, Gould was then himself "fairly prominent in Sydney, against the imperialist war," and

---

175 Ibid., pp. 231 and 234. James Jeffrey interviewed the author after the publication of his book. Tibor Méray said that he discovered "the icy ruthlessness in him ... In Hungary he knew very well indeed the best hotels, restaurants, bars, entertainment places, wines and brandies ... He also knew one or two, perhaps three, middle-ranking functionaries ot the totalitarian regime. But he had not the faintest idea about the country or its people". *Weekend Australian*, March 22-23, 2008.

176 *The Australian Literary Review*, June 4, 2008, pp. 4 and 12.

177 *The Weekend Australian*, March 22-23, 2008.

he adds: "We were correct." Now he is willing to express his "scepticism about Burchett, or more properly my sadness about him." He sees solely "Burchett's political crime agaisnt the socialist project in the 20th century … that when the facts became clear he didn't draw up an objective balance sheet of Stalinism." Gould is still "deeply committed to rebuilding the socialist project."[178]

The most substantial and judicious review from several others was published by Robert Manne under the title "Agent of influence: Reassessing Wilfred Burchett."[179] He writes: "At present two Australians, Ross Fitzerald and Simon Nasht, are reported to be making films on Burchett." Then he lists some "leading left-wing academics … and journalists" who are still supporting Burchett, "despite everything they know about the human catastrophe of Communism,… despite the pyramids of corpses." He talks about the "post-Cold War intellectual inertia, an unwillingness to reexamine judgements made during the Cold War."[180] Toward the end of his summary Manne comes to this conclusion: "In the end, Wilfred Burchett, despite his very considerable talent and his genuine instinct for human equality, based his life on a false faith.… All his books written after 1945 were spoiled by grotesque political misjudgement and propagandistic intent."[181]

CONCLUSION

Burchett was not just a traitor to his countrymen. As a very influential writer, he used his pen to fight for Communist causes and regimes. He

---

178   *Ozleft: An independent voice on the left,* June 4, 2008.
179   *The Monthly,* June 2008, No. 35, The Monthly Essays, pp. 1–12.
180   Ibid., p. 1.
181   Ibid., pp. 11–12. Even in 2009 some perpetual dreamers did not give up trying to defend the liar and traitor Wilfred Burchett. Almost daily during February and March, they claimed that most of the time he was on the right side during the Cold War and that probably he was not member of the CPA his whole life, or that it really did not matter! Their silly statements were almost daily published in *The crikey: Telling you what they won't.* It is a regular and ample newspaper in e-mail format. They kept attacking either Professor Manne, Tibor Méray's book, or the February 4 reprint of my chapter devoted to Burchett. Among other names, they called us *McCarthyists.*

helped to mislead many people around the world about the fraudulent and murderous movement. How was it possible that so many people insisted on believing him? Unfortunately, people are gullible. Once they decide to believe in some political ideology, it is difficult, if not impossible, to persuade them of the truth. It is possible to lie and misrepresent and still be trusted, as Burchett and others proved again and again. Reason is a rarely used quality. Not only children love fairy tales. Many people prefer believing patent nonsense, hoping for a savior, be it an individual or a movement. Lying professionally can be a good career.

In a way, Burchett's career was successful. For a country boy who left school at fourteen, he did incredibly well. He learned several languages, drank a lot of liquor, met many important people and considered some of them—Chu En-lai, Ho Chi Minh, Fidel Castro—as his friends; he published many books that were influential, as well as innumerable reports for both Communist and non-Communist newspapers; he was well paid and provided for by a succession of Communist regimes and was highly valued for services rendered to their propaganda machine. However, how worthy of admiration was the cause for which he lied so often, and for whose victory did the regimes he glorified murder so many millions of their own people? He was a systematic liar for an unworthy program. For the cause of human reason it is humiliating that even such liars and traitors as Burchett can be celebrated with admiration years after their death, in spite of the fact that the ugly truth has been well established and documented.

3

Historian Humphrey McQueen: Admirer Of Mao Tse-Tung

o o o o o o o o o o o o o o o o o o o o o o o o o o o o o o o

When the history of this century is being written, its
reality will be seen as the era during which the eternal
hopes of humanity were began to be realized.

Humphrey McQueen (1987)

Throughout his teaching and writing career, Humphrey McQueen
claimed to be a scientific Marxist. Most of the time he used the
vocabulary of materialist Marxism, and his books are full of terms
such as imperialism as the final stage of monopoly capitalism (Lenin),
class struggle, exploitation, bourgeois and petit-bourgeois, and, of
course, proletariat. However, he strikes me as an idealistic and basically
romantic revolutionary, following an impossible dream which keeps
proving—as he himself admitted—to be just a mirage.

There are several sympathetic features that distinguish him from
other, more mercenary or prevaricating combatants of the Australian
Left, such as Burchett or Milner. Often he picked up the cause of the
Aborigines. He spent years writing on art and literature. He is sometimes
able to acknowledge his mistaken presumptions. He is an entertaining
speaker and writer,[182] but the amusement often tends to be at the expense

---

182 For instance, see his brilliant trailer, "Down Under Buñuel," *Meanjin*,
Vol. 35, No. 2 (1976), pp. 219–221.

of scholarship. He regularly overextends his argument, exaggerates his contention, and virulently attacks his opponents, and even his friends, in order to protect his fixed idea, his mantra of Marxist dogmatism. He can be a prickly fighter. He interests us as a Maoist Australian revolutionary.

Do you remember the exciting times when Mao Tse-tung was the icon of restless young people and middle-aged dreamers who thought that the yearned-for ideal revolution had finally arrived? Militarily organized Chinese masses were waving the *Red Book of Mao's Thought*, mostly culled from his speeches when he was still courting the peasants and not yet enslaving them. The fashion was to wear Chairman Mao's caps; Andy Warhol was creating multiple portraits of Marilyn Monroe and Mao Tse-tung; Mao's poetry, calligraphy, and swimming were celebrated as revelations; some enthusiast in Australia seriously proposed that there should be barefooted doctors in the kangaroo country since Mao had them in his underdeveloped empire; and Gough Whitlam tried to persuade startled South-East Asian leaders that they should join a new Pacific bloc including "neutral" Red China. These were exciting times. Millions of Chinese peasants were dying, victims of several misguided policies of the Great Helmsman,[183] who so much loved his peasants that every day his satraps had to select for the aging dictator a fresh supply of young peasant girls so he could pass on his venereal disease.[184] Everybody on the Left had a great time. Paradise was just around the corner.

FORWARD TO A REVOLUTION WITH PROLETARIAN PIANISTS

McQueen was born in Brisbane on June 26, 1942. His first book, *A New Britannia: An Argument Concerning the Social Origins of Australian Radicalism and Nationalism*,[185] was published by Penguin in 1970. Its short bio ends with: "In 1968 he was foundation chairman of the

---

183 See, e.g., Roderick MacFaruhar, *The Origins of the Cultural Revolution 3: The coming of the cataclysm 1961–1966* (New York: Columbia University Press, 1997).

184 Dr. Li Zhisul, *The Private Life of Chairman Mao: The Memoirs of Mao's Personal Physician* (New York: Random House, 1994).

185 Ringwood, Vic: Penguin Books Australia, 1970.

Revolutionary Socialists in Melbourne." On the second page of his own introduction, the word revolutionary or its plural appears in three short sentences altogether four times.[186] Clearly, we are in the presence of a very revolutionary agitator.

Manning Clark's lukewarm foreword might be explained by McQueen's devastating criticism of Clark's favorite poet, Henry Lawson, whom McQueen proved to be a militarist fascist and racist.[187] Clark reminded McQueen, "a member of the 'New Left'" whom he ranked rather disparagingly among "these latter-day Robespierres," that they were not the first fighters for humanity.[188] In the original and discarded version, Clark compared McQueen to a bulldozer.[189]

McQueen's book emphatically concluded (on page 236) that the proletarian class "can have no solution to its problems other than the establishment of a Communist society." Also (on page 188) we can read, "Marxism is mature socialism. Its acceptance depends upon the appearance of a working class that can see no future within capitalism." Nevertheless, large parts of the book present a lamentation about the poor quality of the Australian working class. McQueen can be comforted that even here he emulated his guru. Lenin did not like the Russian proletariat very much. McQueen too found his country's workers truly frustrating, because they were much more interested in economic issues such as wages, working hours, and quality of life than in their assigned revolutionary mission.

Instead of class warfare, "the degree of amicability reached in employer–employee relations was possible in the skilled trades because of a prosperous economic environment" (p. 205). Instead of conspiring for a revolution and adoring Marx, "it was not accidental that Australians chose a racehorse and a bushranger as their heroes since both expressed the same get-rich quick, Tatts syndrome" (p. 140).

---

186 Ibid, p. 12. Writing about an Australian would-like-to-be-a-Maoist-revolutionary, Paul Hollander says: "His political attitudes evolved from 'a vague leftism' to Maoism, influenced by numerous 'highly visible' Maoists at Monash University in Melbourne, which he attended." See his book *The End of Commitment: Intellectuals, Revolutionaries and Political Morality* [Chicago: Ivan R. Dee, 2006], p. 255.

187 *A New Britannia*, op.cit., pp. 104–116.,

188 Ibid., p. 8.

189 Humphrey McQueen, *Suspect History* (Kent Town, S.A.: Wakefield press, 1997), p. 115.

Instead of sacrificing themselves for the coming revolution, workers wanted to get rich or at least comfortable. "Gold contributed to the consciousness of the laboring class in a number of ways all of which served to reinforce the belief that there was something to be gained under capitalism – perhaps the most prized of all possessions, independence" (p. 146). The gold engendered widespread prosperity. "Higher wages were the first economic consequence of the gold discoveries in 1851" (p. 144). Workers could buy their own houses and invest in land and shares (p. 145). "Gold had ... important effects in the formation of the petit-bourgeois consciousness of nineteenth century Australian labourers" (p. 19). Worse, according to McQueen, was that "property became a paramount concern of Australian workers; this was symbolized by the piano" (p. 18). He returns to its terrible influence several times in a chapter entitled "Pianists" (pp. 117–19). He counted them, the anti-revolutionary monsters: "About 700,000 pianos were reportedly brought into Australia during the nineteenth century. The piano was not the preserve of the middle classes. It was the pinnacle of working-class aspirations.... A working class that could afford such luxuries wanted nothing to do with revolution" (p. 117–118). Or with revolutionaries! What could the Marxists do? Become piano tuners? The only audience available to preachers of the gospel of revolution then were bourgeois intellectuals, artists, professors of history, politics and education, students who in a few years became academics themselves, and journalists.

Another reason why McQueen found the Australian working class frustrating was its experience with democracy. He agreed that "in Australia there was plenty of democratic socialism. *Undoubtedly the most significant consequence of this long 'democratic' experience for the working class in Australia has been the ideological limits it has placed on socialist thinking*" (p. 187).[190]

---

190 My italics.

LEFTISTS INSIDE THE CAPITALIST MEDIA

Since the workers refused to see reason, McQueen decided to attack the capitalists himself. Unfortunately for McQueen, he was still unable to get the Marxist-Leninist ball rolling.

In 1977, McQueen published a scathing attack on *Australia's Media Monopolies*.[191] My university library copy was heavily underlined by one or more wholeheartedly agreeing readers. But another reader tried to spoil the consensus by scribbling on the front page: "Beware ... this guy is a Communist to the most extreme degree! Q: What's Black and White, But Red All Over?"

In his introduction, McQueen stated the reason for his book: "The collapse of the Whitlam government during the second half of 1975, plus Whittler's further destruction during the Iraqi affair in February 1976, made the Australian people acutely aware of the power of the media" (p. 1).

Many authors studied the media; McQueen decided to use their discoveries, since none of them employed the Marxist approach. He proposed to see them "in the context of monopoly capitalism, and ... in terms of the requirements of a system based on class exploitation" (p. 1). Why not? But then comes the funny part: "I no longer read newspapers, listen to radio commentaries or watch the television news" (p. 2). He reassures his readers who ask, "how can I write a book about the media if I do not take stiff dose at least twice a day?" by quipping "I know about the world precisely because I do not read papers, listen to current affairs broadcasts or watch the TV news." (Ibid.) That might be a good line, but it does not make him seem qualified to judge the contemporary media. However, he believes that all he needs to comprehend the current scene is to read and reread Marx from the second half of the nineteenth century and Lenin from the beginning of the twentieth. He explains that "because only Marxism has produced the knowledge needed to understand the monopoly stage of capitalism, Marxist concepts are used throughout this study of Australia's media monopolies" (p. 4). He then asserts that "monopoly capitalism is the enemy of every creative, decent human possibility" (p. 5). The first chapter, "Advertising: The key link," does not persuade

---

191   Camberwell, Victoria: Widescope.

me that advertising "provides unintentional ideological defenses of capitalism" (p. 2). In today's world, people need to buy to live, and advertising helps them to choose. Communist countries advertised their dictatorial leaders. McQueen probably would not mind seeing his cultist teacher, Lenin, in every square or omnipresent statues of his even blooddier successor, Stalin, but the moment they were able, workers in Communist countries demonstrated what they thought about this type of advertising by rushing to tear them down from their pedestals and demolish them. Of course, not only Communist dictators do it. Sadam Hussein's pictures were everywhere in Iraq. It is the same type of self-aggrandizement by despots. I prefer the competing advertisements in democratic countries, although I do not follow them either.

McQueen blamed the Australian media for "disastrous examples of misreporting" in their "accounts of China since 1949" (p. 130). He claimed that in 1962, "on People's China ... there were constant reports about mass killings and oppressions" that were erroneous (p. 131). In fact, Chinese Communist leaders later admitted that the terror and mass killings were much worse than was reported by the capitalist media. A hard man to satisfy, he wrote (on page 183), "Even if all the media were completely honest, accurate and unbiased in all their political comment and reports, they would still uphold the interests of capitalism." He just knew!

No doubt, in Australia the ownership of the media was too concentrated. Media moguls Murdoch and Packer get their own chapters, but McQueen was unable to prove any media monopoly; only duopoly or oligopoly. He did not mention that advanced capitalist states have laws prohibiting monopoly. And, of course, he did not consider the complete monopoly of ownership of the media in his preferred socialist countries, a monopoly no capitalist could dream of, since it included all media along with all means of production and armaments.

McQueen does not know Lenin well enough. His ideological father did not claim that he created a socialist state; he was more modest, calling it state capitalism. Only Stalin much later pretended that he achieved true socialism. McQueen should think about state capitalism a little more. It might be that in our era when capital is needed for accumulation in any system of government in order to invest it and keep employment as high as possible, there is no other workable arrangement if we do not want billions of people to starve and die and so return to a primitive mode of hunting and harvesting. In 1977, McQueen could dream about socialism because he did not acknowledge the depressing situation in all states calling themselves socialist.

According to him, "by constantly playing up murders and robberies, the media reinforce the view that capitalism is in tune with human nature." He does not acknowledge murders in socialist countries, occurring even without media reports, and those often committed by the dictatorial systems themselves (p. 191). His doubtful statement was heavily underlined by a sympathetic reader. McQueen concluded his argument about murders and robberies: "Socialism is seen as impossible and unnatural." In socialist countries, crime often became the province of official state institutions, employing the villains for their own murders and robberies.

In order to bring about this old platonic dream of an ideal society where all people would be good and happy, McQueen in chapter 11 suggested "A People's Network." It is more anarchistic and entertaining than Lenin's recipe of a tightly organized conspiratorial party in charge of a revolution in his *What is To Be Done?* McQueen's "activists involved in particular battle against imperialism" should use methods similar to those that dissidents in China and other Communist countries tried to employ in their battle against totalitarian oppression and exploitation. McQueen wrote, "In addition (to chalking on footpaths, painting slogans on the walls, speeches, leaflets and posters) we must develop new skills—such as street theater (puppet theater if you have stage fright)" (p. 207). His activists are working for socialism, which according to him "is the central demand of the Australian people" (p. 208). Such a naïve populism was seriously recommended in a country where the Communists or their fellow-travelers had many representatives in the media and academia that often helped them to create a hegemony! (This is a favored concept McQueen took from Gramsci.)

For McQueen and "inside outsiders" like him, the world was divided into two inimical camps. He imagined that the bourgeois capitalists formed a united conspiracy that had to be opposed by a conspiracy of people like him. However, he himself admitted that the class enemy he hated was not decisive enough for its own good: "For as long as the capitalist-controlled media are open to us we should not be afraid to use them—in our way, and for our own purposes." As he admitted elsewhere,[192] McQueen wrote for Murdoch's weekend editions of The *Australian* for three years. He was well paid in spite of his vitriolic attack on Rupert Murdoch in the book discussed. The idea of a capitalist conspiracy naively exaggerates and simplifies a much more complex situation. For instance, another, definitely not Right-wing historian, Frank Cain, was able to print his doubts about the existence of the Venona decrypts and Milner's spying (as discussed elsewhere in this book) in the *Weekend Australian* on July 6–7, 1991 (Review p. 4) and on July 20–21, 1991 (p. 24). No doubt, capitalists try to enlarge their profits and fortunes and power, often to the detriment of each other rather than their employees, since they discovered that workers who can buy what is produced increase profits and that contented workers are better workers than unhappy ones. Of course, unemployment still troubles all economies including Australia's, but socialist states too either had to accept tens of millions of unemployed workers as in China or underemployed as in the Soviet Union. Capitalist workers still have to fight against their employers or against conservative governments to achieve better wages and standard of living, but at least they have unions as well as sympathetic parties and socially minded individuals to support them, while in the so-called socialist states, the unions were used by the dictators against the workers and not for them. Communist states often re-established slavery. Reformed or former Communists, such as Radoslav Selucký, talked about return to feudalism.

Because Communist states' economies proved to be much less efficient, more bureaucratized and corrupt than capitalist ones, for years there has been a trend observable in almost all of them to introduce practices they criticized in private capitalism, to privatize and decentralize. Democratic liberalism and private enterprise won the contest, and you do not have to read Fukuyama to realize it is a historical fact. "The Russian and Chinese revolutions and the Nazi conquests during the Second World War saw the return, in a magnified

---

192 *Tom Roberts* (Sydney: Macmillan, 1996), p. 729. The CPA successfully infiltrated the non-Communist press: "Press coverage was facilitated by a sub-editor of *West Australian* newspapers who was a party supporter... Once again, publicity was achieved via a party member occupying a sub-editorial position with the *Melbourne Herald*." McGillick, *Comrade No More*, p. 140.

form, to the kind of brutality that characterized the sixteenth century....
Authoritarian dictatorship of all kinds, both on the Right and on the
Left, have been collapsing."[193]

PROBLEMS WITH APPLIED MARXISM-LENINISM

As a circumspect revolutionary socialist, McQueen attuned his
message to the prospective audience. In 1977, the same year that his
book *Australia's Media Monopolies* was published with its touching
revolutionary advice to paint slogans on walls and sidewalks, he
composed a much more serious prescription to those initiated into the
magical science of overthrowing the capitalist state. His article "National
Independence and Socialism" was published in the *Melbourne Journal
of Politics*.[194] He again invoked Lenin's 1916 thesis about imperialism
being the last stage of monopoly capitalism. "Without making any
attempt to argue its validity," he restated "the Marxist-Leninist position
of the State," namely that "the state is an instrument which organizes
capitalist class oppression. It must be smashed and its place taken by a
dictatorship of the proletariat in order to achieve socialism" (p. 69).

McQueen did not question why all Communist takeovers did
not smash the state, but on the contrary strengthened it enormously.
Terminology was more important than reality. The absolute absence of
proletarians in the leadership of Communist states was not an issue as
long as they called themselves a "dictatorship of the proletariat."

According to "National Independence and Socialism," "the Fraser
government rules on behalf of U.S. Imperialism and its Allies" (Ibid.).
But then comes a moment of unintentional humor as McQueen, a
committed Maoist, denounces Soviet crimes as well. This is confusing
given McQueen's championing of Soviet leaders. He wrote:

> Every time US Imperialism suffers a reverse, the Soviet
> Union is there trying to impose its control. Thus, for
> every blow which the Australians strike at the US, we

---

193   Francis Fukuyama, *The End of History and the Last Man* (New York:
Avon Books, 1993) pp. 11 and 12.
194   *Melbourne Journal of Politics*, No. 9, 1977, pp. 68–79.

must strike one of equal force at the Soviets in order
to prevent them taking over as the leading faction
inside the Australian bourgeoisie (pp. 70–71).

That reminds me of a Czech folk tale. A cobbler killed seven flies
in a day. He advertised this on a poster, and it was believed that he had
really slew seven villains. And so he had a great career and married the
king's daughter. McQueen's claim to be swatting at the great imperialist
flies of the US and the Soviet Union is as genuine as the cobbler's
poster.

McQueen's plan for the Australian working class (in spite of
their preference for pianos and gold and property and democracy)
was clear. It "has its own world outlook—Marxism-Leninism—Mao
Tse-tung thought." He then called for "the United Front with the
national bourgeoisie, the national petit-bourgeoisie, and the national
salaried workers." And, of course, "all classes" will be "united under the
leadership of the proletariat and of its vanguard party" (p.75).

The writer of this political program did not specify which vanguard
party. Out of the three Australian Communist parties, after their split,
he must have been referring to the tiny Maoist SPA (Marxist-Leninist)
of Ted Hill, and not the breakaway Socialist Party of Australia or the
original, now rumpled, CPA. The problem was that when he could
not unite even these three vanguard parties, how much chance did he
have with the bourgeoisie and petit-bourgeoisie plus the piano-playing
proletarians?

Socialist revolutionary dreamers had numerous obstacles, but they
were undaunted. The dream was still only that, but for them it was
already a sort of virtual reality.

SOME OTHER BOOKS BY MCQUEEN

Compared with his major misconceptions, many distortions in McQueen's books are minor, such as his claim in *Social Sketches of Australia 1888–1975*[195] that the Comintern agitator Egon Kisch, who caused a stir when he visited Australia in the thirties, "had been in one of Hitler's concentration camps." For a short time during the war, Kisch was in one of the French resettlement camps. In another book of McQueen's, *The Black Swan of Trespass: The Emergence of Modernist Painting in Australia to 1944*,[196] he sins by "vulgar Marxism" by claiming that "imperialism brought Picasso (a Communist) into contact with African masks" (p.125). That is just a part of his assertion that the "monopoly stage of capitalism" had a major role in development of "modernist art." (Ibid.) It was a very indirect role at best.

In the book *Suburbs of the Sacred*,[197] McQueen alleges that in Australia, "portraiture emerged as a bourgeois art form." From this fact he concludes that the bourgeois class existed already in the long history of Egyptian dynasties in Ancient Greece and Rome, and during the Renaissance, since portraiture flourished then and there! Another doubtful assertion in *Suburbs* brings us back to his political views and writings: "Marx revealed how the products of human labour appeared to oppress the workers who made them.... Humanity would remain a stranger to its own being until there could be a revolutionary reconstruction of society at large" (p. 216).

That is a very mythical statement. Such a return to revolutionary Marxism is disappointing, since McQueen's book published six years earlier was more mature and sensible than all his previous political publications. *Gone Tomorrow: Australia in the 80s*[198] seriously, from the point of view of a disillusioned socialist, explored "what went wrong during the 1970s, and why" (p. 5). According to McQueen, "Whitlam exuded the sweat of failure" and was narcissistic (pp. 168–69).

---

195   Penguin, 1978, reprinted 1986, p. 153.
196   Sydney: Alternative Publishing Coop. Ltd., 1979.
197   Penguin, 1988.
198   London: Augustin Robertson, 1982.

McQueen, like other more revolutionary Leftists, preferred Jim Cairns who "rose as a silent challenger to Whitlam's leadership"[199] (p. 169).

Although this book is more solid than usual, based on a lot of research, the reader finds some exaggerations. "As the choice between socialism and barbarism gained fresh meaning, people of conservative temper, people such as Patrick White, Ronald Henderson, Manning Clark and Judith Wright, found themselves firmly on the Left."[200] As usual, the author also claimed that Australia was "a military, economic, political and cultural dominion of the United States" (p. 221).

The disappointment was not caused just by the failure of Whitlam or by his dismissal:

> Experience since the Paris Commune of 1871 shows how difficult socialism is to achieve, let alone to sustain; and even where socialism has been established it was accompanied by abuses that socialists still hope to abolish or suppress. Bitter disappointments arose when racism, sexism and other inequalities survived the establishment of socialism in Russia and China. From these reverses we should learn that socialism is not a single answer to all the world's problems. Some of today's despair exists because socialists expected too much from socialism or wanted improvement too easily (p. 226).

These were brave words. McQueen went even further, questioning implicitly some of the basic tenets of Marxism-Leninism. Out of Hegelian determinism and dialectics he kept only a much transformed and idealistic dialectic of hope and despair: "Humankind is not utterly fixed or our history entirely programmed in advance.... If hope is another opiate, it too is the kind of drug that helps us to endure the pains of defeat, at once softening the blows and steeling us for further

---

199 The life-long Communist, Ralph Gibson, next to his photo called him "Hero of peace. Jim Cairns, a founder of the post-war peace movement and opponent of the Vietnam War." See the last page, 256, of his volume *The Fight Goes On: A Picture of Australia and the World in Two Post-War Decades* (Maryborough, Vic: Red Rooster Press, 1987).

200 p. 190.

fights.... Perfection is neither possible nor desirable while improvements are both" (pp. 226–27).

With the help of Engels (who until then was not his preferred Marxist classic to quote) and of his pamphlet *Socialism: Utopian and Scientific* (1880), McQueen dared to further revise his ideological frame of mind: "There is a sense in which all socialists remain utopian since we begin by accepting that things can be made better.... The development of Marxism does not mean that utopia is dead.... Reform is more likely to be attempted than is revolution, but reform cannot hope for success, unless, like revolution, it marshals a counterforce of active support from Australia's working people" (pp. 228–29).

McQueen's *Gone Tomorrow* represented a courageous effort to learn from experience. Out of the whole baggage of Marxism-Leninism not much was left. Reforms and revolution both depended on the support of the working class which was obviously lacking, and we know how critical of it the author was in his first book. Out of the dialectical foolproof engine of history, what survived was only the dialectics of despair and hope.

The next book McQueen published, *Gallipoli to Petrov: Arguing with Australian History*,[201] would seem to be a throwback to Marxist tenets that the author managed to overcome two years before. The impression was at least partly caused by his reprinting studies written before 1982. But even in his introduction, he raised "the genius of Marx," and writing "as a Marxist" he declared that "class struggle is the crux of Marxism" (p. x).

Pathetically, he wrote about "triumphant proletarian revolutions" (p. 44), displaying an almost incredible lack of knowledge of counter-revolutionary coups d'état committed against everybody, including workers and socialists, beginning in Petrograd in 1917 and continuing in Prague in 1948, Warsaw in 1944, and Budapest in 1956; Soviet imperialist seizures of power in the Kaukazus in the twenties and the Baltics in the forties, as well as in Kabul; or takeovers by intellectuals and militarists with the help of peasants in China in 1949. There was not a single *proletarian revolution* to speak of (except those that he does not acknowledge, in February–March 1917 in Russia and in October 1956 in Budapest). What is more, not a single one of them was triumphant in the sense that people, and not the party dictators, prospered.

---

201   Sydney: George Allen and Unwin, 1984.

He returned to his detestation of the excellent journal *Quadrant* (pp. 180–195) and used and over-used the terms "bourgeois" and "petit-bourgeois" when disagreeing with opinions expressed (pp. 199–217).

On one hand, McQueen overstated the danger from the Right by asserting: "Within weeks of assuming office, Menzies set about turning Australia into a police state. The pretext was his promise to ban the Communist Party. The aim was to destroy the trade union movement and remove all opposition to the new demands of the US" (p. 170).

On the other hand, he admitted that the Communist Party of Australia really represented a mortal danger. "If intraparty disputes in Australia have not resulted in physical liquidation of opponents, the only reason for this reserve is that the party has lacked the state power to get away with judicial murder" (p. 236).

McQueen also acknowledged that "in the past the CPA came to be seen as a Soviet agency" and that "the CPA (M-L) got itself into the same predicament over China" (p. 237). All in all, "Australian revolutionaries have to begin by accepting Stalinism as part of their inheritance instead of using Stalin as a devil theory with which to get rid of all the things they dislike" (ibid.).

JAPANESE REWARDS AND HOPES

McQueen left teaching at universities in Australia in 1978 and became a freelance writer; sometimes he was supported by the Australia Council's literary fellowships. From 1985 to 1987, he was a prominent member of the committee to review Australian studies in tertiary education and co-authored its large report *Windows onto Worlds* (1987). In 1988 and 1989, he acted as associate professor at Tokyo University. Two books resulted from this stay: *Tokyo World* (1991) was written in the form of a diary, and *Japan to the Rescue* (Port Melbourne: William Hinemann Australia, 1991) was based on solid research. Surprisingly for an author who declared himself to be a Maoist, there is not much praise of, or even regard to Communist China in the book. McQueen, as is his habit, does not positively value Australian friendship with the United States whose changing relationship toward Japan he described. He suggested repeatedly that just as his own negative preconceptions of the Japanese gave way to appreciation, so the Australians should abandon their prejudices and see in Japan a potential protector. The theme is stated clearly in the last passage of the book: "The question is: who will rescue us from ill-informed nervousness about Japanese and Indonesian ambitions, and thus from our dangerous dependency on US power? The answer is ourselves" (p. 345).

SUSPECT REVOLUTIONARIES

McQueen has been a very uneven author. After another solid book, devoted to the painter *Tom Roberts* (1996), appeared a tract, almost unanimously characterized by critics as "venomous," *Suspect History: Manning Clark and the Future of Australia's Past.*[202]

It looks as if all his temperance and rationality vanishes the moment his revolutionary socialist nerve center gets upset. Then the social scientist who wants to be taken seriously gives way to the raging polemicist. What disturbed his peace of mind in this instance was "an eight-page spread on Manning Clark as a Soviet spy" in the August 24, 1996 *Courier-Mail of Brisbane* (p. 1). The word spy appeared only in the first edition of the paper and was eliminated by the editor, but the claim, unproved until now, that the Australian prominent historian received the highest Soviet Order of Lenin remained. It was based on accounts of two prominent figures who remembered seeing the award on his coat.

Defending Manning Clark, but in the process also criticizing him, McQueen viciously attacked many people who had nothing to do with the *Courier-Mail* piece, "abusing just about everyone else to the right of Mao Tse-tung (to whom Humphrey apparently remains loyal).... Dripping with venom."[203] Another critic of the book wrote, "McQueen is not only very nasty; his book is also generous with lazy errors of fact."[204]

Several reviewers were astonished by the author's lack of self-criticism when he wrote, "The only apology I need to make for forty

202 Kent Town, SA: Wakefield Press, 1997.

203 Padrick McGuinness, "Variety in the Spies of life," *Sydney Morning Herald,* June 26, 1997, p. 17.

204 Robert Manne, "Battle for History's High Ground," *The Weekend Australian,* June 7-8, 1997, p. 23.

years of Leftism is to the memory of my parents and grandparents for not trying harder to bring an end to the injustices that blighted their lives and continue to injure a majority of the World's people."[205] The critics reminded him of the tens of millions that were victims of the Left during his Leftism. Some people have harder skins than others. However, even the Chinese Communists disappointed McQueen. He called them "the Market-Leninists."[206]

Since I also became a target of McQueen's revenge for two articles I published in the *Courier-Mail* some time after the controversial eight-page spread, I still owe him an answer, correcting his distortions of facts. The first article that McQueen did not like was based on archival documentation from Prague. In spite of all the accumulated proofs to the contrary, he tried to whitewash the traitor and spy Ian Milner. He asserted that Milner always maintained his innocence and that "left-learning experts remain divided on the issue."[207] Experts in what, exactly? It does not matter if somebody's opinions come from the Left or the Right. What should matter is what is correct and proven by facts. Anyway, it seems that since Lenin's seizure of power, McQueen's brand of Leftism means accepting or ignoring the existence of concentration camps, tortures, and mass murders. Such Left-leaning experts may not be the best ones to consult.

McQueen wrongly claimed that "Milner's file with the Czech Interior Ministry reports that from his arrival in Prague in 1950 he was unhappy."[208] That is not exactly what the file stated. That is what I claimed in my report. The file, as I related, said only that he tried to go back to New York. Milner was not then "busy securing the publication of Australian writers in Czech," as asserted by McQueen.[209] I did not find any trace of such an effort, not even in some twenty pages of bibliography published in his memoirs. My comments were supposedly partisan and not skeptical enough. To cast doubts on the Prague police files, McQueen also quoted the best long-time expert on Eastern Europe, Timothy Garton Ash. (Since Ash is not a Communist,

205 *Suspect History,* p. 179.
206 See his srticle "The Murdoch Press and the Australia Council," *Australian Book Review,* No. 184, September 1996, p. 25.
207 *Suspect History,* p. 57.
208 Ibid., p. 62.
209 Ibid., p. 63.

McQueen called him a "Thatcherite.") Ash said that the secret police "had to meet productivity quotas" and so may have exaggerated or invented Milner's service.[210] That was an argument against 164 pages of police reports by seven of Milner's handlers throughout many years who highly praised his excellent work sending them over one hundred intelligence notices on people he knew!

Finally, McQueen was sure that he had found me out and delivered a knock-out: "So carried away did Hruby become that he lost track of the chronology of events in his native land. He wrote that ... Milner began to supply Czechoslovak secret services with confidential material on Australian situations and personalities.... Those secret services must have been very secret indeed, since the Nazis still occupied his country in 1944."[211]

Again, I just quoted Prague documents. McQueen as a historian should know that during WWII, Czech secret service, led by General František Moravec, reported their very valuable spying activities not only to President Beneš in his London exile, but also to British and Soviet secret services. Also, Czech Communists often used the pronoun „we" when talking about their joint activities with the Russians.

The second article of mine that McQueen objected to was a comparison of two mistaken believers in Lenin and Soviet Communism, "Czech Professor Hromádka and Australian Professor Clark." (It forms part of this book.) There I have to admit that by quoting Manning Clark from memory I might have made a mistake. Although I surely did not invent the expressive sentence McQueen questioned, namely that "he [Clark] hoped to see rivers of blood flowing through Australian streets because only then the Australian phoenix would be able to rise from the ashes and fly" (his page 134). I was not able to find it in print. I must have heard it on the radio or TV, but since all the printed statements of Clark I was able to check, though coming close to it, never contain the whole drastic image, just parts of it that could be put together as the quoted sentence, I might be wrong. Memory is not dependable and so I have to apologize to both Clark and McQueen. On the other hand, McQueen did not tell the whole truth either when he wrote, "What Clark told university students in 1978 was that if reforms were not achieved, that he feared violence might erupt" (ibid.).

---

210 Ibid.
211 Ibid.

In the Wollungong University draft of Clark's graduation address of May 12, 1978, the historian was not too worried. He expected a conflagration:

> Of course now "Land of Hope and Glory" belongs in the dustbin of human history [Trotsky's 1917 image].... It looks as though we here in Australia are in for a great period of upheaval. There is going to be turbulence.... I believe that this is essentially the calm before a great storm—that a tempest will blow or if I may change the image that a cleansing fire will sweep over the ancient and barbaric continent of Australia and during that fire great madness will occur and maybe, although I hope it won't occur, there might be a fratricidal war—a civil war—we are going to be tried in a fiery furnace.... The great question we have to face is whether we human beings will be able to rise out of the ashes after the fire has passed through.... Even if terrible things happen in our country and I think probably they will, people who stand on entrenched ground will still hear the music of the spheres.[212]

In the text of Manning Clark's speech I find only one expression of hope that the apocalyptic vision of his would not occur, but several affirmations that it will. In the printed, edited version of his address, entitled "The Future of Australia," the following statements can be found:

> Anyone who has a sense of the past and has antennae for the present must feel as though he is possibly on the edge of a volcano in Australia.... We would become a society with a past but no future. A society which will be swept into the dustbin of history by those who will not tolerate the existence of privilege.... There's a great deal in our past which is consistent with the cruelty and barbarity of human beings to each other....

212 See pages 2, 4, and 6 of the draft.

Our country is probably quite a suitable setting for
barbarity by one group to another.... Our labour
camps would be in the heat because that matters
in Australia, it's the cold that matters in Russia....
Lawson when he was young and had great faith, said
if you don't find those answers, then we needn't say
the fault is ours "if blood should stain the wattle."[213]

On May 13, 1978, one day after his speech at Wollongong University,
the *Perth Weekend News* published excerpts from an interview with
Clark: "'The election of a more radical Labour Government could lead
Australia into civil war,' Professor Manning Clark said in Melbourne
today." The paper then quoted parts of the speech about the storm, the
cleansing fire, and fiery furnace (always with his "it will"). Then came
quotations from the interview:

He said he believed the parties opposing Labor were
"digging their own grave" [Marx!].... Should civil
war occur, he *hoped* that a new class would emerge
to dominate life in Australia. This would be a merger
of intellectuals and the working people. [Stalin!] He
said today that he *hoped* that the new class would not
be oppressive. "My belief is that this is a time when
domination is being challenged, of one class over
another, man over woman and that the movement
towards abolition of this domination *will lead* to a
period of turbulence," he said. He was trying to get
people to think about the future.... He had no time
scale in mind but felt that dramatic changes would
take place in Australia over the next 20 years.[214]

---

213 *Monogrph 3*, 1–8, pp. 5–8.
214 Italics are mine. In the printed version of Manning Clark's Canberra
     and Wollengong address as it appears in his collection of "Lectures
     and Speeches 1940–1991," *Speaking Out of Turn* (1997), some of the
     images of future turbulence remained, others disappeared. See pages
     30–33.

Again in the interview as in his address, *Manning Clark was predicting the future turbulence more than fearing it*. He liked to act as a visionary, a prophet. At times it even seemed that he would have liked to push developments toward a revolution.

Professor Clark was in his biblical mood making the sort of prophesies of doom that were close to his heart, as he was influenced by them early in his life. After the dismissal of Whitlam as prime minister, the *Australian* quoted him on November 12, 1975:

> The great hope of the Whitlam Government was that it could make changes taking us into the future without violence – without a bloody revolution. If a conservative government gets a grip again, the next step forward for change would be much more likely to be violent.… I think the world has moved on from conservatism.… The historic forces are so strong now that [Mr. Fraser and governor-general] they'll be pushed aside.

He then took this opportunity to again use his beloved Trotsky slogan about the dustbin of history.

On the January 7, 1976, Manning Clark wrote in the *Australian* about "the dying decades of a capitalist society" and compared Sydney and Melbourne to Sodom and Gomorrah. He blamed the reforming governments of Scullin and Chifley that, like Whitlam's, "hesitated and then faltered when it was confronted with that choice, to which it had no answer, between reaction and revolution." The elections in favor of Fraser on December 13, 1975 "will go down in history as that day which converted the radicals from the ballot box to industrial action, from parliamentary to direct action." As he often did, invoking the supposedly healthier Communist part of the world, the professor again claimed that: "It may be the day which proved once and for all just how hopelessly wedded we, as Australians, are to the petty-bourgeois values—to that very sickness which the progressive part of the world is shedding and destroying. It may be that the Whitlam years prove we can only march forward by destroying our old corrupt society root and branch." Again, he prophesied the whirlwind and blamed it on the gravediggers.

Later, more will be said about the strange visionary world of Manning Clark. Several chapters will unveil his illusions about Lenin and the world conspiracy so successfully started by the Russian revolutionary. For the moment, I want to suggest that in spite of differences of outlook between the two historians—Clark mixing Old Testament Ecclesiastes with clichés coined by Marx, Lenin, Trotsky, and Stalin, and McQueen propagating his Maoist United Front—both in the second half of the seventies expected and worked for a major upheaval in Australian society. Both were dangerous revolutionary dreamers.

4

A Tormented Mythmaker: Manning Clark

How much more grievous are the consequences of anger than the causes of it.

Marcus Aurelius

Several earlier citations from Manning Clark's pronouncements prepared us for consideration of his mind, his worldview, and his own self-assigned role in Australia. What were the formative influences and life experiences that led this prominent historian to such a group of fixed ideas that persisted over decades of his university teaching, writing, and public activity?

The more I read him the more I became convinced that he was not only a tormented but even a haunted man—terribly worried about his loss of religious faith, about the hopelessness of life without belief in God and Christ, and anxious to find a new faith in Lenin and his attempt to bring about a paradise on earth supposedly through justice, equality, and brotherhood of men. It is almost painful to follow his internal conflict about which path to follow, which way to go personally and as a society, twisted between two absolutely contradictory programs, but hoping to mix them together to combine Christ with Lenin. A few more quotations from a volume of his autobiography should demonstrate his basic attitude:

She [my mother] probably planted in me the thirst to believe.[215] I had given up all hope that God would work a great marvel in this world. Here was a group of people telling me they could do what He had failed to do. They would build a heaven on earth.... I wanted to believe.[216] Maybe salvation would come from Russia and a new society, like the Phoenix bird, would rise out of the ashes of the corrupt society of Europe ... the world's first Communist society?[217]

In his autobiography, Clark keeps coming back to his loss of faith in basic Christian dogmas: "Maybe that is the greatest delusion of all—that there is someone, somewhere, who can help.[218] What if Rome is based on a lie? What if Christ did not rise from the dead? What if God did desert Christ on the Cross?... That left man as god."[219]

In spite of his ardent wish to believe either in God and Christ, or in Lenin and his Communism, he could not rid himself of doubts about both: "I was also ill at ease with their rejection of Christ.... They slid into ignoring humanity's oldest problem, namely the origin of human evil.... So I was just as divided about the future-of-humanity men as I was about the believers in the kingdom of God. I wanted to believe..."[220]

Manning Clark projected his own dilemma of loss of faith and need to believe into society. The "clergyman's son"[221]—as he calls himself—was always looking for his own and society's promised Saviour: "Where did humanity's salvation lie and who would be the saviour?[222] I believed in the role of Labour to change the world, but was often ill-at-ease in the company of revolutionaries.[223] Then, as ever for me, there were two questions: Did

---

215   Manning Clark, *The Quest for Grace* (Ringwood, Vic.: Penguin Books Australia, 1990), p. 246.
216   Ibid., p. 15.
217   Ibid., p. 58.
218   Ibid., p. 11.
219   Ibid., p. 32.
220   Ibid., p. 16.
221   Ibid., p. 68.
222   Ibid., p. 112.
223   Ibid., p. 118.

God exist and if He did what was He like? Was humanity capable of achieving the aims of the French and the Russian revolutions?"[224]

This dichotomy of faith and doubt was projected into Clark's construction of his *A History of Australia*. At the end of volume two, we read about a miracle that could happen in Australia: "There something of an extraordinary nature might turn up one day on that shore when men liberated themselves from the curse of Adam's fall. There men, freed at last from the stain of the Old World, freed too from the convict's clanking chain, might see that heaven and hell were priests' inventions, and come to trust the brotherhood of man."[225]

Volume three concludes by a similar prophesy, repeating almost the same words in the epilogue: "As British philistinism and industrial civilization began to leave their mark on the ancient barbaric land ... some Australians began to dream: that they could banish the Old World errors and wrongs and lies, that Heaven and Hell were priests' inventions and that they could build a paradise in the land that belonged to them."[226]

Since Clark never showed any deep study and understanding of Russian history, he probably knew about the growth of nihilism only from his devoted reading of Dostoyevsky, who as a Christian believer was very much worried about the possible consequences of the loss of faith in God and Christ by some prominent representatives of the Russian intelligentsia, as he demonstrated in such novels as *The Brothers Karamazov, Crime and Punishment,* and especially *The Possessed.*

Clark was preoccupied by his own loss of faith in God and the Christian life. Projections of his own issues with nihilism on to modern society as a whole were often expressed in his books. He blamed bourgeois capitalism for society's spiritual woes. He liked to express it in biblical terms, as in the sixth volume of *A History of Australia*: "The people killed their gods. The people turned to the worship of the Golden Calf.[227] History has blurred the vision of Eden, allowing Mammon to infest the land.A turbulent emptiness seized the people as they moved into a post-Christian post-Enlightenment era."[228]

224   Ibid., p. 120.
225   Melbourne University Press, 1968, p. 349.
226   Ibid., 1973, p.
227   Ibid. 1987, p. 500.
228   Ibid.

Here we come to the self-imposed mission of a prophet historian that Manning Clark assumed, at least partly to rid himself and his nation of the nihilism brought upon by the loss of faith: "It is the task of the historian and the myth-maker to tell the story of how the world came to be as it is. It is the task of the prophet to tell the story of what might be."[229]

In the fourth volume of *A History of Australia*, Clark—in the usual way of prophets, expecting doom and salvation just around the corner—wrote in his conclusion about the life of man without God. Indeed, that theme takes front billing in this volume along with the impending breakdown of bourgeois society, succeeded by an age of ruins, which is still with us. But a promise of salvation follows; however, it is a conditional salvation: "I have had the good fortune to live at a time when a great debate took place on the nature of man and the future of society. I have the impression that the debate will not go on for much longer, that either the men who know the way forward will take over, and shut up all doubters and dissidents, or the barbarians will shut us all up in their own way."[230]

This either/or prediction was signed by Clark on March 3, 1977. Fourteen years earlier, while commenting on the conflict between Menzies and Dr. Evatt over Petrov's defection, the Australian historian sent a similar message to his readers (obviously counting himself among the "others"):

> Just as the publicists ... probed the origin of evil and the causes of human suffering ... others argued that this preoccupation with evil and the counseling of resignation symbolized the spiritual sickness of bourgeois civilization. For them, only the destruction of bourgeois society could liberate the creative gifts of the people and restore to their literature and their art the hope and confidence of men who knew the way forward for humanity.[231]

In his writings, Clark repeatedly claimed that he and his friends on the Left knew the way forward. He found this way in his childhood

---

229   Ibid.
230   Ibid., p. x.
231   *A Short History of Australia* (Sydney: Mentor Books, 1963), p. 244.

and remained faithful to it all his life: "My political education began in Belgrave by a man named Carter, part-time owner of a garage in the main street. He told me about the Russian Revolution of 1917 and told me it was the beginning of a new era in the history of mankind. I was tremendously excited by what he had to say."[232]

As a student at the University of Melbourne, Clark graduated to the cheap brochures published by the Left Book Club. On the basis of "much reading" he came to the belief that a change in the ownership of the means of production, distribution, and exchange would produce ultimately a change in human behaviour. By removing the main causes of human vileness, evil would disappear.[233]

This fallacy helped to bring to Communism not only Manning Clark but many other people who like him lost faith that God, Christ, and religion could change mankind. The idea of a dichotomous search for salvation and eradication of evil was expressed again in the same volume: "Today there are only two great beliefs in Australia—two tremendous utopias. There are those who believe in the dream sketched by the Communist Manifesto. Then there are those who believe in the last paragraph of the Apostle's Creed."[234]

Clark did not even mention the growing number of rationalists who do not trust either of the two utopias. Although at the end of his life, faced with imminent death, the historian returned to the second utopia and wanted to be buried in the Catholic cathedral, until then he followed and fought for the first utopia. The decisive moment came when in 1958, two years after the Russians crushed the genuine people's and workers' revolution in Hungary, Clark visited the Soviet Union, all expenses paid by the brutal suppressors of Hungarian freedoms. The tormented man found the promised paradise: "I was still a child of unbelief, who had never lost the thirst to believe. Russia was filling with culture the vacuum where God had once been."[235]

Clark's book *Meeting Soviet Man*, in spite of some mild and polite criticism, is a paean to the redeeming quality and historical mission of the Soviet Union:

---

232 *Quest for Grace*, op. cit., p. 248.
233 "Themes in 'A history of Australia'" (1978), in *Occasional Writings and Speeches* (Melbourne: Fontana/Collins, 1980), p. 83.
234 "Rewriting Australian History," (1954), Ibid., p. 7.
235 *Quest for Grace*, op. cit., p. 219.

1917 began the new era in the history of mankind.[236]
Here, indeed, was the key to the Soviet experiment
– the attempt to create the good life for all without
the comforts or support of religion[237].... Driving
back to Moscow in the dusk, with the darkness slowly
enveloping the car, one felt that glow which comes
from being close to achievement, and a sense, too, of
being in a country which was recapturing its bearing
and the ideals of 1917.[238]

There are several observations to be made to dampen the
enthusiasm of Clark who so much wanted to believe that a new history
of mankind began in 1917. First, he never shows real knowledge of the
supposed first year of the new Russian and world history. His extremely
limited grasp of the year 1917 comes from Soviet propaganda films and
brochures. He never mentions the fact that the only genuine people's
and workers' revolution Russia then experienced was the February
Revolution, which opened up prisons and installed democracy with
free elections and the usual freedoms of the press, assembly, and speech.
What Lenin and Trotsky arranged, the assumption of absolute power
in October, was not a genuine revolution but a carefully and capably
orchestrated coup d'état after which all the recently gained freedoms
were very quickly eliminated; the secret police was re-established with
much more cruel efficiency than under the Czars, and torture and
executions were taking place on an unprecedented scale. The freely
elected Constituent Assembly was closed down and the Bolsheviks
brutally ruled against the wishes of three fourths of the population.

What Clark praised as "the ideals of 1917" were either *democratic
principles of Lenin's opponents* or Lenin's populist slogans that he refused
to practice. Clark's idealized picture of saviour Lenin is so obviously
untrue. At many points in his book, he demonstrates the incredible
delusion of an unwavering believer, of a dangerous mythmaker (his
own word): "Lenin ... he was an architect of a new society ... his
humanity is never lost, nor is the idea of Lenin as a pilgrim.... Why

---

236 Sydney: August & Robertson, 1969, p. 114.
237 Ibid., p. 116.
238 Ibid., p. 68. Clark overestimated the changes. The propaganda idol
     Stalin was replaced by the idol Lenin.

did Lenin—a man who seems to have been Christ-like, at least in his compassion—have to die, and this other one take over from him? Why do Stalins always come to the top?"[239]

As will be documented in the third part of this book, Clark did not have any understanding of the real Lenin and the real October Revolution engineered by Lenin, Trotsky, and Stalin. On the obligatory visit arranged by his hosts to the Lenin Museum, Clark mused: "We ... were seeing the lovable Lenin, the lover of humanity, the man who was gentle with woman and child, who wanted us all to be nice to one another ... the Lenin of the humanist faith ... an example, an inspiration."[240]

Here the historian who wanted to serve his nation by becoming a mythmaker fell victim to a propaganda myth which he then continued to spread. Another occasion for devout veneration of one of the most criminal political leaders of the century—matched only by Hitler, Stalin, Mao Tsetung, and Pol Pot—presented itself to Clark in Moscow in 1970. Rewarded by the Lenin Jubilee Medal, Clark, the "mosquito" who was "asked to talk about an elephant," thus extolled the cruel Russian dictator:

> There lived at least two personalities in Lenin. One was the teacher of humanity ... a person who was like Magellan or Columbus, but not so much in the opening of the new world as in the belief he gave people that it was within their ability to create it. There was also the man of political genius in Lenin – the person who advanced all courageous ideas for the non-dogmatic management of government.[241]

Clark in his adulation also declared "Lenin as one of the greatest teachers of humanity," and proclaimed contrary to all evidence that "this great love of life stayed with him to his death," and that "he

239 Ibid., p. 12. The eminent historian, Robert Conquest, whom Clark should have read among many others, called it "my favourite nomination for Lenin-mania." To the "Christ-like, at least in his compassion" Lenin he added Clark's statement that Lenin was "as excited and lovable as a little child." See his review "Terrorists," *New York Review of Books*, March 6, 1997, p. 6.
240 *Meeting Soviet Man*, op. cit., pp. 47–48.
241 The *Courier-Mail*, 24 May 1997, pp. 30–31, and *The Australian*, 16 June 1997, p. 11.

wanted a good life for everyone." Clark ended his idolization of one of the greatest destroyers of lives by asserting that "he was one of those mighty and great people, one of those giants, who are leading the world to creation and well-being."[242]

In his oration, Manning Clark again showed a preference for the secular when he emphatically announced: "He was the result of the Enlightenment. By this I mean that he completely rejected the Judaeo-Christian view of the world and its conception of a man's place in the universe."[243]

Clark, like Peter, denied his master when he agreed with Lenin that Dostoyevsky did not belong to the great achievers of the human spirit.[244] He did this in spite of the fact that the great Russian writer had always served him as a window into the Russian soul, although Clark never, at least not publicly, recognized in the Bolsheviks the monsters of Dostoyevsky's *Besy*. Only in Communist leaders who followed in Lenin's footsteps was he willing to accept Dostoyevsky's premonition and warning: "The most illuminating images on what happened in the Soviet Union since the death of Lenin came from the prophetic writings of Dostoyevsky."[245]

He never acknowledged that all the horrors of Stalin and other Soviet dictators were based on Lenin's foundations and example. For Clark, "Lenin was so great, his vision so correct, his knowledge of human history and society so profound and exact, that now some of the work of the survivors is being seen more and more as an aberration, a deviation."[246]

Clark often talked and wrote about Lenin as a man of the Enlightenment. That is, of course, a very poor understanding of the true Lenin. Maybe only in his refusal to believe in God and Christ could he be seen as a follower of the Enlightenment. Lenin was much more led by tougher German ideologies than by French or British and American Enlightenment philosophers. While living in Geneva, Lenin carefully studied Clausewitz and applied his militaristic view of political activism. He surely was not a friend of liberty and freedom of speech

242 Ibid.
243 Ibid.
244 Ibid.
245 *Meeting Soviet Man*, op. cit., p. 86.
246 Ibid.

or a believer in reason as were the men of the Enlightenment. That is another of Clark's basic misunderstandings of Lenin and Leninism.

In 1978, he fondly recalled his Melbourne days and properly identified *hate* as one of the major sources of his Leninist faith: "It was immensely comforting to mix with men and women who believed that a day would come when the 'shits' no longer told us what to do, or how to behave, or what to believe. In Melbourne in those giddy days we were all great haters very gullible."[247]

The third step in Manning Clark's confirmation as a believer in the Soviet Union's mission of salvation, after the garage man and the Left Book Club, was made by his trip to the promised land: "By 1956, or certainly by 1958 after the journey to Russia which erased some of the doubts about the capacity of mankind for better things, the author was in part a believer in the Promethean message of the Enlightenment.... The author would be writing on the assumption that the world should belong to the Prometheans, to the visionaries, to the men of hope, while knowing that such men were always likely to be crushed in Australia."[248]

Clark then revealed the key to his six volumes of history of Australia, the important point of view that served as its major theme: "Was Australia going to remain a semi-colonial or provincial member of the American way of life, a society of men and women bewitched and charmed by Greed and titillation of culture? Or was it going to fulfil the future sketched for it by the prophets of the 1890s and create a society free from the infamy of capitalist society and the new greyness of spirit of all those societies created so far on the principles of 1917?"[249]

The only criticism of the Soviet-type societies that Clark ever publicly expressed was their greyness of spirit or popism, as he sometimes called their suffocating discipline and enforced unanimity. However, he still ardently contended that they were preferable to democratic bourgeois capitalism. He was worried "about our role in this march of humanity forward from the darkness into the light."[250]

---

247 "Themes in 'A History of Australia,' *Occasional Writings*, p. 83.
248 Ibid., pp. 85–86.
249 Ibid.
250 *A Discovery of Australia* (1976 Boyer Lectures, ABC), p. 14.

To me it was rather depressing that in December
1949 when one third of the population of the world
was marching forwards, we chose to stand still. It
was even more depressing in December 1975 when
we showed the world that we did not much mind if
someone turned the clock back. We were still a nation
of petty-bourgeois property owners.[251] We seemed to
prefer darkness of the womb; we seemed to be pitifully
afraid of the light.... [We] have assumed the role of
the twentieth century last ditch defenders of a corrupt
and decadent social order.[252]

Manning Clark thus spoke as a very superficial propagandist,
spreading Stalin's slogans of "marching forward," "petty bourgeois
property owners," and "a corrupt and decadent social order." Klement
Gottwald's CPCZ campaign's slogan also was the cliché "Forward!" In
the same series of lectures, Clark, as a historian prophet, revealed that
he expected Australia's parliamentary system "to be replaced either by
some variety of a people's democracy, or the spread of a new barbarism
over our continent."[253] He also claimed that "one of the tasks of a
historian is to prophesy the victor-to be" and "whichever Marxist group
seizes power in Australia is not likely to be very merciful or generous
in their judgment of those who stood in their way."[254] In his *Quest for
Grace* Clark, he even prophesied that "maybe a victorious and purified
Russia, a Russia which rediscovered the humanism of Marx, would
light a 'cleansing fire' in Australia."[255]

Twelve pages later, Clark confessed to his naïve faith in backward
Russia—backward in both its Czarist and Soviet versions: "I also held
a messianic view of the role of Russia in world history. Russia would

251 Ibid., p. 15.
252 Ibid., p. 31.
253 Ibid., p. 49.
254 Ibid. Clark even claimed that "the American thesis on foreign policy
     ... exposed Australia to the danger of being on the losing side in a
     world war." *A Short History*, op. cit., p. 240.
255 Ibid., p. 122.

save Europe from decadence and corruption. Russia would save Europe as she saved it in 1812."[256]

Since this book to a certain degree is based on a comparative perspective, it should be remembered that the Czech philosophy professor and later president of the Czechoslovak Republic, T.G. Masaryk, acquainted himself much more deeply with Russian history and literature, as evidenced in his thorough study, *The Spirit of Russia* in its English translation, *Rusko a Evropa* [Russia and Europe] in Czech. (The two volumes were issued between 1913 and 1921). He did not share the doctrine of Slavophilism with its messianic role for autocratic Russia and, on the contrary, warned of its backwardness. He was also critical of the similar messianic role the Bolsheviks ascribed to themselves. When Bertrand Russell went to the Soviet Union to visit Lenin, he saw the facts and denounced Leninism in his book *The Practice and Theory of Bolshevism* (1920).

Manning Clark's visionary program for his nation, however, was not based on study and profound knowledge. Its whole foundation rested on flimsy hopes of restoring his loss of faith in God by faith in Leninism, replacing the so much hated bourgeois liberalism, capitalism, British philistinism, and American culture's titillation and consumerism.

The reader probably by now realizes that Clark not only talked and wrote in clichés, but that he also thought in clichés. Capitalism was always rotten, the bourgeoisie doomed, to be thrown in "the dustbin of history." He also quoted again and again Lawson's "blood on the wattle," Dostoyevsky's statement "I want to be there when everyone suddenly understands what it has all been for," and, of course, "the ideals of 1917." A deep thinker he was not. Rather a propagandist equally adept at convincing himself. It is a testament to the provincialism of the Australian Left that for so long he could be celebrated as some kind of national icon, protected from criticism. There are ideas in Clark's work that one could support, such as republicanism, freeing Australia from its dependence on the British monarchy, the overdue acceptance of the Aboriginal population into the mainstream, and the need to overcome provincialism. During the period of his writing for *Quadrant* he lost some of the silliness. However, his own unrepentant abandonment of

---

256 Ibid., p. 134.

society's better prospects in favor of the Russian brutal experiment in totalitarian domination was completely wrong—and itself provincial.

At the beginning of this chapter devoted to Clark's misguided view of humanity's progress, I mentioned that in my view he was not only tormented, but also haunted. With the help of a few more quotations from his writings, I will explain what I meant and why it influenced his view of the world and its destiny.[257]

Manning Clark suffered from a profound sense of personal guilt. His oft-repeated characterization of the social order as "corrupt and doomed" was at least partly based on his Christian belief that corrupt and sinful people were doomed. He felt that he himself was a very guilty man who desperately needed salvation. On one page in his autobiography, he wrote that "maybe a victorious and purified Russia ... would light a 'cleansing fire' in Australia." Juxtaposed to it on the next page we can read, "My sarcasm and my jokes were a mask to protect the man within, to protect an innocent boy who had managed to survive all the descents into the gutter unstained."[258] Four pages later, he reminisces, "Rages and attacks of the 'sillies', drunkenness, the easy way out, will hang around for years. When they were finally conquered, the memory of those past follies never grew dim."[259]

On the same page and in many other instances, Clark called these sins "the Dionysian frenzy." Later, he is a little more specific, writing about "the buffoonery, the showing-off, and the Friday-night descent into hell."[260]

Clark's book devoted to his favorite author, *In Search of Henry Lawson*, to a large degree is based on his self-projection onto the writer. He talks about his haunting dualism, of "the Dionysian and

---

257 "What comes from inside the historian influences what he sees." Manning Clark, *A Historian's Apprenticeship* (Melbourne University Press, 1992), p. 1.

258 *Quest*, op. cit., pp. 122–23.

259 Ibid., p. 127.

260 Ibid., pp. 184–85. According to *Collins English Dictionary* (1991), "Dionysus or Dionysos, the Greek God of Wine, fruitfulness, and vegetation, worshipped in orgiastic rites. He was also known as the bestower of ecstasy and god of the drama, and identified with Bacchus;" "and Dionysian ... wild or orgiastic." Clark took it over from Nietzsche.

Christian, the flesh and the spirit, human uproar and respectability."[261] Lawson's part Nordic origin brings in Ibsen, whose characters "were haunted by some sexual or financial disgrace in their past."[262] Clark remarks on Ibsen, "He had the courage and the strength to win the battle over the forces of destruction within himself."[263] On Lawson, though, he says, "a time came when a man had to acknowledge and accept the unmistakable evidence of his own swinishness."[264] Several times he comes back to Lawson's "Dionysian frenzy"[265] and stresses that Lawson was also "hoping ... that somewhere over the horizon there was salvation."[266] As in his autobiographical writing, Clark uses the very same imagery of "the descent into hell in the beer shops."[267] There are other features of his self-portrait in Lawson's image, but let us move to another revelation of Clark's feelings of guilt.

The correspondence between Manning Clark and Kathleen Fitzpatrick from 1919 to1990 was the subtitle of a book published in 1996 entitled *Dear Kathleen, Dear Manning*.[268] Clark had a bypass operation in September 1983 and in the hospital was disturbed thinking about his life: "I look on much in the past with great regret and remorse ... and all those follies which can never be undone or atoned for, or made right. Enough of remorse, of self-laceration, and regrets. I can only hope that Christ was right when he advised us to let the tares and the wheat grow together. The tares of my Melbourne days troubled me greatly in St. Vincent's."[269]

In the first volume of his autobiography, *The Puzzles of Childhood*, Clark wrote about himself as passion personified: "I wanted it all now.... There were to be wild years in which I nourished the terrible delusion that others may be dirtied in the gutter, but not me. That innocent one who had been wounded by the world, he could never be

261 Melbourne: The Macmilian Company of Australia, 1978, p. 2.
262 Ibid., p. 4.
263 Ibid.
264 Ibid., p. 17.
265 Ibid., pp. 48 and 71.
266 Ibid., p. 79.
267 Ibid., p. 72 again p. 95 twice.
268 Edited by Susan Davies (Melbourne University Press).
269 Ibid., p. 54.

besmirched. There would be many years in the fog, in which I would hurt many people and be hurt in turn by many others."[270]

Mysteriously, he wrote about "a boy's descent into Hell—into what the mystics identify as the 'dark night of the soul'."[271] He complained that the father did not help him and "My mother begins to cry whenever it happens. Tears stream down her cheeks."[272] Several pages were devoted to his mild form of epilepsy, but Clark did not explain the connection since he admitted in the context: "There was much doing of what ought not to be done – and I had to find the strength to live with that, to live in the knowledge that one day one must forgive oneself."[273]

Although Clark repeatedly claimed that he lost his faith in God and that Lenin and Communism successfully replaced the void and nihilism in his own soul and in society, he was haunted by the possibility that Christianity was right after all. Especially toward the end of his life, he returned to his religious faith, as recalled, among others, by Philip Adams: "With the passage of time it was the old-time religion, not the recent ideology, that proved the more powerful. Not long before he died I interviewed Clark for two hours on the wireless and he told me that he had a "shy hope" of the existence of God. And of an afterlife."[274]

Not all is yet known about Manning Clark's private life that might have influenced his public stance and also his haunting feelings of guilt. Rumors about his womanizing and about his bisexuality seem to be supported not only by his rather frequent confessions of sinfulness, but also by a strong hint of his homosexuality in *The Quest for Grace*. Remembering his grief caused by the premature death of his close young friend, Noel Ebbels, and his foreword for a book of documents that Ebbels collected on the Labour movement, he wrote: "My loss was so great that I risked revealing what mattered to me most in life. I

270   Ringwood, Vic.: Viking, Penguin Books Australia, p. 211.
271   Ibid., p. 212.
272   Ibid.
273   Ibid.
274   "Dictatorships of popes and proletariats," *Weekend Australian*, Review, p. 1, 21–22 June 1997. Under the title "Hero of the Left" Peter Charlton and Peter Kelly quoted Dr. Ian Spry, son the director of ASIO, Brigadier Sir Charles Spry, that "Clark had been provided with a mistress who worked in the Soviet Embassy in Canberra and that this relationship continued for some years." *Courier-Mail*, 12 September 1998.

confessed in public my love for Noel. The mockers of Melbourne had
the evidence they wanted, 'I told you so ... ha, ha, ha!' I also implied
that the words of Christ and the Russian revolution were the great
hopes for humanity. This statement was greeted with uproar."[275]

On the next page Clark called his foreword "my hymn of love
and praise." A few pages later, Clark recalled a conversation with Dr.
Evatt:

> In 1954 Dr. Evatt, who was then leader of the
> Australian Labor Party, expressed a wish to ask me
> questions about Ian Milner. Someone had told Evatt
> that I had known Milner well in the mid 1940s....
> He wanted to know all about Ian Milner from me,
> or so he said. But he had already made up his mind
> about Ian Milner, and nothing I told him had the
> slightest influence on him. By then he saw himself as
> the object of a gigantic conspiracy to destroy him. His
> mind was like a chessboard on which he had placed
> all the pieces in their place. The fact that the position
> did not correspond with the facts did not cause him
> to change his mind. On that know he was nowhere
> near that place. But Evatt would not budge.[276]

The book was published one year before Manning Clark's death.
In the convoluted way by which these important confessions, or near
confessions, were revealed, was he indicating two dark secrets of his
Melbourne life? Concerning the first opening of his heart, what would
have mattered about the hint of homosexuality was not so much the
time's strict disapproval, but rather his understandable worry that Soviet
agents could have used it against him at any time to pressure him into
collaboration. The second intimation is even clearer: Dr. Evatt in 1954
was staunch in his belief that the Petrov affair was just a sinister plot,
and Ian Milner, among others, was not a spy for the Soviet Union,
but a victim of the Cold War spy mania. If Manning Clark tried to
tell Evatt the opposite, he must have known by then, if not ten years
earlier, that Ian Milner helped to provide vital information to Soviet

275 Op. cit., p. 202.
276 Ibid. p. 208.

secret services through Walter Seddon Clayton. According to some private information, Clark was present when Milner met Clayton. That makes Clark's assertion that in Milner he preferred the poet more understandable. He most probably had known about Milner's treachery since the mid-forties.

When Clark was writing about Jim Cairns we can again recognize features of his own self-portrait: "Most of the time Jim looked desperately unhappy.... He was a wrongs righter—a man who had been the victim of a great wrong, who elevated the curing of his own wound into a national cause. I never knew what that wound was. I still ponder whether perhaps he did not know, or, if he did, that it was too painful for him to talk about to anyone."[277]

While writing about feelings of guilt, Clark also proved to be guilty of rather ungentlemanly behavior toward his wife Dymphna: "We both lived in the shadow of the avengers and the punishers: *there were ghosts in the past of both of us.*"[278]

A MISLEADING SEER

Manning Clark often stressed that he wanted to serve his people as a seer, a prophet, a visionary pointing the way forward. The trouble was that his vision was faulty, misleading, and dangerous, leading to catastrophe if followed. He claimed to have insight in a field which was not his own, which he refused to study, and in which he trusted propaganda slogans and clichés. Even his knowledge of Christ was flawed: he was not "the founder of Christianity" as Clark professed.[279] Jesus was a Jew and died as a Jew. Other men founded and constructed Christianity.

His hate of his own bourgeois class, his lack of real understanding of the lauded proletariat, his hate of Great Britain and the United States, his shortsighted condemnation of private capitalism, all this along with a naïve belief in Lenin as the savior of humanity was in line with the Stalinist plan of a historical march forward over the graves of dissenters. Clark was even considering Australian concentration camps in the

---

277 Ibid., pp. 154–55.
278 Ibid., p. 37. My italics.
279 Ibid., p. 155.

hot desert[280] and the denial of paper to write on to non-Communist historians.[281] He was not a democrat in his repeated expressions that parliamentary democracy was probably doomed and that "the ballot box was not the way forward in Australia ... that there must be a 'lick on the lug', that in Australia either blood must stain the wattle, or Australians must join the British and the New Zealanders as the darling dodoes of the twentieth century."[282]

Clark's manifestations of political foolishness cannot be dismissed as minor lapses or side issues because they represent his *Weltanschauung*, his prophesy and perspective by which he saw his self-assigned role as his nation's leader and saviour. In 1954, he wrote prophetically: "History, to be a great history, must have a point of view on the direction of society. It also must have something to say, some great theme to lighten our darkness—that, for example, the era of bourgeois liberalism, of democracy, and belief in material progress is over, and that those who defend such a creed are the reactionaries of today.... The historian ... must know one big thing—and feel it deeply".[283]

Twenty years later, Clark confirmed his worldview based on two irrational, apocalyptic, and murderous utopias, Christianity (during parts of its history) and Marxism-Leninism: "Those two secular prophets, Karl Marx and Leon Trotsky, like the metaphysical prophets of the Old Testament, instructed us how we can liberate ourselves from moral infamy."

In fact, rather than liberating anybody from moral infamy, Professor Manning Clark, Ian Milner, Humphrey McQueen, and other well known or not so well known Leftist illusionists, wittingly or unwittingly, consciously or unconsciously, by their activities and propagandist writing and teaching were helping Soviet conspirators to advance their plan to replace democracy with totalitarian dictatorship.

---

280 "Are We a Nation of Bastards?" *Meanjin*, Vol. 35, No. 2, 1976, p. 218.
281 Ibid.
282 *Quest*, op. cit., p. 199.
283 "Rewriting Australian History," *Occasional Writings and Speeches* (Melbourne: Fontana/Collins, 1980), p. 19.

PART II
Agents, Informers, Spies, And Conspirators

1

Times Of Twilight: From Alliance To The Cold War

A few years around 1945 were marked by hopes shared by people in democratic countries that anti-Fascist cooperation would continue, that the Soviet Union had passed the age of terror and would liberalize its system of government. It was a time of illusions by some and for others a time of learning about the true and continuing nature of the Communist regime and its worldwide conspiracy. Democratic intellectuals and politicians, especially those believing in socialism, felt the need to change capitalism in order to avoid repeating recent economic crises and their terrible consequences.

The suffering of the peoples of the Soviet Union and their great contribution to victory in World War II persuaded many people that everything should be done to facilitate future cooperation. Soviet leaders allegedly feared a capitalist encirclement threatening the success of their revolution. It was believed that what was needed was to offer the Communists friendship without suspicion and prove it by welcoming them with open arms.

I

In Australia, Dr. Herbert Vere Evatt as Minister for External Affairs and attorney-general from 1941 to 1949 "was responsible for the Security Service but was notoriously lax about security." His "right-hand man with respect to foreign policy matters was Dr. John Wear Burton Jr." As Desmond Ball and David Horner reported, "they believed in the construction of a new world order in which power would be replaced by humanitarian principles."[284] Both were against the creation of an Australian counterespionage agency and did not suspect the Communists of spying in Australia.

They believed in the theory and practice of open diplomacy. Dr. Burton "encouraged his departmental officers to be as forthcoming as possible with Soviet representatives in Canberra." Although Soviet spies such as Ian Milner and Jim Hill gave no credence to open diplomacy, "to some extent at least, Jim Hill was simply practicing what some of his superiors were preaching." According to Robert Manne, "the Federal Member for Mackellar, the volatile anti-Communist activist, W. C. Wentworth ... on May 7" referred "to Dr Evatt's appointment of Dr Burton ,a young Communist sympathiser', as Secretary of the Department of External Affairs." Burton repeatedly defended Milner: "Milner's responsibility was readily apparent. What was more surprising was Dr Burton's response. When Milner leak was brought to the attention by Sir Frederick Shedden, Burton defended Milner as a ,safe security risk'."[285]

No doubt such a naïve and suspect attitude substantially facilitated Soviet espionage. However, it was not just an Australian phenomenon. It was part of a worldwide age of innocence when the end of a horrible war encouraged hope in brotherhood and unity, of purpose based on goodwill.

In England, Professor Harold Laski wielded great influence not only in the British Labour Party, but also in Australia and Europe. (According to Tony McGillick, Evatt was a personal friend of Laski.) On November 22, 1946, he entertained eleven of his friends, including

---

284   *Breaking the Codes: Australia's KGB Network, 1944–1950* (St. Leonards, NSW: Allen & Unwin, 1998), pp. 150–151.

285   Robert Manne, *The Petrov Affair: Politics and Espionage* (Sydney: Pergamon, 1978), pp. 79, 103, 181 and 183. Christopher Andrew in his new book *The Defence of the Realm: The Authorized History of MI5* (London: Allen Lane, 2009) describes how, after the discovery of leaks in the Ministry of Foreign Affairs [Ian Milner], the urgent mission to Australia to install an efficient counter-intelligence agency by Sir Roger Hollis and Sir Percy Sillitoe of M15 was met by "the abrasive Evatt" who "skillfully probed" their cover story so that they had "to reveal the true source" [Venona] that even President Truman did not know about (but Stalin did). See pp. 369-370.

seven members of Parliament, in order to tell them about his impressions of visits to the United States and the Soviet Union. Interestingly, ten pages of his comments—in Czech—were found in the Prague State Central Archive.[286] In the opening statement it was emphasized that Laski impressed his guests by the earnestness of his declaration and by the correctness of his conclusions about the political situation in the Soviet Union. He insisted that it was necessary to reach lasting friendly relations with the USSR as soon as possible. Laski "expressed his conviction of and confidence in the sincerity of Russian politics aspiring to permanent peace as well as the invincibility of the Soviet Union in any future military conflict that certain war-mongers in Great Britain and above all in the United States want to provoke."[287]

Harold Laski pointed out that British foreign policy toward the Soviet Union must be changed. As he explained in the major part of his dinner address, his deep trust in Soviet leaders' good intentions was based on his private conversation with Stalin.

When Laski was in Moscow together with a British parliamentary delegation, someone in the Kremlin told him confidentially that Stalin would like to have a talk with him. Laski suggested that a few other members of the delegation should be invited too, but Stalin insisted that only Laski should come while other members of the delegation would be kept watching a movie; Laski would claim to be unable to attend. When the delegation was bored with the film and wanted to leave, they were prevented from going and told that the best part of the movie was to come later. Laski then spent two and a half hours alone with Stalin, playing cat and mouse with a master of the game.

Politely, the Soviet dictator requested Laski's opinion about what should be done to improve mutual relations. Laski disliked Molotov and

---

286 SCA, 100/24, 101, 1148. The document was found by Dr. Vilém
    Prečan then from the Institute for Contemporary History in Prague.
    He kindly provided a copy for me. Tony McGillick, *Comrade no More*,
    (West Pert: McGillick, 1980), p. 225. Laski used here the favored term
    of Stalinist propagandists. For example, on September 19, 1946,
287 Ibid. Stalin's pretense of American war-mongering is obvious from
    his statement of 12/16/1949 to Mao Tse-tung: "America, though it
    screams war, is actually afraid of war more than anything; Europe
    is afraid of war." See "Stalin's Conversations with Chinese Leaders,"
    COLD WAR INTERNATIONAL HISTORY BULLETIN (Washington,
    DC), Issues 6–7, Winter 1995/1996, p. 5.

pleaded for a change in Soviet diplomacy, closer cultural cooperation and improvement of trade contacts. Talking to his guests, Laski praised Stalin's patient attention and his assertion that he would do all in his power to bring about changes. Laski naively fell for a ruse when Stalin pretended that in the Politburo there were three factions: one aggressive and led by Molotov; one peaceful and led by himself; and the third in the decisive middle ground. In order to win them for his policy of friendship and peace, Stalin demanded changes in British foreign policy. Ernest Bevin must be replaced as British foreign minister, after which Stalin could replace Molotov. He assured Laski that if Britain fulfilled its nationalization of industry, transport, and finances, etc., with a systematic foreign policy and internal reforms, it could reach the same degree of socialist development as the Soviet Union, maybe even more. Because of the presence of the capitalist class, it would need more time and perseverance, but it is possible to achieve socialism by democratic-socialist methods.

All that was music to Laski's ears. Although Stalin openly proclaimed that Britain should join the Soviet Union in opposing American imperialism and cut off discussions between British and US military staff, Laski did not grasp that all Stalin was interested in was detaching Britain from its major ally, thus making it easier to conquer. (As will be shown elsewhere, his agents had carefully drawn plans for it, including assassinations, shutting down transportation, etc.) As in Australia, in England it was easy to appeal to anti-American prejudices.

Stalin had absolute power as he proved again and again by replacing or even judicially assassinating members of the Politburo, heads of secret services, and most generals, including the chief of staff. Yet, he innocently claimed to Laski that he could not make changes in the armed services as long as the British military continued cooperating with the American general staff. And this learned British political scientist accepted it as a fact.

At the end of his report to the assembled dinner guests, Laski mentioned that he went to see British Prime Minister Atlee, informed him about Stalin's proposals, and urged him to replace Bevin. He also suggested that Atlee should go to Moscow and offer Stalin Britain's goodwill, friendship, and large-scale economic help in order to insure the building of democracy and socialism in the peace that the world so needed. Atlee, a more realistic politician, answered that he was willing to go to Moscow but not before spring.

Laski implored his influential guests to join him in attempts to alter British foreign policy and detach Britain as fast as possible from the war-mongering Americans. Stalin obviously achieved his aim with Laski, but luckily not with the British government.

How was it possible for Prague to so quickly receive a detailed report of a private dinner at Laski's home? The answer might be found in the incomplete list of invited guests. Named in the report are deputies L. V. J. Callaghan, B. Stross, Richard Crossman, J. Reeves, E. F. M. Durbij, Mrs. B. Ayerton-Gould, Carol Johnson from the parliamentary section of the Labour Party, and, strangely, "four other invited guests." Since it is known from revelations of Czech secret service agents that they were using a few Labour Party deputies as informers, did one of them provide the Czechs with the detailed report? He would have been as keen to hide his contribution as his handlers.

Opinions of a few of Laski's contemporaries will be quoted. Laski's naïve misjudgment of Stalin contrasts markedly with that of George F. Kennan, who knew Stalin well. In his *Memoirs 1925–1950*, we can read:

> An unforewarned visitor would never have guessed what depths of calculation ambition, love of power, jealousy, cruelty, and sly vindictiveness lurked behind this unpretentious facade. Stalin's greatness as a dissimilator was an integral part of his greatness as a statesman.... The most impressive of all was his immense, diabolical skill as a tactician. The modern age has known no greater master of the tactical art. The unassuming, quiet facade, as innocently disarming as the first move of the grand master at chess, was only a part of this brilliant, terrifying tactical mastery. [288]

Laski also adopted Soviet slogans about American war-mongering at a time when US forces were quickly being demobilized and other authors, on the contrary, complained about American lack of concern

288 Boston & Toronto: An Atlantic Monthly Press Book, Little, Brown and Company, 1967, p. 279.

about obvious Soviet imperialism. John A. Lukacs, considering the last stages of WWII, wrote under the heading, "American lack of realism: the friendship with Russia" that "Washington tended now to subordinate everything to the grand plan of American-Russian collaboration"[289] and "in Washington the fully unrealistic illusions about global cooperation dominated the scene."[290] These illusions led to the sacrifice of hundreds of thousands of Russians who were forcefully sent to the USSR where they were executed or perished in the Gulag.

It came as a shock to Australians and other democratic leaders when they realized that Soviet espionage was active against their countries both during the war and after its end. A theoretician on international politics noted, "The Soviet state has ... greatly refined, perfected, and organized bilevel diplomacy, which combines traditional international relations with conspiracy of subversion."[291]

Soviet KGB major operator Oleg Gordievsky together with Christopher Andrew in their solid review of such secret activities and of the slow grasp of them by Western politicians remarked: "Mackenzie King, Canada's Prime Minister since 1935, was even more naïve than Roosevelt about Soviet espionage in his own capital. At first he disbelieved Guzenko's story. When finally persuaded by it, he told his diary how shocked he was at the thought that the Soviet Union had spied on a wartime ally."[292]

What the Soviet spy who deserted his KGB masters had revealed to the surprised Western leaders, Vladimir Petrov would reveal a few years later too at least for some incredulous Australian counterparts. In the meantime, Soviet aggressive policies in the Greek civil war, in Poland, Hungary, Rumania, and Czechoslovakia, in violent denunciations of and military threat to Tito's Yugoslavia, and finally in its attempt to push Western allies from East Berlin, persuaded the West that Soviet

289   *The Great powers & Eastern Europe* (New York: American Book Company, 1953), pp. 585–86.
290   Ibid., p. 602.
291   Ivo D. Duchacek, *Nations and Men: An Introduction to International Politics* (Hinsdale, Illinois: The Dryden Press, 3rd ed., 1975), p. 235.
292   Christopher Andrew and Oleg Gordievsky, *KGB: The Inside Story of Its Foreign Operations from Lenin to Gorbachev* (London: Hodder & Stengton, 1990), p. 305.

imperialism had to be resisted and that peaceful cooperation was just a dream. It was a slow learning process.

Henry Kissinger was more realistic than Laski. Looking back on the post-war situation he wrote, "Moscow's renewed ideological hostility increasingly challenged our comfortable wartime assumptions about postwar international harmony."[293]

In his book on *American Diplomacy 1900–1950*, George Kennan commented on "the innate antagonism between capitalism and Socialism" when he wrote, "There can never be on Moscow's side any sincere assumption of community of aims between the Soviet Union and powers which are regarded as capitalism."[294]

In his *Memoirs*, George Kennan revealed the frustrations that led him to send the famous "Long Telegram" of February 22, 1946 from Moscow which helped to wake up American leaders to Soviet dangers and prepared the future policy of containment: "Over the eighteen months I had now spent on this assignment in Moscow, I had experienced unhappiness not only about the naiveté of our underlying ideas as to what it was we were hoping to achieve in our relations with the Soviet government but also about the methods and devices with which we went about achieving it."[295]

American foreign policy then embarked on a brilliant series of programs that helped to strengthen West European moral and determination to resist what was beginning to look like an unstoppable Communist advance to the Atlantic and Mediterranean oceans. The Truman Doctrine was announced on March 12, 1947 after repeated protests over Soviet anti-democratic actions in Poland, Romania, and Bulgaria led nowhere. It stated: "The peoples of a number of countries of the world have recently had totalitarian regimes forced upon them against their will.... Totalitarian regimes imposed on free peoples by direct or indirect aggression, undermine the foundations of international peace and hence the security of the United States."[296]

---

293 *White House Years* (Boston & Toronto: Little, Brown and Company, 1979), p. 60.

294 New York: A Mentor Book, The New American Library, 1954, p. 109.

295 Op. cit., p. 290.

296 Quoted in Frederick H. Hartmann, *The Relations of Nations* (2nd ed., New York: The Macmillan Company, 1962), p. 441.

On June 5, 1947, Secretary of State George C. Marshall announced the inspired plan that led to the improvement of West European ravaged economies and stabilized governments menaced by both internal and external Soviet aggression. Alas, the military pact of cooperation, NATO, came too late for Czechoslovakia. A Communist coup d'état, successfully masquerading as a people's revolution, achieved total power by constitutionally legal means (at least on the surface).

Czechoslovak President Eduard Beneš became a victim of his premature attempt at coexistence with the Soviet Union. While studying before WWII in France, he became a socialist. The collapse of his dream of collective security guaranteed by the League of Nations and the tragic Treaty of Munich that delivered his country to the mercies of Hitler persuaded him that he could not trust Western powers. He felt that the safety of the State relied on cooperation with the Soviet Union. He believed that having informed Stalin about the Tukhachevsky plot, Stalin was obliged to him for saving his life. (Beneš was just used by the KGB and Gestapo.)

During the war, Beneš already trusted the Soviet Union and founded his policy to a large degree on expected Soviet domination of central Europe. The head of the Czechoslovak secret service organization in exile, General František Morevec wrote in his *Memoirs*:

> My persistent impression was that in return for the Communists' consent to his continuation in office, Beneš had committed himself in Moscow to several matters which he did not immediately divulge to his London entourage.... In our émigré circles it produced political confusion and moral collapse. The opportunists and the fearful began to flood into the Communist camp, where they saw the best prospects for their future.... The Communists' single-mindedness, organization and intransigence contrasted sharply with the chaos, impotence and fears of the democratic group.[297]

---

297 Frantisek Moravec, *Master of Spies: The Memoirs of General Frantisek Moravec* (London: Bodley Head, 1975), p. 232.

General Moravec described his disappointing experiences with Soviet secret service agents during the war. To him it was clear "what we could expect from the victorious Soviets after the war. But my efforts to convince Beneš that we could not trust them were in vain."[298]

To a large degree, Beneš represented prevalent opinion in Czechoslovakia—especially in its western, Bohemian and Moravian part—that the way to go was with the Soviet Union.

The illusion of Slavic brotherhood and fear of German revanchism played as big a part in this anti-Western and pro-Soviet orientation. Czechoslovakia also suffered by political naiveté and lack of democratic, anti-totalitarian leadership. Naturally, as in all countries conditioned for a takeover, anti-Communism was promulgated as something very indecent and even dangerous in the post-war situation. The result was that in the twilight era of Czech democracy, between May 1945 and February 1948, the Communist conspiracy was not matched by any solid and sustained defense of democratic values. General Moravec again described the uneven contest between those who knew that what they were after—total power—and those who did not dare to suspect or prevent it:

> Commissars had been introduced into all army units under the cover title of 'education officers'... The Communists also started at once to organize Czechoslovak youth. At the same time the Communists organized a vast network of spies in every building, domestic or commercial, watching and often denouncing completely innocent people.... Thus, in the characteristically Communist way, everything was prepared in advance of the takeover. The event itself, in February 1948, was largely a formality. The methodical Communist preparation contrasted sharply with the indecisiveness, delay, misconceptions and lack of realism on the side of the democratic leaders.... Beneš regarded the Communist party as one of the parties in a multiple-party system, not taking into consideration that this party did not

298 Ibid., p. 235.

recognize any democratic principles and was preparing
a coup almost publicly.[299]

My professor at Charles University, Dr. František Kovárna, one
of the most open defenders of human rights during bloody purges in
other Eastern European countries, was a leading cultural light in the
second largest Czech party. He did not even recognize that a putsch
was happening after it had obviously started, and later told me, "Such
things are not done in a democracy." Unfortunately, they are done by
anti-democrats.

The learning process about the true nature of the Communist
march to power was slow and painful, allowing the Communists to
achieve so much so fast. Some time after the coup, President Beneš
resigned and sent a message to exile leaders that the major mistake of
his life was to trust Stalin and the Communists. It was too late.

In an important book published in 1994, Stephen Koch wrote:
"It seems to me likely that it took many enlightened people in
the West so long to recognize that Communism is monstrous
because Communism is a monster born from the ideals of the
Enlightenment, and the Enlightenment is necessary, indeed
indispensable, to the hope of civilization in our era.... If the
evil of fascism was obvious, the evil of Communism presented
tremendous obstacles to lucid recognition."[300]

299 Ibid., pp. 248–49.
300 *Double Lives: Spies and Writers in the Secret Soviet war of Ideas Against
the West* (New York: The Free Press, 1994), p. 109.

2

Traveling Conspirators

Three years after the devastation of World War II ended, several events of 1948 seemed to be signaling Stalin's intention to terminate years of domestic stabilization, of digesting Eastern European satellites, and of temporary tactical cooperation with the West. The coup d'état of Prague, the denunciation of the Yugoslav Communist dictator Tito, and the Berlin blockade were parts of a new strategy in Europe. Stalin was preparing for expansion or war. Expecting the collapse of Western economies, he decided that it was time to incorporate into his empire the remaining parts of Europe. French Communists originated a wave of strikes and openly talked about welcoming the Red Army and joining the battle on its side. A vigorous peace movement propaganda campaign was intended to demobilize Western powers and to remove the only military advantage they possessed, namely the atomic bomb.

This trend went against the prevalent mood in the rest of the world that hoped for continuing cooperation in order to rebuild societies that were badly shaken by both war and decolonization. Outside of the Soviet Union, many Communist parties' leaders believed that in the new situation they should fulfill their national duty and join forces with other parties for the sake of their own countries.

II.

In this conflict of contradictory positions, leading representatives of the Communist Party of Australia (CPA) decided to embrace the Stalinist call for the rejection of unity of purpose with bourgeois parties and

135

work for the radical pursuit of internationalist revolutionary goals, and not only in Australia.

A few documents found in the archives in the Czech Republic can throw some light on their involvement. Stalin's radical change from one policy line to a new and opposite one obviously created some difficulties. The leaders of the CPA took over Stalin's slogan of opportunism in order to fight against its supposed representatives in Great Britain and several states of Asia. They were active in trying to establish a Communist regime in Australia, but also entertained much larger ambitions. To reach their goals, they traveled widely between Sydney, Rome, Paris, Prague, Moscow, and Peking with stopovers in several Asian capitals.

At the same time that Stalin was purging his own and other Communist parties in Central and Eastern Europe, Australian comrades attempted to help him in London, New Delhi, Burma, Malaysia, and Vietnam.

The chronologically first document in the Prague archives dealing with that affair is from February 3, 1949. In a letter sent from Sydney, the secretary general of the CPA, Lance L. Sharkey, informed the leader of the Communist Party of France, Jacques Duclos, about his fight against opportunism in several Communist parties. Duclos was working for the Soviet intelligence network in charge of the Asian theater of operations.

According to this letter, the Central Committee of the CPA decided in January 1948 that it should criticize the CP of Great Britain at the first opportunity, because "Australia is one of the best places where such criticism could originate." The letter continues: "I [L. L. Sharkey] criticised [Harry] Pollitt's pamphlet "Looking Ahead" [in Czech, Hledíme vpřed] in an article that was published in the press organ of our bourgeois press on the anti-strike standpoint of the CP of Great Britain at a time when our Party on a grand scale led strikes for a forty hours working week and much higher wages."[301]

As in France and Italy, such strikes were coordinated by Moscow and intended to disrupt democratic societies, preparing them for a Communist seizure of power.

The epistle of L. L. Sharkey to J. Duclos continues:

---

301   State Central Archive (SUA), 100/3/25/91d.

> In February 1948, I traveled to India as a delegate to the Congress of the CP of India. There I discovered that my criticism of Pollitt's pamphlet circulated in all party organisation of the CP of India and played a major role in the fight against the opportunistic leadership of Joshi. Under his influence the CP of India supported [Lord Louis] Mountbatten's solution and the Central Commitee was carrying out the same policy of resistance to strikes and class war as the English CP, on the basis that India is now "free" and the Party has the duty to build this new "free" India.[302]

In his letter, L. L. Sharkey mentioned that during his meetings with comrades of various Asian parties, he often heard about a so-called Palme Dutt-Joshi Axis as responsible for such a defeatist policy. During his visit and by letters to members of the Central Committee of the CP of India, Palme Dutt persuaded them that they would benefit from the new Labour government. Therefore, Sharkey realized that the leadership of the British CP and especially Palme Dutt were responsible for Indian Communists' support for the Mountbatten solution. Sharkey concluded this part of his letter to J. Duclos: "In order to help in the fight against Joshi's opportunism I had to sharply attack to defeat Joshi and achieve his removal from position of Secretary General of the Central Committee."[303]

The peripatetic Australian Communist then had to fix the problem of Malaysia. In June 1948, the Communist Party of Malaya embarked upon an insurrection and proclaimed that a Communist republic should be created by August 1948. In his letter to Duclos, L. L. Sharkey reported: "During my visit to Malaysia I found out that in the Central Committee existed a group proposing return to British imperialism and its false projects for a consolidation in the country. I had to reveal the role of labourist imperialism and the politics of the CC of the British CP in order to smash the influence of this right wing and to prepare the Party for coming battles."

---

302 Ibid.
303 Ibid.

L. L. Sharkey discovered other centers of opportunism in Asia. In Burma, the dragon of opportunism was lifting its head. Palme Dutt helped the local CP to get five deputies in the Parliament, while the "semi-Trotskyist party SAMA" got fifteen. As a result, the CP of Australia criticized the CP of Great Britain. According to L. L. Sharkey, "the Congress of the British Empire's parties, under the leadership of Palme Dutt, almost completely ignored the fight against British imperialism and concentrated its fight on American imperialism."

L. L. Sharkey saw the situation in Vietnam as being similar. He tried to influence the development there with his sharp talk with a Vietnamese representative in Calcutta. Toward the end of his letter to Jacques Duclos, the secretary general of the CPA defended his own party against criticism. He acknowledged that the party was much stronger in trade unions than in the parliament. However, he did not know what to do about the party's weakness. Could the French Comrade offer some advice? Sharkey then complained that the British CP rejected the Australian critique. Its leaders "often use revolutionary phraseology while in fact remaining reformists."[304] The Australian Comrade promised to send more information on Asia.

III.

L. L. Sharkey was not the only Australian Communist traveling around the world in order to help Soviet leaders to prepare their world revolution. On the eighth of April 1949, Comrade Ernest Thornton, member a of the CC of the CPA and the secretary general of the Federated Ironworkers Union, appealed in Prague to the CP of Czechoslovakia (CPCZ) to take a stand on the Australian criticism of the British CP. (It was Thornton who while in Prague submitted a copy of the letter by L. L. Sharkey to Jacques Duclos.) Comrade Glaserová, secretary of Bedřich Geminder, head of the international department of the CPCZ CC, submitted a report to him:

> Comrade Thornton also affirms that in the opinion
> of the CPA, the British CP not only committed
> opportunism in its relations with the Labour Party

---

304 Ibid.

and in many mistakes in the colonial question when it often defended the point of view of the British Empire, but that in many instances it was guilty of anti-Soviet politics. For instance, two months ago, the *Labour Monthly*, edited by Palme Dutt, published an article by G. B. Shaw about the Michurin theory and Lysenko's debate that was entirely directed against the standpoint of the Soviet CP. And in his commentary Palme Dutt praised that article.[305]

(Charlatan Trofim Lysenko claimed that, following the Marxist tenet that "man can change everything," biological heredity can be transformed by environment. Stalin praised him and allowed him to eliminate many Russian scientists who did not share his view that a "new Lenin-Stalin man" could change anything that he wanted to.)

Thornton also quoted Pollitt's two-year-old statement that Communist parties of the British Empire should pay attention not only to Stalin's pronouncements but also to opinions expressed by the British Party. Thornton begged Comrade Geminder to give him a chance to discuss it with him. Thornton had something else on his mind. The Communist Party of Japan complained that it was not getting any material from Europe. Everything bound for Japan should be sent to his address at his trade union office: "It is less probable that it would be censured. The Australian Party knows how to forward information material to Japan."

As Paul Christopher of the *News Weekly* commented, "Thornton saw nothing unusual in offering the Ironworkers Union as a conduit for clandestine communication from a foreign government and its intelligence service."[306]

At the end of his submission, Thornton denounced one of his comrades, John Fischer, for his alleged anti-Soviet views. Fischer's wife dared to voice hostile opinions about Communist Czechoslovakia.

On June 1, 1949, Ernest Thornton returned to Prague. He was accommodated in the luxurious Palace Hotel and then went to the similar plush Hotel Dixon at the lavish spa in Štrbské Pleso in the Slovak High Tatras. He needed rest after the exhausting fight against

---

305 Ibid.
306 March 22, 1997, p. 17.

British and American imperialism. He liked it there and decided to stay a few days longer. His flight to Paris had to be postponed. A series of Soviet and Czech cables and letters, preserved in the Prague archives, were assuring that all possible comforts were available to the revolutionary proletarian apparatchik.

In January 1950, Thornton was asked by Prague to send "regularly every month a short survey of the most important developments from a trade union point of view," so it could be published in the Czechoslovak union press. These intelligence reports were to be sent confidentially from Canberra in a diplomatic bag. Two such reports soon arrived.[307]

Half a year after his previous peregrination around the world, Thornton was again on the road. En route from Rome to Moscow to attend the Soviet Trade Union Congress, he wanted to stop in Prague on April 6, 1950, and requested by cable to be met at the airport and to be accommodated for two days.[308]

A few weeks later on May 18, 1950, the Czechoslovak chairman of the press department of the Ministry of Information and Culture, Dr. Burián, reported on a short visit by the "leading Australian trade union functionary, Ernest Thornton."

> He was passing through Prague on the 6th May on the way to Budapest. The same day he was supposed to fly to Budapest, but the plane *did not depart* and Mr. Thornton was assigned to hotel Pension, Ruzyně [close to the airport]. On the order of the representant of the secretariat of the Central Committee of the CPCZ the press section of the Ministry for Information and Culture assumed the responsibility so that the same day, after an agreement by the party with the manager of hotel Pension, Mr. Thornton in company of Comrade Kleinová left for Prague where he was put on in the hotel Palace [a much more luxurious hotel reserved for prominent State or Party visitors] in order to make it possible for him the next day to take part in the celebrations of the anniversary of the

307   pres/3984/50-ev/RůzB.
308   SÚA, 93/25/3/1950 DYT.

liberation of the Republic. Because it was not viable to get a ticket to the tribune or to hotel Ambassador, Mr. Thornton watched the review from the press section of the Ministry of Information. On the 7th May, Mr. Thornton flew to Budapest.[309]

As usual, several offices received a copy of this secret report. Comrade Reinerová from the Presidium objected that such a report did not merit classified status and circulated it. Dr. Burián defended his action by stating that Comrade Thornton had no permission to stay in Prague and legally was not allowed to leave Hotel Pension, and that everything was arranged on the direct order of the secretariat of the CPCZ CC.

Soon after that on July fourteenth, Thornton requested Prague unionists to welcome his wife who would be flying to Prague from London on her way to Moscow. His Prague contacts replied that it would be best if she joined Walter Stevens who was going to Moscow on the thirty-first. They wanted to know if it was up to the Czechs to arrange for her ticket from Prague to Moscow.[310]

Thornton served as representative of the Austral-Asian secretariat of the World Federation of Trade Unions in Peking. Comrade Jack Hughes announced this in Prague before he left for Rome on December 22, 1950. As reported by his Prague comrades, he was worried about the secrecy of Communist intercontinental communications, so he demanded: "The mail that Thornton sends to Australia goes through the Prague agency New China to Mrs Muriel Springhall, Association of Supervisors, Engineers and Technicians, ASSETT, telephone London MAYfair 8541. Comrade Hughes asks if this mail between London and Prague could be sent in a different way than normally because it concerns questions of great importance and there is a danger that mail sent from the Chinese agency and back could be censored."[311]

---

309 SÚA, 100/3/25/94
310 SÚA, ZK/97323/50-ev/Ruz./A3.
311 SÚA, 100/3/25/27.

IV.

The next document discovered in Czech archives partly answers the question of where the money needed by the perambulatory comrades was coming from.

On July 20, 1951, Ernest Thornton wrote a letter from the Prague hotel Alcron to "Esteemed Comrade Geminder!" He petitioned him to take care of fourteen young Australian Communists. He said that he had already discussed everything with (Soviet) Comrade Kuznetsov in Moscow. An internal memorandum sent to the political secretariat of the CPCZ dated July 25 reads:

> The CP of China invited them in order to save them from prison [?] and wants to send them to Party schooling. Because of problems with passports they could not travel through Hong Kong and had to go through Europe.... Comrade Thornton arranged for them to travel from Marseille to Zürich and then to fly to Prague.... Czechoslovak visas should be issued separately since their Australian passports would probably be marked "Not valid for Czechoslovakia." All expenses will be paid by Comrade Thornton who received the needed capital from the CP of China.[312]

According to the letter from Ernest Thornton, the group of young Australians, supposedly saved from Australian prisons, was led by Comrades E. Aarons and Kenneth Davidson Gott, a journalist whose British passport was issued in Peking. Were the names of these fourteen Communist apprentices known in Australia? How did they fulfill expectations invested in them?

Eric Aarons wrote in his *Memoirs* about "The Great Adventure":

> In June 1951 John Sendy, Keith McEwan, Bruce Lindsey and I with nine other young Australians (I was the oldest) boarded the Italian ship, MV *Surriento*, in Sydney, on a serious assignment—which also just

---

312   Ibid., 73, 75, 91.

happened to be the adventure of a lifetime.... Should
the existing leadership be wiped out or incarcerated,
my instructions were that our group was to form the
nucleus of a new 'leadership in exile'. Our passports
were stamped as not valid for the Chinese People's
Republic and other socialist countries. We traveled
incognito in the guise of simple tourist. Most of us
were in the first class because tourist class was booked
out....

They were put up "in Prague's biggest and poshest
and almost empty, hotel, drinking the delicious and
very potent Czech export beer."[313]

V.

Let us return to Comrade Sharkey who liked to influence developments
in Asian Communist parties. He flew to Prague on August 5, 1952.
It took him ten days to get there from Australia because he and his
wife stopped in Jakarta, Singapore, Calcutta, Karachi, Beyrouth,
and Zürich. Comrade Sobotka, who reported on his meeting with
Sharkey in the capital of the Czechoslovak police state, was appalled
by problems that the Australian visitors had to experience on the way.
First, Australian passports were not issued for travel to the Soviet Union
and people's democracies, but after interventions, Sharkey managed to
get over this hurdle. ("He knows well our consul in Australia, Jaroslav
Kafka.") Second, at the airport in Malaysia, they were welcomed by
the police who did not allow them to talk to anybody, did not permit
journalists to approach them, and transported them to a hotel where
they questioned Comrade Sharkey for two hours about the aim of his
travel. No one was admitted to their room, not even a waiter. Food was
brought to them by the police, but they did not eat anything, afraid
of what might be mixed in it. The police took them to the airport in a
police car and put them on an airplane.

313 *What's Left? Memoirs of an Australian Communist* (Penguin Books,
1993), pp. 73–77 and 79.

In a discussion with Sobotka, Sharkey complained about Australian workers: "They are willing to fight for economic improvement of their situation, are ready to go on strike, but they have no appetite for the study of Marxism-Leninism. That's one of the problems of great consequence that the Party could not solve."[314]

This complaint sounds familiar. Lenin had blamed Russian workers for economism, saying they did not give a damn about a world revolution. All they cared about was their standard of living, so aristocrats like Lenin, middle-class bourgeois dreamers, and intellectuals have to fight for the workers who will not fight for themselves.

The secretary general of the CPA was flying to Moscow. He had been invited to come for medical treatment of his ailing heart. From Moscow he would return home through China, said his Prague interlocutor at the end of his report. Comrade Sharkey left a gift in Prague: a historical flag of the workers' movement in Australia, the design a white cross in a blue field with stars. Australian workers carry this flag during rallies, reminding them of the first clash of Australian gold miners with employers in EUREKA. Sharkey would have liked to stay longer in order to get to know life in Czechoslovakia, but he had to rush to Moscow.

EPILOGUE

When Western allies, alarmed by Soviet and Chinese plans of expansion in Western Europe and South Eastern Asia, decided to contain Stalin's enlargement of his empire in Europe by the Marshall Plan and NATO, Stalin murdered several advisors who almost managed to get him involved in an unwinnable war, and turned his aggressive energy in a historically typical Russian switch to the other side of the huge Euro-Asian empire, to Korea in Northern Asia. Australian Communists moved with the tide. (The role of the supposedly non-Communist journalist W. G. Burchett was examined in another chapter.)

---

314 SÚA, 100/3/25/94/.

3

How To Make A Revolution

Not all members of the CPA were as well connected in Moscow or Peking as L. L. Sharkey or Ernest Thornton. They were major players in Soviet world planning. Other comrades who were active in supporting roles depended on their recommendation and often tried to gain support from Prague operatives who were not always interested in petitioners who seemed to be volunteers. Some of them were even suspected of being Western spies or, during the witch hunts of the late Stalin years, Trotskyites and Titoists.

MELBOURNE AND PRAGUE SCHOOLS OF REVOLUTION

According to Comrade Stephen Murray-Smith, Prague was attractive to young Australian Communists because it seemed to them to be the center of a successful young revolution. There they hoped to learn to prepare and execute a revolution in Australia. While serving their apprenticeships in Czechoslovakia, they were used by local and Soviet agents to spread encouraging news about the supposedly extraordinary successes in building a socialist people's democracy.

The young revolution was in fact a capably Soviet-orchestrated putsch with some Czech and Slovak modifications. Since 1947, the Soviet Union insisted on the CPCZ's total seizure of power. Klement Gottwald's leadership was blamed for a lack of decisive action. Even during the actual seizure of power in February 1948, serious disagreements emerged between Prague and Moscow.

The former Soviet Ambassador to Prague, Valerian A. Zorin, was sent to Prague to supervise the takeover. A historian of the Prague coup, ex-Communist Karel Kaplan wrote that Zorin delivered Stalin's two point message: First, proceed with the immediate seizure of power, and second, request military assistance from the Soviet government. Gottwald accepted the first suggestion but refused the second. He claimed that everything was well prepared and under control. Foreign intervention would provoke an unfavorable impression, both domestically and internationally.

While visiting Crimea in September of the same year, Gottwald tried to explain to Stalin his refusal to request Soviet armed intervention. Finally, Stalin assented to his reasoning and even praised him.[315] In Communist parlance, the so-called Czechoslovak way to socialism became the preferred method of reaching sovereignty in democratic states with a developed industrial base.

The plan was to use the same approach in Australia, and that was what Australian Communists were learning in the Prague revolutionary school. The most systematic methodology of the Prague School was gradually published by Jan Kozák and adopted by Soviet strategists of world revolution. The titles of his contributions explain the lessons of the Czechoslovak putsch which was carefully prepared and staged as a people's revolution: 1)"Feasibility of a Revolutionary Utilisation of the Parliament During the Transition to Socialism and the Role of People's Masses,"[316] 2)"On Some Questions of the Strategy and Tactics at a Time of the Outgrowing of a National and Democratic Revolution into a Socialist Revolution: 1945–1948,"[317] 3)"For the Clarification of Methods of the KSČ Central Committee in the Struggle for Gaining the Majority of the Nation in the Period Before February 1948."[318] The systemic revolutionary strategy was considered so important that even the United States House of Representatives decided to publish Kozák's

---

315 Karel Kaplan, *Pět kapitol o Únoru* [Five Chapters on February] (Brno: Doplněk, 1997), p. 353.

316 *Příspěvky k dějinám KSČ* [Contributions to the History of the CPCZ], Vol. 1, No. 1 (Autumn 1957).

317 Prague: *Rudé právo* [Red Justice], 1956.

318 *Příspěvky k dějinám KSČ*, No. 2, March 1958.

instructions under the title "The New Role of National Legislative Bodies in the Communist Conspiracy."[319]

Most of some fifteen young Australian Communists who worked in Prague for the Communist International Union of Students (IUS) in the late forties and early fifties came from the University of Melbourne. There they studied for the intended Australian and world Communist revolution. Among their teachers were Ian Milner and Manning Clark.[320] According to Desmong Ball and David Horner, while teaching at the university, "Milner was a secret but very active member of the Communist Party, having joined the Melbourne University branch soon after his arrival in Melbourne in March 1940." Students received thorough instruction from him during extracurricular activities.

From 1941–42, when the party was illegal, Milner became the leading (but covert) organizer and recruiter for the university branch, which often met at his flat at 163 Flemington Road in North Melbourne. According to an account given to ASIO on July 8, 1954, Milner would select and "cultivate" students and, "after inviting them singly to his home on a social basis, would subsequently invite them to Communist Party study groups or Communist Party Branch meeting. He would arrange to meet recruits at street corners and escort them to the various party meeting places in North Melbourne."[321]

In 1944, Ian Milner invited Manning Clark to join him in teaching—and indoctrinating—students at the University of Melbourne.[322] In his pro-Communist confession, Clark wrote: "I

319 Committee on Un-American Activities, 30 December 1961.
320 Clark wrote: "Later Humphrey McQueen joined us as an apologist for Marxist history ... Bruce Kent and Daphne Gollan, both strong in the faith of Karl Marx, showed the students how the laws of history explained the French, the Russian and the Chinese revolutions." *The Quest for Grace* (Ringwood, Vic.: Penguin Books Australia, 1990), pp. 213–14.
321 *Breaking the Codes: Australia's KGB Nework, 1944–1950* (St Leonard, NSW: Allen & Unwin, 1998), pp. 258–59.
322 Describing the influence of the student guilds affiliation through the AUS with the "Communist-dominated International Students' Union operating from Prague," Tony McGillick remarked, "I lived to see this remarkable and frightening transformation of our universities from tranquil seats of learning into hot-beds of Marxist subversion." *Comrade No More*, p. 33.

had no misgivings about our society in Australia being swept into the dustbin of human history by the Communists in their self-appointed role as the vanguard of the revolution. I had been tempted to become the buffoon of the Left-wing intelligentsia in Australia."[323]

The historian also acted as recruiter of his students to the Communist Party. For instance, "he tried unsuccessfully in the late 1940s to convert and recruit to the Communist cause as the great cause of world progress," Denis Austin O'Brien, the oldest brother of associate professor at the University of Western Australia, Patrick O'Brien, who wrote:

> At Melbourne University Clark introduced Denis to members of the CPA, which was operating through the Labour Club. According to former CPA identity and leading left-wing intellectual, the late Dr Ian Turner, the Labour Club had been established as a Communist front organisation to push Stalin's general line and to recruit party members at the university.... Clark told me that their attempts to recruit Denis to the Communist cause through the club failed miserably.... Whereas Clark was in quest of totalitarian order, Denis was in search of free spirit.[324]

After their graduation, Leftist Melbourne University students often went to Prague to finish their political education "at the Communist Party training-school in Prague," as O'Brien remarked.[325] One of them was Ken Gott:

> Careers in student politics did not necessarily end with graduation. The International Union of Students had been formed late in the war and afterwards set up its headquarters in Prague.... Like most student

---

323 *A Historian's Apprenticeship* (Melbourne University Press, 1992), p. 3.

324 "Death of a Free Spirit," *Courier-Mail*, 14 September 1996, Monitor, pp. 25–26.

325 *The Saviours: An Intellectual History of the Left in Australia* (Richmond, Vic.: Drummond, 1977), p. 86.

associations in the western world, the N.U.A.U.S
saw the I.U.S. as becoming increasingly Communist-
dominated, particularly after the Communist
coup d'etat in Czechoslovakia early in 1948.... The
Australian Student Labour Federation became the
local affiliate of I.U.S. and a lot of Labour Club
people went to Prague to work in its headquarters.
Ken Tolhurst abandoned his commerce course to go
to Prague in 1948. After his return in 1949, Noel
Ebbels and I worked there. Steve Murray-Smith
also settled in Prague.. Ebbels, after two years in
Prague, came back to devote himself to student and
youth organising work for the Communist Party....
Another young student, Dave Bearlin, left his course
to become a wharfie in the interests of the party....
Murray-Smith came back from Prague and worked
for the Peace Council.[326]

Out of the whole group, the Czechoslovak secret police, as far as I
could determine, showed marked interest only in two of them: Ebbels
and Murray-Smith. Ebbels, who during WWII served as an Australian
Naval Intelligence Officer, had two files in Prague. One was destroyed
in 1989, the year of the Velvet Revolution when the secret police tried
to wipe away its footprints, and the other someone borrowed and never
returned. There was no indication of who, when, and where. The only
remaining trace of the file reveals that it concerned passports and visas.
The impression that Ebbels was recruited by the Czech secret service
as an agent and that he helped it to provide passports and visas for its
exploits against his own country is probably not farfetched.

The other file concerned S. Murray-Smith. He was also mentioned
in the papers devoted to the Czechoslovak commercial attaché in
Australia, marked only by the first letter of his name "Z" (Žižka), who
allegedly was "maybe the first and for long the only [?] Czechoslovak

---

326 Ken Gott, "Student Life: The Forties … The Other R .S. L.," *Melbourne University Magazine*, pp. 27–28, as quoted by O'Brien, *The
Saviours*, op. cit., p. 86.

agent in Australia between 1952 and 1956."[327] It mentioned that Murray-Smith was going to the Soviet Union.

In an interview with Patrick O'Brien in 1975, Murray-Smith's close friend, Ian Turner, whose expulsion from the CP in 1958 led to Murray-Smith's resignation, talked about the instruction received at the University of Melbourne by himself and other young Communists and socialists in the forties:

> The basic political organisation from the Left's point of view at University were the *CP* branch which, at its peak in 1946, had about 120 members, and the *Labour Club* ... which of course was the united front organisation, with the Communists probably constituting the decisive force in it.... Obviously the party branch discussed ideas about what the *Labour Club* ought to be doing and then put them up.[328]

In 1946, Turner studied Manning Clark's course on history and was influenced by him, as were the other Melbourne University students. The young comrades, with additional preparation in Prague, went to work for the CP's revolutionary aims in carefully selected places: in the labor unions, in organizations of young people, and in the supposedly idealistic and non-party Peace Council. Ian Turner, who himself worked on Soviet peace propaganda, soon went to work as a carriage cleaner in order to strengthen the party's position in the Australian Railway Union.[329] In an interview with late Professor O'Brien, he said: "The Australian Peace Council was formed in 1949. I was involved in the initial formation of the Council which was a conscious Communist decision of course." The interviewer asked: "At that time Brian Fitzpatrick's *Australian International News Review* gave enormous publicity to the various peace councils. Was Brian consciously aware that the show was basically organized by the Communists?"

---

327 Private information from the Office for Documentation and Investigation of Communist Crimes, Ministry of the Interior, Prague, Czech Republic, on October 7, 1998. Later "Z" was identified as "Zdeněk".
328 Typed "Interview with Ian Turner," pp. 14–15.
329 Ibid., p. 22.

Turner's answer was a simple, "Yes." About his own infiltration of the union he said, "I might have ended up as Industrial Officer of Assistant State Secretary, or something like that."[330]

When Professor Eugene Kamenka prepared the "University Lectures 1970," Ian Turner spoke on "The Significance of the Russian Revolution." He acknowledged that "the revolutionary socialists outside Russia ... were attracted, mothlike, to the flame of Soviet power,"[331] yet he was still "under the influence," blinded by his Leninist vision that distorted and falsified the horrific Russian experience—very much like his teacher, Manning Clark. In 1975, Turner still missed the "extraordinary feeling of belonging to some kind of very large and very extended family with international ramifications."[332]

PRAGUE'S DRAWING POWER

Let us now review some other members of the Prague colony and other Australian visitors who were similarly attracted by the exported "flame of Soviet power" into Czechoslovakia.

In 1949, Comrade Glaserová, secretary of the then still very powerful Bedřich Geminder, sent Geminder a note advising him that an Australian, Jack Hutson, who was teaching English at the labor unions headquarters in Prague, would like to remain in Prague. Hutson arrived in Europe in 1947 to attend a youth festival and after that worked as a mechanic in Yugoslavia. When the Soviet led Cominform denounced Tito, Hutson moved to Prague and worked as an official correspondent for the party paper the *Guardian*. He requested a new confirmation by this paper that he would continue to be its correspondent. Geminder

---

330 Ibid., Turner interview, p. 19. Brian Fitzpatrick was expelled from the Australian Labor Party in 1944 for his support of the CPA. See AA Canberra, series A6119/90, item 2471, p. 52. "Brian Fitzpatrick of the Australian Council for Civil Liberties" was "the most talented polemicist for the anti-Petrov cause." Robert Manne, *The Petrov Affair,* op.cit., p. 241.

331 *A World in Revolution?* (Canberra: The Australian National University, 1970), p. 19.

332 Turner interview, p. 19.

shortly answered that if he did not have a new confirmation by The *Guardian*, he could not be accredited as a foreign correspondent.[333]

On March 12, 1947, John C. Henry addressed the General Secretary of CPCZ from London. He said that he would reach Prague by train together with Comrade Gerard Peel and requested a week's accommodation in a Prague hotel. Henry wanted to look over a nationalized factory. He was especially interested in obtaining information on worker–management relations. He introduced himself as a member of the Political Committee of the CPA. He attended a conference of Communist parties in the British Empire in London as his party's delegate. In the same capacity as a fraternal delegate, he also took part in the Congress of the CP of Great Britain. Comrade Peel was his consultative delegate from Australia at the London Conference.[334]

Another document from the Prague archives bears the signature of L. L. Sharkey, general secretary of the CPA, attesting that on March 12, 1953, J. C. Henry, member of the Secretariat and Political Committee of the CPA, "is visiting the Soviet Union in order to receive medical treatment." Sharkey requested Czech assistance.[335]

On June 10, 1949, Dr. Jan Kabourek, head of the foreign department of the unions' headquarters, ÚRO, told the general secretariat of the CPCZ that the ÚRO invited E. V. Elliot, general secretary of the Seamen's Union of Australia, for a week-long visit to Czechoslovakia. Kabourek stressed that Elliot was a member of the CPA Central Committee and played a major role in the boycott aimed at Dutch ships which had already lasted four years. The suggestion of his invitation came from the chairman of the CPA, R. Dixon, and the president of the Metal Workers Union, E. Thornton.[336] Comrade Elliot was in no hurry to get back to his seamen since as late as August 19, 1949, Dr. Kabourek requested that airport customs not create any difficulties for him; he would be taking with him a cut glass vase given to him by Czechoslovak trade unionists. He was a guest of Czechoslovak and Hungarian labor unions.[337]

---

333   SUA 100/3, 25, 91.
334   Ibid.
335   Ibid.
336   Ibid., Pres. 111392/49.
337   Ibid., Pres. 145178/49-t.

On May 19, 1949, another member of the CPA, A. Brotherton, wrote a long letter from Prague to Dr. Zdeněk Hrdlička, Ministry of Information and Culture. Brotherton requested a position in Prague and he stressed that it should be secure. His Communist credentials were impressive. He became a member of the CPA in 1941, "at that time illegal." He worked for the Australia-Indonesia Association translating and publishing Indonesian propaganda material including a booklet by Sjahrir, "Our Struggle." He worked for the CP of Vietnam, the Malay CP, and for the Indonesian Information Service in Singapore and Bangkok. In Shanghai, he was employed by the Soviet press agency, Tass, boarded a Soviet ship to Vladivostok, and then proceeded to Prague through Moscow. He knew English, French, Malay, and Indonesian. In Prague, it was decided to check his CPA credentials (he carried a party recommendation from April 1947) and find him a job.[338]

On the April 25, 1949, the cultural attaché of the Czechoslovak embassy in London, Aloys Skoumal, sent a letter to the fourth department of the Ministry of Information and Culture in Prague, suggesting that the Australian painter Noel Counihan be invited to Czechoslovakia for two to three weeks. From Ian Milner's *Memoirs*, we know that he was a close friend of Milner.

According to Skoumal, Counihan was a progressive artist, connected with Australian labor unions and the CPA, not only by the selection of his artistic subjects, but also by his political activities. He had been drawing caricatures for the CPA organ *Guardian Newspaper*.

In his letter, the attaché enclosed an album of Counihan's caricatures, "60 Counihan Cartoons from the Guardian." The painter was sent to Europe and to the Paris Congress of the Defenders of Peace at their expense. Among his references was one by Gabriel, the cartoonist of the *Daily Worker*, and others by Paul Hogarth and writer Jack Lindsay. (As Ian Turner said in his interview with Patrick O'Brien, a member of the party enjoyed "really an extraordinary feeling of belonging to some kind of very large and very extended family with international ramifications."[339])

After Prague, Counihan planned to spend some time in Poland and Hungary. Five days after his arrival in Prague, the Ministry of

---

338 SÚA 100/3, 25, 91, 107572.
339 Turner interview, p. 19.

Information advised officials that a decision "must be made in a great hurry! Today." Counihan was then invited to spend two weeks during the second half of May in Prague. "Since it concerns a prominent guest whose visit is from the point of State propaganda very important … expected cost would come to Kčs 12,000."[340]

It looked like an invasion of Australian Communist painters in Prague. The cultural attaché in Paris recommended to invite Roy Delgado who carried a reference from the CPA testifying to his long membership in the party and his reliability. The vice president of the Studio of Realist Art in Sydney commended that it would be desirable to oblige Delgado's wishes. Delgado reached Prague on October 3, 1949, where he met Czech artists and obtained orders for work from the magazine *Tvar* (Form).[341]

Australian "gifted, progressive painter, and Communist," George Sampson, who was being supported by the unions, came to see Mrs. Jílovská of the Ministry of Information and Culture on September 12, 1949. He asked for an allowance for an excursion to southern Bohemia. He was given five hundred Kčs.[342]

On the first of August, 1919, F. R. Coursier was more demanding. In his letter to Dr. Rudolf Popper, the press department of the Ministry of Information, he wrote that although his "experience lies in radio," his wife "is a professional artist" with a "main interest in portrait painting." The Coursiers were both Londoners, settled in Australia since 1937. Coursier stressed that his wife belonged to the social-realist school and used her maiden name, Olive Long, professionally. They had "largely the sense of creative frustration" in Australia. Coursier was looking for a new home. He anticipated that all of his four children would go to school and added, "The children themselves need more than the purely physical advantages of this country." He mentioned that "Joris Ivens, the film director, who is probably still in Prague, knows us well and will vouch for us." He wanted to work in Prague for two years.

Dr. Popper contacted Comrade Vančura, chairman of the Anglo-Saxon department of the fourth section of the Ministry, and emphasized that Colonel Sheppart, whom Coursier mentioned as a reference, was a dependable and very active friend of Czechoslovakia who had had

340 SÚA 100/3,25, 91, 106221.
341 Ibid., 117145.
342 Ibid., 113191.

Popper as his guest the previous year. The couple also were very active members of the CPA.[343]

The same ministry's fourth department registered that Norman Rothfield from Australia—not a painter, for a change—arrived in Prague in 1950 to "learn about our successes on the way to socialism." He was a cofounder of the Australian Peace Council and had a recommendation from the Jewish Council to Combat Fascism and anti-Semitism (a Communist front organization). The bill for a lunch in Hotel Ambassador came to Kčs 210.[344]

Australian citizen and member of the CPA, Mrs. Wills (maiden name McMillan), who came to Europe to attend the Peace Congress in Paris, had been living in Prague for a month in Hotel Šroubek. Comrade Glaserová called this to the attention of her boss, Bedřich Geminder, of the International Department of the CPCZ CC, on September 26, 1949. Comrade Wills wanted to proceed to a festival in Budapest but did not get a visa. As a correspondent of various Australian progressive journals, she had a personal letter from the general secretary of the party, L. L. Sharkey. She carried a membership card of the CPA, however, without a name in it. She claimed this was because the party expected to be declared illegal. She received a visa to travel to Bulgaria, but her request for financial support was refused. Comrade Šváb, of the secret police, noted, "If her visa is not valid any more, she should leave."[345] Her Communist credentials were found inadequate.

COLONEL SHEPPARD

In 1948, with the beginning of the witch hunt on suspected Titoists and those connected with certain party leaders, CPCZ leaders were more cautious. Finding victims was preferable to becoming one. Torture and execution threatened many party members. Australian Communist Mrs. Newbigin (never identified by her first name) was caught in the net. On the twenty-third of December 1949, a Prague comrade whose name cannot be deciphered sent to Bedřich Geminder a copy of a coded cable from the London consulate's Comrade Bystřický (the cable is not

343   Ibid., 111568.
344   Ibid., 118091.
345   Ibid.

available). The cable said that "the Australian Newbigin, allegedly a longtime member of the CPA," planned to fly to Prague. In view of her recommendation by Colonel Sheppard, whose request for a visa was some time ago rejected, her request for a visa was questionable.[346]

On January 3, 1950, Hanuš Frank of the department A VI-4 investigated the case and sent Geminder a "record of an interview with the Australian citizen Mrs. Newbigin." He reported that he met her in his office. She did not have a party card or CPA references. In Sydney, she gave Vice-Consul Halla A£250 and asked him to transmit the money to Prague where she planned to spend her holidays. She wanted to study life in the ČSR. She was involved in some party affairs such as organizing help for Greek children. She traveled to Europe on the same vessel as Colonel Shepherd (sic), but she said she did not talk with him on the ship. Here, Hanuš Frank pointed out that the trip lasted four weeks. He mentioned that Shepherd (sic) was a personal friend of the Yugoslav minister of foreign affairs, Bebler. After the war, Shepherd (sic) worked in Australia for a "free Greece" and took part in propaganda campaigns in favor of Czechoslovakia. He delivered hundreds of good lectures on Czechoslovakia and accompanied them with propaganda films. "At the moment," Hanuš wrote, "Mrs. Newbigin is taking part in a week-long tour of the country with the Czech travel agency Čedok." Murray S. Smith, Telepress' correspondent, told Hanus that he considered both Mrs. Newbigin and Colonel Shepherd (sic) as dependable friends of the ČSR. After Comrade Geminder read all that, he wrote on the first document: "1. Refuse. 2. She arrived without permission."[347]

Colonel Sheppard became subject to a thorough inquiry by the Prague government. In the state central archives, I was able to copy no less than twenty-one pages of documents. Many people were involved in the development of his case. As before, he wanted to come to Prague again and obtain the necessary visa. However, in this time of fear of imperialist or Titoist machinations against the People's Democracy of Czechoslovakia, everyone was under suspicion. Finally, in spite of some warm recommendations, he did not get his visa.

The first of the documents I copied is from September 28, 1948. In a report by Comrade Rohan of the main CPCZ daily *Rudé právo* to

346 Ibid., 150/3, p. 29.
347 SÚA 100/3125, 91, 150s, pp. 29 and 39.

Comrade Rosemanne, Colonel Sheppard appears to be a paragon of Communist virtues. During World War II, he fought with the Allies on all fronts: in Greece, Lybia, Crete, Palestine, Cyrenaica. In the Australian army, he became a brigade general. Toward the end of the war, he was seriously wounded and volunteered to go to Greece and distribute gifts. There he discovered that Great Britain was following an imperialist policy that did nothing for the Greek people. He managed to persuade Dr. Evatt to invite Minister Porfyrogen, who was obviously an anti-British representative, to the United Nations assembly. Rohan noted, "Sheppard is not a Communist, but he is a very decent, progressive man who feels close to us."[348]

On the twenty-eighth of October 1949 (when Czechs celebrated the founding of the ČSR), Colonel A. W. Sheppard sent a long and bitter letter to Dr. A. Kosta, Ministry of Information, Prague, Stalin Avenue 3. He was writing from Rome. He felt sorry that he was kept waiting six weeks for an entry visa. He asked what he should say to his friends in Greece and Australia, "that the story about an Iron Curtain is all a myth?" People would be expecting a full report from him. "What shall I say to the people who listened to me in 112 meetings in which I showed that Czechoslovakia has a fine socialist system." Sheppard then denounced the Czech representative of heavy industries in Australia, P. Morawetz, who "is the most ardent anti-Communist among the Jews" and in a letter "says why he believes that Jews should not ally themselves with Communists," yet Morawetz can freely travel to Czechoslovakia while Sheppard cannot.[349]

On November 2, 1949, Dr. M. Burián of the Ministry of Information and Culture sent a "secret" (twice underlined) two-page letter to Comrade B. Geminder at the International Department of the CPCZ CC, concerning A. W. Sheppard and his visit to the ČSR. Burián repeated all the merits of the colonel already listed here and revealed that Sheppard wrote to Dr. Kosta on September 15, 1949 that he would like to get a visa for Prague in Rome since Sheppard did not want the visa to appear in his Australian passport. Burián also mentioned Comrade Newbigin's wish to visit Czechoslovakia.

However, on the second page of his letter to Geminder, Burián enumerated problems Colonel Sheppard presented. Sheppard had

---

348   SÚA 100/3, 25. 91.
349   Ibid.

visited Yugoslavia several times and was friendly with some local functionaries, especially Bebler. Comrade Maximos claimed that although Sheppard helped the Greeks, his services were not as great as he claimed. When Dr. Popper questioned who was financing Sheppard's expensive trips in Europe, Maximos told him that the help he got from the "democratic Greeks" was too small to cover it all. It was not clear where most of the money came from. Maximos doubted that the Yugoslavs paid Sheppard as their agent. During his stay in Prague, Comrade Dixon said that the colonel had some good qualities, but that the CPA considers him as a kind of adventurer, unsuitable for party membership. Rohan thought that the Czechoslovak Ministry of Defense could gain some information from Sheppard based on his experiences with the Australian army. He cooperated with the Czech delegation to the UN, but there are many things that are unclear about him. "In view of recent international experiences, had to be taken into account even more strictly than before."[350]

On November 9, 1949, A. W. Sheppard dispatched another sad letter to Dr. Kosta, this time from London. Sheppard understood that he would not get a visa to Prague and asked for two favors: that letters sent to him from Australia be forwarded to his address in London, namely, the Commonwealth Bank of Australia; and that a "small amount of money to my credit for articles" sent to the Czech press agency ČTK should be sent to the same address. "The amount in question is not very much: but to a thirsty man a drop of rain is like a river." He also wrote, "Apart from anything else, I shall never cease to be grateful to Czechoslovakia for what your country has done for my Greek friends." He added, "I shall not let it change my deep-seated convictions of the rightness of the course your country has followed in the past, and I hope shall continue to follow in the future." On the back page of this air letter, Sheppard mysteriously postscripted, "Perhaps you may care to ask Dr Popper or Mrs Reinerova what was my opinion and advice about a certain journalist whom you have only just expelled. Perhaps, after all, I am your best friend."[351] (I think he had Wilfred Burchett in mind.)

This secret letter was considered so important that it was circulated to the very powerful Minister of Information and Culture, Comrade

---

350 Ibid.
351 Ibid.

Václav Kopecký; his deputy, Comrade Lumír Čivrný; another deputy, Comrade Hušek; Presidium's chief, C.Dr Novák; and Comrade Reinerová.

Madame Reinerová became the addressee of Sheppard's next epistle sent from Paris on November 29, 1949. He complained that his correspondence sent from Australia to Prague was not forwarded to him by Dr. Kosta. "In the name of common decency," he requested her to send the letters to Copenhagen since he was going on a lecture tour of Scandinavia. "I had hoped to be able to say good things about Czechoslovakia, as I had on my previous lecture tour." He stated that he knew the cause of his troubles in Prague: "A man named Trachtenberg, who left Australia while the C.P. was considering a hearing against him, has written letters to Mr Rohan alleging untruths against me."
Sheppard wrote:

> We had been friends. But I found that he had been pestering my wife in many bad ways, and I ordered him out of my house. Later, I found out that during the war he had been an agent in the service of the Australian Security Service, spying on foreign nationals, especially Slavs.... These facts were placed before the Communist Party, and a hearing was pending, when he decided to leave for Poland. The ease with which he got his passport and clearance from Australia should have been sufficient to show what he was ... a special agent in Poland beyond a shadow of a doubt.

At the end, a carefully formulated threat was expressed: "I am here as the representative of several left-wing newspapers, whose readers will want to know why I have been refused permission to enter Czechoslovakia, but I am not prepared to do that at this stage, unless my letters are not returned.... But believe me, I am not writing in an unfriendly spirit as I know the difficulties you must face there."[352]

---

352 Ibid.

S. MURRAY-SMITH AND OTHERS

Now we return to S. Murray-Smith with whom this chapter began. On March 30, 1950, Hanuš Frank from the Information Ministry had a telephone conversation with the Telepress correspondent. Frank was informed that Colonel Sheppard and Murray-Smith had founded the Australian-Yugoslav Society in Sydney. Frank invited the Telepress man to his office and then wrote a report on their conversation. He was told that Sheppard gained great popularity in Australia with his lectures on Czechoslovakia. Many Australians visiting Prague were referring to him as a great friend of the ČSR. However, recently the Australian Communist press had been warning against his activities. Obviously, the colonel overestimated his chance of criticizing socialist Czechoslovakia in the Communist press.

Murray-Smith informed his Communist interlocutor about alleged clashes in the new Australian government between Menzies and his more pro-American foreign minister, Spender, who wanted to replace Menzies at the first opportunity. Smith also informed him about preparations for a large peace congress in Australia. Murray-Smith was successfully trying to establish a wide network of Telepress correspondents in British colonies and dominions. That would allow the Telepress bulletin to become a new important source of information for the Ministry of Information. In view of all that, Hanuš Frank recommended further close cooperation with Murray-Smith.[353]

On April 5, 1950, Rupert Lockwood wrote a very long letter in Warsaw to "My Dear Edith" in Prague. At its end, he had this to say about Sheppard (and it was circulated in the Ministry of Information in Czech, marked "Secret!"): "I suppose you heard that it was now definitely established that Colonel A. W. Sheppard, who visited Prague some time ago, is a bribed Titoite (sic) agent and Intelligence spy. He has been very disruptive recently in Australia and in Scandinavia. I have some interesting information about him."

Lockwood complained about "the flood of displaced persons who bring slanders against every one of the People's Democracies." Therefore, he wrote several articles for the *Tribune* and "Comrade Dixon has also done lecture tours." He was "rather reluctant to leave

---

353   Ibid.

Australia at the present juncture," but he "received several insistent cables from the World Peace Committee in Paris, asking me to attend the third session of the committee in Stockholm." They paid all his expenses since "the presence of a delegate from Australia was 'indispensable.'" He addressed meetings in Sweden and Norway. He was glad that the exiled Czech tennis player Jaroslav Drobný "has been playing an exceedingly bad game of tennis in Australia." It proved to him that "emigration from the People's Democracies is apparently not very good for morale." He called the Menzies government "pro-fascist," and meeting Phillip Jessup, "the American 'roving ambassador'," he was pleased that he could "still talk to some of these imperialist clowns and butchers." He assured Edith that he "may be the last Communist out of Australia for some time," but he praised "a powerful united front movement developing against the Government." He was optimistic. "It is possible that united workers' resistance may bring down this reactionary government before another year has passed." Lockwood hoped to come to Prague again and praised them for getting "rid of that nuisance John Fischer at last."

He also would have liked "to have a talk with some of the Australians in Prague."[354] At the end of his comments on Murray-Smith's letter, Prague official "Janák" complained, "It is strange that the paper took so long from June 24 to get to the cadre department in spite of the fact that it concerns such a weighty matter." Since Lockwood's letter was private, and "Comrade Edith" was assigned to him as an interpreter who "allowed Dr Burián's press section to inspect the letter" so that he could report on it only on June twenty-fourth, the delay was understandable to a degree. Jandák also wrote, "Necessary measures were carried out."[355]

In the agonizing times of party purges and political or even physical elimination of comrades, it was easy for the secret services and purgers to find proofs of treason or alleged spying by imperialists or Titoists. The comrades kept denouncing each other, and it was up to the authorities to decide whom to purge and whom to trust, at least for the moment. The cadre files were filled with an abundance of negative reports that could be used any time it suited the persecutors: "Their

---

354 Ibid.
355 Ibid.

dossier of all the leading politicians made them the real rulers of the country. They could produce a charge against anyone at any time."[356]

The man Lockwood mentioned as unworthy of Czech Communists' hospitality, Comrade John Fisher, defended himself in a letter sent on April 22, 1951 from Rome to the international department of the CPCZ CC. According to its Czech translation, it was received on the second day of May. Fisher wrote that he was glad that "a certain misunderstanding about his good name in Czechoslovakia and elsewhere was removed." He said he had recently received an official communication from the CPA confirming that the party as a whole did not have anything against him. It mentioned that although some members did not hold this view, the party did not know anything potentially damaging about him. The message was sent to him and to relevant comrades by the chairman of the Control Commission of the CPA, John Hughes. He issued the declaration while he was in London as a delegate to the Second World Peace Congress.[357]

The previous year, on December 27, 1950, Hughes, in his official capacity, talked with J. Glaserová, Geminder's secretary, and vouched for Comrade Burchett: "The Australian Party is content with his work and is certain that he is good comrade. The Party would welcome if his name was cleared, as well as the name of his wife."[358]

The last document in this series describes visitors to Prague, both welcome and unwelcome. They were there to witness and eventually report on the glorious people's democracy in Czechoslovakia. Here is an example of how the system worked to try to persuade people that a Soviet-type Communism would be beneficial to other countries.

On the second day of 1951, Secretary Glaserová informed her boss, Comrade Geminder, that Comrade James Healy, member of the CPA CC, chairman of the Waterside Workers' Union, and delegate at the Peace Congress, wanted to discuss the invitation of an Australian delegation to the ČSR. Healy had just returned from the USSR and Poland, where at meetings there it was agreed to invite delegations from Australia. Unionists and, if possible, cultural workers, doctors, etc. would be included. In every such delegation would be a responsible

---

356   Eugen Loebl, *My Mind on Trial* (New York and London: Harcourt brace Jovanovich, 1976), p. 146.

357   SÚA 100/3, 25, 91.

358   Ibid.

comrade. Geminder noted on the memo, "Take up with the Unions (Kolský, Zupka)."[359]

Geminder probably had other, more important and personal things on his mind. Beginning in the middle of the previous year, several leading Communists had disappeared. He must have known that Stalin had sent his experienced interrogators to Prague. They taught members of the Czech secret service how to force arrested comrades to admit guilt. Eugen Loebl, the minister of foreign trade and a member of the CPCZ CC, was interrogated for several months, and finally arrested in December 1950. Several Slovak leaders were denounced publicly as bourgeois nationalists.

When Stalin switched from supporting Israel to courting Arab states, Zionism was attacked as treasonable. Translated into plain anti-Semitic language, that meant that any comrade of Jewish origin could be used as a scapegoat in the developing show trial against traitors. Geminder, a former member of the Comintern's executive committee in Moscow, was of German Jewish origin. Soon he would be arrested and taught self-denunciation through torture at the so-called Slánský trial. In a book written much later, Eugen Loebl reported the satisfaction of one of their interrogator-torturers: "Only Geminder has trouble," he said. "His Czech is so bad that he has trouble saying his lines."

The Australian Communists who were so eager to learn from their Czech comrades about leading the young revolution were being offered new and unexpected lessons to be used at home. Most of them needed further proof of Communist cruelty and dishonesty before they would grasp the truth.

While in Prague, Murray-Smith worked for Telepress which was a state and party agency responsible for disseminating news to the international community. Of course, most of it was Communist propaganda.

Telepress was under the control of Bedřich Geminder, the major Soviet representative in the ČSR and probably the strongest man in the republic. He had his own direct lines to the Kremlin. When Stalin decided on one of his periodic purges, he was hanged in the infamous Slánský show-trial in 1952. Chaos reigned in Telepress after his "departure," as it was described at a meeting of its members. Cliques formed and tried to destroy each other by denouncing each other to higher party

---

359 Ibid.

organs. The Telepress lost almost eight million Czech crowns. It was decided to request help from Moscow in order to determine the fate of Telepress. "In Telepress there are foreign correspondents who were not checked out and who were put there by Geminder."[360] It is not surprising then that Murray-Smith experienced some difficulties and his previous enthusiasm about the young revolution was threatened by more realistic considerations.

On September 15, 1949, from his home in Terronská 6, Prague XIX, S. Murray-Smith wrote a recommendation for comrades Kurt Merz and Blanche Chidzey to the international department of the CPCZ. He vouched for them as "active members of the Australian Communist Party of a number of years standing." They were "anxious to spend a couple of weeks in Czechoslovakia to study certain aspects for which they have commissions from some militant union papers and the party press." He offered several credentials of Czech Communist officials and of Ken Tolhurst of the International Union of Students, his compatriot.[361]

On June 9, 1952, S. Murray-Smith back in Australia wrote a letter to Mr. Vergeiner, foreign correspondent, ROH, in Prague. ROH was an abbreviation of the Revolutionary Union Movement, supreme organ of the unions serving the State. He wrote: "Dear Comrade Vergeiner: I am writing to you as a former member of ROH to appeal for your help in regard to my employment with Telepress. As you know, I worked for Telepress in Prague from 1949 until 1951, being a member of ROH during that time. In the first half of 1951 I returned to Australia to work as Telepress correspondent in Australia."[362]

Murray-Smith complained that from February until April he had not received any salary in spite of the fact that he was told he would be paid. Only in June had he learned that "Telepress had been closed down in early April ... without notifying Telepress correspondents or subscribers." He kept spending "a large amount of money on Telepress' behalf *after* the organisation had in fact closed." His bill came up to £180 sterling as salary and £72 sterling "for cables sent to Telepress." Murray-Smith stressed that he was in a very difficult financial situation aggravated by a new baby:

360   SUA 100/3, 25, 91.
361   Ibid.
362   Ibid.

> I have worked hard since returning from CSR to explain the new life in CSR to Australians, and have traveled over 6000 km to address nearly 100 meetings on the subject. I have also written a booklet on present-day CSR which has been published. [Its title reveals its content: *There Is No Iron Curtain.*] You can understand why I am embarrassed when people say to me: "How can an organisation in a socialist country treat its employees as Telepress has treated you?"

Two weeks later, Murray-Smith's call for justice was answered by the international secretary, Dr. Jan Kabourek, who assured him that soon he would be paid.[363] S. Murray-Smith did not become discouraged, at least not yet. In the Spring 1953 issue of *Meanjin*, he attacked Andrew Fabinyi's "reckless statement" that "Australians and New Zealanders buy more books per head of population than any other people in the world."[364] He was obviously either ignorant or lying when he claimed that "Writers are free to write as they wish, and the 30 publishing houses in Prague ... have a free and uncensored choice of the books they will publish." Against all overwhelming evidence to the contrary, he wrote: "The result has been a new flowering of Czechoslovak literature— naturally, since it is arising in a new society, accompanied by birth and growing pangs, but fundamentally healthy, optimistic, confident."

Such slanted information was unashamedly spread throughout Australia. In the next issue of *Meanjin*, Andrew Fabinyi corrected some of the untruths of Murray-Smith, but could not claim that he had lived in Czechoslovakia as Murray-Smith had.[365]

Murray-Smith's naiveté (or propensity to misinform) was so great that he reported on the judicial murder of the former general secretary of the CPCZ in the show trials of 1952 by praising "the best traditions of Western legal principles."[366] Principles that apparently were behind the horrid spectacle of leading Communists being tortured and forced to recite memorized confessions in the court. Only three out of fourteen were not hanged.

---

363 Ibid.
364 Vol. XII, No. 3, pp. 339–41.
365 Vol. XII, No. 4, pp. 466–67.
366 Patrick O'Brien, *The Saviours*, op. cit., p. 101.

When Murray-Smith returned to Australia, he joined the Peace Council and worked for it until 1958. In 1955, he founded a strongly pro-Communist journal *Overland*, but left the Communist Party in 1958. When he founded the journal, he still expected the revolution to come in Australia in 1959, as he told Patrick O'Brien in a long interview in 1975, and added, "In fact we were hopelessly out of bloody touch with everything."[367]

---

367   "Transcription of Taped Interview," p. 36.

4

Comrades Cloaked In Wool: Exporting Wool For The Benefit Of The Communist Party Of Australia

A few documents discovered in the Prague archives demonstrate the inventiveness of leaders of the CPA in subverting Australian democracy by channeling part of the profits from local wool growers into the coffers of the party. After World War II, Czechoslovakia was not the only country interested in obtaining large credits for the buying of Australian wool. France, the Netherlands, and Finland requested financial assistance. Other countries, including Italy, were thought likely to make further requests.[368] The treasury informally indicated to the French minister that "large credits" were "impossible because of our vulnerable economy." It was suggested that "even a credit of ten million sterling would be embarrassing because we would be faced with similar requests from other European countries." The Australians proposed a small credit of five million pounds for two or three years "as gesture of goodwill."[369]

In October 1946, Czechoslovakia requested credit of one million Australian pounds for purchase of wool in excess of an agreed upon quantity.[370] Australia granted a credit of five hundred thousand pounds during July 1947. Poland was receiving £1,500,000 worth of wool as

368   AA, A2910/1/428/1/177/7.
369   Ibid.
370   Ibid.

part of a gift of six million pounds from surplus.[371] The Czechoslovak government also approached New Zealand with a request for wool credits.[372]

By September 1948, Czechoslovakia obtained a credit of one million sterling pounds.[373] In September 1949, the same credit for the purchase of Australian wool was granted to the Czechoslovak government that was by then fully in the hands of the Communist Party. Copious documentation of the exchange of letters between the two governments and banks exists in the Australian archives in Canberra.[374] The secret deal involving the CPA and Prague is revealed in the Czech archives. Before we get to it, some Australian authorities' suspicions and discoveries of improper trading practices should be mentioned.

On November 15, 1949, First Assistant Secretary F.H. Wheeler, wrote to the secretary of the Department of Commerce and Agriculture in Canberra, calling his attention to the confidential foreign report of The *Economist* entitled "Czech Export Plot."[375] Another letter written on the same day to the Australia House in London was more specific: "The credit extended by Australia is used by Czechoslovakia to buy wool for textiles sold to Canada at prices nicely calculated to be below the British ones." Between 1947 and 1948, the share of Czech share of woolen products imported to Canada increased forty fold.[376] Other documents remind readers that "the whole of Czechoslovak industry has been nationalised, as have import and export trade and internal distribution." Internal prices were unknown and therefore it was hard to establish proof of dumping.[377] On Christmas of 1949, a representative of the Board of Trade, Commercial Relations and Exports Department in London laconically remarked, "This is the way the Czechs do business with hard currency countries." And "Czechs are doing the same thing on motor cycles to Australia."[378]

---

371   AA, A2910/1/440/1/68.
372   AA, A2910/1/428/1/177/7.
373   AA, A2910/1/440/1/68.
374   Ibid.
375   AA, A2910/1/440/1/68.
376   Ibid.
377   Ibid.
378   Ibid.

In spite of the Czech business practices, as the Australian government trade commissioner, C. J. Crane, wrote in a memorandum for Canberra's Department of Commerce and Agriculture, the British authorities did not protest because they were doing the same thing and therefore did not want to press the matter.[379]

The involvement of prominent members of the CPA is politically more interesting. In 1950, Jack Hughes was acting as chairman of the Control Commission of the CPA which in itself is a very important function since he was in charge of checking on and eventually purging CPA members. However, at the same time, he was marketing research director of the Australian Merchandise & Enterprise Pty. Ltd. in Sydney. As can be proved from a document discovered in the Prague archives, he had full authorization to investigate trade and other activities connected with exporting from and importing to Australia.[380]

The story behind the testimony of the managing director of the company, Mr. Alfred White, comes to light in other documents found in the same archive. On December 18, 1950, a secret report for Comrade Bedřich Geminder explained the reasons for the existence of the exporting/importing company. (At that time, Geminder was probably the most important agent of the Soviet Union in Czechoslovakia.) According to this document, Norman Freehill, member of the CPA, was returning home from the World Peace Congress through the ČSR when he requested a favor of the Czechs:

> Soon the CPA will be forced into complete illegality. To facilitate contacts between individual States of the Australian Union and in order to gain finance for Party activities, the CPA recently established a commercial enterprise, the Australian Merchandise & Enterprise Pty. Ltd., Sydney, 72 Pitt Street, that has a solid commercial base. This firm, first of all, should serve as a cloak for Party activities. The firm will have branches in all Australian States and a European office in London. It wants to direct its commercial relations mainly to people's democracies, especially the ČSR and Poland. This firm will be able to deliver

---

379   Ibid.
380   SCA, 100/3/25/91/7.See also SCA, 02/2/58/472/63.

> an unlimited amount of wool and other merchandise
> in accordance with need, and is interested, first of
> all, in buying newsprint paper from the ČSR, cars,
> etc. In Australia there is not enough of newsprint
> paper; it would be used for Party needs and also
> for sale. Comrade Freehill will represent the firm in
> London.[381]

Obviously, the CPA was ready for all eventualities. Had Prime Minister Menzies succeeded in his attempt to make the party illegal, it would have continued legally as the Australian Merchandise and Enterprise Pty., Ltd. Just a simple change of name. Comrade Freehill clearly had arranged everything with Comrade Roháč from the Czechoslovak embassy in London, along with its cultural attaché, Comrade Skoupal, and Comrade Zemánek from the ČTK (Czechoslovak Press Agency), all of whom he refers to in his statement.

At the same time, Freehill asked Geminder to transfer a letter to Jack Hughes, the chairman of the Central Commission of the CPA, who, as Freehill said, "would probably ... travel through (Czechoslovakia) on his way to Italy." He requested that the letter be destroyed in four days if Hughes did not show up.[382]

Hughes apparently did come to Prague. It emerges from another report to Geminder that Hughes appealed to Geminder to support his company by having the CPCZ enter into commercial relations with it. He again stressed its importance as a cloak for the survival of the CPA in case of its banishment. He also enclosed the confirmation of representatives of the firm quoted above and his own right to act on its behalf.[383]

The CPA, however, was allowed to remain legal. There are no further documents to be found relating to the woolen cloak of secrecy in the Prague archives from 1950; yet in 1957, the question of how to combine the undermining of Australian democracy with trade popped up again.

---

381   SCA, 02/2/58/472/66. The Australian address of the company was identical with the address of the CPA.

382   Ibid.

383   SCA, 100/3/25/91/7. See also ACA, 02/2/58/472.

A document prepared on March 20, 1957, by Comrade Jiří Hendrych, at that time the second most powerful man in the party hierarchy, proposed a substantial "Help to the Communist Party of Australia." Under this title, the submission to the next meeting of the all-powerful Political Bureau of the Central Committee of the CPCZ gave Comrade Hendrych the task of "examining suggestions by Australian comrades (General Secretary Comrade Sharkey and Comrade Hill) for joint business activities between Czechoslovak foreign trade and their Australian business firm."[384] The document was marked "Strictly Secret!" A short summary explained the project:

> During the visit of our delegation to the Eighth Congress of the CP of China, Comrade L. Sharkey, General Secretary of the CPA, suggested to Comrade V. Kopecký and Comrade V. Krutina that we should trade with an Australian company that is of interest to the CPA. This firm would distribute part of its profit to the CPA. The proposal was dealt with by the Sixth Department of the CPCZ CC.[385]

The core of this deal was repeated and widened in an enclosed information:

> Comrade Sharkey drew our attention to the fact that only himself and Comrade Hill, member of the Politburo of the CPA, knew about the affair. He also stressed that it was very important, especially after the case agent Petrov which led to the breakoff of diplomatic relations between Australia and the Soviet Union. He requested our permission to discuss these matters with our Consul General for Australia and New Zealand, Comrade Jandík... The International Department of the CPCZ CC considers that it is possible in principle.[386]

---

384 SCA, A-ÚV KSČ, 02/2/134/174/1-2.
385 Ibid., f. 1.
386 Ibid., f. 3.

In Sydney, Consul General Jandík became involved as proposed by Sharkey. In April 1957, a cable sent by Jandík conveyed this message:

> I inform you: We are dealing with a serious and well funded firm Dekyvere which buys Australian wool for overseas customers. One of the co-owners of the firm made an advantageous proposal according to which we would buy corded wool in Australia and in exchange we would export our own merchandise that is mainly for consumption. We would obtain special licenses for it. The trade could go as high as one million pound sterling [exactly the previous amount of the Australian government's granted credit!] I know from reliable sources that one partner of the firm, Marcel Dekyvere, is a personal friend of two federal ministers, and that in Australia he and his wife enjoy high social status. The CPA would share the profits from realized transactions. The second partner of the firm, Victor Dekyvere, will come to Prague in May to have discussions with Centrotex. The Dekyvere firm does not know that we are familiar with their arrangements with the CPA. Our Ministry of Foreign Trade was informed about this project.[387]

How long did this fascinating arrangement to financially support the intentions of the CPA last, and how well did it do? Clearly some people highly placed in the Communist government of Czechoslovakia and elsewhere knew about it. How much money did the CPA manage to get out of the secret deal? It was new and innovative in Australia, but it was a well-established practice in Europe.[388] In Italy, for instance, the

387 CzMFA, 013 669/57-ABO-3.
388 According to Karel Kaplan in *Majetkové zdroje KSČ v letech 1945–1952*/Property Resources of the CPCZ 1945–1952/ *(Prague:* Ústav pro soudobé dějiny /Contemporary History's Institute/, 1993), the Communist party began to collect illegal funds already before the 1946 elections by secret trade dealings with Austria, Poland, Hungary, and Romania. In 1947 (till 1951) for this purpose was established a company called Eupex. The company smuggled American cigarettes from Belgium through Czechoslovakia mainly to Austria and Germany but

Communist Party was able to obtain huge amounts of money from trade with the Soviet Union, Czechoslovakia, and other people's democracies. The supposedly anti-capitalist conspiracy successfully conspired to get its share of profits from commercial access to Communist countries. What comes to mind is Lenin's statement that capitalists will sell the Bolsheviks the rope with which to hang them. In this case, rope made of wool.

---

also to Italy, Finland, Great Britain, Island, Yugoslavia, and France. For illegal trade with Switzerland another company was created, Technotex.

5

Suspect Roles Of Czechoslovak Consuls In Australia

According to *Collins English Dictionary*, Australian edition, 1991, a consul is "an official appointed by a sovereign state to protect its commercial interests and its citizens in a foreign city." After World War II, the Czechoslovak consul general and his large staff—representing a country that was sovereign only in name—interfered improperly in Australian domestic policies in at least five areas:

1.   They maintained contacts with individuals of the Communist Party of Australia (CPA) and of the extreme left wing of the Labour Party for the purpose of garnering information and trying to influence and aid their activities.

2.   They met and entertained trade unionists in order to gather information useful to Soviet and Czechoslovak secret services and to encourage their revolutionary dreams.

3.   They tracked Czech and Slovak refugees who settled in Australia to spy on them rather than aid them by keeping agents in their ranks. They regularly supervised, as well as led, the actions of the large Czechoslovak circle in Sydney. They secured their own preferred people into elected positions during annual general assemblies.

4.   They propagated the supposedly successful socialist achievements of people's democracies through

film, books, brochures, lecture tours, and organized visits by public officials whom they attempted to seduce for their own political aims. Such propaganda formed a large and costly part of the consulate's efforts to influence Australian development to a Communist state.

5. The Czechoslovak consulate regularly sent secret political reports on Australian politicians and policies to Prague. Both secret codes and couriers were used to deliver them. Czechoslovak consuls assisted Soviet secret services and their agents in Australia.

The archive of the Czech Ministry of Foreign Affairs in Prague proved to be rich source of documentation for this rather unusual functioning of the Sydney and—to a lesser degree—Melbourne consulates. Other documents were found at the state central archive containing proof of illegal activities of Communist Party's main organs. So far, these documents cannot be complemented by the Czechoslovak consulates' local archives since—as the post-Communist Czech Ambassador in Canberra suggested—they disappeared and might be in Moscow. However, ample Australian archives in Canberra can add to our knowledge of what was happening.

Trained specialists of the Czechoslovak secret service, acting under the cover of the consulate in Sydney and later also in Melbourne, took over the important outpost in Australia soon after the coup d'état of February 1948. However, since the middle of World War II, the consulate had been operated as a branch of Soviet espionage.[389]

According to Desmond Ball and David Horner, from 1943 to 1948, the Czechoslovak consulate in Sydney employed in a vital position a man who perfectly represented the ambivalence of Czech and Russian interests. Constantine Johannes Tenukest was born in Russia in 1906, but like many thousands of Russians and Ukrainians who fled the Soviet Union, he found refuge in democratic prewar Czechoslovakia.

---

389 "The KGB relies heavily on the intelligence services of Soviet satellites counries in carrying out both its active measures and espionage operations." Amy W. Knight, *The KGB: Police and Politics in the Soviet Union* (Boston: Unwin Hyman, 1988), p.285.

He became a Czech citizen and arrived in Australia in 1938, before Czechoslovakia was divided and taken over by the Germans.

As a clerk in charge of coding and decoding important confidential messages coming from the Czechoslovak government in London exile, and from 1945 from liberated Prague, he was familiar with ciphers used by the Czechs. One of his closest friends in Australia was Feodor Andreevich Nosov, who acted as a newspaper man representing the Soviet press agency TASS. Nosov was recruited by the KGB and between 1943 and 1950 played a very important role gathering secret information, delivering it to Moscow, and cultivating a large group of Australians willing to reveal secrets to the friendly Soviets. He had easy access to Dr. Evatt's ministry. His friends included members of the well established spy ring formed by Australian traitors including Katherine Susannah Prichard, Walter Seddon Clayton, Rex Chiplin, Allan Dalziel, and Alfred Hughes. Tenukest later revealed some of his experiences to Australian authorities.[390]

The Czechoslovak consul general in Sydney, Dr. J. Němeček, invited agent Nosov for lunch, as he described in his letter to Prague of October 21, 1946. He sent the confidential "Political Report No 3: The Communist Party of Australia" on June 29, 1947, well before the putch:

> In Australia the number of Communists is relatively insignificant.... The party since its beginning twenty-five years ago had a definite influence on the structure of the workers' movement mainly through trade unions.... L. L. Sharkey is the chairman of the party; he is an old member. In 1935 he studied in Moscow where he was elected into the Communist International.... Many members of the Party dominate the major trade unions, such as the Federated Ironworkers and Munitions Workers Union, Miners' Federation, Sheet Metal Workers Union, Boilermakers Society, Seamen Union, Waterside Workers Federation, Ship Painters and Dockers' Union, Building Workers' Union,

---

390 *Breaking the Codes: Australia's KGB Network, 1944–1950* (St Leonards, NSW: Allen & Unwin, 1998), pp. 134–35; and Statement of Constantine Johannes Tenukest, CRS A6283/XR 1, item 56, ff. 12408.

Clerks Union, and Hotel Club and Communist
Party has great influence in other unions, especially in
Teachers' Federation, Actors Equity and Fire Brigades
Union.... Method and tactics are adapted to special
local conditions of the workers' class that enjoys a
high living standard and benefits from a good and
strong Labor government.... Particularly cautious is
the Communist Party versus the unions that are very
sensitive to political interference. Here the technical
proceedings are doubly methodical. Its candidates to
leading positions in the unions are never nominated
or presented directly by the party of as comrades, but
regularly pushed in the so called preliminary caucus as
specialists or capable leaders. Therefore union leaders
who are distinguished members of the party are rarely
labeled as Communists.[391]

The next report on the political situation, which reached the
Ministry of Foreign Affairs on December 12, 1950, was not any more
informative but marked by slanted and aggressive vocabulary:

The transition of the Australian industry from
peaceful to war-time production was accompanied
by introduction of Fascist methods into political
and public life. 1. The government uses all possible
means of propaganda to inflame martial hysteria in
Australia ... 2. The government in all possible ways
tries to destroy and annihilate the activity of the
progressive movement of the working class so that it
could then exercise its politics without opposition. The
first action of this policy is a law on the dissolution
of the Communist Party.... The Australian capitalist
class is attempting to liquidate workers' trade unions
by splitting them in various fractions.... Especially
the Australian Workers Union's leaders can be hardly

391 Consulate's No. 2170/47, Cz. Foreign Ministry's (MZV) No.
146925, arrived 12. VII. 1947.

distinguished from a group of capitalists in Queensland since their interests are closely connected.[392]

[It's touching how the author worries about the threatened rights of the Australians while he represents a country whose government already had abolished all such rights of its citizens!]

The Catholic wing of the Labor Party was blamed in particular for its supposedly close cooperation with the employers.

Between these two political reports basic changes took place in Czechoslovakia and within its diplomatic representation in Australia. In February 1948, the Communist Party of Czechoslovakia (CPCZ) seized total power and several of the state's delegates resigned from their positions in protest.

The honorary consul in Adelaide, Raymond H. Cato, closed his office on March eleventh.[393] The next day, the chancellor de carrière from the Sydney Consulate, Karol Tököly, called the Department of External Affairs and resigned: "Mr. Kotaly (sic) stated that he felt unable to carry on since the recent coup in his country. The rest of his staff in Sydney were of the same mind and were also resigning. He wished to remain in Australia indefinitely."[394]

Karol Tököly was a demobilized captain in the Czechoslovak army in Britain during WWII. He was charged with commercial affairs. He arrived in Sydney on April 13, 1946.[395] In his letter of resignation, he wrote: "The recent political developments in Czechoslovakia ... are against the democratic principles of my country.... I do not feel inclined to acknowledge the present Czechoslovak Government as a true Government of our people."[396]

The Czechoslovak consulate general informed the Department of External Affairs that Mr. Josef Felix was appointed as vice-consul until the arrival of Consul General Karel Sakh.[397] This message was dated March 22, 1948, yet the situation was apparently not stabilized since on December 6, 1949 another vice consul, Jiří Halla, tendered his own

392   MZV 158970/50.
393   Australian Archives (AA), A1838/265, item 1515/1/10/3.
394   AA, A1838/278; 1515/1/10/1.
395   Ibid.
396   AA, A1067/1; IC46/15/15/2.
397   Ibid.

resignation in a letter to Dr. Burton. On the nineteenth of December, Burton was informed by Vice Consul Josef Felix that he was in charge of the office "until the arrival of Consul General Mr. Hanuš Frank."[398]

A protracted conflict about the premises occupied by Jiří Halla led to a court case. The consulate wanted him to leave the apartment immediately while Halla requested permission to remain until March sixth when a new place would be available for him.[399] Halla was treated as a traitor. The man who administered the revenge was Vice Consul Josef Felix, who in a short time would change his mind and also resign. It is a revealing story.

Felix was first appointed as vice consul in Melbourne on February 12, 1948 by Karol Tököly, who informed the Australian Department of External Affairs that Josef Felix was fifty-four years of age and during the war served in the Czechoslovak army in exile both in Russia and England holding the rank of captain. However, the appointment proved to be premature since on July twenty-eighth, Consul General Karel M. Sakh requested Secretary John W. Burton to accept his appointment on June twenty-ninth, one month before his written request.[400] It was announced by the *Commonwealth of Australia Gazette* only on the nineteenth of August.

The happy solution did not last long. In March 1951, Josef Felix announced that as a consular representative for the dominion of New Zealand, he would spend four weeks of his annual leave in New Zealand and Jindřich Jakš would be in authority during his absence.[401] Before his departure, he informed the Australians that Jaroslav Kafka had been accredited to the general consulate as vice consul. The proper acknowledgment sent back was, however, answered not by Jakš who was supposed to be in authority, but by Kafka on behalf of Felix. The legal and consular section of the department made this comment for the secretary: "The matter is referred to you in view of the differences of

---

398 It was complicated. Cyprian Slimák was supposed to come as con-
     sul general on October 1, 1948. However, Prague decided to send
     Jindřich Jakš instead. On twentieth of January 1950, the Department
     of External Affairs confidentially requested a report on him "in view of
     Slimak's case." AA A441/1; 1951/13/1661.

399 AA, A 1838/1; 1515/1/10/6.

400 Ibid.

401 AA, A1838/278; 1515/1/10/1.

opinion which apparently exist in the Czechoslovak Consulate General in Sydney, and of possible repercussions from Mr. Felix if provisional recognition is proceeded with."[402]

On the thirtieth of March, Vice Consul Jaroslav Kafka had the honor to inform the Australian authorities that Josef Felix had been transferred to the Prague Ministry of Foreign Affairs.[403] On April second, Josef Felix requested permanent residence in Australia and in a long letter explained his reasons:

> Being appointed in the year 1947 by the Democratic Government of the Republic of Czechoslovakia to the Consular Service in Australia, I carried out my duties obviously according to the regulations and stipulations of the International Law avoiding any interference in internal political matters of this country. I continued to carry out my duties in the same manner when the present Czechoslovak Government seized power in the year 1948. Although I have many times been requested to furnish political reports regarding Ministry, I have always refused to comply with such requests, as this is opposed to my conscience and democratic principles for which I fought in the last two world wars on the side of the Allied armies ... To remain further would be against my dignity.... As an opponent of the present regime in Czechoslovakia it is quite impossible for me to return to that country as it would mean exposing my life to danger and therefore I beg the Australian Government to grant to me political asylum in Australia.[404]

---

402 Ibid.
403 Ibid. Jaroslav Kafka wrote to the Department of External Affairs in Canberra that Jindřich Jakš was going on his annual leave to Czechoslovakia from December 13, 1951 until the end of February 1952. In April, he announced that Jakš has been transferred to the Ministry for Foreign Trade in Prague. Interestingly, the Passport Control Department of the Foreign Office confidentially warned in May 1952 that Jakš "should not be granted a visa for the United Kingdom without prior reference to this department." AA A441/1; 1951/13/1661.
404 AA, A1838/278; 1515/1/10/1.

The legal and consular section prepared for the minister a review of the case and included a two page confidential note about remarks Mr. Felix made on the sixth of February to the external affairs officer. He advised then that when Mr. Jakš arrived as a commercial specialist one year before, he was not fully trusted in Prague and his wife and children were kept in Prague as hostages. When Mr. Felix was asked to supply political information on the Australian Administration of the Mandated Territory of New Guinea, for example, or to submit a draft resolution for peace to the Australian parliament, he refused to do so.[405] He was also asked to organize a peace movement among the Czech community. "He told them that he did not know any Czech nationals who would join such a movement."[406] He decided to wait for the arrival of the newly appointed Consul General Frank. However, he did not arrive, supposedly due to ill health. The real malady was probably political. A week later, when Jaroslav Kafka came instead, he refused to do the work assigned to him by Felix and claimed that he was sent to Australia to perform political functions only. Kafka previously worked as a mechanic in a factory. He was not a professional diplomat. "Mr. Felix came to the conclusion that Kafka was an emissary of the Communist Party."[407] This whole sentence was underlined in the confidential report to the secretary of the Department of Foreign Affairs. Kafka asked Felix for information on papers subscribed to by the consulate. When told that the consulate received the *Herald* and *Telegraph*, Kafka criticized Felix for not subscribing to the *Tribune* and said that "this is the only paper where one can read anything true."[408]

The daily papers informed their readers about the affair. On the April 5, 1951, the *Daily Telegraph* reported that Mr. Felix "feared for his life" if he returned to Czechoslovakia, quoting him as saying, "This is a beautiful, democratic country. Here I am free." On April sixth, the *Sydney Morning Herald* reported that Felix told the Australian authorities that he suspected Kafka "had already contacted Australian Communist Party officials" and "when he took over the Consulate he altered all locks on safes and doors and kept the keys himself." Fearing for his life should he returned to totalitarian Czechoslovakia, he also

405 Ibid.
406 Ibid.
407 Ibid.
408 Ibid.

mentioned, "My wife and three sons disappeared mysteriously in German concentration camps in the last war."

On April 27, 1951, the *Sydney Telegraph* reported that Josef Felix was able to remain in Australia. It quoted the Minister for Immigration, Holt, who said: "It is understood that Mr. Felix served the Allied cause in both world wars. It has been established that he upheld the democratic way of life, and does not constitute a security risk."

It is interesting that the ASIO file on this issue included the United Nations Economic and Social Council's Commission on Human Rights thirteen-page decision entitled "Activities of Various Organs of the United Nations in Connection with the Right of Asylum." For Australians it was a new experience. They had to learn to cope with totalitarian systems of government and their consequences for democratic states. However, dangerous dreamers persisted in their admiration for police states.

It is worth mentioning a "Top Secret and Personal" note that the director-general of security, C.C.F. Spry, sent A. S. Watt of the Department of External Affairs. The colonel complained that he felt "that the interval between FELIX's first approach and our learning about it may have meant the loss of valuable information."[409] In an immediate reply, Watt told Spry that he "shall ensure that if any further cases of this nature come to the notice of my department, your Service is immediately informed."[410] Dealing with totalitarian states involves a long and difficult learning process.

As was suggested by one of the the previous chapters, the interlude between alliance and Cold War misled many people into believing that cooperation between democracies and the Soviet Union would and should continue indefinitely. Before we judge such naïvité too harshly, it is important to remember that this was a time of great flux. Power relations between Communist and democratic states were shifting, and individuals within those systems were being moved from one position to another. It was only later, when people's positions became permanent and the true nature of Communism evident, that everyone was forced to chose a side.

Before the coup d'état of February 1948, representatives of the Czechoslovak government might have served their country either as

409   Ibid.
410   Ibid.

declared Communists or socialist sympathizers. For instance, before the coup, Dr. Němeček, whose "Political Report No. 3" was quoted above, acted in some instances much as Communist agents would act later. In his reports to his Minister of Foreign Affairs in Prague, he referred very favorably to Dr. Evatt several times, praising Evatt's reorganization of the Department of Foreign Affairs in Canberra. Němeček also defended Evatt against Right-wing press accusations that he allowed his ministry to be influenced mainly by the Communists.[411]

Dr. Němeček also propagated the progressive line of his Prague superiors when he sent his deputy to introduce Bert Williams to the Sydney circle of Czech and Slovak compatriots after Williams's return from student congress in Prague.[412] What is of more than passing interest is his inviting of Soviet agent Nosov to lunch. This secret Soviet agent was posing as a press representative of the USSR and was serving as the contact for Clayton's spy network.[413]

Vice-Consul Jiří Halla, who resigned after the coup d'état, was doing what his government asked him to do previously. Colonel A. W. Sheppard acted as an intermediary between Halla and the Communist Party of Australia. It was revealed in a document sent from London to Prague by "Bystricky 2248/D" marked No. 700. The document reached an unnamed office in Prague on December 22, 1949 (No. 7825/49). It expressed Colonel Sheppard's worry that someone at the consulate in Sydney would discover what Halla had told the Australian police about him. At Halla's request, Sheppard regularly supplied news about the political and economic situation in the Far East. Obviously, before

---

411   Ibid.

412   See his report to MZV, 30.7.1946 and 21.1.1947.

413   On the May 23, 1946, reported by Dr. Němeček on July 18, 1946. Bert Williams, acting as a secretary of the Federation of the Democratic Youth (a Communist front), was expelled from France on March 9, 1950. He moved to Prague to continue his work from Czechoslovakia. On March eighteenth, the CPCZ CC's Committee for Assistance to Fraternal Communist parties decided to permit him to stay. As support for the decision, it was stated that Williams has been a member of the CPA since February 1942 and secretary of SFDM since November 1945. This "strictly secret Record No. 1" was in agreement signed by the CPCZ Secretary General, Rudolf Slansky, who was angry that he received a copy only on the twentieth and there was no date of session. State Central Archive, 100/1, 58, 454, p. 196.

his resignation, Halla served his masters in Prague as an informer. The
acting consul general, Josef Felix, also managed to slant his political
reports to Prague by giving the Communist perception of events, as in
his review of the Australian elections of December 1949. His message
was typed in English on January 19, 1950:

> The main reason for the victory of the Liberal Country
> Party lies in the Australian class composition. The
> industrial proletariat accounts for below 50% of the
> electors.... The socialist vote was extremely small, the
> Communist Party losing in comparison to last year as
> a result of the increased incomes of some sections of
> the proletariat and the attacks on the Party from all
> sides.... The proposals for social welfare are extremely
> reactionary.[414]

The situation in the Ministry of Foreign Affairs in Prague was
complicated before the coup. Although Jan Masaryk served as Foreign
Minister, he traveled a great deal, and the administration and direction of
the Ministry was in the hands of an experienced and devoted apparatchik
of the Communist Party, Dr. Vlado Clementis. Therefore, as was the
case in many important ministries, the Communist Party had almost a
free hand to pursue its own and Soviet policies, including preparation of
Communist takeovers at home and abroad. It is difficult to decide who of
the ministry's employees was a Communist, an agent, or just a sympathizer
fulfilling Prague requests as a part of his lucrative employment.

One of the last actions Josef Felix took as the acting consul general
was to declare that "from the 1st October, 1950, the honorary consul,
Mr. Norman L. Burnell has been relieved of his duties" and that "the
honorary Consulate of the Czechoslovak Republic in Perth, Western
Australia, has been discontinued." He sent the letter only much later, on
January 5, 1951.[415] The *Commonwealth of Australia Gazette* published
its notification on February 15, 1951, and the new acting consul
general, Jaroslav Kafka, acknowledged news of the notification only on
July 19, 1951. Dealing with the changing personnel and policies at the
Czechoslovak consulate general in Sydney must have been frustrating.

---

414   Announced to the MZV on the 21.10. 1946.
415   AA, A1838/265; 1515/1/10/9.

6

Jaroslav Kafka: Czechoslovak Acting Consul General In Sydney, 1951-1954:

Uncertainties about personnel at the consulate ended with the arrival of Kafka. He was born on February 28, 1922 in an industrial and mining town in Bohemia. Because of its strong tradition of Communist orientation, the town was called "Red" Kladno. Kafka was selected to represent the new generation of Communist diplomats. Being a mechanic and coming from a workers' family, his background was considered appropriately proletarian. He arrived in Sydney on January 23, 1951 with his wife Věra, born the same year as her husband, and two small children. Prior to his appointment to Australia he worked in the Ministry of Foreign Affairs in Prague for eighteen months.[416]

Because Australian officials witnessed several resignations of Czechoslovak diplomats since the coup d'état in February 1948, an attempt was made to persuade the new man to follow their example. Early in 1952, Leo Carter led the operation code-named Cabin. On February twenty-second, he sent a memo to his boss, P.S.O, B.2., originally marked top secret. He met the previous acting consul general, Josef Felix, who told him that it was "most unlikely that Kafka will seek to remain in Australia." He had no profession or trade suitable for Australia, and his own and his wife's parents were still in

---

416   AA, A6119/90. Item 2462, Kafka Vol. 1, f. 17.

Czechoslovakia. But Felix was "awaiting a suitable opportunity to make an approach in an indirect manner."[417]

On March tenth, Leo Carter sent another "Top secret, personal" letter to "Principal Section Officer, B. 2." A man identified only as "known to Jaroslav Kafka" approached him, and the following conversation ensued:

> —Greetings. I hope you don't mind me calling on you.
>
> Kafka: Well, I am not exactly pleased, but I can give you 15 minutes.
>
> —I heard rumors that you may eventually decide to stay in Australia.
>
> Kafka: I can only tell you that it never entered my mind and assure you that it never will.
>
> —Well, in case it ever does, would you be kind enough to let me know?
>
> Kafka: You are giving me enough of troubles as it is and don't force me into making the life of your relations harder than it is.
>
> —Well, this is news to me. Could you tell me how are my parents?
>
> Kafka: They are well looked after.
>
> —Thank you, Mr. Kafka, and just in case you change your mind, let me know. You could possibly be of more use to your country if you do.
>
> Kafka: Please do go. I have no time and I never will find it necessary to contact you, of that I am more than positive.

The conversation must have taken place in Czech since Kafka's knowledge of English or German was minimal, although he was supposedly fluent in Russian. At the end of the memo, Carter remarked that Josef Felix had not yet made his approach and that he was "waiting for an opportunity to do it in a diplomatic manner.[418]

---

417 Ibid.
418 Ibid., ff. 15–16.

The regional director, N. S. W., G. R. Richards, in a March seventeenth memorandum for headquarters, ASIO, wrote that Felix was still waiting, and although the defection seemed most unlikely, "The seed has been sown and the visit by Felix may throw fresh light on his attitude."[419]

It was part of a learning process in dealing with Communist governments to realize the difference between the old school of diplomats and the new that was carefully screened and prepared for service abroad.

Another top secret document sent by Director-General Richards was more realistic in acknowledging that Kafka "was an emissary of the Communist Party," but again highly underestimated Kafka's mission by claiming that "his main purpose would appear to be to work amongst the Czech Community." In fact, it was one of his minor functions in spite of his dutiful attention to its Sydney branch. This document of June 23, 1952 also mentioned that Kafka contacted Soviet agent-diplomat Vladimir Petrov, Clive Evatt, Alfred White, Izrael Conway, all important Communists, as well as Soviet diplomats-cum-agents Galanin and Pakhomov.[420]

Kafka was regularly followed by counterespionage agents from the outset, and his telephone was tapped. During his first stay, hundreds of pages of secret reports were devoted to him. During his second diplomatic mission, this pile grew into thousands of pages of witness briefs. Most of them are only external observations, and even his telephone conversations when read are frustrating since he obviously suspected bugging. However, there must have been someone at the embassy imparting inside information to the ASIO, so that soon Kafka's real pursuits became evident.

In a review of Kafka's "Activities and Associates" from January 1951 to July 1954 when he was acting as vice-consul, it was recorded that "he was in close and regular touch with identified cadre and co-opted workers of the R.I.S. [Russian Intelligence Service] and leading members of the C. P. of A." Among the Australian Communists named were Chiplin and Bresland, both cited by the Royal Commission on Espionage (1955) as contacts of the RIS, "under the code names 'CHARLIE' and 'COOK' respectively."

419   Ibid., f. 18.
420   Ibid., ff. 31–36.

The review mentioned that Kafka "had received a primary education only," but that a Czech exile revealed that Kafka attended a special school for secret agents in Doksy. He belonged to "the higher organisation of the Secret Police." Another source reported that Kafka was sent to the USSR to get special training. During eight or nine months prior to his posting to Australia, he became a member of the MVD (Soviet Ministry of Internal Affairs).

It was established that between 1951 and 1954, Kafka was acquainted with and regularly met the following "cadre workers and collaborators of the Russian Intelligence Service": Ivan Pakhomov had two functions; officially he represented the news agency TASS (1950–1952), while secretly he was an MVD cadre worker, and from April 1951 until the end of that year was also in charge of spying as temporary MVD resident. After Pakhomov returned home, Victor Antonov took Pakhomov's place from June 1952 to April 1954. Galanin's official mission was to act as the commercial attaché, but he also was an MVD collaborator (1950–1952). Kovaliev replaced Galanin from 1952–1954 in both functions. Plaitkais, attaché at the Soviet embassy in Canberra from January 1952 to April 1954, was an MVD "EM" worker.

After Chiplin and Bresland, the other prominent Australian Communists who were listed as often being in company of Kafka were L. L. Sharkey, secretary to the Central Committee of the CPA, "who, according to Petrov, received $25,000 from the M.V.D. funds which were handed over to him by Antonov"; president of the CPA, Clifton Reginald Walker (alias R. Dixon); Herbert Bovyll Chandler, member of the CC CPA and the printer of the official newspaper of the CPA, the *Tribune*, in whose possession were found secret documents including information on ASIO personnel and their license plates numbers; and finally, James Healy, member of the CC CPA.[421]

Naturally, even spies have a more or less normal side to their lives, and their secret and more important functions are often carefully hidden by activities that look very innocent, such as family visits, lunches, dinners, parties, exercise, celebrations of national revolutionary holidays (November 7, May 9), and viewing films.

Kafka was well selected. It was reported to his surveyors that he was "a pleasant type of person, very fond of his two children, a boy about 3

---

421   AA, A6119/90, item 2464, Kafka Vol. 3, ff. 88–92.

and a girl about 5, who attends school in the Bondi area,"[422] where the family settled. Kafka was interned in Germany during World War II for three years; he was arrested soon after the destruction of the village of Lidice that was suspected of protecting Heydrich's assassins. Both Mr. and Mrs. Kafka were members of the Catholic Church, and he was not a gambler as was his close friend and associate at the consulate, Josef Tříska, who was described as "an inveterate gambler ... continually in debt through his gambling habits." The report also revealed that "Kafka said that he liked Australia and that the climate was very beneficial to his two children."[423]

In January 1952, Kafka was involved in a car accident,[424] but his wife's use of their Škoda car was more questionable. She was reported as having obtained a driver's license only in July 1953: "It is of distinct interest that Mrs. Kafka has apparently been driving for some time without a license of any sort."[425] She requested a visit from a Roman Catholic priest on October 16, 1952.[426] On December 18, 1952, she was treated for a cut finger in the surgery of Dr Bialoguski.[427] Since the Petrov affair, he was well known for his role as a double agent—Soviet and Australian—who later persuaded the Soviet diplomat to request asylum. The contacts between the Kafkas and Bialoguski became more frequent and cordial. For instance, they visited his home on the July 30, 1953, and he was invited to their home two days later.[428] On September 30, 1953, Kafka together with Antonov went to a party at Bialoguski's home to help raise funds for the NSW Peace Council. Kafka often met Soviet agents covered by diplomatic immunity as employees of the Soviet embassy. For example, he was in contact with Victor Antonov, the TASS and MVD operator, in 1952, on the twenty-seventh of February, the seventh and eighth of November, the sixth and twelfth of December; in 1953, the nineth of January, the twenty-second of February, the third and thirtieth of May, the thirtieth of June, the thirty-first of July, the first, fourteenth, and thirtieth of August, and

422   AA, A6119/90, item 2468, Kafka Vol. 7, f. 12.
423   AA, A6119/90, item 2462, Kafka Vol. 1, ff. 48–50.
424   Ibid., f. 32.
425   Ibid., f. 149.
426   Ibid., f. 151.
427   Ibid., f. 153.
428   AA, A6119/90, item 2463, Kafka Vol. 2, f. 40.

the twelfth December. In February 1954, Kafka and Antonov took a trip together to Newcastle.[429]

In the same period, Kafka continued to meet other Soviet officials, especially Vladimir Petrov who became close to him and for whom Kafka occasionally provided special services. He met Petrov as often as Antonov. A secret source reported that on the occasion of a film showing organized by Kafka on December 6, 1952, "Petrov and Kafka were talking together for a considerable time in another room of Kafka's home."[430] The Czechoslovak acting consul general provided Petrov with a Czech camera that the Soviet agent-diplomat requested and with two Czech photographic enlargers.[431] Kafka himself was observed on June 11, 1953, in Darwin taking "about eight photographs of the RAAF Air Radio Section and the D.C.A. Radio Control Tower at the Airport."[432] A source related that on March 14, 1953, "Petrov was again enquiring about passport blanks." Petrov hoped to pick them up at Kafka's party on March 28, 1953.[433]

After his defection, Petrov told the ASIO's agent Richards that he met most of his Australian contacts at Kafka's home. For example, in May 1952, he met Charles Bresland (code name COOK), who was supposed to "pick out special students in the Sydney and Canberra

---

429 AA, A6119/90, item 2468, Kafka Vo. 7, ff. 516, 8, 18, 19, 21, 22, 24 and 25

430 Ibid., f. 18. On January 19, 1953, Kafka sent a letter to the Ministry of Information and Culture in Prague reporting his successful "Film Propagation in Australia." On the same day of Petrov's long talk with Kafka, the Czech film *Přehrada* ("*The Dam*") was shown. The film was based on a propagandist novel by Marie Majerová in which workers stage a revolution in order to seize power from a democratic-capitalist government. It was well chosen for an audience of "several general secretaries of progressive trade unions, members of the CPA CC, Peace Councils of Australia and editors of the Communist paper *Tribune*." It was an instructive film. Kafka praised another film very popular with Australian clubs, *Vánoční sen* (Christmas Dream). He wrote, "Thanks to this film and plum brandy the local censor is well-disposed to us." Kafka also stressed that the CPA intensively used Czech films during its election campaign.

431 AA, A6119/90, item 2468, Kafka Vol. 7, ff. 12, 17, 107.

432 AA, A6119/90, item 2462, Kafka vol. 1, f. 124.

433 Ibid., f. 102.

Universities" to be sent to the Soviet Union to the Komsomol Congress. Bresland, as the head of Eureka Youth League, selected himself and another student identified only as Bocquet. Petrov gave each three hundred pounds toward their fares through China and handed them passports. (He needed passport blanks from Kafka.)[434]

At Kafka's home, Petrov also met Communist officials Sharkey, Dixon, Chandler, Maher, Henry, and Blake. He stated, "I have met them conspiratorially. I have not met Chandler in a conspiratorial way."[435] Clearly, one of Kafka's functions was to act as a facilitator, introducing important contacts to Petrov. Since I have found no recent file on Kafka in the archive of the Ministry of the Interior in Prague,[436] it is probable that he worked directly for Soviet secret services.

Petrov also met Clive Evatt, chief of the Australia-Russia Society, at one of Kafka's receptions in order to "build up a network."[437] At receptions held at the home of Kafka, Petrov kept meeting Rex Chiplin, who according to Pakhomov was an agent with the code name CHARLIE.[438] Pakhomov usually met Chiplin at his office at the Communist paper *Tribune*, since he "was instructed [by Moscow] to reduce to a minimum his meetings with Chiplin in the press gallery and other places and should only accept information from him in fully advantageous conditions." To Richard's question "Is Chiplin still active as an agent?" on April 13, 1954, Petrov answered, "Yes."[439]

The close association of the Soviet "temporary resident" of Soviet intelligence in Australia, Vladimir Petrov, and the Czechoslovak consul general in Sydney, Jaroslav Kafka, ended in 1954 when Petrov defected. Kafka left for New Zealand soon after to serve as acting consul general in Wellington.

---

434 AA, A6119/90, item 2463, Kafka Vol. 2, ff. 1, 9, 10.
435 Ibid., f. 2.
436 Private information from Patrick Virkner who in July 1998 was put in charge of a new special file on "Collaboration of Australian Communists with the Czechoslovak Regime in the ČSR in the Fifties," founded in order to facilitate my research by the "Office for Documentation and Investigation of Communist Crimes" at the Ministry of the Interior of the Czech Republic in Prague. (Later closed down.)
437 AA, A6119/90, item 2463, Kafka Vol. 2, f. 3.
438 Ibid., f. 19.
439 Ibid., f. 18.

On July 30, 1954, Kafka and his family boarded the RMS *Monowai* to occupy first class cabins 159 and 160. They took with them "a Škoda car and a considerable amount of heavy baggage."[440] The Communist businessman Alfred White gave Kafka a farewell party on July seventeenth and was observed in their cabin among a large group of well-wishers who used to meet with Kafka, often when he was acting consul general in Sydney. Emanuel Victor Elliot, his wife Valens, Josef Tříska, the lawyer S. I. Conway, and Della Nicholas were among those present.[441] The same people would welcome the Kafkas back in a year on the fourth of July and bid them farewell on the nineth when the Czech family left for Genoa on a month long voyage, occupying first class births 1920 and 1921. [442]

Kafka's work in Australia was considered satisfactory in both Prague and Moscow. In 1959, he returned to Australia for several more years as full consul general. Interestingly, he came back when the Soviet Union ended its boycott began as punishment of Australia for having instigated the defection of Petrov and his wife in the dramatic scene at Darwin airport.

440   AA, A6119/90, item 2462, Kafka Vol. 1, f. 226.
441   Ibid., ff. 227-28.
442   AA, A6119/90, item 2463, Kafka Vol. 2, ff. 43 and 48–50.

7

Political Use Of Australian Writers

According to Karl Marx's prophesy, history will bring about the proletarians' victory over bourgeois capitalists. Lenin decided that workers could never do it on their own, so he added the necessary group of political manipulators, the so-called avant-garde of the proletariat, the Communist Party. When in the twenties it became obvious that even that was not enough to guarantee an expected world revolution, Willy Münzenberg proclaimed, "We must organize the intellectuals": The revolution *needed* middle-class opinion makers—artists, journalists, "people of good will," novelists, actors, playwrights ... *humanists*, people whose innocent sensitivities weren't yet cauterized to nervelessness by the genuine white-hot radical steel.[443]

From the thirties on, a capable international cabal of Communist controllers devoted itself to winning over and inspiring prominent writers, actors, journalists, professors, and artists to support "good causes" selected by Soviet secret services that would help to destroy the image and defenses of the West, while at the same time enhancing the popularity of the Soviet Union and its satellites. It was a tricky and delicate enterprise that involved flattering influential people, inviting them to the Communist countries, preparing huge banquets for them, treating them to the best amenities, and taking them on sightseeing tours to carefully selected places where well-trained specialists would approach them "spontaneously," praising the benefits of Communism.

---

443 Stephen Koch, *Double Lives: Spies and Writers in the Secret Soviet War of Ideals Against the West* (New York: Free Press, 1994), p. 19.

It was very costly but worked beautifully. Many Western intellectuals were duped into believing and further spreading the Big Lie.

Australian writers participated in this worldwide stratagem. Documentation of their seduction and voluntary propagation of Communist myths was preserved in Moscow in the state literary archive. Peter Coleman reported on the following examples:

> Katherine Susannah Prichard not only helped to organize an efficient spy ring around Walter Seddon Clayton in the forties[444] but also was paid a life-long retainer by the Soviets. Dymphna Cusack and her husband were well treated all over the Communist bloc. She received generous "royalties" for her plays produced there and expressed pride when they were given "a brick from the then newly erected Berlin Wall." Alan Marshall was charmed by the Russian edition of his *I Can Jump Puddles*. Frank Hardy and Judah Waten were treated to free trips to the Soviet Union "with good hotels, chauffeured cars, splendid banquets (there were so many visitors in the 1960s that Judah Waten called it 'the Australian invasion.')" Dorothy Hewett, in addition to such services, received "free medical treatment in Soviet sanitarium." They repaid their KGB benefactors by dispensing Soviet propaganda so long as they themselves believed it. Hewett and Hardy later ridiculed their own previous enthusiasm.[445]

My research in recently opened Prague archives complements Coleman's findings in Moscow.

In 1951, Frank Hardy visited Czechoslovakia. During his stay, the Czechoslovak Ministry of Information prepared twelve pages documenting his visit and its political use. According to this source:

> Frank Hardy, foremost progressive Australian writer, visited Prague with his wife on the 5th September together with a part of the Australian delegation to the Festival of Youth in Berlin. He was scheduled to

444   Desmond Ball and David Horner, *Breaking the Codes: Australia's KGB Network, 1944–1950* (St. Leonards, NSW: Allen & Unwin, 1998), pp. 233–40 and passim.

445   Peter Coleman, "Stalin's Literati" and "Turning from Stalin," *Courier-Mail*, 29 August and 5 September 1998, pp. 28 and 28.

travel to the Soviet Union, but the Soviet Embassy in Prague did not have any communication from Moscow. The Czechs helpfully extended his entry visa by eight days. The Hardys departed for Moscow on the fifteenth and were invited back for two weeks as official guests.

On November second, Hardy returned to Prague alone. He was invited to spend a few days at the castle in Dobříš which was given by the government to writers who were willing to sing the praises of the government. Many Czech writers (especially Catholics) were then political prisoners, condemned on trumped-up charges, spending twenty or more years in jail.

Hardy met several Czech official writers and "enjoyed his stay in Dobříš … he used it for working on the collections of material that he picked up in the Soviet Union and in Poland." On the fifth of November, he returned to Prague and was put up in the luxurious Hotel Paris.

He visited a state literary agency and discussed the problem of payments for two tons of paper for publication of his books in Australia. There was no problem, as long as he was willing to serve the Communist cause.

Hardy went to a prison in Pankrác where he wanted to see a room where executions took place and the cell in which the Communist journalist Fučík had been incarcerated by the Germans during the war. "He needed it for his work devoted to Fučík."

Fučík was a leader of the Communist Party underground during the Nazi occupation. After the war, the party made a hero of him, claiming that in spite of horrific tortures, he refused to reveal anything to the Nazi interrogators. A book published in many languages was supposedly written by this phony hero in prison and smuggled out. Gradually, it became known that to avoid torture, Fučík revealed everything that he knew about the underground organization. On walks in Prague, accompanied by his Nazi friend, he was used as an agent provocateur for compromising unsuspecting comrades. The book was written mostly by his wife after the war.

Hardy also wanted to talk to some prisoners. Two officers accompanied him while he interrogated three inmates. Naturally, they knew the terrible consequences if they dared to complain. Since Hardy knew no Czech, the officers in translating the prisoners' words could say anything they wanted. Hardy was very much impressed by "the willingness and love of those two members of the Ministry of the Interior which they devoted to their work." The writer of this document also stressed that Hardy "departed with a very positive impression because this way he could practically verify the principles of re-education of criminals as we suggested to him in previous discussion."

On November 7, 1951 a press conference with Hardy was organized in the club of the journalists. Of course, only state journalists could use the paper provided by the government to write on, as Manning Clark once stated would be the case in Australia when the pro-Communist dreamers came to power.

Frank Hardy was welcomed with open arms when he wanted to discuss publication of his work in Czech translation. The remaining details of the printing of *Power Without Glory* were debated. He promised to send to the publishers his collection about Henry Lawson and a selection of revolutionary Australian stories and poetry, three manuscripts, and six books of various novels from Australian literature. In the future, he would send all his work for translation into Czechoslovakia. The man in charge of Hardy's visit was enthusiastic about the prospect of publications of Australian revolutionary literature and about the life of Australian workers. Hardy, of course, was happy about the money and fame he would get.

The departure for London led to this comment by his hosts: "Frank Hardy, in spite of the shortness of his stay in Czechoslovakia, was very much used politically."

According to a financial statement at the end of the report, the visit cost the Ministry twenty thousand Czech crowns. In addition, Hardy carried much more luggage than was allowed. It was necessary to pay for 1,700 Czech crowns worth of British pounds for the extra weight. The state bank refused to release so much precious foreign exchange. Interestingly, in spite of the opposition by the state bank, the government decided to pay it anyway, as the report says, "because Hardy was very well used politically."[446]

Another series of documents found in the Prague archives concerned Australian writers Dymphna Cusack and her husband Norman Freehill.

---

446 CzMFA, 129601/5/1959.

On December 15, 1959, the director of the Czechoslovak Ministry of Education and Culture, M. Hudeček, wrote to the Australian Department of the Ministry of Foreign Affairs in Prague that it was not willing to receive these two writers as official guests, but that the Writers' Union should take care of them in February 1960. The letter included four pages of information on both writers taken from a longer communication obtained from the Czechoslovak embassy in Tirana where both writers lived as guests of the Albanian government for four and a half months. They also enjoyed hospitality for the same duration from the East German Communists, as well as two years in China and unspecified lengths of time in Hungary, Poland, and the Soviet Union. Comrade Freehill was in Czechoslovakia for the third time.

Two Czech writers reported later that Freehill offered himself as an agent. He approached the writer Petr Pujman, son of the celebrated Czech Communist writer Marie Pujmanová. At that time Pujman acted as international secretary of the Czechoslovak Writers' Union. Freehill, thinking that Pujman was an agent of the secret police, told him that he would be submitting reports on his discussions with Czech writers who trusted him as an Australian and were not afraid to talk freely with him. He asked Pujman if he should deliver his reports to him or someone in the Ministry of the Interior (police).[447]

The pages received from Tirana highly praised the Communist-oriented novels and plays of Dymphna Cusack. It was stressed that her work was widely published in Communist countries and that she often appeared on Australian television. Her articles from China and other Red countries found their way not only into both Communist and non-Communist publications, but were also covered by the Australian Broadcast Company (ABC). Both authors, according to the report, were very active in the peace appeals, peace movement, and peace congresses organized by the party between 1950 and 1959.[448]

447 "Among the more offensive reports in the Moscow archive are the reports of Norman Freehill, Dymphan Cusack's husband. He kept Krugerskaya informed (and through her, the KGB) of the 'deviations' of both Australian and Soviet writers." Peter Coleman, "Memento Moscow," *The Weekend Australian*, Review, 16–17 January 1999, p. 10.
448 SCA, 122.144, 125.499 and 126.442/ all IV/5, 1951. In October 1951, another fighter for the Soviet peace, Rev. Bill Hartley, vice chairman of the Australian Council for the Defense of World Peace, requested a similar favor as Frank Hardy. He wanted to visit some

Obviously, both writers were also exploited politically. Their hosts knew how to flatter and reward them financially, along with extended hospitality for services rendered. It is interesting that in spite of the outstanding help provided to the Communist cause by Cusack and Freehill, the Ministry of Education and Culture was not itself willing to host them—a much higher honor they had offered the previous year to a much-less-published author, Manning Clark. The then completely unknown editor of some local historical documents was considered to be much more important than a world famous writer.

"disciplinary educational camp" in order to refute his government's inflammatory propaganda comparing this educational institution existing in all People's Democracies with Nazi concentration camps. After his return from a Peace Congress and a few days in Prague on his way to Australia, he would address miners and workers concerning his experience. Well-known Communist "poet" and party activist, Ivo Fleischman, acting as director of the department IV/5 (cultural contacts), wrote in his recommendation that their own contact officer would serve as interpreter and, therefore, "we think that the matter is for us tolerable enough to agree to the request." SCA, 124.191/51-IV/5, 26. 10. 1951. Dymphna Cusack enjoyed her stay at the Dobrís Castle and from there wrote to Petr Pujman that in such a lovely prace propaganda in her writings takes precedence from truth. AMFA, Fond TO-O, 1945-59 Australie, kr. 2, sl. Zajezdy 1958-59, c.j. 130838.

8

Miloslav Jandik: Czechoslovak Consul General In Sydney, 1954– 1959

A few noticeable circumstances accompanied the appointment and arrival of the new Czechoslovak consular representative to Australia. At the end of 1953, the acting consul general, Jaroslav Kafka, told Mr. Stuart, head of the protocol, Department of Foreign Affairs, that he would stay approximately six months to complete the handover. However, he left for Wellington, New Zealand two months later. The establishment of the Royal Commission on Espionage had a lot to do with it.

He also said, "I do not anticipate any increase of consular staff," only a small expansion in the commercial staff.[449] That proved to be the case, except the expansion was not at all small. Commercial staff acted as secret agents and spies. In Prague, Dr. Karel Kaplan, prominent historian of the Communist takeover of Czechoslovakia and author of many books on the criminal proceedings that followed, confirmed what had been long suspected, that all such diplomats worked with special assignments of undercover activities for the Czechoslovak and Soviet spy networks. (Kaplan began his career as a young devoted Communist apparatchik, helping to collectivize independent farmers. As a trusted comrade of worker's origin he was given access to party secret archives when it was decided to review the history of Stalinist show-trials of the fifties. He was horrified by the facts he discovered

---

449   AA, A6119/90, 2469, Jandik Vo. 1, f. 19.

and became a historian of the crimes committed, as he put it, by a gang of criminals.)[450]

Miloslav (sometimes spelled in documents as Miroslav) Jandík came to Australia as a Czechoslovak secret police agent. His code name was KUČERA. He signed up as an informer on April 27, 1954 and was told that he should depend on Soviet comrades.[451] (According to the Ministry of the Interior archival files, he continued working for the secret police until January 1981, twenty years after he had left Sydney.)[452]

The consular staff was increased substantially. Australian authorities counted five more members. By January 1954, there were six, and by July, eleven. Instead of one vice-consul, there were now three plus the consul general. Instead of two commercial officers, there were three, and instead of three clerks, there were now four.[453] There is an obvious connection between the departure of Soviet diplomats (and agents) from Canberra and Sydney, who left in protest after the defection of the Petrovs[454] and the substantial increase of Czechoslovak diplomats (and agents).

On May 5, 1954, the "Esteemed Comrade Viliam Široký," the Czechoslovak prime minister, received a letter from the Ministry of Foreign Affairs informing him of plans for representation in Australia. It began: "Esteemed Comrade! In connection with the gross provocation by Australian authorities against the USSR that led to an interruption of diplomatic relations between USSR and Australia, I am submitting to you information about the state of mutual relations between the ČSR and Australia, especially concerning the staff of Czechoslovak consulates."

---

450   See pages devoted to Kaplan in my book *Fools and Heroes: The Changing Role of the Intellectuals in Czechoslovakia* (Oxford: Pergamon Press, 1980), pp. 39–41.

451   AMV, 40403, f. 19–22 and 25–26.

452   AMV, 40403/II workfile, f. 47–50.

453   AA, A6119/90, 2469, Jandik 1, f. 44.

454   Accrding to Christopher Andrew and Vasili Mitrokhin, *The Mitrokhin Archive II: The KGB and the World,* Vladimir Petrov was "the most senior Soviet defector since the Second World War." His wife Evdokia also acted as a Soviet spy (London: Allen Lane, 2005), pp. xxvii–xxviii. Jaroslav Kafka, Zdeněk Žižka, and Comrade Popelka knew Petrov very well and cooperated with him as spies before his defection.

The letter enumerated nine employees and said that "for the year 1954 we plan a staff of thirteen. Another consulate will be created in Melbourne with a staff of five in addition to the Sydney personnel." That means that the number of Czechoslovak diplomats (agents) would double in order to replace the missing Soviet delegates. The official dispatch also stipulated, "In Australia besides the ČSR (and until recently also the USSR) no other people's democracy has any diplomatic nor consular representation."

The attention of the prime minister was called to the "most numerous group of post-February emigrants (over 12,000 people)." The writer claimed that Czechoslovak emigrants were "recruited" in Western Germany. "A group of Czechoslovak post-February emigrants took an active part in provocative actions at the Sydney airport on the occasion of the departure of the Soviet citizen, wife of the former worker of the Soviet Embassy, Petrov." And so the letter ended as it began, blaming Australia for a "provocation" against the Soviet Union.[455]

Jandík arrived in Sydney on June 2, 1954 and assumed his duties on June tenth.[456] Australia did not have any diplomatic representation in Prague, so the large increase in the number of Czech and Slovak diplomats provoked some interest. The Australian *Daily Telegraph* of July 2, 1954 called attention to this lack of parity and expressed the obvious suspicion that the large number of Czechoslovak arrivals just a few weeks after the departure of Soviet diplomats amounted to a replacement of Communist agents by a new set of Communist agents. The independent fortnightly of Czechoslovaks in Australia, *Pacific*, quoted from the *Telegraph* that all the newly arrived comrades had diplomatic passports and immunity, even the typist. The consulate would have some fifteen employees when one includes local people settled in Australia, all known Communists.[457]

The Department of External Affairs in Canberra inquired about any possible objection to its granting visas to Jandík and his family, but was assured by both the ASIO and British embassy in Prague that there were no adverse records obtainable.[458]

---

455 AMFA, 410.620/54-ABO/3.
456 AA, A6119/90, 2469, Kafka 1, ff. 22 and 176.
457 AMFA, 415.879/54-AB0/3.
458 AA, A6119/90, 2469, Jandik 1, ff. 3, 5, 17.

Jandík was born on August 3, 1919 in Plzeň in Western Bohemia. His wife, Ludmila, was four years younger. Their son was born in 1948. Both of Jandík's parents were members of the CPCZ since its foundation. The consul had four years of real gymnasium (high school) and graduated from a business academy. He was employed by the credit bank at Škoda Works in Plzeň for eight years followed by a successful career as an official and director of nationalized coal and mining enterprises. Starting in June 1953, he was employed by the Ministry of Foreign Affairs in preparation for his diplomatic mission. His curriculum vitae claimed that he spoke Russian, German, French, and English, but Canberra officers Tange and Stuart noted that "his English was not very fluent and the conversation with Mr Tange was a limited one." Jandík repeated Kafka's line, agreed upon in Prague, that "his office was endeavoring to build up Czechoslovakia's export trade to Australia" and that was why so many new "experts" had to come.[459]

On the same plane that brought Jandík to Sydney was a new vice consul, Milan Jurza, ten years Jandik's junior, with his wife. In his memo to the principal section officer, B2, a travel officer reported that Jandík and Jurza "carried from the plane as diplomatic baggage a large brown sealed kit bag which contained what appeared to be a solid and very heavy metal object." Although other baggage was left unattended, "the kit bag was never left alone nor did they allow airport portage to handle it. It took two men to carry it." [460] From Prague documents we know that it was a new huge safe "for keeping secret and confidential papers."[461] Jandík drove a new Škoda car.[462] Later he replaced it with a fancier Mercedes.

On July 20, 1954, Jandík accompanied Kafka to Wellington to establish a new consulate. Jandík's responsibility as consul general extended to New Zealand, and Kafka would act as vice consul there.[463] Jandík left Sydney for Wellington again on the tenth of August.[464] In the meantime, on July 12, 1954, another Czechoslovak consulate was opened in Melbourne.

---

459   Ibid, f. 33.
460   Ibid., ff. 22–23.
461   AMV, 40403/0040, f. 26.
462   AA, A6119/90, 2469, Jandik 1, ff. 22–23.
463   Ibid., f. 42.
464   Ibid., f. 39.

I. Zdeněk Žižka (WILLIAM)

Zdeněk Žižka's mission and its history merit some attention. Zdeněk Žižka was previously sent by the Ministry of Foreign Trade to Sydney in March 1952, during Kafka's term as vice consul. In the middle of 1953, it was decided that Žižka would be sent to Melbourne. On July 1, 1955, the minister of foreign trade expressly stated in his letter to the deputy minister of foreign affairs that "the Ministry of Foreign Affairs would impose on Comrade Žižka only the most important tasks so that most of his working hours would be henceforth devoted to foreign trade commission."[465]

However, according to police files in Prague kept secret until recently, Zdeněk Žižka was really a secret agent sent to Australia by the Ministry of the Interior. (His file contains complaints that he was not effective, did not establish any important contacts, and "on top of it, was directed from Prague by letters that he mostly did not receive.")[466] He signed up as an agent on February 23, 1952 and was given the code name WILLIAM. His task was to inform on Czechoslovak refugees in Australia, search for informants among them, and report on uranium mines, their use, and also on other industrial plus military secrets.[467]

As was documented in another chapter, there is no mention in the Czech secret police files that Jaroslav Kafka might have worked directly for Soviet secret services. I was assured by the officials of the Prague Institute for the Investigation and Documentation of Communist Crimes that there are files that remain inaccessible even to them.

According to the letter quoted, at the beginning of 1954, Comrade Žižka requested his recall to the center for "pressing reasons." Although a new delegate was sent to Sydney by the Ministry of Foreign Affairs as his replacement, "relevant officers are informing us that the replacement for Comrade Žižka has not yet been cleared up." Obviously, the matter was bureaucratically complicated because three ministries were involved. The deputy minister of foreign affairs, "Esteemed Comrade Dr. G. Sekaninová-Čakrtová," was reminded that "besides the completely justified family considerations, a quick recall of Comrade

---

465 AMFA, 419.874, AB0/3.
466 AMV, 40046, f. 70.
467 AMV, 40046/4226, ff. 13–21 and AMV, 40046/020, ff. 27–28.

Žižka is urgent because of significant duties that would be entrusted to him in the center."[468]

Consul General Jandík (KUČERA) still had to request an action as late as October 31, 1955, when he set a message from Sydney explaining the urgency of Žižka's recall: "Poor health of the wife of Vice Consul Žižka was to a large degree caused by her longing for her children and that could seriously harm the functioning of the office in Melbourne. I request an approval for sending her back to the ČSR for good."

His plea was finally accepted.[469] Czechoslovak authorities, like other similar regimes, often kept family members, mainly children, of its representatives at home as a precautionary measure against the general tendency to use a foreign trip or a foreign assignment for defecting into exile. According to an evaluation by captain Hledík of the Czechoslovak secret police, however, not only Žižka's wife's homesickness was involved in his dismissal, but also his heavy drinking habits.[470] (Žižka was later sent to New Zealand and worked there as an agent from 1960 to 1961.)[471]

II. PEACEMAKER JOSEF HROMÁDKA

Still, before Žižka could return to Prague, one of the major tasks he had to fulfill, a task that conveniently straddled both foreign affairs and police interests, was to make a success of the mission of Professor Josef Hromádka to Melbourne and other major Australian cities.

Hromádka was a theologian belonging to the international group of evangelical Protestant preachers who believed that Communism was misunderstood and that it really strove to achieve a just, brotherly community of people who would rid themselves of greed and live happily ever after in friendship. At the beginning of February 1948, he wrote, "Even in the theological perspective socialism is closer to me than bourgeois democracy." After the establishment of the totalitarian Communist regime, he substituted his socialist faith for the reality of Communist dictatorship: "If today's work of socialist construction

---

468 AMFA, 419.874, AB0/3.
468 AMFA, 419.874, AB0/3.
469 AMFA, 424.274/55-AB0/3.
470 AMV, 40046/020, ff. 27–28.
471 Ibid., ff. 19–22 and 27–28.

collapsed, socialization would not stop, but would be carried on after a new catastrophe. Desperately would we then try to revive Klement Gottwald and Antonín Zápotocký."[472]

Gottwald and Zápotocký were venerated by the Party propagandists as enlightened "workers' presidents." Communist historian Karel Kaplan, who studied minutes of their party and government meetings, called them rather more appropriately "members of the gang of criminals" who were cynically sending their friends to the gallows.

Professor Hromádka landed at the Sydney airport on September 9, 1954. He was welcomed by Consul General Jandík.[473] Hromádka reached Melbourne the fifteenth of September, and until his departure for Perth six days later, Zdeněk Žižka was responsible for the success of his propaganda lecture tour. The professor was devoted to the Soviet peace movement and widely traveled praising the alleged Communist love of peace and damning the alleged Western capitalist preference for war. As were many others, he was duped by the false alternative spread by the Soviet Union and willingly served its cause. He, of course, believed that the peace-loving Communist states were threatened in their building of beneficial Communism by Western imperialism.

The top Soviet agent who defected to the West, Oleg Gordievsky, drew on his own experience inside the Soviet secret service to describe the mirage pursued with such vigor by Professor Hromádka and his many cohorts:

> The World Peace Council [was] the most important of the post-war Soviet front organizations.... Originally based in Paris, the WPC was expelled in 1951 for 'fifth column activities,' moved to Prague, then in 1954 to Vienna where it was banned by the Austrian government in 1957.... In fact, the WPC continued to operate in Vienna under a cover organization, the International Institute for Peace.... The WCP claimed to be funded by contributions from supporters— 'national peace committees' in almost every country.

472 Josef Smolik, *Josef. L. Hromáddka: 'Zivot a dílo*/Life and Work/, [Prague: Ekumenická ˇskola /Ecumemical School/, 1989, pp. 106 and 111.

473 AA, A6119/90, 2469, Jandik 1, f. 25.

> In reality, its funds came overwhelmingly from the
> Soviet Union which by the late 1970s was providing
> almost 50 million dollars a year. The WCP followed
> faithfully the line laid down by the International
> Department of the Soviet Communist Party's Central
> Committee, which coordinated the work of front
> organizations.... The peace campaigns ... were
> directed uniquely against the West.[474]

On September 30, 1954, in his capacity as Melbourne vice consul, Zdeněk Žižka sent a long report to the Ministry of Foreign Affairs in Prague. First, he stressed that the announced arrival of Professor Hromádka excited Czechoslovak migrant circles. They attempted to prevent his arrival and even sent a request to Prime Minister Menzies that he be refused a visa. Menzies did not respond, despite the fact that "the government did not welcome Hromádka's visit."

When the immigrants could not prevent his arrival, they at least tried to disrupt his speeches.[475] In contrast, the "progressive circles" became very much interested. They hoped to get from him a true account of life in socialist Czechoslovakia to compare with the bleak picture painted by the immigrants. Many people attended his addresses. Hromádka was able to finish his first speech in spite of disturbances created by the emigrants who were protected by the police rather than thrown out. The second public oration "was marked by such enormous attendance and such a reception as Melbourne had never experienced before."

According to Žižka, "his address was being interrupted all the time by applause of agreement." He estimated that some seven thousand people were present and only some five of them attempted to disturb the meeting at its start.

Žižka praised the police who took the violators of peace out of the hall so that "Professor Hromádka was able to explain the efforts of the Czechoslovak people to achieve peace in the whole world." Hromádka's popularization of that effort created much local interest

---

474 Christopher Andrew and Oleg Gordievsky, *KGB: The Inside Story of Its Operations from Lenin to Gorbachev* (London: Hodder & Stoughton, 1990), pp. 419–21.

475 AMFA, 419.378, ABO.

in the ČSR. Many people came to the consulate asking for literature on Czechoslovakia. Most of them were students. (Did progressive professors use the occasion to request essays from their students on Communism and its love of peace?) Žižka was impressed by waterside workers from the Communist led trade union who created special personal bodyguards who never let Hromádka out of their sight and protection. With this letter were included thirty clippings from Australian newspapers.[476]

It clearly was an occasion for the usual misuse of genuine ideals for subversive propaganda. The whole Leninist experience was from the beginning based on such fraudulent misuse of positive sentiments and values.

In the executive group of the Peace Council were these prominent Australians: Reverend Ald Dickie, Reverend Frank Hartley, Reverend Vic James of the Unitarian Church, John Rogers of the Australia-Soviet House, Alec Robertson, editor of *Tribune* (a Communist paper), and Ian Turner. Jim Cairns was close to the council, as was the Presbyterian Gwyn Miller. The Soviet peace movement was very attractive to Protestant churchmen and to extreme Left-wing intellectuals. It worked as intended.

In February 1956, Professor Hromádka came to Australia again, this time to take part in another Soviet front organization, the World Council of Churches. He was a member of its action committee.

III. MYSTERIOUS FLIGHTS

The Australian archive in Canberra contains hundreds of documents sent to the ASIO by its agents or contacts who were busy observing the movements of the large number of Czechoslovak diplomats, especially Consul General Miloslav Jandík. They noticed that he regularly traveled to Jakarta, Indonesia, for a few days before returning to Sydney. Such short visits took place in May and June 1955, for example. During Jandík's vacation spent in Prague, Bedřich Hála traveled to Jakarta in June 1956, and after his return to Sydney, Jandík again flew in February and November 1957.[477] One telegram sent to the Australian

---

476   Ibid.
477   AA, A6119/90, 2469, Jandik 1, f. 62.

embassy in Jakarta suggested that "it would be helpful if you could throw any light on the purpose of these visits."[478] A report on telephone conversations remarked that Jandík sometimes canceled planned trips to New Zealand "at very short notice" in order to fly to Jakarta. The duration of his stay in Indonesia was always very brief.[479] The ASIO suggested that his visits to Jakarta might coincide with the arrival there of Czechoslovak or Soviet couriers. It was "noticed that when Jandík departs either for Jakarta or New Zealand, he carries only a brown crocodile leather briefcase. When he returns, it is well filled."[480]

Jandík flew regularly to New Zealand (e.g., in May, June, and August 1955, after the inaugural flight in August 1954, and again in October and December 1956). He might have been attending not only the Czechoslovak consulate, but also the Soviet embassy in Wellington.

A secret report from the Australian embassy in Jakarta informed the Department of External Affairs that a new trade agreement between Prague and Jakarta was being negotiated, including substantial credits for machinery imports. From a later revelation by defecting secret agents, it is now known that the machinery was in fact a large quantity of armaments of both Czech and Soviet manufacture. An ASIO memorandum of January 17, 1958 observed that "it is probably correct to assume that the visits of Hála and Jandík (approximately four every year) to Jakarta are timed to coincide with the visits of Czech couriers." Local Communist leaders were also suggested as possible contacts.[481]

Frequent cancellation of booked flights and fresh bookings soon after also characterized Jandík's three month family vacations in the ČSR. The consulate had problems with constant changes of plans.

478 Ibid., f. 64.
479 Ibid., f. 83.
480 Ibid., f. 65.
481 AA, A6119/90, 2470, Jandik 2, f. 37. From 1955 on, following Soviet advice, Czechoslovakia began to deliver large quantities of imported Soviet and Czechoslovak armaments, and aircraft to Indonesia. Former major of the Ministry of the Interior, Ladislav Bittman, described it in his book *Špionážní oprátky* /Espionage Gallows/ (Prague: Mladá fronta, 1992). The otherwise carefully prepared coup probably failed because of disagreements and competion between the pro-Soviet faction on one side and the pro-Maoist faction on the other, as well as by the incomplete assassination of all the Indonesian generals.

Jandík was singled out in a secret report by comrade Eduard Bílek entitled "Evaluation of the activities of the General Consulate in the first half of 1954." Bílek states, "In the present situation, Consul General Jandík is forced to spend a large part of his working hours coding and decoding dispatches at the expense of intelligence service and other business." This evaluation also emphasized that it was important "to judge if social contacts were properly exploited as a form of political agenda." In contrast to the usual aid consuls provide their citizens in a foreign country, the report called attention to the existence of some twelve thousand Czechoslovak immigrants and the need to supervise them. It was proposed that "the Consulate General should include in its working program the elaboration of a plan, as detailed as possible, on the activities of the emigration."[482]

Another time, a consular report acknowledged that "consulates do not have the right to establish contacts with their own countries by couriers," so comrade Pudlák was put in charge of the courier section of the Sydney consulate.[483] In another dispatch they admitted that by international law the Czechoslovak consulate was not allowed to code its messages. At least they knew what was illegal, even if they did not act accordingly. Consul General Jandík's grasp of the English language did not make much progress. On January 4, 1955, an ASIO report noted:

> He speaks very little English and his intelligence and cultural standard seem to be very low. It is extremely difficult to conduct business with him because of his limited capacities and lack of language, and consequently he appears to be unable to judge and decide for himself. Jandík is nominally the first employee of the delegation but all members are very secretive regarding their ranks.... Frequently, the person from the Embassy who is to be contacted in a business deal is changed. These occasions cause a great deal of difficulty, and the successor is apparently not informed of the details of the previous work.

482 AMFA, 413.757/55-ABO/3.
483 Ibid., 170.443/54 AB0/3, Annex 2.

The report also mentioned that "another Embassy employee, Mr. [Zdeněk] Toman, recently had his fourth car accident."[484]

IV. COMRADE POPELKA

It is well known that official titles of Soviet and their satellite secret agents had nothing to do with their real rank and function. Sometimes the embassy driver, or as in the case of Petrov, its second secretary, was its real boss, working for the espionage agencies. Therefore, the repeated claim that the large number of newly arrived representatives of the ČSR commercial attachés was due to the importance of mutual trade did not make much sense, since the mutual trade was relatively very small.

The case of Comrade Václav [his first name is almost never given] Popelka illustrates some of these points. The first mention of a so-far unnamed *resident agent* preparing himself for his role as a Czechoslovak leading secret agent in Australia can be found in a report from First Lieutenant Bohuslav Dub written on April 14, 1954. It dealt with his proposal to gain the clandestine cooperation of the future consul general in Australia, Miloslav Jandík, for serving as the medium for facilitating all the activities of the forthcoming *resident*. Jandík should be bound to the secret police and facilitate the agent's work. Interestingly enough, the future resident comrade Popelka knew him and together with comrade Jirásek recommended him as a dependable comrade.[485]

Four days later, Dub explained the situation and his duties to Jandík. Popelka would be his *subordinate*, but the ambassador would *depend on him* in all security measures. Jandík would call Popelka's attention to interesting cases and people he would be meeting. He would facilitate Popelka's actions against Czechoslovak exiles by lending him a car and giving him free time.[486]

Two years later, first Lieutenant Jílek complained in a memorandum of April 3, 1956 about Jandík's lack of cooperation. Comrade Popelka, the resident, contacted Jandík in May 1955 when the deal was supposed to start. Although Popelka had not sent his report yet, the

---

484   AA, A6119/90, 2469, Jandik 1, ff. 100 and 102.
485   AMV, 40403, f. 19.
486   Ibid., f. 25.

police interrogated its collaborators (agents) Svatoš and Plachý. They reported that Jandík did not create for Popelka the expected conditions for his work, so that he could not properly accomplish his mission.[487]

According to another report from June 25, 1956 on first lieutenant Jílek's meeting with Jandík, Prague received quite a bit of worthwhile information from Sydney about the uranium mine in Darwin, technological details of production, the most modern weapons, and contacts with Australian pro-Soviet officials (e.g., Dr. Herbert V. Evatt; the Russians praised the report on useful contacts with him). However, Jandík's assistance to comrade Popelka did not improve. When Popelka wanted to fly to Jakarta for mail from Prague, Jandík did not allow it. His explanation was rather facetious: "What if this lad (in Czech a scornful expression *kluk* was used) fell in the ocean! For that I cannot take responsibility." The important mail from the Prague secret police thus remained uncollected. Jandík insisted that he and Popelka had "good friendly relations," but he alone was responsible to the Ministry of Foreign Affairs for the office work, and therefore even for Popelka. Jílek said that Popelka had bought a new car, a Fiat. Jandík continued his report, "He is an honest and good comrade but too much *at ease* [in the original *lážo-plážo*]. He's not a *top dog* [*špička*] and could use more dash. His linguistic imperfection creates for him great problems. It makes it very difficult for him to talk with an Australian." In conclusion, First Lieutenant Jílek remarked that Jandík's relation to Popelka was more like that of a father to his son or of an older brother to a younger. He was not under Popelka's control as he should be. "The whole time, KUČERA did not realize that in the conspiratorial matters he was subordinate to Popelka and he should accept his orders.... He assumed that they were independent of each other and equal."[488]

The problem, of course, was in the original contract where it was stated that Popelka would be his *subordinate*, but that Jandík should *depend on him* in security matters. At the next meeting in the Prague café Slavia, on June 26, 1956 (reported on July fourth), Jílek again discussed this misunderstanding with Jandík at length and assured his superiors that everything was now clear to his interlocutor, but Jandík and Popelka's relationship and its influence on their spying was much on his mind. Accordingly, he mentioned that Jandík (KUČERA) did

487 AMV, 00403, ff. 8–9.
488 Ibid., ff. 11–14.

not want to talk about Popelka and always tried to change the subject. Finally, Jandík again opened up a little. Jílek reported that Jandík said:

> Australia is a hard drinking country, but one has to know how to do it. Popelka doesn't know how and at such moments does not control himself. He forgets our goal when he talks with a person we are interested in. Thus, for instance, there occurred a certain squabble between Žižka (WILLIAM) and Popelka when at a drinking session Popelka expressed himself negatively about KUČERA, and WILLIAM did not agree with it. Jandík does not know what it was all about, he does not care but is grieved by it. Another time, in a similar situation, he (Popelka) disclosed his mission in front of another commercial delegate (Svatoš).

Jandík repeated that Popelka did not know how to drink and should stop. "He is not a bad worker, he is only slow, everything takes him a long time to do."

Jílek again stressed that the best cover for secret work in Australia is the mask of a commercial delegate. The police did not pay much attention to them. However, Soviet delegates knew much better how to buy when prices were low. Czechs did it all wrong, buying when prices were high. "Thus we incur losses in millions."

At the end of his report, Jílek mentioned that Popelka was being attacked in the Australian press in connection with an effort by Soviet countries to encourage their emigrants to return home. Such written personal encouragement was often taken by the exiles as a threat to their relatives at home. "Even acts of violence occurred." The police appealed to immigrants to report any such visit by a "red spy."[489]

We know what really happened at the drinking session the ambassador was hesitant to talk about. Just how friendly the relations between Jandík and Popelka were can be discovered in another report about a meeting with Žižka (WILLIAM) on July 4, 1956. The critical part of the report begins with the obligatory statement that Žižka liked Popelka but continued in a different way: "Popelka does not control

---

489   Ibid., ff. 15–19.

what he is saying [in Czech "*nevidí si do huby a pouští si ji na špacír*"]. He should get some rest and *face the music* [*"dostat trochu do těla (spucunk)"*] and be punished. Everybody knows about his mission." Žižka did not like his contempt for other comrades. About Jandík, Popelka declared, "I will shit on that KUČERA. I will do him in." (In Czech "*Na toho já se vyseru, toho já odkrágluju.*")[490]

Another report on a meeting with KUČERA in the café Slavia on August 20, 1956 shows us what kind of fish was caught in their spying nets: "A certain Zoubek visits Popelka frequently. Popelka described him as a violin virtuoso and former conductor. He is a notorious drinker and half crazy. He would like to return home but is lacking funds and requests subsidy from the consulate. Popelka meets him very often but Jandík thinks that there is no hope for getting any solid work from him after his return home."[491] The Prague center suggested that the difficult relationship between Jandík and Popelka made it imperative to keep Popelka in Melbourne. From dispatches of November 15, 1957 and February 5, 1958 by Popelka from Australia, it seemed that it was definitely decided that Popelka would be superior to Jandík and give him orders, for instance to concentrate his attention on Sydney University.[492]

Comrade Popelka was recalled to Prague in the middle of 1958, and in the final evaluation of Jandík's mission in Australia, we can read that although he was bound to facilitate Popelka's work, he did not himself show any initiative.[493]

V. POLITICAL USE OF SOCIAL LIFE

Let us see how "social contacts" were being used, as mentioned previously, for "political work." In a report only recently made public on the "Evaluation of the activity of the Consulate General in Sydney and of the Consulate in Melbourne during the first half-year of 1955," "the use of films for propaganda purposes was praised as among the best by foreign offices." According to the Czechoslovak Foreign Institute,

---

490   AMV, 40046/II, ff. 71–73.
491   Ibid,, ff. 21.
492   Ibid.
493   Ibid., f. 34.

"the Consulate General devotes considerable attention to compatriots' circles [spying on them] and effectively is helping the progressive Czechoslovak Circle in Sydney [by influencing its annual elections of officials by its two own employees – old time settlers]." The Comrade Minister Sekaninová-Čakrtová sent them a coded letter with further instructions about improving their work among the compatriots-immigrants.[494] On April 10, 1956, Jandík and Mládek invited V. G. James, musical director of the ABC, for lunch. Mládek picked James up at his office.[495] On May 9, 1956, they invited James to a party at the Pickwick Club.[496]

Systematic care was taken of a few prominent trade unionists. On January 18, 1956, Jandík was entertained by several trade union leaders at the Trades Hall. He traveled from Sydney in the company of the federal secretary of the Seamens' Union, Eliot Valens Elliot: "They are spending a short holiday in Brisbane." Della Nicholas, who was living with Elliot, arranged a party for ten people, including Jandík and Eliot, who would bring a few bottles of beer.[497] The consulate discussed the screening of Australian trade union films in the ČSR with Edward Charles Roach from the Waterside Workers Federation. On the May 22, 1956, N. I. Levy from the Waterside Workers Federation was included in these talks, and they decided to send two films to Prague. Jandík would take them there. The third film, *Pensions for Veterans,* had to be completed within a week with music and dialogue. Czechoslovakia, of course, was not interested in films that would present Australia favorably.[498] Although E. V. Eliot already had two tickets for the Olympic Games, Jandík bought three additional tickets for Eliot's secretary, her husband, and niece. On the way through Sydney on December 10, 1956, they were invited by Jandík and went together.[499] "They were on a first name basis."[500]

A large reception was always organized by the consulate for the anniversary of the liberation of Prague by the Red Army on May 9,

494 AMFA, 420.885/55 –AB0/3.
495 AA, A6119/90, 2469, Jandik 1, ff. 100 and 102.
496 Ibid., f. 49.
497 Ibid., f. 89.
498 Ibid., f. 114.
499 Ibid., f. 123.
500 Ibid., f. 158.

1945.[501] (In fact, Prague was freed from the Germans by the anti-Soviet army of General Vlasov a few days before.) The eleventh anniversary was celebrated by two parties. In the afternoon, some 150 guests drank cocktails. That was for officials such as diplomats, university representatives, and the ABC, led by the program director, businessmen, and journalists. Czech food and Czech drinks were served. The more intimate reception then took place in the evening in the apartment of the consul general. In his report to his ministry in Prague, Jandík stressed that taking part were:

> First of all, general secretaries of trade unions, members of the CPA CC and representatives of progressive organisations. A special significance to the evening commemoration was given by the presence of Soviet and Chinese trade union delegations that became very popular in Australia. Upon their arrival, the cordial entertainment changed into a real demonstration of warmth between the Soviet, Chinese, Czechoslovak and Australian peoples. Serving of Czech meals and drinks considerably contributed to the evening's success.[502]

Australian archives in Canberra contain three reports to the ASIO about these two parties, twelve pages long altogether. It is interesting to compare them with Jandík's self-congratulating report. Yes, all the CPA leaders were present as well as several trade union secretaries: E. V. Eliot, Pat Clancy, Tom Wright, Jim Healy, and others. Rex Chiplin celebrated as well as Mr. and Mrs. Jack Barton. The Russian delegation arrived rather late, almost four hours after the party began. The consul general patiently waited for their arrival and only then, ten minutes before midnight, began to welcome the guests, many of whom had already left. The Chinese left soon after the first toasts, spending only fifteen minutes talking through an interpreter with Lance Sharkey and Jack Hughes. An incident occurred when "Jack Hughes in a drunken

---

501   Ibid., f. 209. See e.g., Peter Biskup, "Sergei and Nikolay: The Tale of Two victims of Stalinism," *Westerly,* Spring 1998, pp. 40–5, esp.p. 45 on.

502   AMFA, 41662/56/786/15 AB0-3.

condition was involved in a lengthy conversation with Frieda Brown."
Ted Rowe rebuked him and cutting remarks followed before Hughes
moved away. After the departure of the Russians, only some twenty
to twenty-five people remained. Sharkey became drunk very fast, and
"Hughes, J. B. Miles, Bert Williams, and a number of others exceeded
their capacity and were quite drunk and yet were reluctant to move
away from the bar area."[503] The difference between the consulate's
elevated picture of international revolutionary brotherhood and the
more realistic Australian description of a drunken melee is striking.

The Soviet trade union delegation was treated to a dinner between
the afternoon and evening parties in the Hotel Morris. E. V. Eliot,
Della Nicholas, and James Healy of the Waterside Workers Federation
also attended. After the dinner, they all went to the evening party.[504]

Even in the absence of documentary proof of spying, it is clear that
the influencing of Australian politics through monetary corruption
and the constant courting of important Communists and their
sympathizers was important. It strengthened the spirit of a common
international fight against the alleged enemies of progress and socialism.
The camaraderie, though often in a drunken stupor, of the elitist group
of outsiders committed to a revolutionary seizure of power was thus
systematically encouraged on the foreign soil of a sovereign country.

Rex Chiplin (Soviet code name CHARLIE), a journalist for the
Communist *Tribune* and constant Soviet spy contact since World War
II, collaborated very closely with Jandík (KUČERA). Chiplin called on
Jandík at the consulate on April 26, 1956[505] and May twenty-second of
the same year.[506] When Jandík, accompanied by his family and Bedřich
Hála's wife, departed from Sydney airport for Prague on May 26, 1956,
Rex Chiplin traveled with them.[507] He was going to meet Ian Milner
to consult with him about his reaction to revelations of the Royal
Commission on Espionage. "On departure Chiplin stated that he was

---

503   AA, A6119/90, 2468, Jandik 1, ff. 124–26 and 128–130.
504   Ibid., ff. 133–38.
505   Ibid., f. 111.
506   Ibid., f. 146.
507   Ibid., ff. 148, 152, and 163.

traveling on business and would be away from Australia for a period of about two weeks."[508] His airfare was paid by the Czechs.[509]

After his return to Sydney, Chiplin went to see Jandík on December 9, 1956, and six days later on the twenty-seventh when they were overheard calling each other by first names. On January 18, 1957, Tříska informed him that "the old man" wanted to see him. Other times, Chiplin called the consulate, asking to see Jandík, e.g., 2/15/ 1957, 5/21/1958, 11/21/1958. On the last day, Chiplin brought newspaper clippings to Jandík, and he came to see him again on December 19, 1958.[510]

Every year, the consul general with help of his employees Josef Tříska and Václav Mládek, facilitated the elections of suitable Communist leadership of the Czechoslovakian Club in Sydney. On September 8, 1956, Jandík addressed the annual meeting and "spoke about the wonderful progress being made in Czechoslovakia.... He also said that a Christmas present would be sent from Czechoslovakia ... to each of the members' children."[511]

Taking care of trade unionist leaders, on February 25, 1957, Jandík invited Jim (James) Healy of the Waterside Workers Federation, Comrade E. V. Eliot, and his wife Della Nicholas to dinner.[512] Healy was leaving Sydney for an international conference of transport workers in Hamburg, followed by a visit to the ČSR.[513] He had already stayed in Prague at the beginning of 1951. This time, the CZCP CC invited him for two weeks, and he remained between the seventeenth and twentieth of May and the fourth and fifteenth of June 1957. The interruption was caused by his attendance of a transport conference in Bucharest, Romania. Before coming to Prague, Healy visited Great Britain, Sweden, Norway, Denmark, Belgium, Holland, and East Germany, "mainly studying the situation and working conditions in transport." He traveled with his wife "who works for the Australian progressive movement." He had discussions with officials of the CZCP,

---

508 Ibid., f. 150.
509 Ibid., ff. 145, 156, and 161.
510 Ibid., ff. 176, 178, 185–87, 21|9| and 227. Also AA, A6119/90, Jandik 2, ff. 55, 54 and 56.
511 AA, A6119/90, 2469, Jandik 1, ff. 188–89.
512 Ibid., f. 229.
513 AMFA, 3603/57.

the trade unions, and the World Union Federation. They were taken sightseeing which included visits to several factories all around the country and workers' housing developments. Pilsen brewery and river ports in Bratislava and Komárno figured on the route. Two industrial and mining centers arranged discussions with the Healys "on the struggle of the CPA." Czechoslovak radio prepared an interview for its foreign broadcasting about their impressions of the country. Healy suggested visiting exchanges of Australian and Czech miners and founders. He also promised to send an article about the fight of Australian workers and unionists to be published in the Czech trade union press. According to this source, "They will use information about the building of our economy and social provisions as well as about the growth of the living standard of our workers during the last years, once they return to Australia."[514]

In 1961, Consul General Kafka requested from Minister Václav Kopecký that Healy should be again invited to the ČSSR. As a footnote to a report on the invitation, someone wrote by hand at the bottom, "According to a telegram from Sydney Consulate, Healy died."[515]

As a guest, Healy, of course, did not have to pay for anything. Sometimes even the airfares for the visitors were paid by the Czechs, as in the case of Victor George Goss. On May 28, 1957, the URO (Central Union Council) demanded that the Ministry of Finance pay for the flight of a "progressive trade unionist Victor George Goss, Australian citizen, who visited Czechoslovakia and was invited by Soviet union to visit the USSR." The director of the international department of URO, Edvin Chleboun, simply wrote, "Since the Comrade does not have any money to pay for his flight, we request permission to buy him a ticket." The price was 1,197 Czech crowns. Permission was granted the same day.[516]

Eleven days before that, Comrade Chleboun demanded from the VM-KSVB foreign department that another Australian citizen, Fanny Waten, born February 21, 1916 in Perth, WA, who arrived by invitation by URO to take part in a music festival, should stay, all expenses paid by the Czechs, in the ČSR as a student "in order to get

514   Ibid., 411/112/0260/549.
515   Ibid., 411/112/117.276.
516   Ibid., Fond TO-0, 1945-1959, 650.890.

acquainted with the Czechoslovak educational system and the life of our working people."[517]

The central organization of Czech unions had the adjective revolutionary in its title. A world revolution obviously was a costly business. Many Australian Left-wing enthusiasts knew where to turn for support and took advantage of it. Out of many such favors extended to Australian unionists, two should be mentioned: John Hadge King, secretary of the Australian Miners' Union, was treated to fourteen days at a cost of 1,810 Czech crowns. The same budget was allowed for the visit of Francis Henry Cockerill, secretary of the same union. Both were invited in December 1953 by the ÚRO secretariat.

In the absence of Soviet diplomatic representation, the Czechoslovak consul general took care of Russian scientific delegations when they flew to Australia for conferences. On October 13, 1953, six Russian agricultural specialists on their way from Manila to New Zealand landed at Sydney airport. Consul General Miloslav Jandík and Vice Consul Jiří Nováček picked them up and took them to a hotel.[518] Ten days later, two Russian scientists and an interpreter arrived to attend a UNESCO conference on Arid Regions in Canberra. Jandík took them to the airport and "remained with the party until they boarded the aircraft."[519]

Richard Dixon (Clifton Reginald Walker), president of the CPA, was sometimes in contact with Jandík, as on April 9, 1957 and June 23, 1959, when he had an appointment at the consulate.[520] However, Jandík's connection with Allan Dalziel was much closer. Jandík had dinner with him on February 25, 1959. Lidia Janovski booked them a table at All Nations Club for June 26, 1959, but Dalziel "reprimanded her" the next day because on the twenty-sixth, both "attended a function which caused considerable embarrassment to both." All three then met in Dalziel's office on July 1, 1959. On July fourteenth, Dalziel was informed by Jandík's wife that they would soon be leaving Australia and that his old friend Jaroslav Kafka would return to Sydney. On the day of the Jandíks's departure, July 31, 1959, Dalziel came

---

517 AMO, 822/57.

518 AA, A6119/90, 2469, Jandik 1, f. 197.

519 Ibid., f. 204.

520 AA, A6119/90, 2470, Jandik 2, ff. 8 and 78.

to the airport. A very large party was present to bid them farewell.[521] Probably the most conspiratorial friendship between two agents, code-named KUČERA and DENIS, continued after Jandík gave Dalziel his Prague telephone number, as is clear from an intercepted long-distance telephone conversation between Judah (Leon) Waten, Les Haylan, and Allan Dalziel on October 7, 1960, when "old Dal" discussed it with Waten, an old Communist ally.[522]

The departure of the Jandíks from Australia was not completely happy. The previous year, on July 8, 1958, Mrs. Libuše Hála, wife of the Czechoslovak vice consul, mentioned that Mrs. Jandík was unhappy about leaving their son behind when returning from their vacation in Czechoslovakia.[523] On June 3, 1959, "Mrs. Zofia Szeminska, wife of the late Polish Consul General, informed Mr. (sic) Marta Zielinska, that she had got rid of Mr. (Miloslav) Jandík, who, when he left her, was fairly drunk."

The Czechoslovak Club said good bye to Jandík on July 18, 1959 with a dance.[524] However, in Prague, his bosses in the Ministry of Foreign Affairs and especially those in the Ministry of the Interior, who had sent Miloslav Jandík (KUČERA) to act for three years as consul general in Sydney, were not content with his performance. They expected more from him. He was not willing to risk anything. His tasks were to safeguard the consulate from spies, to provide cover for Comrade Pavelka, the resident agent, and many other duties. He knew that he was being followed by the ASIO and did not want to harm his reputation as consul general.

He lived in disgrace for a few years in Prague, but in 1972, they co-opted him again. He was targeted at the embassy of the German Bundesrepublik in Prague. From 1975 until 1981, he was active in the embassy in Romania. His masters, again, were not happy with him. His information was coming only from official channels. The final verdict was negative: "In spite of his ability, he did not fulfill our expectations.... People did not like him for his self-seeking utilitarianism.... He becomes a pensioner."[525]

521 Ibid., ff. 61, 77, 78, 80, 82, and 69.
522 Ibid., f. 75.
523 Ibid., f. 47.
524 Ibid., ff. 61 and 7.
525 AMV, 40403/II.part of his working file, ff. 47–50.

CONCLUSION

Obviously, in spite of its sending to Australia several agents in various capacities and masks at the same time, Prague secret services had to cope with several serious problems. Language skills were poor. Distance from home and from children had a negative influence, especially on women. Men had problems with heavy drinking. Often they disliked each other, were unable to cooperate fruitfully, and their spying activities faced technical and managerial difficulties. Even when they could make useful contacts and discover military secrets, they did not follow through with them. That is all just as well, bascause their intentions, of course, were illegal and harmful to Australia.

9

Jaroslav Kafka: Czechoslovak Consul General In Sydney, 1959–1962

After four years in the Ministry of Foreign Affairs in Prague, Kafka was sent back to Australia to replace Miroslav Jandík as consul general on August 14, 1959. It was considered highly unusual for the same man to be reappointed to the same post in a higher function than previously. The regional director of the ASIO, H. C. Wright, noted: "Kafka's departure coincided with the Petrov[526] Affair; also, his return has been timed with the re-establishment of the U.S.S.R. Embassy in Canberra.... The official attitude is one of keen interest in KAFKA."[527]

It was also noted that Kafka had six officers in his trade section, in spite of the distance of the consulate from town, which was "something of an obstacle to an office properly concerned with the development of trade."[528]

A long review of Kafka's "Activities and Associates" called attention to the fact that "he was acquainted with identified cadre workers and

---

526 According to Christopher Andrew and Vasili Mitrokhin, *The Mitrokhin Archive II: The KGB and the World* (London: Allen Lane, 2005), pp. xxvii–xxviii, Vladimir Petrov was "the most senior defector since the Second World War." His wife Evdokia also acted as a Soviet spy (Ibid.). Jaroslav Kafka, comrade Václav Popelka, and Zdeněk Žižka all knew Petrov very well and before his defection used to cooperate with him closely.

527 AA, A6119/90, 2463, Kafka 2, f. 115.

528 Ibid.

collaborators of the Russian Intelligence Service and with leading members of the Communist Party of Australia." Five MVD cadre workers and collaborators were named: Pakhonov, Antonov, Galanin, Kovaliev, and Plaikais; as well as two CPA apparatchiks, known from Petrov and Venona cables by their code names COOK and CHARLIE, namely Charles Desmond Bresland and Rex Chiplin.

Following his return to Australia, Kafka resumed his close contact with the new set of Soviet diplomats-agents: the ambassador, Ivan Fedorovich Kurdiukov, "who has a background of intelligence activity in North Korea prior to 1948;" Ivan Fedorovich Skripov, "First Secretary, who has been identified ... as having been an Intelligence Officer between 1952 and 1957 when he was a Second Secretary in the Soviet Embassy in London;" and Ivan Efimovich Skarbovenko, second secretary, who "as Consul ... occupies a position similar to that held by Sadovnikov and Petrov, both of whom prior to 1954 were Residents in Australia of the M.V.D." The review concluded, "Kafka is an R.I.S. collaborator who has been schooled and trained in Russia."[529]

Colonel C. F. Spry in his secret report to "Dear B-" imputed, "Kafka is in a very favourable position to carry out intelligence activities."[530]

As we already know from our first chapter devoted to Kafka, he cultivated "leading trade union officials and members of the CPA. Among these were Healy, Elliot, Dixon, Blake, and Chandler." Businessmen who were often invited to his parties and to his home or restaurant meals included: Alfred White, Laurie Malco, and Cecil Holmes. Kafka's great interest in the Czech community in Sydney was noted as well as his close friendship with its secretary, Klobušiak.[531]

A SATELLITE?

Soon after his arrival in Sydney on August 18, 1959, Kafka traveled to Canberra to pay respects to the chief of protocol, Landale, and to the Soviet ambassador, Kurdiukov.[532] A journalist from the *Sun* met Kafka at a reception and found that "he was still smiling happily." When the

---

529   AA, A6119/90, 2464, Kafka 3, ff. 88–92.
530   AA, A6119/90, 2463, Kafka 2, f. 133.
531   Ibid., f. 86.
532   Ibid., f. 116.

journalist reminded Kafka of his departure after the establishment of the Petrov Commission and suggested that it was "unusual for a Soviet satellite to send back someone who was here when all that was blowing up," Kafka did not lose his diplomatic temper: "'A satellite?' he said, smiling gently. 'I do not regard my country as a satellite of anything. Would you call Australia a satellite of the United States?'"[533]

However, from some fourteen hundred folios of observations of Kafka's visits, parties and telephone conversations by Australian agents, it soon becomes apparent that Kafka was either an extremely helpful fellow to his friends or was regularly used by his Soviet masters as a subservient subordinate. He not only met them almost every week, offering them his apartment for overnight or for much longer stays, but made himself useful on many occasions. The Russians often requested his services when they could have used the telephone themselves or ordered their secretaries to make arrangements.

For instance, when a Russian scientist called Kafka and wanted to talk to him, he did not take a taxi to Kafka's home. Although the consul general was leaving the next day for a ten-day holiday in Queensland and told him that his time was very limited, Kafka drove to the university to pick him up.[534] When Pavel Fedorovich Safonov flew into Sydney on August 11, 1960, he called Kafka and "his man" met him with his car at the airport.[535] In July, Makarov and in October 1960 Safonov wanted to buy a Czech car. With Kafka's assistance, the normal price of £968 was reduced to £525.[536] For Safonov it went down to £325.[537] The Kafkas bought a knitting machine for I. S. Andriyenko.[538] Mrs. Kafka made an appointment for Mrs. Andriyenko to see a doctor.[539] In February 1961, Smirnov asked Kafka if the offer to take him and Tatiana Petrovna Nicolaeva to Kangaroo Valley still stood and "readily accepted Kafka's offer to give them a lift to the concert."[540]

---

533   "Back in Orbit, Mr Kafka," 18.8.1959.

534   AA, A6119/90, 2463, Kafka 2, ff. 178–79.

535   Ibid., f. 183.

536   Ibid., f. 170.

537   AA, A6119/90, Kafka 3, f. 58.

538   Ibid., f. 175.

539   Ibid., f. 182.

540   AA, A6119/90, 2465, Kafka 4, f. 33.

On February 16–17, 1961, "Smirnov made a request to Mr. (Jaroslav) Kafka … for a lift from the City…. Kafka arranged to pick him up at the Town Hall at 1915 hours."[541] Skripov called May 10, 1961 saying that he could not remember the address of the Polish consul general, and Kafka arranged to pick him up together with the Ambassador and take him there.[542] Kafka was present regularly at the airport for the arrivals and departures of Soviet ambassadors and other Soviet officials.[543] He booked seats for Mr. and Mrs. Andriyenko to see the film *Gone with the Wind* on September 28, 1961.[544] On October 26–27, 1961, Andriyenko asked Kafka to send his cleaner to Andriyenko's flat.[545] Four days later, Andriyenko called Kafka: "Listen, Jaroslav, could you tell the cleaner to go and clean the house there?" Kafka: "Good. Good."[546] Andriyenko: "Left a message at the home of Mrs. Vera Kafka asking for his things to be packed for him."[547] Mrs. Skripova informed Mrs. Kafka that her husband had a bad toothache and needed a dentist. The appointment was made by the Czech consul's wife.[548] On March 26, 1962, the Soviet ambassador "informed" Mrs Kafka that he and his wife would like to visit them. "Mrs. Kafka promised to arrange for her husband, Jaroslav Kafka, to pick the Kurdiukovs up at their hotel at 1100 hours."[549] A Soviet embassy official, Dorofeev, asked Mrs Kafka to ask her husband to find accommodation in Sydney for Kurdiukovs.[550] He did.[551] Mrs. Andriyenko requested the Czech consulate to arrange an appointment at the hairdresser.[552] Finally, Makarov entreated Kafka to send someone who spoke Russian to the airport to meet Mrs. Zimenkov. Kafka promised to go himself or to

---

541 Ibid., f. 37.
542 Ibid., f. 48.
543 Ibid., f. 185, and 2466, Kafka 5, ff. 5, 39, 44, 68.
544 Ibid., f. 85.
545 Ibid., f. 132.
546 Ibid., f. 138.
547 AA, A6119/90, 2467, Kafka 6, f. 29.
548 Ibid., f. 40.
549 Ibid., f. 96.
550 Ibid., f. 123.
551 Ibid., f. 128.
552 AA, A6119/90, 2468, Kafka 7, f. 65.

send Mr. Vodička to meet her. Makarov then asked Kafka to assist her with the customs declaration.[553]

Minor Secrets

In the hundreds of pages of documentation of Kafka's or his comrades' contacts with their Soviet counterparts at the consulate, only later in the files does one find more than just outside observations. Several pages that I was not allowed to see might be more interesting. The diplomats-agents ostensibly kept meeting for a swim, a picnic, or volleyball, but surely more was going on than meets the eye. On the telephone, knowing that they were being listened to, they often spoke in code.

Among the rare moments of undiplomatic pronouncements was Alexander Smirnov's statement that he regarded members of the embassy staff as "scoundrels." Both Smirnov and Varfolomeev agreed that "they are all the same, complaining about overwork."[554] When on January 14, 1961, Kafka answered Safonov's request to call him back, Safonov said, "Rung you just from boredom," but after a while, they discussed the Polish consul's, Zielinski, appeal for political asylum. He was due to go back to Poland. Safonov said, "Better without him (laugh)." Kafka added, "Prostitutes always love money." The Australian agent who listened to the conversation commented, "Kafka's Russian is very bad."[555]

One of the Czechoslovak consulate's employees, Jaroslav Šimek, was asked by a contact where Kafka was. Šimek said that he did not know, but "if you can find the beer, you will find Kafka. That's all he does."[556] The Polish defector, Dr. Zeilinski, had a different opinion when asked about Kafka: "He gave the impression of being a young man with great ambition." He also said that Kafka and the former Polish consul general, Czeslaw Kasprzek, "were very close to one another." Many folios in Canberra archives confirm this and that Kafka contacted Polish diplomats much more often than during his first term of duty in

---

Australia. Often Soviet officials while in Sydney met both the Czechs and the Poles; sometimes even the Yugoslav consul was present. But I did not find a single occasion when the Polish diplomats or their wives proffered similar services to the Russians as did the Czechs.

Soviet and Czech couriers took no more flights to Jakarta or New Zealand. They regularly delivered or picked up messages in Australia.[557] On one occasion, Australian secret services became worried about Kafka's attempts to cultivate "an officer of the Department of External Affairs." In March and April 1961, this unidentified officer—several folios were withdrawn—attended the International Conference on Diplomatic Contacts. Kafka tried to get personal and political information about him through Allan John Dalziel "who had been twice allotted code names by the R.I.S. as established by the Royal Commission on Espionage (1955)." Rex Chiplin and Rupert Lockwood were also approached concerning the same officer by the consulate's employee, Josef Tříska, at Kafka's instigation. The officer was warned "to be constantly on the alert for any signs of 'cultivation' and not to fail to report without delay anything at all about which he has the slightest suspicion."[558]

As was mentioned before, Kafka was helping the Soviet agents by acting as a facilitator, inviting their targets to his home for parties attended by the Russians. It seems highly probable that he was offering the same service to the Polish diplomats-agents. On December 13, 1961, Kafka informed the Polish consul general, Benedykt Polak, that "the two people whom he wished to introduce to Polak are not yet available as they have been busy with the Elections."[559] Previously, on April 7, 1961, Jaroslav Kafka and Czeslaw Kasprzak met for a meal in a restaurant (Rainauds) with Alan John Dalziel and Leslie Haylen; Dr. Evatt attended too.[560] Kafka and a Polish consul went several times to the CPA center at 40 Market Street, Sydney, to call on Lawrence Louis Sharkey or Laurence Aarons. They spoke while taking a walk around the block in order to avoid listening devices.[561]

---

557   AA, A6119/90, 2463, Kafka 2, ff. 158, 159, 161; 2464, Kafka 3, f. 75; 2465, Kafka 4, ff. 141, 150; 2468, Kafka 6, f. 90; 2469, Kafka 7, f. 98.
558   AA, A6119/90, 2465, Kafka 4, ff. 173 and 189.
559   AA, A6119/90, 2466, Kafka 5, f. 186.
560   AA, A6119/90, 2465, Kafka 4, ff. 73–74.
561   Ibid., f. 60.

Kafka had a very close relationship with Skripov, first secretary of the Soviet embassy. In February 1963, the Australian government declared Skripov *persona non grata*, and he had to leave the country. Kafka's relationship with the second secretary, Skarbovenko, went on unabated. Petrov reported that Skarbovenko was "highly trained in intelligence service."[562]

Receptions given by other states' consuls were handy occasions for useful encounters. On October 29, 1959 at a reception organized by the honourary consul of Turkey, Comrade Kafka talked at length with the German consul general, Brunhoffen, who showed warm feelings toward Czechoslovakia. "His wife in a particularly sharp way criticized the Nazis' actions during WWII." This part of the consul's report was in Prague heavily underlined by some official—the signature looked like Nový—at the Ministry of Foreign Affairs who added this remark: "In the third section it was registered for further documentation. 28.11.59."[563] I would guess that it was decided to contact the German consul general or his wife with a proposal of a closer cooperation with Czech secret services. Like some Australians mentioned elsewhere, they seemed to have been offering themselves as collaborators.

As if to confirm the suspicion that the Czechoslovak consulate was opened in Melbourne in July 1954 in order to allow several more Communist diplomats-agents to come to Australia and replace the missing Soviet intelligence officers, soon after the Soviet intelligence officers returned, the Czech Melbourne outpost was closed down. When the previous consul, spy Zdeněk Žižka (code name WILLIAM) returned to Prague, Eduard Bílek supplanted him. Bílek arrived in October 1956. After the difficulty with Žižka's wife missing her children, Bílek's child was able to accompany his mother.[564]

The Czechoslovak consulate in Melbourne had its part in the political use of social contacts as directed from Prague (and Moscow). For example, Vice Consul Bílek reported by an airletter to the Ministry of Foreign Affairs in Prague that he had arranged a three-hour dinner for March 6, 1959 for three leading members of the CPA and their wives. Another dinner lasting three hours was prepared for the chairman of the CPA in Victoria, J. F. Johnson, and his wife on April seventeenth.

---

562   AA, A6119/90, 2468 Kafka 7 f. 173.
563   CzMFA, 3481/59.
564   AA, A6119/90, 2469, Jandik 1, f. 194.

Three hours seemed to be the norm. On November 14, 1958, the workers of the CPA in Victoria were the guests of honor.[565]

On July 7, 1960, W. G. A. Landale, Department of External Affairs, recorded his conversation with Kafka who told him that his government had decided to temporarily close down its consulate in Melbourne. Eduard Bílek had been recalled to Prague. He mentioned two reasons for the closure other than the suspicion expressed above: the consulate in Melbourne interfered in trade projects initiated in Sydney, and Czechoslovak exports to Australia had not increased.[566] On July 15, 1960, the consulate was officially closed, and Vice Consul Bílek returned the service gun No. CZ 50, caliber 7.65 mm to Comrade Kafka.[567]

Kafka's reports to the Ministry of Foreign Affairs that I was able to see in Prague are a little more revealing than the ASIO's observations, though the vital intelligence and coded messages are missing. For instance, on October 5, 1959, the consul general mentioned a lunch to which he was invited by the Soviet ambassador, Comrade Kurdinkov. "On this occasion various pieces of information about this country were exchanged." On August twenty-sixth, the head of the mission arranged a lunch in the restaurant Bamboo for the councilor of the Soviet embassy, Comrade S. Safonov, and the Second Secretary Skarbovenkov. Comrade Šimek also took part. "During the lunch various experiences of this country were talked over," and on August twenty-ninth, Kafka and Vice Consul Šimek were invited to his apartment for a dinner by the secretary general of Waterside Workers, E. Elliot. "During the dinner the Australian trade union movement was discussed."[568]

On November 11, 1959, Vice Consul Comrade Lukáš prepared an evening meal for the Polish Consul Zielinsky. Consul General Kafka and his wife took part and reported to Prague: "Constantly we have been trying to improve relations with the Polish representatives in Sydney without success; Soviet comrades have the same experiences."[569] The situation changed after Zielinsky's defection. On November 23, 1959,

---

565   CzMFA, 1115/59-Bi, 1187/59-Bi and 639/58.
566   AA, A6119/90, 2463, Kafka 2, f. 166.
567   AA, A1838/1, 1515/1/10/17.
568   AMFA, 3329/59.
569   Ibid., 3593/59.

Kafka invited the chairman of the CPA, Dixon, and his wife for dinner. "The evening was used for a friendly private interview."[570]

The message sent by a courier on February 29, 1960 was more informative about the previous day's stay at the weekend house of the former deputy and minister Clive Evatt: "He is still very well informed about the political events in Australia. We discussed the situation and diverse trends in the Australian Labor Party."[571]

COURTSHIP OF TRADE UNIONS

Leading trade unionists were cultivated with special care. In his regular review of social contacts Kafka reported to his ministry by a courier:

> On January, 29, 1960 in the residence of the head of the office, a reception was organized for important representatives of the Australian trade union movement. These were the main guests: General Secretary of the Waterside Workers' Federation, J. Healy; General Secretary of the Rolling Mill Workers, T. Wright; General Secretary of Boiler Workers, H. Grant; General Secretary of the Seamen's Union, E. Elliot; Secretary of the Building Workers' Union, P. Clancy; President of Building Workers' Union, F. Sullivan; General Secretary of Welders' Union, T. Rowe; correspondent of *Questions of Peace and Socialism*, E. Thornton; writer F. Hardy; General Secretary of Miners, E. Ross; and Editor of the *Tribune*, W. Brown, who just returned from his trip to the Soviet Union and the ČSR. Altogether, forty-four guests were present as well as nine employees of the Consulate. The aim of the evening was to strengthen mutual bonds and thus facilitate eventual future concrete requests.... For the event thirty pounds were spent and out of our stock for representation we used

---

570   Ibid.
571   AMFA, 2259/60.

42 bottles of Australian wine, 8 bottles of whisky and 200 cigarettes.[572]

The green tree of revolution obviously must be well taken care of to prosper and bear fruit. Special attention was paid to the general secretary of the Seamen's Union, E. Elliot. On September 30, 1960, he was invited to dinner together with Dalziel, the secretary of Les Haylen, general secretary of the Rolling Mill Workers, former councilman of Sydney, T. Wright, as well as Conwey, a lawyer.[573] Elliot treated the Kafkas to a dinner on January 10, 1961. "During the evening we talked about the problems of the trade union movement and it was decided to invite some eminent reformist unionists to a reception in our residence."[574]

Not all discussions were productive, but important confidential information could be transmitted to the Czechoslovak Foreign Ministry. An airmail letter was sent from Sydney on November 10, 1961, reached the ministry on the twenty-first, and took two hours and fifteen minutes to decode that evening:

STRICTLY SECRET! COPYING FORBIDDEN! For the CPCZ CC. Member of the CPA CC, General Secretary of the Seamen's Union, Elliot, told me that the Australian Party is very dissatisfied with the progress of the 22nd Congress of the CPSU. In their opinion constant references to mistakes committed in the past put weapons into the hands of the reaction. The activity of the Party is thus targeted to explaining history and the march forward is slowed. However, he emphasised that the Australian Party is conscious of the necessity to keep a fighting unity and will never allow her disagreement with the congress line to break through to the public. Kafka 87. For the coder. Tell me what table to use for contact with Wellington.[575]

572   Ibid., 2120/60.
573   Ibid., 3230/60.
574   Ibid., 2038/61.
575   Ibid., 14839/61.

On December 15, 1961, Kafka entertained members of the central committee of Australian trade unions: P. Clancy, E. Elliot, T. Wright, and their wives. "We discussed activities of the unions and possibilities of them using our propaganda materials; I will use the information obtained in future reports."[576]

On April 30, 1962, Consul General Kafka informed his ministry of his meeting with the secretary general of the Building Workers, Purse. They talked about mutual exchanges of delegations. The Building Workers' Union had already invited unionists from the (East) German Democratic Republic in 1960, and was then hosting a Soviet delegation. "They always plan the visit for a whole month and take the visitors to all Australian capitals and centers where they organize receptions with short speeches and discussions." The guests paid for their own travel, but local unions paid their expenses in Australia. "They would like to offer a similar program to us." The secretary of the Building Workers' Union in NSW, Clancy, had visited Prague a year before.

Elected to the politburo of the CPA, Purse was also a member of the party. "The visit would gain wide publicity because almost all Australian trade unions united in the federal A.C.T.U. are now engaged in an active fight to lead it."[577] Communist state officials in charge of unionists who did not have any right to freely elect their own representatives spread misleading propaganda during their visits in an attempt to infiltrate the ACTU. Had they been victorious, they would have tried to change the Australian system of democratic unions into an organ of a Communist state.

On July 12, 1962, Kafka invited Comrade Elliot to lunch in a restaurant along with the Polish consul general who requested the meeting. The consul general wanted to become better acquainted with the seamen's unionist in order to extend the list of labor union leaders to invite to Polish receptions.[578]

When it was known that Kafka would soon be recalled to Prague, Elliot invited him and the Polish consul general to a farewell dinner in his home on September 2, 1962.[579]

---

576   Ibid., 4213/61.
577   Ibid., 1629/62.
578   Ibid., 2392/62.
579   Ibid., 2739/62.

MEETING CPA LEADERS

One month after their dinner of November 23, 1959, Richard Dixon, president of the CPA, called on Kafka on the morning of December sixteenth.[580] The visit was repeated on July eighteenth the following year.[581] Other CPA representatives met the Czechoslovak consul general more often. The editor of the *Tribune*, Paul Francis Mountier, complained to Kafka in October 1960 that his own contributions to the ČTK, the Czech press agency, were not paid.[582] In May 1961, Mountier contacted Vodička and then Kafka because he wanted to get in touch with the Soviet Ambassador Kurdiukov but did not want to go to Canberra.[583] Mountier called on Kafka in September and October 1961.[584] On April 13, 1962, Kafka invited Mountier for lunch in the Bamboo Café and then reported to Prague in a "special report," No. 1672/62, which is not available.[585]

Comrade Bert Chandler "wanted to discuss a matter" with Kafka on August 9, 1960[586] and on January 23, 1961 contacted him saying that the friend Kafka wanted to see, L. L. Sharkey, had just returned from Hong Kong.[587] On August 24, 1960, Laurie Aarons of the headquarters of the CPA requested to see Kafka.[588] In the evening of April 17, 1961, the Kafkas were expecting Sharkey for dinner, but he did not show due to "a misunderstanding."[589] On November 29, 1961, "at the request of the Soviet Embassy," Kafka prepared a dinner in his home for members of the CPA Politburo, Aarons and Robinson. "During the evening we discussed the course of the election campaign and the situation in political parties." Kafka said that he would use the information in his report.[590]

---

580 AA, A6119/90, 2463, Kafka 2, f. 139.
581 Ibid., f. 174.
582 AA, A6119/90, 2464, Kafka 3, f. 64.
583 AA, A6119/90, 2465, Kafka 4, f. 121.
584 AA, A6119/90, 2466, Kafka 5, f. 129.
585 AA, A6119/90, 2467, Kafka 6, f. 117, and AMFA, 1629/62.
586 AA, A6119/90, 2463, Kafka 2, f. 182.
587 AA, A6119/90, 2464, Kafka 3, f. 139.
588 Ibid., f. 21.
589 AA, A6119/90, 2465, Kafka 4, f. 95.
590 AMFA, 4020/61.

Again, on January 8, 1962, "at the request of the Soviet Embassy," Kafka invited the general secretary of the CPA, L. Sharkey, president of the CPA, Dixon, members of the Politburo, Aarons and Robinson with their wives to dinner at his home. (All this was heavily underlined in Prague with a red pencil.) However, "due to an unexpected engagement," the Ambassador Kurdiukov was not able to attend. "Information gained about political and economic events in Australia is being used in our report."[591] So another dinner was prepared for January sixteenth. This time the Soviet ambassador flew in, accompanied by his secretary, Dorofeev. They dined with Sharkey and Aarons. "A special report was sent by airmail."[592]

Former Senator Bill (William Robert) Morrow stayed in a close contact with the Czechoslovak consulate general. On November 21, 1960, Morrow and the secretary of the Peace Council in NSW, Geoffrey Ronald Anderson, were invited for lunch by Kafka who then reported to his ministry that various personalities of the Australian Labor Party were discussed as well as the activities of the peace movement. As Kafka promised, "the information will be used in my report on the LP."[593] A long report was sent on January 12, 1961. We have both its Czech original and its English translation thanks to the Australian archives in Canberra. A few samples might be of some interest. It begins:

> The Australian Labor Party is based on the working class, but it cannot be characterised as a working-class party.... It is remarkable that, for instance, in the parliament of New South Wales there is not a single Catholic among all the members of the Liberal Party, whereas all the members representing the Labor Party are Catholics.... The party is forced to put into practice various reforms, but it has never taken a determined stand against capitalism. The ALP's only basic principle is that of maintaining its anti-Communist policy.... The majority of its representatives have a real panicky fear of being branded as collaborating with or supporting the CP of A.... The removal of

591   Ibid., 1041/62.
592   Ibid.
593   Ibid., 3475/60.

Dr. Evatt, who was appointed Chief Justice of N.S.W. several months ago, has somewhat strengthened the position of the ALP, but it has still not achieved the desired unity. In place of Evatt was elected the almost "dead cert." Calwell, but much trouble and enmity and much militant "campaigning" were caused by the election of the deputy-leader of the Opposition. To this position E.G. Whitlam, a young and very capable lawyer from N.S.W. was elected.... His election was a definite compromise in an effort to prevent the election to this office of either E. J. Ward or L. C. Haylen.... Enmity even went so far as to lead to an exchang of blows between Ward and Whitlam.

The writer characterized Ward as "the best and most fearless speaker in parliament," a "leftist," but with "a gift for demagogy, unprincipled in part." Haylen was praised for his book *Chinese Journey* because "it is very objective" (sic) and it "has not made him very acceptable to the majority of labor members, who are markedly conservative." Both Ward and Haylen were commended as "the best fighters in the ALP." Regrettably, "the Labor Party has always kept well away from the entire peace movement." The Labor Party "like the Menzies coalition, considers the Australian peace organisations to be Communist."[594] Kafka signed this document that was clearly based on Anderson's and Morrow's opinions.

On May 19, 1961, Morrow and Kafka lunched together.[595] On August sixth, Morrow was presented with the Soviet International Peace Prize.[596] On April 19, 1962, the Soviet ambassador hosted a lunch in honor of the bearer of the Lenin Peace Prize, W. Morrow. Kafka was also invited. The Soviet ambassador announced that Senator Morrow might be invited to the World Council of Peace meeting in Moscow in June and recommended that the Czechs invite Morrow for a week.[597] On July 3, 1962, the Consul General Kafka arranged a lunch with Morrow and informed him that no decision so far was made about

594   AA, A6119/90, 2464, Kafka 3, ff. 114–122.
595   AA, A6119/90, 2465, Kafka 4, f. 133.
596   Ibid., f. 176.
597   AMFA, 1672/62.

his invitation to the ČSSR. All the information that Morrow rendered about the Australian delegation to the Peace Congress was sent to Prague by airmail.[598]

When Kafka was recommending to the Ministry of Foreign Affairs (on May 4, 1962) that Morrow should be invited, he included this comment: "Morrow is a very good orator and an expert on the history of the Australian workers' movement. Therefore I assume that he could be exploited by Czechoslovak radio. Morrow has been a member of the CPA for many years, but this information for tactical reason should not be publicized in order not to harm his activity in the peace movement."[599]

Several more lunches and telephone calls between Morrow and Kafka took place before the senator departed for the Peace Congress held in Moscow July 9–14, 1962.[600] When Morrow returned from Moscow and Prague on the thirteenth of September, Kafka hosted him for lunch. They talked about his experiences abroad and agreed that the Czech consulate would lend the senator many films for an extended period of time, so the peace movement could distribute them. Morrow already had given two half-hour long lectures on the ABC. He discussed also his stay and experiences in the ČSSR.[601]

On September 22, 1962, the secretary of the Peace Movement, W. Morrow, invited "distinguished functionaries of the Peace Movement" to his home and acquainted them with experiences from his journey to the USSR, ČSSR, and Japan. Polish and Yugoslav consul generals were in attendance. Morrow used this occasion for saying good bye to Comrade Kafka.[602]

The struggle for the Soviet style of peace (see Hungary in 1956 and so on) was a two-way street: Communist peace propagandists traveled to Czechoslovakia and other similar regimes in order to tell

---

598 Ibid., 2392/62.

599 Ibid., SP4966/025872.

600 AA, A6119/90, 2467, Kafka 6, f. 158; 2468, Kafka 7, ff. 48, 53, 80, and 91.

601 Ibid., Kafka 7, f. 152, and AMFA, 2739/62. From 1961, the Czecho-slovak Communist government was allowed by Soviet authorities to officially add another "S" to its abbreviated title as the only other Communist state to have reached the honorary (and fictive) stage of completed socialism.

602 Ibid., and also AA, A6119/90, 2468, Kafka 7, f. 154.

the enslaved populations that capitalism was much worse; then they flew back to Australia in order to inform their compatriots about the marvels of countries building socialism. Senator Morrow was just one of such traveling missionaries.

Another was W. E. Gollan, member of the Peace Council of NSW. On December 1, 1961, Kafka invited him for lunch along with the secretary of the council, G. Anderson. They discussed inviting Gollan to the ČSSR.[603]

The lunch took place two weeks before the consul general sent a coded airmail letter to the Prague Ministry of foreign Affairs:

> W. E. Gollan is a well known member of the CPA of long standing. He is also Director of one of the major schools in Sydney. In spite of the persecution of the Party, he has been able to keep his position, since he is recognised as the best pedagogical educator in N.S.W. and the parents' committee at the school would not allow him to be dismissed. The Central Committee also published his book about education. I am recommending that he be invited to Prague for a week, all expenses paid. Send me your opinion by cable and I will contact him. The CPA CC already secured his delegation to the Soviet Union because his knowledge of the Soviet situation would be widely disseminated.[604]

Careful preparations were made in Prague to welcome Comrade Gollan; a special meeting took place on December 20, 1961 at the Ministry of Education:

> Comrade Gollan will be welcomed at the airport by representatives of the Ministry of Education and the Experimental Institute, eventually also by the Czechoslovak Council for the Defence of Peace. The first day he will be welcomed by Comrade Kujal, who is the Director of the Experimental Pedagogical

603   AMFA, 4213/61.
604   Ibid., 14770/61. It was marked "Strictly secret!"

Institute. He will devote himself to Gollan for four days. Also Comrade Mařan and one of the inspectors on the methods of the Institute will be at his disposition. The first day a more exact program for his stay will be discussed and co-ordinated with the Czechoslovak Council for the Defence of Peace and the CPCZ CC. [Obviously, the connection between the Party and the Peace Council was close.] The Pedagogical Institute will arrange visits to special schools and the Museum of Comenius [the famous seventeenth century educational reformer of Czech origin]. The Ministry of Education will cover all the expenses of the visitor for one week and will take care of the transportation and visits of cultural establishments, e.g., Laterna Magica. He will be shown films.... He will receive gifts, especially writings by Comenius. Comrade Černý was already in contact with him since the session of the World Peace Council in Stockholm. He will arrange a visit to Lidice. According to Comrade Škopek from the CPCZ CC, Comrade Gollan will be officially received at the CPCZ CC.[605]

Comrade Gollan clearly enjoyed all the attention and hospitality, since on April 13, 1962, the consul general sent another letter informing the ministry that Gollan suggested that the Australian delegate to the Congress of the Peace Council in Helsinki, Suse Wolf, born April 12, 1938, "intends after the Festival to spend one year working in one of the socialist states." Kafka recommended her strongly: "The Comrade is a member of the Party, has a university education and teaches English. The Party is interested in her having a chance to work in Czechoslovakia. In a few days, she is departing from Australia by ship and therefore a decision about her employment or refusal of it should be given to her sister who lives in England. Comrade Wolf will also contact the leader of our delegation during the Festival."[606]

The budget for hosting and indoctrinating Australian Communists about the blessings of the Soviet system of government must have been

605 Record of the meeting, no marks, copy in my possession.
606 AMFA, 4161 St, KPR, G, K1, 5, K0025.020.

large. I will quote just a few samples of many visits paid for by special agencies.

The secretariat of the CPCZ CC invited five Australian Communists studying at the High Social School in the USSR for ten days in Czechoslovakia. On August 19, 1959, it prepared a detailed program of their stay and recommended providing each with five hundred Czech crowns pocket money and one thousand Kčs worth of souvenirs to the whole group.[607]

The consulate general in Sydney regularly arranged visits by prominent trade unionists to Czechoslovakia. The Trade Union of Employees in Mining and Energy in Prague reported on a visit by Comrade Bill Parkinson, president of the Miners' Federation, to the ČSR on July 17–24, 1961. He was invited while he was in Germany during his world tour of Europe and Asia. He visited England and from Prague continued his trip to the Soviet Union and China. He was also identified as a member of the CPA CC.

Bill Parkinson, accompanied by Comrade Rudolf Šimák, head of the trade union's organizational and educational work, was taken to the North Bohemian brown coal area and to the mines in Kladno:

> He was keenly interested in questions of work safety, wage policy, hospital and social insurance. In a discussion he talked as a conscious Marxist with complete openness; besides words of approval he did not hide criticism where he saw shortages.... During the initial conversation at the trade union central committee he could not understand our preferential treatment of miners working underground at the expense of above ground miners both in terms of wages and shorter working hours. Only after discussions with miners ... he grasped that miners' preferential treatment is necessary during the building of socialism.

Naturally, he was not told the political reasons; the conditions in the old mines were horrible, and Soviet Union's strict demands for fast industrialization and war production were the real cause. There was

607 SCA, XIII, 379/141.

great turnover of miners who hated the difficult and dangerous work and high wages were needed to attract desperate workers.

Parkinson was impressed by the hospital and social insurance, complained about the situation of Australian miners as "serious and difficult," and stressed that next to the unions of seamen and dockers, the Miners' Federation was one of Australia's most progressive unions: "In the battle for world peace and in the fight against warmongers and imperialist bases, the Australian miners stand in the first rows of the working class."

In the conclusion of the report, it was "hoped that Comrade Parkinson's visit strengthened mutual ties." Clearly, intellectuals allowed themselves to be fooled by propaganda easier than experienced unionists: "Shortages witnessed by him must be remedied. The Director of the mine

Centrum boasted about the solarium in workers' baths. Though, when Comrade Parkinson wanted to see it, it was discovered that for a long time it has been unusable. Also in the mine Nosek the workplaces were in a mess that directly threatened work security."[608]

Kafka continued to cultivate Bill Parkinson by inviting him for lunch at the Bamboo Café on September 27, 1962.[609] Parkinson prepared a report on his overseas trip for the central council and made speeches to the Sydney Trades Hall and elsewhere.[610]

A relay system existed among Communist regimes by which delegations to be influenced were transferred from one country to the next in order to strengthen desirable impressions. For example, three Australian unionists traveled from Poland to Czechoslovakia and then to East Germany. Alfred James Harris, president of the Australian Union of Brick Makers, Stonecutters and Ceramics in Victoria; Peter Campbell, president of the National Council of Australian Union of Painters and Decorators, Brisbane, Queensland; and Valentine Moloney, member of the Australian Union of Auxiliary Workers in New South Wales, arrived in Czechoslovakia from Poland on October 18, 1961. They were shown workplaces and housing developments in

---

608   Archive of the ROH (Revolutionary Trade Union Movement), no numbered file, copy in my possession, 3 pages. See also AA, A6119/90, 2465, Kafka 4, f. 146, and 2466, Kafka 5, ff. 111 and 113.

609   AA, A6119/90, 2468, Kafka 7, f. 166.

610   AA, A6119/90, 2466, Kafka 5, f. 131.

Ostrava and Pardubice on the way to Prague. Everywhere discussions with functionaries and workers were arranged during which the major topic was fighting for peace and against German and Japanese rearmament, encouraged by American warmongers and imperialists. Comrade Campbell explained that the CPA did not support unification of all trade unions as it existed in people's democracies, because in such a move the conservatives would manage to dislodge many progressive leaders who find it more useful to infiltrate individual unions and thus hold power in them. On October twenty-third, East Germans took over the delegation on the frontier of Czechoslovakia.[611] There, in the heavily armed Soviet satellite, the propaganda fight for Soviet peace and against alleged fascization of Western Germany would continue, so that the delegates could report on it to other unionists once back in their own countries.

All such activities were carefully coordinated with Soviet agents. Thus, Consul General Kafka reported to his superiors in Prague that he had entertained the Soviet ambassador, his secretary Skripov, General Secretary Sharkey of the CPA, and his deputy Aarons. The evening was devoted to deliberations about the composition of the Australian delegation to the Congress for General Disarmament and Peace as well as political developments in Australia.[612]

Jaroslav Kafka was recalled to Prague and left Sydney on October 3, 1962. Thirty people, mostly Czechs, were at the airport to see him off. As Australian "Travel Control" reported, "Andrienko [the Russian name was transcribed either as above or as Andriyenko or Andrieenko] from the Soviet Embassy was most prominent standing beside Kafka most of the time." The Polish consul general, Polak, was also present.[613]

Almost seven years of Jaroslav Kafka's activities in Australia were very useful to Soviet intelligence. Although we can only be sure that his duties included acting as facilitator for the recruitment of agents and informers by Soviet spies accredited as diplomats or journalists, it was certainly more than that. One of the most successful Soviet agents in Canada and the USA was repeatedly told by KGB handlers: "We want you to search for progressives everywhere, particularly among politicians and journalists, and we want you to report about anyone

611   Archive of the ROH, no file number, a copy in my possession.
612   CzMFA, 2392/62.
613   AA, A6119/90, 2468, Kafka 7, f. 172.

interesting you meet, progressive or not.... We must constantly hunt for 'progressives.'"[614]

One of Kafka's main targets was Leslie Clement Haylen who referred to Kafka as his "mate." Kafka cultivated him constantly with the help of Alan John Dalziel who believed that Haylen should be deputy leader of the Labor Party, important for a future revolution. However, Haylen was just one of many progressives so managed.

---

614   AA, A6119/90, 2465, Kafka 4, f. 171 and 89; AA, A6119/90, 2463, Kafka 2, f.175. John Barron, *KGB Today: The Hidden Hand*, (New York: Reader's Digest Press, 1983), pp. 323 and 331.

10

Informers

Stanislav Levchenko, a Soviet agent who defected to Japan in 1979, used to recruit informers for his country. He described how in training courses for Soviet operatives, methods suitable for seduction of foreigners were summarized under the abbreviation M.I.C.E.: money, ideology, compromise, and ego. These were recommended as elements of the recruiting process: meals, flattering the ego, focusing on the need to be clandestine, and encouraging abandonment of former loyalties.

West Australian journalist, Nicholas Partridge, who called my attention to the above passage in his unpublished manuscript, "Agents of Influence: The K.G.B. and Australia," also included the following example, by now well known, of the Australian MICE being caught by Soviet CATS:

> Mr. Fergan O´Sullivan, a journalist in the Canberra Parliamentary press gallery—who later became Dr Evatt´s press secretary—had compiled a "Document J" which gave thumbnail sketches of forty-five other journalists in the press gallery with character weaknesses which could be used as pressure points for blackmail or recruitment by Soviet intelligence.[615]

The K.G.B. Moscow Center must have been very grateful; such information was most precious for them. Further, on September 25,

---

615 Stanislav Levchenko, *On the Wrong Side: My Life in the KGB* (Washington: Pergamon-Brassey´s 1988), pp. 106. 88, 127 and 241. Robert Manne in his book *The Petrov Affair: Politics and Espionage (1987)* has much more on this topic.

1985, on ABC TV, Rupert Lockwood admitted that he had written similar profiles in the Soviet embassy in Canberra.

Secret until recently, the archives of the Communist Party of Czechoslovakia (CPCZ) and of the Czech Ministry of Foreign Affairs in Prague contain many documents proving that the methods listed above were successfully used by Czech and Slovak secret agents— masked as diplomats—for obtaining crucial information from Australian legislators, trade unionists, and businessmen at a very low price, sometimes just the price of a meal. Some Australians showed a marked lack of loyalty to their own country, preferring to serve the interests of the USSR. They might have believed that they were furthering the interests of a world revolutionary movement that was replacing decadent capitalism. However, they were favoring a merciless and conspiratorial dictatorship at the expense of their own democratic system. Lack of knowledge does not exculpate their guilt. In politics, innocence can be equal to recklessness and treason.

In the fifties and sixties, the Czechoslovak consulate general in Sydney was an important source for Communist secret services. As we have already seen, Australian elected representatives and other local personalities were often most willing to offer precious intelligence information about their colleagues and the political and economic situation in the country. Monthly reporting by Sydney consul general Jaroslav Kafka, and later by his replacement from 1962, Vladislav Kraus, demonstrate the extent of this information gathering.

At a dinner on February 23, 1959 for Federal Deputy Les Haylen and the personal secretary to Dr. H. V. Evatt, Allan Dalziel, both gentlemen "promised all imaginable help" to Czech authorities.[616] On June 26, 1959, the Kafka was ivited for a meal by the secretary of the leader of the parliamentary opposition, Dalziel. Labor Deputy Haylen also took part with his wife. According to a Prague document, "the head of the Consulate was informed about the program of a trip by

---

616   Alan (John) Dalziel met Kafka very often, usually in company of Leslie Clement Haylen or Lydia Janovska, alias Lydia Mokras(ova) who spoke Czech and worked in Czechoslovakia as a nurse before the Communist coup d'état. She was suspected of working for the Australian police because she was close to Dr. Bialoguski, who persuaded Petrov to defect.

an Australian parliamentary delegation and about the names of the participants."[617]

That was only the first instance of revelations facilitating Czechoslovak preparations for use or misuse of the Australian delegation. Another document from the archive of the Czech Ministry of Foreign Affairs is even more compromising. The councellor of the Australian embassy in Paris, Allan Philip Renouf, who in Warsaw was advising this delegation during its visit to Poland, rushed to Prague in order to secretly inform Czechoslovak authorities about his Australian colleagues. They would reach the Czechoslovak capital only one or two days after his arrival on September 6, 1959. Voluntarily, he offered the surprised Czechs a thorough characterization of all five members of the delegation that he was supposed to serve! In a secret report of the visit, it was stressed by a Czech operative, with obvious appreciation, that "he acted in a very friendly way" and offered his comments "without any question from our side:" "Renouf labelled the leader of the delegation, W. C. Haworth, as an outspoken enemy of our regime, while he expressed favourable opinions about the other members."

These represented the Labor Party, while Haworth was a liberal. For whom did Renouf really work? As a reward for his voluntary services to a totalitarian regime, he requested and obtained a trip to the Castle Karlstein and the Slapy Dam. His other wish to meet, as he declared, his friend Ian F. Milner (the Soviet spy and Czech undercover police agent) was not satisfied since he was not in Prague; at least that is what he was told.[618]

Dalziel (Soviet code name DENIS) often had dealings with Kafka. For instance, on November 30, 1960, the consul general invited him for lunch in a restaurant. He then reported to Prague that "individual personalities of the Australian Federal Parliament were discussed."[619] After such meals there was always something to communicate; another lunch on February eighth with Haylen and Dalziel was followed by "a special report sent by airmail."[620] On the twenty-third of the same month, Kafka's invitation to Dalziel was readily accepted.[621] Dalziel

617 AMFA, 2901/59.
618 AMFA, unmarked report of five pages, copy in my possession.
619 AMFA, 3475/60.
620 Ibid., 2317/61.
621 AA, A6119/90, 2465, Kafka 4, f. 36.

was not only a frequent informer on Australian individuals. He also served as a propagandist for Czechoslovak Communism and defender of its policies on the ABC.[622] In his book *Australia's Spies and Their Secrets,* David McKnight is inconclusive:

> By 1958 the taps revealed that Dalziel had become friendly with Lidia Mokras (nee Janovski). The contact between her, Dalziel and the Czechoslovak Consulate was of great interest to ASIO which believed that after the Soviets pulled out of Australia following Petrov's defection, the Czechs had probably taken over their espionage activities.... Dalziel's contact with the Czechs was confined to Sydney consular representatives.[623]

There was no lack of willing informers: on November 21, 1960, the Czech consul general invited the secretary of the Peace Council on NSW, Anderson, and former Senator Morrow for lunch: "We discussed activities of the peace movement and Australian Labor Party; we will send you information."[624]

An old friend of the Czechoslovak consulate, businessman A. White, buyer of wool for the Chinese People's Republic, invited Kafka for dinner: "At the dinner table we discussed the contemporary economic

---

622 AA, A6119/90, 2464, Kafka 3, f. 42.
623 NSW: Allen & Unwin, 1994, p. 102. In an interview with Rod Moran, Desmond Ball said: "Another major area of investigation that might be fruitful concerns Alan Dalziel, Dr Evatt's personal secretary." The professor was "almost certain" that the Soviet embassy had access to Australian secrets thanks to Dalziel who "was meeting with Nosov on a weekly basis." Nosov was their agent. Further, "there was a connection between Dalziel and Zaitsev." Col. Victor Zaitsev "was the first GRU (Soviet Military Intelligence) resident in Australia ... between 1943–48.... An ASIO report of December 29, 1949 records that the former 'showed secret papers to (Zaitsev) whilst the latter was in his office.'" See Red Moran, "Reds under Aussie Beds," *West Australian, Big Weekend,* January 23, 1999, p. 5.
624 CZMFA, 3475/60.

and political situation in Australia. I will use the new information in my reports."[625]

It is deplorable that these more secret files are not yet found or have disappeared. That is also true about another coded letter, sent by courier, concerning the November 22, 1961 meeting with Senator Armstrong after his return from Czechoslovakia. They met at a reception given by the Lebanese consul general.

On September 18, 1962, the consul general sent from Sydney by courier a secret "Characterisation of Social Contacts." Out of his list of *thirty-nine willing informers,* let us examine at least a few persons who were well known at that time.

At the head of the list is Alfred White (the address of the named informer is always given). Kafka stated that White's buying of wool for the Chinese Communists was done on the recommendation of the Czechs. The consulate also built him a network for the sale of Soviet watches. Why? "He is always willing to answer our questions or help us at different opportunities."

Husband and wife J. and Viena Barton, CPA members, were both praised for their eager cooperation. She specialized in conferences for women. Together they were hosted in Czechoslovakia and on their return addressed many audiences on the blessings of Communism, especially for women: "Mrs Barton very obligingly offers information about progressive organisations' activities." These organisations also benefit from the Bartons' willingness to accommodate their meetings in "their large apartment."

Not everybody mentioned in Kafka's letter was hailed without reservation. The retired director of an Australian glass company, V. K. Gray, who visited Czechoslovakia in 1958 and was very hospitably treated, helped to broadcast several programs on Czech glass and ceramics. "We keep friendly contacts with him," but it "is very tiring because he is a senile duffer, but for the moment we consider it useful."

Eliot Elliot, general secretary of the Seamen's Union for thirty years, "readily informs us about trade unions."

L. L. Sharkey, general secretary of the CPA: "At the request of the Soviet Ambassador, while he is in Sydney, I organize meetings in

---

625 CZMFA, 4020/61.

my apartment; Sharkey is becoming forgetful and so Laurie Aarons accompanies him all the time."

L. Aarons "has many good memories of his stay in the ČSSR and became a great propagator of our successes."

Nick Abound, owner of a textile enterprise, visited Czechoslovakia several times on business. "He acts as an intermediary between the Labor Party and industrialists: former Senator Armstrong is one of his large shareholders." Abound and Kafka helped each other. Kafka arranged invitations for him to foreign embassies, and Abound invited Kafka to parties in his home "where it is always possible to get acquainted with influential personalities."

Bert Keasing, director of CPA bookstores and treasurer of the Australian Soviet Friendship Society, "transferred documents to me about the visit of Comrade Kisch in Australia that I have sent to the Institute of the CPCZ History."

B. Parkinson, CPA member and president of the Coal and Shale Employees Federations, was commended by Kafka because "he had procured for us good documentation of modern mining equipment used in Australia."

The information was considered vital in Prague. In the Ministry of Foreign Affairs it was marked, obviously for future use, "Please transcribe the characteristics on cards for documentation."[626]

One year later, on December 27, 1963, the new consul general in Sydney, Comrade Kraus, who "knew his predecessor, Jaroslav Kafka, very well,"[627] sent a long letter by courier marked "SECRET!" and entitled "Report on a Conversation with the Federal Deputy of the Labor Party, Tom Uren." One week earlier, Kraus had invited Uren and his wife for dinner. The consul general commented: "Uren is an honest man and inside of the Australian Labor Party belongs to the Left. In the Parliament—in contradiction with the majority of the A.L.P.— he conducts himself courageously.... He condemns the reactionary politics of the Menzies Government."

Next is a choice paragraph showing how the Czech state functionary felt superior to his humble Australian interlocutor: "Tom Uren, although much of Marxism-Leninism is not clear to him, has a sincere admiration for countries of the Socialist Bloc and sees in them

626   Ibid., 072/62.
627   AA, A6119/90, 2468, Kafka 7, f. 181.

an example for progress to socialism in Australia. He thinks that the policy of peaceful co-existence is creating conditions for Australia to reach socialism by parliamentary means. [He understands that progress by way of gradual reforms.]"

From the text that follows this evaluation of Uren's lack of ideological maturity, one can observe the importance of the abandonment of former loyalties as was taught in the school for Soviet foreign agents: "He expressly affirmed that the majority of leading functionaries of the A.L.P. are people who first of all are looking for their own personal profit and only after that are ready to do something for the benefit of workers. Careerists who use the A.L.P. as an instrument for their own advantage and enrichment, repel the ranks of honourable workers who are members of trade unions and who have class consciousness."

Tom Uren further mentioned that although he was not a Communist, "he saw in Communists his allies." He expressed the hope that in the future a truly socialist party would be created in Australia: "He characterized Calwell as a Right-winger who at the moment was the best person to unify the party and actually serves as a brake to anti-Communism."

After Uren described the situation in NSW and in Victoria as influenced by their respective archbishops Gilroy and Mannix, he praised Dr. Cairns as "the most capable personality in the A.L.P.; in the future, he could become its leader." Uren also complained about February 1963 revelations spread in the press that he and other A.L.P. deputies often met with Soviet diplomats. He did not deny the accusations but described them as "hysterical."[628]

A nice supplement to the previous statement by Uren is the concluding part of another long secret report sent by courier from Sydney on May 31, 1965. Consul General Kraus thus informed the Prague Ministry of Foreign Affairs: "On May 19, the Soviet Ambassador Loginov arranged a lunch in his residence for federal deputies of the A.L.P., Dr. Cairns and S. Benson, and I. Both deputies informed the Soviet Ambassador about the planned increased military budget and expected higher taxes to be passed by the coming August session of the Parliament."

Furthermore, as reported by Kraus: "Cairns informed that in Melbourne the protest movement against sending Australian soldiers

---

628 AMFA,076/63.

to Vietnam develops favorably. There is a continuing problem with the lack of unity in the A.L.P.... He does not like the announcement of the Chairman of the A.C.T.U., A. Monk, who opposed protest strikes in connection with the sending of Australian soldiers to Vietnam."[629]

Twelve days previously, at another reception in Canberra at the Soviet embassy, Czechoslovak Consul General Kraus attempted to influence Senator Hendrickson and deputies B. Bryant, M.H. Nicholson, and W.C. Coutts on the Vietnam question.[630]

Soviet interests in Australia were well served by the Czechoslovak consulate general under all three representatives, Kafka (twice), Jandík, and Kraus, and by their social contacts, used for political purposes and as willing informers. As Manning Clark liked to say, Australia was where two worlds collided, the center of a battle between good and evil, or more accurately, in contrast to his naïve view, between a reasonably democratic system and a shrewd but dangerous totalitarian world.

---

629   Ibid., 2156/65, f. 4.
630   Ibid.

11

Harry Stein: "Tropical Organizer Of Immigrants"

As was noted earlier, Czechoslovak consuls did not show any interest in helping compatriots who had landed in Australia as political refugees. All the attention paid to them was devoted to preventing them from influencing the Sydney Czechoslovak Club that was led by Communists, and to spying on them as long as they remained democrats. For that purpose, the consuls used informers who infiltrated all the other Czechoslovak societies in Australia.

They also engaged the cooperation of a Communist agitator who for many years had a full time job with the CPA as migrant organizer and supervisor. On July 10, 1962, Consul General Jaroslav Kafka entertained in his home two members of the CPA CC, W. Brown and H. Stein. In his report to the Ministry of Foreign Affairs in Prague, he wrote, "Comrade Stein has been commissioned to work among emigrants; he wanted to clarify the situation of Czechoslovak refugees and possibilities of penetration by the party in their ranks." Kafka also said that Stein was asked to supply information concerning Chinese migrant associations in Australia. As we know, Kafka closely collaborated with Chinese Communist agents and often acted on their behalf. On July 18, 1962, Kafka invited Stein for lunch; Stein handed over information on Czechoslovak immigration, and Kafka then sent a special report to Prague (not available).[631]

Harry Stein continued his oversight of Czech and Slovak immigrants in Australia. For instance, on February 19, 1964, Kafka's

---

631   AMFA, 2392/60; Sydney letter of 7.27.1962.

successor as Sydney consul general, Vlastislav Kraus, invited Bill Brown, Alec Robertson, Harry Stein, and six editors of the *Tribune* to dinner. On December 17, 1964, Comrade Litavsky dined with Stein and his wife.[632]

From the 1930s on, Harry Stein was one of the most assiduous activists of the CPA. According to some reports (later to be quoted), he received his assignment for specialized party work directly from the Comintern in Moscow. From the beginning, he radiated the enthusiasm of genuine believers in the success and fulfillment of the world revolution. Although his name was not even mentioned in the recent monumental first volume of the history of the Communist Party of Australia until 1942, *The Reds*, by Stuart Macintyre,[633] he represents the connecting link between pre-war and post-war Communism in Australia. Australian archives in Canberra contain three bulky volumes of files devoted to his activities until 1962. (They are heavily censored.)

Stein was born on February 1, 1919 in Carlton in Victoria. His Jewish parents came from Palestine and were naturalized as British subjects. In Melbourne in the late thirties, Harry was known as Stenhouse. In 1936, he acted as secretary of the Young Communists' League. He was also associated with the League of Young Democrats and led the Eureka Youth League in Victoria.[634]

In order to get to Spain, he embarked in September 1937 as an assistant steward on the S.S. *Otranto*. He used the name Harry Stein and kept it.[635] After some time spent in England, he was active in Melbourne in June 1939. The next year, as a "prominent member of the Australian Labour League of Youth," he functioned as assistant secretary and treasurer of the League of Young Democrats. He called himself "Organiser of the New Deal for Youth." In 1945, he served as national welfare officer of the Eureka Youth League and the next year was elected secretary of its Victorian branch, to be confirmed the following year. He edited the *Youth Voice* and was a member of the Jewish Committee of the CPA. He also participated in the activities

632 Ibid., 1350/64, and AMFA, 1033/65, Sydney 1.7.. 1965, f. 2.
633 St Leonards: Allen & Unwin, 1998.
634 AA, A6119 XRI, 245, f. 2 and AA, A6119/90, 2478, Stein Vol. 3, f. 47.
635 AA, A6119 XRI, 245, 2.

of the Kadimah Youth organization. All these groups as well as the Communist dominated Labor Club —where Stein also operated— were introducing their members to the Communist Party. Harry Stein was also active as country organizer.[636]

Beginning in 1947, Stein concentrated on youth festivals which became a popular trap for young people's enthusiasm and willingness to serve the supposed ideals of peace, love, and international friendship. He took a prominent part in the Melbourne "Youth Parliament," another device used by Communist parties in many countries. Selected as the leader of the Eureka Youth League delegation, he participated in the first World Youth Festival in Prague.[637]

The atmosphere of these festivals was enthralling. The Communists bathed in the glory of the Red Army's victories and Stalin's example of how to march toward to the glorious future without wars and capitalist exploitation. The organizers capably staged the meetings with red flags waving, parades with marches (toward the glorious future), and folk dances. These looked like spontaneous expressions by young people of various Communist states, but were produced by professional groups of dancers—another very successful Soviet mastery of stagecraft.

The youthful Czech enthusiast and poet, Pavel Kohout, celebrated by the party as a great writer despite the cheap tendentiousness of his silly verse, later wrote, "It was an era of great faith that around the corner was the time when the best ideals of humanity would be realized."[638] In his 1969 autobiographical *Diary*, he confessed, "We were charlatans who passed ourselves off as surgeons."[639]

Another Czech writer, and Communist enthusiast around 1948, Milan Kundera, in a partly autobiographical representation of these times, later wrote: "Jakub was living in a world where human lives were readily being destroyed for the sake of abstract ideas. He knew the faces of those arrogant men and women: not evil, but virtuous,

---

636   Ibid., ff. 3, 4, 5, 10, 77; and AA, A6119/90, 2471, Stein Vol. 2, ff. 54 and 57.
637   AA, A6119 XRI, 245, f. 77.
638   "What I Was...," *Literární noviny*, 21 March 1964, p. 3.
639   *Aus dem tagebuch eines Konter-Revolutionärs* (Luzern: G.J. Bucher, 1969), p. 46.

burning with righteous zeal or shining with jovial comradeship; faces reflecting militant innocence."[640]

I witnessed the crazy enthusiasm Soviet propagandists could provoke when during the *Sokol Slet* (gymnastic rally) in Prague, all male spectators around me became highly excited when Soviet motorcyclists drove around the stadium with skimpily clad bosomy women on their shoulders. Such circus performances were effective after wartime frustrations and could inspire in willing targets the will to participate in the Communist world revolution against misery and strife. They had so much vitality and contagious faith! It was very tempting to join them, the once and future victors.

Harry Stein attended the Prague World Youth Festival as manager of Graeme Bell's dixiland band of seven musicians, supported by the Eureka youth league. They were disappointed in him and complained when he left them for six weeks: "He was merely using them to extract money to cover his personal expenses." In December 1947, Stein requested more money from the band in order to proceed to Yugoslavia. They suspected that there he attended not only the conference of the World Youth Fellowship but also a meeting of the cominform that appointed him as its represesentative in Australia. "Stein was constantly writing copious notes, and invariably carried quantities of papers in a briefcase." He went to Paris and stayed there during the serious Communist-inspired strikes. The band members suspected that he "had joined up with the organisation merely for the sake of a trip to Europe." He was telling them that they "should ensure being on the winning side by supporting the Communist cause" and that "he knew what the future held in store."[641] (Manning Clark used very similar expressions in his book *A Short History of Australia* (1963), pp. 240 and 244. Did they read the same Stalinist pamphlets?)

When Harry Stein reached the Melbourne port on January 20, 1948, the Customs House searched his baggage for prohibited books. They found an extensive library of Communist propaganda brochures in Czech, French, English, Greek, Spanish, and translated reports on the struggle of the Vietnamese, Chinese, Japanese, South African, and

---

640   *The Farewell Party* (New York: Alfred A. Knopf, 1976), pp. 193–94.
641   AA, A6119 XRI, 245, ff. 9–10 and 77; AA, A6119/90, 2478, Stein 3, f. 47.

Yugoslav revolutionaries against capitalism and imperialism.[642] At that time there were many such struggles for independence going on around the world that one could feel sympathy for, though not necessarily in the Communist way, that is for their own party purposes.

Back in Australia, Stein returned to his hectic schedule of propagandistic speaking and writing. On February 13, 1948, the Melbourne *Guardian* reported him as saying that "the people are moving—not in the direction of America, but in the direction of the new life which has sprung up in the East." His pronouncements were heavily anti-American. He denounced the Marshall Plan as an expression of American imperialism. He became a council member of the World Federation of Democratic Youth and was chosen "as leader of the Youth International of the South-East Pacific Cominform Area." This organization was prepared to operate in the event of war with Russia.[643]

In other speeches, Stein used his European travels as a source or misinformation that described the situation in the western and eastern zones of Germany exactly the opposite from how it really was: "Many people wonder why, with the example of Soviet administration so near, there are not more revolts in the Western Zones of Germany which are being robbed by Britain and America. The answer is that there are revolts in Germany, big revolts."

His remarks about divided Austria are similarly laughable: "Soviet administration for the people is miles ahead of the Allies'.... The coming elections should see big changes. The elections will be free because of the presence of the Red Army."[644] (The Communist party badly lost.)

On February 15, 1948, at a meeting convened by the Eureka League, Stein stated that the Australian delegation to the Prague World Youth Festival had forty-three members. He could not discover any iron curtain around Czechoslovakia and, according to him, the country was not dominated by the Communist Party, just led by it.[645] In April 1948, Stein told young people in Adelaide that in contrast to Australia, whose independence was temporarily penetrated by the Americans, new

---

642   AA, A6119 XRI, 245, ff. 11–16.
643   Ibid., f. 77.
644   AA, A6119 XRI, 245, no folio number visible on my copy.
645   Ibid., f. 18.

democracies in Czechoslovakia and Yugoslavia "successfully prevented imperialist penetration."[646]

Observing the many activities of the Eureka Youth League and Democratic Youth Council involving thousands of young people at meetings and at Christmas camps, the deputy director of the Commonwealt Investigation Service, D. A. Alexander, stated that "the League has altered its organization in all States during the past 12 months to fit with the role that the Party may have to play in the event of war with Russia.... Stein is believed to be the leader of the Cominform Area concerning youth."[647] Noel Ebbels, national secretary of the National Union Australian University Students, was taking part in these efforts.[648] Young people working the railways, tramways, engineering shops, factories, stores, and offices as well as apprentices, students, and C.R.T.S. trainees were addressed by Stein; Jack Brown, secretary of the A. Railways Union; and Don Thompson, secretary of the Building Trades Federation, at the Young Workers' Conference in August 1948. (At that time, the CPA played with the idea of staging a revolution.) With the pretext of a fight for better living conditions, they were asked to fight "for a lasting peace and an independent Australia."[649]

Several statements by Harry Stein in his article celebrating "the forward drive of the People's Army of China" remind us of almost identical expressions of Manning Clark when he praised Communist seizures of power against the vast majority of people in many countries as "people's" victories:

> The Russian revolution put the wealth of the country into the hands of the ordinary Russian people.... The Russian revolution meant that one-sixth of the world had broken away from capitalism and begun the socialist world. One hundred million people, after the recent war, also broke away from capitalism and established people's democracies – in Poland, Czechoslovakia, Hungary, etc. The Chinese revolution

646 Ibid., ff. 28–30.
647 Ibid., 40, 44–46.
648 Ibid., f. 40.
649 Ibid., f. 34.

will mean that a total of 800 million people, almost one third of the human race, will be on the road to socialism.... The year 1949 will see the capitalist world rushing into a depression that will make the one of 1927–30 seem like a picnic.... Nineteen hundred and forty-nine will be a year of great struggles, of great change. Undoubtedly it will bring more people of the world along the road to socialism, to a free and happy life.[650]

Next year, Stein eulogized Lea Soong, "a 20-year-old Malayan patriot," whom he met at the World Youth Festival in Prague as "president of the now banned Democratic Youth League of Malaya." Praising the Communist uprising, Stein ended his article: "The Malayan people defeated the fascists [sic] of Japan. They will also defeat their imitators."[651]

In the same issue of *Youth Voice*, a ten-day children's hike spent collecting plants and insects and making maps was praised as following Harry Stein's example of Soviet children.[652] Similarly, everything children were led to do in other Communist countries was always done "like the Soviet children"—an example of gradual sovietization.

The Youth Peace Conference in Melbourne, October 21–23, 1949, was addressed by Harry Stein, Rupert Lockwood (leader of the Australian delegation at the Paris Peace Congress), Jim Cairns (a lecturer at Melbourne University), and the Rev. Victor James (Australian Peace Council).[653]

Harry Stein was very active in the Marx School. His report to National Council, Sydney, March 24–26, is full of noble ideals serving ignoble aims. Well-known American journalist Walter Lippman was called "the American Imperialist" and the Marshall Plan was leading "our people and the people of Britain to slaughter." Stein could see "the new Führers who have taken over from the Nazis their plan of world domination, their slogan of anti-Communism and quite a lot of the Nazi industrialists, S.S. men and others of the Fascist rabble." He

---

650   *Youth Voice*, February 1949; AA, A6119 XRI, 245, f. 48.
651   *Youth Voice*, April 1949; AA, A6119 XRI, 245, f. 50.
652   AA, A6119 XRI, 245, B 2 21/9.
653   Ibid., f. 53.

also said, à la Clark, "these are the two camps in the world today, one standing for peace and democracy and the other for imperialism and war." Extolling Manning Clark's idea of historical writing that would help to prepare the way for an Australian revolution, Stein said toward the end of his long speech: "It is our task to bring the great men of History to the youth, so that they will become acquainted with and understand the noble ideas of men such as Marx and Lenin, of such Australians as the democratic poet Henry Lawson and the Workers leader, William Lane and many others of our own and other lands."[654]

In another long statement on "what is to be done," (à la Lenin) Stein attacked those unionists who excuse their failure to attract followers by claiming "the young workers are being too well paid, their conditions are too good, or they're just disinterested." Stein praised the success of the second W.F.D.Y. Congress in Hungary, attended by over seven hundred delegates. He stressed "the struggle for peace" as if all that was needed was "to struggle." In a few lines of text, the idea of "struggle" was emphasized nine times.[655]

After North Korea attacked South Korea with Soviet and Chinese military support, the Australian "wharfies have demanded an immediate end to Wall Street's [sic] terror-bombing of the Korean people." Harry Stein addressed their meeting.[656] He then praised them, agreeing "with my mate Max Heidke that the wharfies are the salt of the earth."[657]

In March 1954, Stein applied for his passport to be endorsed to spend four weeks in China and three weeks in the Soviet Union. He wanted to go, of course, as a tourist. His passport was cancelled in May. He blamed "the Iron Curtain placed around Australia." A year later, in July 1955, Stein applied again, this time including not only China and the Soviet Union, but also Hong Kong, the United Kingdom, France, and Italy. He again wanted to go as a tourist. This time his request was granted, and in August he departed together with Elliot Frank Johnston. Several other prominent Communists, including Lawrence

---

654   "Marx School Reading Material," AA, A6119 XRI, 245, 7 pages.
655   AA, A6119 XRI, 245, ff. 62–66 and 68–73.
656   *Sydney Tribune*, 9.29.1950.
657   *Challenge*, 11.26.1952.

Aarons, Bernard Taft, and six more, also left for China and the USSR. Among their destinations was the Fifth World Youth Festival.[658]

Upon his return, Harry Stein was given the responsibility of working amongst *aliens*, a designation used by the ASIO throughout its SECRET Report No. 23499. The CPA had not tried to win over the Hungarians coming to Australia after the Soviet military suppression of the people's revolution, but kept advising them to return to Hungary, the sad country they were happy to leave behind. At the CPA National Congress, Stein proposed measures that would please extreme Australian Right-wing jingoist Pauline Hanson; he demanded, in the name of the workers, "the immediate ending of the Menzies mass migration policy":

> No government has the right to continue to bring to Australia 115,000 migrants a year when there are not enough jobs or houses for these already here. For example, every day thirty or forty Hungarian immigrants arrive at the N.S.W.office of the Red Cross, looking for work.... Every week 1660 new migrants land here.... There is a minumum expenditure of £1000 on every migrant that lands in Australia.

Of course, Stein could not mention that the CPA did not like the stories of the horrors of Communism that the Hungarian refugees were bringing to Australia, spoiling the Communist propaganda about the blessings of life in people's democracies. Stein was searching for the nefarious intentions of the Menzies Government: "They have some special reasons for continuing the mass migration policy. That must be the aim of building a researve army of unemployed aiming at breaking down conditions of Australian and foreign born workers and of attempting to weaken the trade unions that they both belong to, or for some military adventures in the interests of monopoly super-profits in an imperialist expansion in South East Asia."

Stein regretted that there was "still a tendency in the Party not to approach foreign born workers." That attitude must change, because there are just too many new Australians to ignore them completely:

---

658   AA, A6119XRI, 245, ff. 118–21, 125–25, 143, 155–56, 158–59, 161–62, and 171.

From October 1945 to September 1957, 1,246,789 migrants came to Australia.... Only about 16% come from countries that now make up the Socialist Commonwealth.... It is true that there are some reactionaries among the migrants, that some of the migrant organisations' leaders are under Menzies' influence.... Our job is to help the progressives unite with the middle of the roaders and isolate the reactionary elements.... These are now about half a million migrants in the Australian workforce. They make up one third of the membership of the Ironworkers' Union. As 73% of the recent additional workers in the steel industry have been migrants they make up a big percentage of the workers in the giant Newcastle and South Coast N.S.W. steel plants. Six thousand work for the Victorian Railways—5000 are members of the N.S.W. A.R.U. almost 65% who work at the G.M.G. plant Fischermen's Bend in Victoria are migrants and at least one in two of every worker in other major plants. Four out of five who work on the Perway gangs around Sydney, 95% of members of the Glass Workers Union and 83% of the membership of the Rubber Workers Union are migrants. They also make up 50% of the workers of the Snowy River Scheme, and more than 20% of all those who work on major public construction schemes.[659]

Harry Stein carefully prepared his agenda based on a statistical survey. He also spent a lot of time attempting to bring about a change in the party's lack of influence on migrant workers. He addressed many meetings, traveled to Adelaide and many other places where he tried to influence recalcitrant immigrants to join his party. His success was very limited. Repeatedly, he stressed that the best target are the Greeks and the Italians. But the Greek association was split into factions and

---

659   *The Guardian, May 1, 1958* and AA, A6119/90, 2471, Stein Vol. 2, ff. 104–105.

suffered from conflicts among its leaders. He interviewed various members, endeavoring to achieve reconciliation.[660]

His tactics were to offer some practical help, win confidence, and gradually try to persuade selected individuals that they should join the CPA. When Oscar Riva, an Italian waterside worker treated to meals in restraurants and coffee lounges, finally wanted to enter the party, Stein suggested that he should first obtain his naturalization. Only then would he get his party card.[661] Stein was observed in East Sydney Darlinghurst areas engaging migrants in friendly conversations.[662] The party prepared booklets written in Greek and Italian.[663] At the CPA meeting in Adelaide, Stein advised that the best way to get 158,000 new Australians into the party was to tell them how to vote and help them with their income tax and other problems: "They should be invited into Party members' houses, and cultivated on a friendship basis which would flatter them." [664]

Stein always carried many propaganda brochures and Soviet propaganda films to show. He attended barbecues and dances.[665] He tried to impress the audience by very exaggerated reports on the economic successes of Soviet and Chinese Communists: "By 1960, China's industrial achievements would exceed that of the United States and Great Britain.[666] It is quite possible and feasible that they [the USSR] will surpass these countries [America and Britain] in seven years and by the time the 12 years plan is completed they will have headed the world in all spheres of industry, etc."[667]

In 1963 the ambitious Seven Year Plan was abandoned as impossible to achieve and harmful to the Soviet economy. Since 1959, Harry Stein had acted with the official party title "Tropical Organizer."[668] He confirmed it in 1960, telling a friend, "I am convinced that I am being trained as a tropical organizer."[669]

660 Ibid., ff. 133–34, 31–32, 21, 23, 70, 33, 60, 62, 67, 82, 93, and 98.
661 Ibid., f. 107.
662 Ibid., f. 108.
663 Ibid., f. 143.
664 Ibid., f. 144.
665 Ibid., ff. 147, 149, and 158.
666 Ibid., f. 167.
667 Ibid., f. 170.
668 Ibid., f. 184.
669 AA, A6119/90, 2478, Stein, Vol. 3, f. 73.

He was as busy as before, traveling to many Australian centers. In Brisbane, he organized an Italian Communist Party of Australia branch and took over control of the Italian Club. He "stated that he had been given the responsibility for traveling 'all over Australia' to make contact with National Groups and step-up Communist Party of Australia activities among New Australians."[670] He boasted to comrades that he received information concerning individual Italians from the Department of Immigration.[671]

While in Brisbane, Stein also attempted to create a Greek Communist Party of Australia branch.[672] He systematically worked on influencing migrants through papers published in their native languages. The Communist editors were not revealed. The Greek newspaper *Neos Cosmos* was published in Melbourne "under the undercover direction of the Communist Party of Australia." It published hints on income tax laws, suggestions of how to prepare tax returns, advice to unionists on how to improve the lot of railway workers, etc. Stein approved, because "it included throughout the paper items of Party propaganda they would also read."[673]

Stein did not like that a Roman Catholic paper, *La Fiamma*, was widely read by Italians who could get it in the Iron Workers' Union offices. The CPA endorsed his proposition that it should have its own Italian publication to counter the Catholic paper. He also tried to "get undercover control of it and change the content of the paper to suit the Communist Party of Australia."[674] On his visits to industrial centers Stein distributed copies in Greek and Italian of a booklet entitled (in English translation) "The Booklet of Legal Information for the Migrants." He insisted that the CPA CC should insure that the *Tribune* also print it in Polish.[675]

Stein wanted to break down the White Australia policy by finding a job in the Papua, New Guinea area to work amongst aborigines and migrants.[676] However, as with all other such initiatives, the primary

---

670   Ibid., ff. 27 and 18.
671   Ibid., f. 29.
672   Ibid., f. 26.
673   Ibid., ff. 6 and 44.
674   Ibid., ff. 5 and 44.
675   Ibid., ff. 58 and 162.
676   Ibid., f. 61.

goal was not to help the addressed communities, but to win them over for Communist Party purposes.

In response to his appeal to Italian members of the CPA to start publishing a weekly paper in Italian beginning in 1961, someone suggested that first it would be necessary to get money from the Italians to help finance it. Stein replied, "That would be very nice but don't worry about the financial angle; that is covered."[677]

When his passport was taken away from him while he was on a ship in Melbourne, he "remarked that the Communist Party had all sorts of schemes worked out to beat the security ban." He also reafirmed to his listeners that in Central Europe there was no such thing as an Iron Curtain.[678] Refugees risking their lives attempting to leave the Communist paradise across mine fields and barbed wire barricades guarded by watchtowers manned with machine guns might have disagreed.

Probably the most hilarious statement of Stein's propaganda addresses was his 1960 claim that "Sir Edmund Hillary was a spy and was sent to the mountains to contact agents and get information on China."[679] This startling revelation about the first person to climb Mount Everest was used by the Communist Party elsewhere.

In order to stir unrest in hostels and camps as happened in Victoria, Stein remarked that he "wanted to activate unemployed migrants" for causing more trouble.[680]

Stein did not forget his Eureka Youth League beginnings. In 1961, he led a series of political classes for young people at party headquarters, 40 Market Street, Sydney.[681] When Australian delegates flew to attend the Eighth World Youth Festival in Helsinki in 1962, Stein was there to see them off at the Mascot Overseas Terminal.[682]

Finally, in the winter of 1962, Stein reported to the CPA branch meeting on Lawrence Aarons's participation at the Indonesian Communist Party Congress. As mentioned elsewhere, at that time Soviet and Czechoslovak political and military assistance to the Indonesians

677 Ibid., f. 124.
678 Ibid., f. 71.
679 Ibid., f. 134.
680 Ibid., f. 174.
681 Ibid., f. 186.
682 Ibid., f. 229.

was in full swing. Stein repeated Aarons's claim that the local CP had two million members officially, though the actual membership was much higher. Sukarno attended the Congress together with some cabinet ministers.[683] From a local migrant organizer, Stein grew into an international political guru.

683   Ibid., ff. 236–37.

12

Vlastislav Kraus: Czechoslovak Consul General In Sydney, 1962-1965

Vlastislav Kraus took up his appointment in December 1962. According to an ASIO report, he knew his predecessor, Jaroslav Kafka, very well. Both joined the Ministry of Foreign Affairs in 1949 soon after the Communist coup d'état. In the sixties, they were the two oldest members on the Foreign Service. In Prague, Kafka helped Kraus to prepare for his new assignment.[684]

A change in policy accompanied the change in personnel. New instructions forbade employing "foreigners or Czechs who were long time residents in Capitalist Countries." Only employees engaged in Czechoslovakia would be permitted to work in the consulates. It meant that old friends of Kafka, such as Joseph Tříska and his wife, had to be dismissed. Tříska was then involved with the work of painting the Polish embassy, a convenient way of spying on its employees.[685]

Otherwise, the old routine of sending regular monthly reviews of social (political) activity continued along with the targeting of five influential groups: the leaders of the CPA, trade unionists, especially under Kraus useful businessmen, Labor Party Leftists, and the Sydney Czechoslovak Club. Leading trade union officials were often also highly placed in the CPA.

---

684 AA, A6119/90, 2468, f. 181.
685 Ibid., f. 180.

President of the Sheet Metal Union, Eliot Elliot and his wife continued to enjoy dinners paid for by the Czechs, as on December 5, 1963.[686] Soviet representatives again took part in such social occasions, as on September 30, 1963, when Comrade Oliva, member of the CPA CC, dined with Kraus and the Commercial Counsel Andreyenko who introduced his successor Treshenkov.[687] At another such occasion on March 28, 1964, the vice chairman of the CPA, Comrade Aarons, was treated to lunch together with Soviet Councellor Safronov and his wife.[688] On February 19, 1964, Kraus entertained the leading lights of the CPA, Bill Brown, Alec Robertson, Harry Stein, and six editors of the *Tribune*.[689] The general assembly of the Czechoslovak Club in Sydney was, - as usual -, well prepared and manipulated. First, Comrade Mládek, on December 8, 1962, informed the consul general about the compatriots' circle's activities. Together they prepared the list of functionaries to be elected, and then on January 26, 1963, supervised as honored guests the proper selection.[690] Acting very much like his predecessor Kafka, Kraus invited his old friend and secretary of the Czechoslovak Club, Slovak V. Klobušiak, and his familly to lunch and dinner on January 11, 1964.[691] They undertook an excursion to "discuss the compatriots" on February twenty-third.[692] Businessman M. Dekyvere drank cocktails with Kraus on the same day, and Mrs. Barton visited Kraus on the fifteenth of the same month in order to "exchange views on some questions of the peace movement."[693] These samples of the Czechoslovak consul general's social calendar reveal the well-established pattern of activities aimed at influencing Australian developments toward socialism, a.k.a. Soviet-style Communism.

Special reports were regularly dispatched to Prague by a courier. A May 7, 1963 letter informed the Ministry of Foreign Affairs about a dinner/buffet prepared on April fifth for "a large group of important functionaries of the Australian trade union movement." It reached

---

686   AMFA, 3108/63.
687   Ibid., 2596/63.
688   Ibid., 1525/64.
689   Ibid., 1350/64.
690   Ibid., 1034/63.
691   Ibid., 1137/64.
692   Ibid., 1350/64.
693   Ibid., 1268/63.

Prague only on June third. Since the matter was rather urgent, the delays seem to be extravagant. Listed as present were E. Elliot, president of the Sheet Metal Union; T. Winter, secretary of the Federation of Communal Employees; J. D. Kenny, vice president of the A.C.T.U.; Frank Purse, general secretary of the Building Workers' Union; and J. Baker, representative of the White Collar Workers' Union, all with their wives.

They discussed policies of the union movement. Kenny told Kraus that the leadership of the A.C.T.U. did not allow its members to participate in congresses organized by associations dominated by Communists. In September 1963, Australian unions planned to have a federal congress that might change that rule. Exchanges of delegations with socialist countries would be possible then, but there would be financial difficulties to overcome. This hint at Communists states' monetary support was immediately understood and rewarded by the consul general who suggested— as he reported to Prague— that "our own delegations, without any doubt, would pay their way to Australia." However, if Australian delegations faced problems with flying to Czechoslovakia, the ÚRO (the Czechoslovak equivalent of A.C.T.U., though highly centralized and completely dominated by the CZCP) could offer a certain subsidy if Czechoslovak airline was used. Kraus wrote, "I called to their attention our air connection between Jakarta and Prague." Kenny promised to arrange a meeting with the president of A.C.T.U., Munk, in Melbourne, or have Munk come to Sydney for a few days. T. Wright mentioned to Kraus that he would be flying to Cuba at Castro's invitation and would like to make a short stopover in Prague.[694] There the head of ÚRO's International Department (with an unreadable signature) remarked in his reaction to that suggestion that the financial promise of assistance might not be exactly right and requested clarification from his superiors.[695]

One year later, on June 6, 1964, Kraus sent another letter to the Ministry of Foreign Affairs with the intention of courting an important functionary of the A.C.T.U.; he forwarded it by a faster courier than the last time. It reached Prague in a week. Note his characterization:

---

694 Ibid., 1611/63.
695 Ibid., 110.450/63/112.788/63-5.

Res: Invitations of the Vice-President of A.C.T.U.,
J. D. Kenny to the ČSSR. He is very active in the
trade union movement as well as in Australian public
life. He was originally a glass factory worker and went
through many trade jobs. In leading positions he shows
himself to be an opportunist who politically belongs to
the center of the Labor Party. In the union movement
his position often changes and it is hard to predict if
in a concrete question he would lean to the Right or
Left [P. H. remarks: the strictly ideological view!]. In
distinction from the position of the Right, he admits
the presence of Communists in trade unions and does
not take part in their push to get them out. He keeps
personal contacts with Communist functionaries. As
are many other Australian trade unionists, Kenny is
a believing Catholic who goes to church and does
not eat meat on Friday. Because of heart disease he
is temperate in drinking alcohol. The fact that J. D.
Kenny does not avoid meeting Communists and to a
certain degree cooperates with them in trade union
problems is positive. He is an honest man and our
friends [P. H.: meaning the Soviets] think that his
visit to the ČSSR would be beneficial.

From June seventeenth to July nineth, J. D. Kenny represented
workers as part of the Australian delegation at a meeting of the
international Labour Organisation in Geneva. His wife traveled with
him. Kraus recommended that Kenny and his wife be invited to visit
Czechoslovakia either before his visit to Moscow or on his way back
home.[696]

In the archive of the International Department of the ÚRO,
two documents about the visit were found. The first was written by
Ms. Kitzlerová on July 22, 1964. She identified herself as a comrade
working for the department. She was in charge of the sightseeing
program for Kenny and George Blayney, president of the Machine
Industrial Workers, whom she called "a zealous Catholic." They were
both with their wives. They experienced many difficulties finding hotel

---

696   Ibid., 2027/64.

rooms and a lack of willingness to help in the busy summer season full of tourists. Although she tried to explain the situation in the mining communities of North Bohemia, the delegation was shocked by old houses unsuitable for living but occupied by workers. "They could not understand why in such an industrially rich territory people cannot have decent housing." Kenny was described as frank: "He says what he thinks." In order to repair the damage, Kitzlerová suggested to invite them again to a spa in High Tatras. "Their main wish is to get to know the truth and see it for themselves."[697] Shocking!

The second report on Kenny's visit was prepared by Comrade Málek and concerned a meeting with four comrades of the ÚRO. At the meeting Kenny declared that no working people desire a war as he found on his travels in the USA, Switzerland, the USSR, England, and Germany. He would strive to keep peace and do away with poverty. He expressed his thanks for the medical care provided to him and his willingness to repay his debt. In agreement with A.C.T.U.'s President Monk, he would facilitate exchanges of unionist delegations.

Kenny asked questions about the Czechoslovak pro-forma five parties and about working hours. The structure of local unions and their financing also interested him. Comrade Pastyřík of the ÚRO repeated the invitation to Australian unionists to visit the ČSSR in 1965 and suggested that leading comrades should spend their vacations in Czechoslovakia.[698]

On November 26, 1963, Consul General Kraus sent to the Prague ministry of Foreign Affairs by courier a substantial and secret analysis of "Anti-Communism in Australia." It was entitled "Extraordinary Political Report No. 7." A few quotations show his ideological perspective:

> Anti-Communism in Australia, as in other developed
> capitalist states, forms an important part of the
> policy of the governing agencies. Anti-Communism
> ideologically justified the active participation of the
> Australian Government in the Cold War on the side
> of imperialist great powers.... At the head of the

697 The document was given to me by an archivist without any file identi-
fication. I have a copy.
698 Ibid.

Australian Government for more than fourteen years
stands the rabid anti-Communist Menzies.... Heralds
of anti- Communism shamelessly lay claims to ideals
of personal freedom, humanism and democracy....
About Communism only all its enemies can talk
"freely." For the defense of their ideas and politics
the Communists have only their own press published
in difficult conditions and in small numbers. Doors
to radio and television are closed to them.... The
monopolistic bourgeoisie's efforts to realise their
policies meets strong opposition from the peace
movement and from Australian unions.... The CPA
concentrates its attention on the unions and the peace
movement. Through them it influences the masses
in order to mobilize them to fight the monopolistic
capitalism and against the most reactionary standpoints
of Australian foreign policy. Therefore, naturally
anti-Communists systematically denounce the peace
movement as a "covert Communist organization."...
They devote much effort to the so-called driving out
the Communists from trade unions where the CPA's
influence considerably exceeds its small membership.

The secret report sent by the Czechoslovak consulate general in
Sydney then addressed "anti-Communist hysteria" and "furious cursing
of the USSR." Parliamentary debates were called "theatrical." The
Democratic Labor Party was "committed to a fanatical fight against
Communism" and represented "generally backward workers and small
clerks." They were "characterized by a fanatical Catholicism and hatred
for everything progressive." Many adherents of the National Civic
Council were denounced as "straight spies of A.S.I.O." The Returned
Soldiers League and the airmen association were reviled: "Political
backwardness of soldiers is considerable." Postwar immigrants were
blamed for anti-Communism.

Very much like McQueen and other Marxist dreamers, the report
blamed the Australian "standard of living" where a house and a car
ownership are more important than politics. Individualism is strong.
Among "Left-wing deputies," Dr. Cairns was especially praised for

his anti-Americanism and his "congruent opinions with the Soviet policy of peaceful coexistence." Deputies Haylen and Uren were also extolled. (Agent) Skripov's expulsion "on the basis of fabricated accusations that he was building a wide network of spies in Australia" was called "hysterical." Revelations about Soviet massacres in Katyn and Solzhenitsyn's description of "innocent inmates in concentration camps" were criticized as "distorted." The film about a whole circus's defection from Czechoslovakia was denounced as helping to feed the propaganda describing Communists as brutal, stupid, and vain— although the desperate escape actually occurred. Professor Frank Knopfelmacher was dubbed "the anti-Communist mischiefmaker."

The report, as was habitual in such surveys had to end on a positive note:

> Soviet citizens by their tactful behavior, high intelligence and education are winning credence; in spite of the local unfavourable political climate their appearances meet with lively interest and are attended even by people outside of the progressive movement, mainly from the intelligentsia.... Trade unionists, cultural personalities and members of various groups of intellectuals are systematically invited to the USSR where they are able to see by their own eyes Soviet life.... We should continue the present policy of inviting Australian trade unionists to the USSR in connection with their trips to Europe and also keep sending Czechoslovak artists to Australia on a commercial basis. Sydney consul general Kraus.[699]

The battle for the minds of influential people was going on in order to ready them to embrace progress when the moment of revolution came. The professional persuaders did not feel discouraged even if the document quoted above could serve as a proof that the CPA existed in a free and legal society. They could publish their papers, but no masses were willing to buy and read them, because they did not share the editors' belief in a workers' revolution.

---

699 AMFA, 032217/63-5.

And so the consulate general helped to arrange many visits of trade unionists. J. Convery, A. Noonan, and F. Braun, went to the ČSSR for a week in August 1963. The problem with trade unionists often was that they asked improper questions while in mines or factories; it was easier to satisfy them in luxurious hotels, spas, impressing them with the horrors of fascism in Lidice, or by sightseeing in historical castles and churches. When bad conditions were found in working places, the usual explanation, as in this case, was that "capitalism left us difficulties" (P. H.: even twenty years after socialist nationalization).[700]

In March 1964, Kraus advised the Ministry of Foreign Affairs that the secretary of the Peace Council in NSW, G. Anderson, recommended that University Professor S. E. Wright, vice president of the Peace Council, and his wife be invited to the CSSR for a week. Their expenses while in the country would be paid.[701]

Kraus continued inviting trade unionists for meals, kept sending them for friendly sightseeing trips in the ČSSR, and often met Soviet representatives both in Canberra and Sydney, but his bosses in Prague were not satisfied. When the next Czechoslovak consul general, Karel Franc, arrived in Sydney in 1965, Vice Consul Karel Nekolný told him that "the best way to describe the mission in Australia of Vlastislav Kraus was that he had ruined everything which (Jaroslav) Kafka had built up." Franc promised that he would "regain the people who had turned against Kraus."[702]

A sample of Kraus's antagonizing important people who had been carefully cultivated for years could be seen in his handling of Eliot Valens Elliot. When Kraus said that he planned to visit Queensland in August 1963. Elliot suggested that he and his wife come with Kraus and introduce him to trade union leaders as he had done for Miloslav Jandík, Kraus flatly refused the offer.[703]

700 Comrade E. Labasta of the *dum kultury pracujících* [Workers' House of Culture], 6 September 1963. I have a copy.
701 AMFA, 108503/5/64.
702 AA, A6119/90, 2468, Kafka 7, f. 189.
703 AA, A6119/90, 2470, Jandík 2, f. 83.

13

Czechoslovak Consulate General In Sydney, 1965–1970, And Australian Consequences Of The Soviet Invasion In 1968

On the first of September 1965, the new consul general Karel Franc arrived in Sydney. For three years he would follow the established routine of contacts with and cultivation of the active or prospective collaborators and agents in view of a hoped-for Sovietization of the continent. Then came the invasion. The brutal military ending to the attempt to replace the usual inhumanity of the Soviet pattern of socialism by giving it a "more human face" had unforeseen effects on many Australian dreamers. It effectually put an end to many years of the subversive work and destroyed the effort of a generation of conspirators.

Before his departure for the new assignment, Franc prepared a *Draft of Relations with the Australian Commonwealth: Foreign Political Orientation of the Australian Government.* According to his draft, Australia supported reactionary solutions of international problems: "Australia was one of the initiators of the shameful campaign against socialist countries in the ONU in the so-called Hungarian and Tibetan questions." Franc pointed at "the affair" with the Soviet spy Petrov as "espionage provocation." Such an arrogant denunciation of all non-Communist attitudes as fierce reaction provoked a systematic blindness and naturally led to a general misconception of international relations. The isolation of conspirators was becoming absolute.

Franc denounced the Democratic Labour Party as semi-fascist and anti-Communist. He regretted that the weak CPA only had a strong position in the mining, unqualified workers and maritime unions. It would be necessary to enlarge the meagre contact with Australian politicians. The goal of creating an embassy in Canberra was not achieved because the Australians claimed lack of finances for their own embassy in Prague.[704]

In the part devoted to work with compatriots, Franc mentioned the number of Czechoslovak immigrants as between twelve and thirteen thousand. He proposed, in order to get them closer to the consulate and to brainwashing, to create cultural clubs of "friends of Czech music" or of "Komenský." Also, an "Association of Australian-Czechoslovak Friendship" could be established after consultation with the CPA [but not with the Australian government!] Practically, it would be a friendship with less than 1 percent of the population.[705]

On March 23, 1966, Franc sent to Prague a secret report by courier about a demonstration in front of the consulate by the association *Pravda vítězí* ("Truth will prevail!"). Some forty people attended. Nevertheless, the consul requested police protection.

The Prague Ministry of Foreign Affairs was regularly sending half-yearly recommendations for further activities. Cooperation with the CPA and attention to "perspective personalities" were always stressed.[706] The other way, from Sydney to Prague, went a report about the coming twenty-first congress of the CPA: "The local Communist Party works in difficult conditions. The workers' living standard is high, most of the workers suffer by trade-union illusions."[707] After the congress, Franc reported that the party is being torn apart by disputes.[708]

On April 24, in his report to Prague the consul general reviewed his visit to the capital city Canberra. The contacts with so-called

704 AMFA, T 1965–69 Angola Austrálie 1, file 411/112, No. 026-524/65-5, p. 1.
705 Ibid., p. 4.
706 Ibid., file 411/411, year 1965 and 1966/67. In the plan for 1966 the necessity of working among the immigrants was again stressed. There is a need "for deeper reporting on the post-February emigration" and "for infiltration among this type of former citizens." Ibid, file 1961–1971.
707 Ibid., file 411/311, 1966/67.
708 Ibid.

progressive Leftists continued. He dined in the parliamentary restaurant with deputies Tom Uren, Dr. J. F. Cairns, Bert James and Gordon M. Bryent, and senators L. K. Murphy, J. M. Wheeldon, and J. L. Cavanaghi. According to Franc, these people in the Labor Party formed a "Marxist wing."

Tom Uren especially recommended more frequent contacts between deputies of both countries because "Dr. Kriegel's visit the previous year by his contacts and political overview made a very good impression not only on ALP deputies but even on coalition parties of the government."[709] [Dr. Kriegel, during and after the Soviet invasion in 1968, would become a *bête noire* for the occupiers for its denunciation. It must have been registered in Australia.]

After the August invasion, Franc for some time continued his work for the Czechoslovak Ministry of Foreign Affairs. Thus a year later, on February 24, 1969, in his "Political Report No. 3," prepared by S. Vodička, he signed even this sentence: "The August events in the CSSR activated the old after-February emigration, mainly the existing organizations, but especially the Czechoslovak Club in Sydney. Anti-Communist elements used the events in the CSSR for a strong agitation."[710] However, then, imitating the example of Petrov whom he previously vehemently denounced as a traitor, he also requested the right of exile.

Prague MFA on October 13, 1969, sent to its remaining representants in Sydney this cautious advice: "Secret! Orders for a discussion on the occasion of transmitting the governmental declaration.... The desertion of consul Franc created an unfavourable moment in Czechoslovak-Australian relations, especially in case of his eventual publications in Australia.... It is not good to directly talk about this question nor to protest."[711]

On October 16, 1968, Karel Franc was replaced in the Sydney consulate by Jaromír Johanes. He had to face some problems. Mr. Homer, chief of the consular and diplomatic protocol of the Department of Foreign Affairs in Australia, complained that the Czechoslovak consulate general in 1969 "ordered for official use 250,000 cigarettes

---

709   Ibid., file 411/117, 1967–68.
710   Ibid., unit Sydney 1969.
711   Ibid., No. 025.388/69-7178

duty-free."[712] Johanes attempted to blame Franc for it and in his report to Prague boasted that he had harmed him by it for the conspicuous black-marketeering with cigarettes, and also with spirits.[713]

Johanes invited into his residence the Soviet ambassador Tarakanov with his wife and the First Secretary Comrade Gorev. On June 10, 1970, he sent a report on it. They discussed "further deepening of cooperation and they agreed about the need to gain Labor senator Murphy, leader of the opposition, for a short visit to the CSSR."[714]

On July 22, 1970, Johanes notified Prague Ministry of Foreign Affairs about the emigration of Mrs. Hartig and her daughters. Her husband used to work for *Skloexport* and the MFA (meaning that he was an agent). Recalled, he returned to Prague without his family. Johanes tried to blame Mrs. Hartig for "a love affair with an Australian of Czech origin, Mr. Liezl." He did not like the "exclusive interview with Mrs. Hartig" bought by *Daily Telegraph, Sunday Telegraph* and *Melbourne Age.*[715]

Comrade Mesjacev became a new Soviet ambassador in Australia. On September 5, 1970 Johanes sent a report by secret courier informing his superiors in Prague about his trip to Canberra. He reported to his Soviet indirect master the defection of the representant of *Jablonex*, Mr. Bartoš with his family, and consulted with the ambassador of the invading power about ways how to face Australian press, authorities, and diplomatic corps. Comrade Mesjacev advised that after bad experiences with Australian press and television it is better to avoid polemics.[716] In another report to Prague, Johanes pressed on the need to soon change the personnel of the consulate. It was promised that it would be done before the end of the year.[717] Obviously, not many Communists were willing to serve the Soviet collaborators.

On March 3, 1971, Johanes complained in his further report about the lack of material support for "work with the emigrants": "Both Polish and Hungarian consulates general are materially much

712 AMFA, T Argentina Austrálie 6, 1970–1974, file 411/117, No. 04
     2/70. On the note No. 1511, 1961–1971.
713 Ibid., file 411/117, 1967-68.
714 Ibid., unit Sydney 1969.
715 Ibid., No. 059/70.
716 Ibid., No. 079/70.
717 Ibid., No. 069/70.

better endowed, also by personnel, to devote themselves to working with emigration more thoroughly and systematically.... The Polish community numbers some 60,000 and the Hungarian some 35,000 persons."[718]

The Soviet invasion of fraternal Czechoslovakia caused a basic change in the position of the CPA. The party, for so long, carefully cultivated by Czech and Slovak comrades, never recovered from the crisis. We are able to document it from"Political Report No. 3" on the CPA situation sent by Johanes on March 10, 1970:

> Already in 1956 in the CPA appeared efforts to drag the party down to anti-Sovietic positions, mainly after the counter-revolutionary moves in Hungary. In a sharp fight the Marx-Leninist line then won, represented by the party's leader Sharkey. But in the leadership began to form a strong rightist opportunistic group led by Comrade L. Aarons who in 1966 managed to replace Sharkey in the function of general secretary of the party. Since that time rightist tendencies keep manifesting themselves ever stronger. .. If after the war the CPA had more than 20,000 members, today's membership is estimated at 3–4 thousand. At least 25% of them are older than 60.

Under the subtitle "Anti-Sovietism and Departure from Proletarian Internationalism" we can read: "For its anti-Sovietic attacks the CPA misused and misuses mainly the development sent in the CSSR during the last two years ... To a precedentless anti-Soviet campaign the CPA moved over after August 21, 1968 (P. H.: the day of the invasion).[719]

A political psychiatrist could be struck by this type of psychotic behavior of his patient who is unable to realize that a comrade could have for his actions not exclusively "anti-Soviet campaigning," but also quite genuine basic dislike of foreign invasions. This part of the report could have carried the so often misused slogan "Resistance of

---

718 Ibid., T Argentina Austrálie 1979–1974, file 4, 411/111.
719 Ibid., p. 5. It is funny to read about "counter-revolutionary moves in Hungary" when the Soviet forces invaded in order to crush the real people's revolution!

healthy forces in the party." On April 4, 1970 Johanes reported on thirteen pages on the twenty-second congress of the CPA: "The party is threatened by an ideological breakdown." The consul's illusions about "healthy forces in the party" proved to be exaggerated: "Out of 130 delegates 118 voted for the group led by Aarons and only 12 for proposals of healthy forces in the party."[720]

On July 21, 1970, Johanes invited for lunch Comrade P. Clancy, member of the Central the Committee of the CPA and secretary of the Union of Construction Workers, who "as the single man of the CC CPA is attacking the incorrect policy of the party's leadership." Clancy, however, was not an altruist. He requested help with a short stay in Prague for four members of a delegation of his union who depart on August 5 to Moscow.[721]

I remember that while I was living in Australia for thirty years, it was obvious that this union had problems with a high level of corruption. For instance, leaders of the union quite often had their own houses built up by construction workers, members of the union, from union funds. In the above quoted case, a milder form of corruption was being used. It was mutually agreed reciprocal support.

Next year, another help was offered to Comrade Clancy. With Comrade Sharkey and his wife he arrived from Moscow. Previously, he had stayed in Prague several times. He stressed that it is important all the time, untiringly, correctly explain the Czechoslovak question, that is being misused both by the reaction and also by the rightists in the CPA, who denounce the events as a brutal invasion. If it were possible to explain the question correctly as a Soviet fraternal help to Czechoslovak socialism, it would be of great help to members of the CPA who cannot agree with the politics of the contemporary leadership of the CPA that condemned it as an invasion.[722]

The only problem was the IF. Since 1971, three miniature Communist parties competed in Australia about the tiny number of comrades. Johanes therefore decided to go fishing in more friendly waters. Certainly not only on his own advice he flew to the Philippines. On April 23, 1971 he was invited to a breakfast by the Minister of Foreign Affairs, General C. Romulo, who informed him that against

720 Ibid,. p. 2.
721 AMFA Prague, file 1970-74, T Argentina Austrálie, box 4, 411/111.
722 Ibid., box 3, No. 0.22.320/71-7.

closer relations with socialist countries, often the argument was cited that their legations misuse diplomatic relations. Johanes then referred to Prague his impression that is would be useful to "concentrate our efforts on helping by concrete actions realistic Philippine forces in their attempts to detach Philippines from their one-sided orientation on Washington."[723] It seems that forces can be not only healthy, but also realistic.

Johanes also flew to Papua New Guinea. On May 15, 1971, he sent to Prague a quite sensible report:

> Many people of Czech origin, allegedly some 100, are working here. Some of them hold functions in the colonial administration. Most of them are members of the so-called post-February emigration.... When I was asked by the head of the Administration about the entry of allied military forces on our territory in August 1968, I explained the significance of the international help of the SSSR and other socialist countries to socialism in the CSSR.

Even there they did not like the invasion! Johanes recommended bigger export of Czechoslovak medicines to Papua New Guinea.[724]

723 AMFA Prague, file 1970-1974, T Argentina Austrálie, boc 4, 411/111.
724 Ibid.

PART III:
Illusions And Reality

1

Agents Or Fools?

o o o o o o o o o o o o o o o o o o o o o o o o o o o o o o o

One is easily fooled by that which one loves.

Molière

The twentieth century, the most murderous in human history, is shameful not only for the massacres of many millions of innocent victims by totalitarian dictators, but also because so many intellectuals helped to support such villians and even admired them as saviours instead of unmasking them and combatting them. Such willful blindness helped to diminish resistance to evil and political criminality of the highest order.

For a Central European observer who happily settled in Australia in 1971 for thirty years, the controversy surrounding Professor Manning Clark sounds very familiar. (These chapters will consider Manning Clark less as a historian and more as a public personality.)

For some sixty years I have asked myself in regards to Cold War history, "Is he or she an agent or just a fool?" Many people in my lifetime, through their irrational beliefs and anti-democratic behavior, confirmed Julien Benda's 1927 thesis on the "treason of the intellectuals" in his book *La Trahison des Clercs*. (Pun on Clark's name intended.)

Out of many possible examples, I would like to show what I mean by describing a person who, at least in Australia, does not provoke such strong feelings as the Czech Protestant Christian, Professor Josef Hromádka. His name will probably be recalled only by some senior Australians or Anglo-Americans because he was highly esteemed in religious circles for his theological writings and, in the fifties, also for his activities for Soviet front organizations, including the World Council of Churches and World Peace Council. Very much like Manning Clark and many other Left-leaning intellectuals, he hated British imperialism and American capitalism—a hate which by itself might have had some reasonable motives—but he also foolishly believed that a new and better civilization was being created in the Soviet Union.[725] Like Manning Clark, Josef Hromádka, although a bourgeois himself, hated the bourgeoisie. Both men foolishly saw in Lenin a Christ-like figure and in Communism a newly realized Christianity. A mixture of irrational hate and naïve illusions led many intellectuals into believing patent nonsense.[726]

Professor Hromádka was worried about a possible atomic war between the superpowers. He worked hard for a reconciliation, hoping that Christians could moderate radical Communists and humanize the movement. Through his influence in religious circles, not only in Australia, he persuaded quite a few Christians that the Soviet Union was basically a peace-loving country that should be trusted. Several of his fellow believers regularly attended conferences around the world, spreading the message about the supposedly

---

725 Very much like Clark, Hromádka believed in Lenin's saving mission. He wrote, "Russian, Soviet revolution may be a great asset in religious history." *Křesťanská revue* [Christian Review], No. 5 [1931–32], p. 105. And also "Lenin's achievement appears to be one of the main pillars of the future organization of human society." Quoted by Pavel Filipi, *Do nejhlubších hlubin* [Into the Deepest Depths], [Prague: Kalich, 1990], p. 352.

726 "Communism is the newest link in the evolution of the Western culture—Christianity." Quoting Hromádka's speech on the 26th March 1949 in Brno, J. S. Trojan et al., *Nepřeslechnutelná výzva* [An Appeal not to Overhear], Edition Oikúmené, 1990, p. 81.

good intentions of Soviet leaders. At this time, Stalin was carefully planning future takeovers. (Australia was scheduled to become Communist, as General Šejna, who knew about the Socialist bloc's military plans, revealed in his book *We Will Bury You*). Stalin was feverishly re-arming in a way that helped to antagonize workers in satellites of the USSR since their standard of living plummeted. Professor Hromádka and other religious leaders were in fact trying to lower Western defences more than change Communism. (I know of only one Marxist who was moderated by these meetings between Communists and Christians: Milan Machovec who wrote an admiring book on Thomas G. Masaryk from a Marxist point of view and even a good book on Jesus Christ. Machovec became a reforming Communist.) Otherwise, the result of such conferences fulfilled the intentions of Soviet propagandists and conspirators, that is to fool Western intellectuals about Soviet leaders' character and intentions so such Western figures would influence the public on their behalf. I along with many other Czechs kept asking myself if Professor Hromádka was an agent or just a fool? [727]

In the second half of the nineties, during my stays in the Czech Republic, I attempted to answer the question. Although I did not have access to secret police archives concerning Hromádka, it seems that he was just a sincere frightened fool. His basic mistake was his belief that Western civilization was doomed and would be replaced by the victorious Leninist civilization. He and the dean of the faculty of philosophy, and my professor, J. B. Kozák, shamelessly collaborated with the Communist Party during their putsch of February 1948. When I repremanded him for it, he replied that there will be a collision between two huge icebergs and that he wanted to join the winning party in time to dress the wounds of the losers. He also sometimes used a similar metaphor of two millstones threatening to kill us all. I told him that the Communists would just use him and

---

727 On September 23, 1958, as the first Czechoslovak citizen, Hromádka received Lenin's award for consolidation of peace and international friendship.

get rid of him once his usefulness ended. That actually happened very soon after.

In Prague in the nineties, I met several of the leading representatives of Protestant churches who shared Hromádka's ideology (a mixture of theology and Leninism), and who took part in pro-Soviet religious political meetings around the world. All of them found their names mentioned in a list of secret police agents published in the unofficial volumes of *Rudé krávo* (a pun on the official party press organ *Rudé právo*; in English meaning "Red Cow" instead of "Red Justice"). They claimed that they were not agents, in spite of the fact that the police allowed them to travel widely every year, which was out of the question for 99 percent of the population. Were they really agents or just collaborating fools voluntarily working for the party and taking advantage of party favors? Now they knew that they had lost prestige and credibility. They distrusted each other. By using them, the Communist Party managed to harm the popularity of Protestant churches to such a degree that they lost some believers to the Catholic Church. For instance, my friend Zdenka Frydrychová/Kubicková who began as a Protestant, moved gradually to the Catholic Church, that for the most part did not share the illusions about the benevolence of Communism (although quite a few of its priests, for other reasons, also worked as informers for the secret police).

On a related note, it is important to remember two significant misconceptions concerning the workings of Communism that people in democratic countries often share. First, not all Soviet agents were contract agents. As long as influential public figures wrote and acted in a way that pleased organizers of the world Communist conspiracy (never doubt its existence!), they did not need to pay them for their voluntary services. Communists preferred not to sign them up as agents. That would destroy their credibility and diminish their power to influence other people; better that they remained supposedly independent thinkers. Lenin said it well right at the beginning when he recommended the utilization of "useful fools" as much as possible.

Second, not all Communist sympathizers and fellow-travelers had to carry a party card. On the contrary, often it was preferable to keep them as free agents. For example, at the end of the Second World War, the leader of the Communist Party of Czechoslovakia, Klement Gottwald, advised General Svoboda, who wanted to become a member of the party, that he should not enter its ranks: "We can use you more as a non-member of the Party!" Accordingly, Svoboda then served in the government as an independent as Minister of Defense and shocked the democrats during the putsch in 1948 by throwing the weight of the armed forces behind the putschists.

Although Professor Manning Clark was probably not a contracted agent of influence in the sense that he was not paid for his services to the Communist cause, he was an "agent of influence" in the other meaning of the word agent, namely as an activist propagating a cause he believed in and publicly supported.

In 1960, two years before the publication of the first volume of *A History of Australia*, after just three weeks in the Soviet Union, Clark claimed in *Meeting Soviet Man* that he discovered a paradise of brotherly and just Soviet society, where people were already happy and smiling. In reality, it was a police state dictatorship based on slavery. Repeatedly in his articles he praised life in people's democracies and alleged that people that in reality lived in misery enjoyed themselves much more than in Western democracies.

He did not shy away from associating with at least one official and paid agent, Ian Frank Milner. This old friend of his, in his capacity as acting head of the Department of Political Science at the University of Melbourne, appointed Manning Clark as a lecturer in 1944. The same year, Milner began to supply Communist secret services with British confidential material on post-war plans in the oceans. He became a full-scale agent for the Czechoslovak spy network in 1949. He also served as a Soviet spy, as is well known. However, when Manning Clark visited Prague in 1958, coming from Moscow as head of an Australian cultural delegation, he met Milner in his hotel his first evening there. (Milner took refuge in the ČSR when his pro-Soviet spying was revealed in 1950.) Manning Clark must have known that his old friend and protector was a double anti-Australian spy, but that obviously did not trouble his moral sense. After a week-long stay in Prague, his last evening there, December 3, 1958, was again spent in Milner's company, this time in Milner's apartment. (It would be interesting to read what Milner, as was his duty, reported to his police masters.[728])

Manning Clark did not mind traveling as a guest to the Soviet Union just two years after the Soviet massacre of tens of thousands of Hungarian freedom fighters and again two years after Soviet tanks liquidated the Prague Spring of 1968 (even Milner liked Dubček!). He made other friendly visits in 1964 and 1973.

He never stopped propagating the compassionate Lenin, in spite of the fact that the cynical and merciless Lenin during his short stay in power managed to murder at least a couple hundred thousand of his compatriots. Lenin even asked his chief of secret police, "Are we killing enough professors?"

---

728   "In 1964, while on study leave, Clark phoned Judah Waten and told that he had 'seen Ian Milner whilst he was overseas'—he had met him in Prague and London—he said that he would tell Watten all about it when he called to visit him." ASIO secret intercept report on Clark-Watten contact, Vic W 223/125 incoming call. Quote by Andrew Campbell, "Double Lives: Three Australian Fellow-Travelers in the Cold War, *National Observer—Australia and World Affairs,* June 22, 2006, fifth page of 10. Here is a testimony on Waten: "Manning Clark House, devoted to perpetuating the memory of Manning Clark,… has published on the Internet an extract from an address by Clark's son Andrew on the occasion of the Judah Waten National Story Writing Competition. Judah Waten was an Australian author. He was also a brutal literary Stalinist.

Ex-Communist writer Dorothy Hewett, at one time deeply involved in Communist literary politics, told me that when writers from the Soviet Bloc toured Australia, it was Waten who called on them and their Australian contacts and told them that if they said anything out of line he would be on the phone to report it to Moscow that night. He also told them that their lives were at stake." Hal G. P. Colebatch, "Manning Clark and Judah Waten", *National Observer—Australia and World Affairs,* April 1, 2004, on the first page of 6.

As for myself, I got a measure of the man when Clark publicly stated that, "We are going to be tried in a fiery furnace" in a possible "fratricidal war" before "the Australian phoenix will be able to rise from the ashes and fly." As a preventive measure for my students, some of whom then believed that guerrillas in the low Darling Ranges, and in the woods around Pemberton, Western Australia, could topple the Australian government, I quoted Manning Clark's statement with the comment that irresponsible public figures who call for a cleansing fire and labor camps do not belong in universities but rather in a mental institution.[729]

From the Soviet point of view, both Professor Hromádka and Professor Manning Clark were "agents of influence," even if they were not contracted as such. They publicly influenced many people who admired their other achievements and they were trusted as independents, more than if they had been members of the Communist Party. From the point of view of Communist conspirators, they were even better than enlisted agents of influence.

Non-enlistment also had an important psychological effect for people like Hromádka and Manning Clark. They had a clear conscience. They did not serve a political party. They were free agents following their own beliefs. In their minds, they were doing their best to defeat "bad people," Western imperialist capitalists, and to help to victory the "good people," the Leninist "humanists." It also flattered their sense of their own importance. It helped to give them prestige, self-satisfaction, and, of course, some welcome emoluments from Soviet gratitude.

In the final analysis, their behavior was rooted in defeatism. They did not feel like democrats who should defend humanism against the barbarians of brown or red fascism. They did not trust that seemingly

---

729 University of Wollongong Graduation Day, 12th May 1978, Clark's "Draft," pp. 4–5, *Weekend News*, 13.5.1978, p. 1. According to ASIO G Q file PF/C/8/10, "Clark had operational contacts with numerous [15!] Soviet intelligence officers [some were KGB/GRU co-optees] whom he met at their residences and at many Soviet embassy functions." Campbell, "Double Lives", *op.cit.*, fourth out of 10 pages.

weak and corrupt democracies could or even should win, so they tried to join the supposedly winning and superior side in time. Hatred for your own people and false illusions about your real enemies can have terrible consequences. Even if they did not sign any contracts as agents, the behavior of so many of the educated Left amounted to treason.

2

Manning Clark's Illusions And The Soviet Strategic Plan

o o o o o o o o o o o o o o o o o o o o o o o o o o o o o o o o o

We had excellent sources in Australia and Canada.... We had productive moles in Australian Intelligence who passed us documents from the CIA and British Intelligence, as well as providing us with information on subjects as varied as the peace movement and the Australian military.

Oleg Kalugin, Spy Master, p. 170

So far a few important facts in the disturbing affair of "agent of influence" Manning Clark and his friend, Czech-Soviet spy No. 9006, Ian Milner, have not been properly considered. For instance, fifteen prominent Australians complained to the Australian Press Council about the *Council-Mail's* treatment of Clark when in an article he was named as a pro-Soviet agent of inluence. Democrats usually view everything from a humane, even sentimental, perspective. That, however, markedly differs from the way steeled anti-democrats, ruthless practitioners of Realpolitik, see it.

In the past, democratic politicians have repeatedly made the same mistake—and it is a very dangerous mistake—believing that totalitarian dictators share their values, scruples, and inhibitions. They refused to realize that their opponents acted according to totally different and much more merciless principles. In case the democrats did not read Machiavelli's *The Prince*, at least they should have learned from the last century's history. Let us recall just a few examples of such dangerous misunderstanding:

1. Until Lenin's successful putsch in November 1917 (falsely glorified as the "October Revolution"), Alexander Kerensky believed that socialists did not have enemies on the Left and that he could trust the Bolsheviks' claim that they were fighting for a workers' democratic system.

2. When representatives of the British government went to Rome in the thirties to see Mussolini and tried to win him over by hinting at English acceptance of Italian fascists' domination of the Mediterranean Sea, Il Duce remarked to his minister of foreign affairs, Count Ciano (who then put it down in his diary, since then published), that such obviously weak people should be given a kick in the pants.

3. When Neville Chamberlain in the famous scene at the London airport waved a piece of paper with Hitler's signature on it as a supposed guarantee of peace, he foolishly trusted a much more unscrupulous man than he was himself.

4. When Czechoslovak President Beneš believed Stalin's word that he would never interfere in domestic affairs of his democratic republic, he showed the same credulity as the other democrats when they all demonstrated their lack of understanding of totalitarian mass murderers, the shrewdest criminals of our age.

Contemplating Australian experiences with public figures such as Professor Manning Clark and his friend, the unmasked spy Ian Milner, we have to look at them and at the events not only from our own humanistic and sentimental point of view, but also from the widely different viewpoint of their Soviet masters. Luckily, capable observers of Soviet political thinking and behavior pointed out some of their peculiar features. Their knowledge has often been based on inside information gained while they were still serving the Communist cause.

For instance, in his book *We Will Bury You* (1982), Jan Šejna described the Soviet Strategic Plan according to which all Europe should have become Communist, the United States isolated and demoralized, and Australia, among others, prepared for a takeover. He wrote: "As First Secretary in the Ministry of the Defense I was a member of the Administrative Department, through which passed all the major Soviet directives. In the sixties, the Strategic Plan was prepared and accepted by all countries of the Soviet Bloc. All had their special assigned tasks, both in its preparatory, political phase, and later military advance to enemy territory."[730]

The whole book is worth reading, but I think Australians should have been especially interested in chapter fourteen, entitled "The Plan for Britain and Australia."[731] It is instructive to realize what kind of intentions Moscow had in 1967 when the plan was finalized, and how foolish all the Leftist dreamers were who trusted the peace-loving Soviet Union. They were part of the plan even if they were playing their roles unwittingly.

As a first step, the plan stressed that in Britain, "progressive forces must take over the trade unions and penetrate the Labour Party."[732] That was nothing new. This strategy was already in use in Australia and many other countries since the end of World War II, and sometimes even before from the beginning of the Second International and the Comintern. That was also the way the seizure of power in Czechoslovakia was prepared during the three years before the coup d'état in 1948. General Šejna remarked that Czech Communists were already subverting British trade unions before 1967.

The next task was to "discredit and weaken the bourgeois leadership in the U.K."[733] The Soviet takeover of Czechoslovakia and other people's democracies provided a model of how to conduct such a smear campaign. Then "sabotage operations" would "cripple

730 Jan Sejna , *We Will Bury You* [London: Sidgwick & Jackson, 1982], p. 109. "One of the basic problems of the West is its frequent failure to recognize the existence of any Soviet 'grand design' at all. Those rejecting this concept unwittingly serve Soviet efforts to conceal their objectives.... The Soviet Strategic Plan for the establishment of their 'Socialism' worldwide does, without doubt, exist." (p. 103.)
731 Ibid., pp. 142–50.
732 Ibid., p. 143.
733 Ibid.

vital British industrial, defence, and communications installations as a prelude to war."[734] In 1964, Alexander Shelepin, head of the KGB, supplied Czech Communist leaders with a list of several hundred names "including leading members of all political parties" in Great Britain. According to Šejna, "action contemplated ... ranged from temporary detention to execution without trial." Assassination of "selected British personalities" was planned even before the takeover in order to "precipitate both a crisis of leadership and a collapse of national morals." In order to achieve their goals, they would have to give their violence the correct spin: "The murders were to take place during their visits to Third World countries, where such killings should be easier.... In this way they would be interpreted as a repudiation of Britain and British imperialism by the developing world."[735] People familiar with methods that were used for takeovers of Central East European satellites by the Soviet Union know that such methods were indeed effective.

British unions were supposed to create a second power and Czechoslovak Communists had to prepare British unionists by special schooling that included sabotage and use of bombs and firearms as their special task. For that purpose, their suitable members were being invited to Czechoslovakia.[736] As some Australians might remember and as Prague archives abundantly confirm, in the fifties and sixties, many trade delegations and groups of young Australian Communists, were invited not only to Prague but also to Moscow and Peking for weeks at a time in order to obtain such specialized schooling for future use.

General Šejna also gives some details about Soviet and Czech political intelligence and military help given to the IRA, which shared the goal of destabilizing Britain. For instance, hundreds of tons of Semtech, the most destructive bomb material produced in Bohemia, were shipped to Ireland.[737]

---

734 Ibid., p. 144.
735 Ibid.
736 Ibid., pp. 145–47.
737 Ibid., pp. 147–48.

Now we come to Australia. Šejna's recollection of this part of the Soviet Strategic Plan is short and takes less than two pages. The methods to be used in Britain were to be used in Australia too, although a little later, and did not have to be described in detail.

During military maneuvers in Bohemia, Soviet Marshal Grechko stressed the strategic importance of Australia. Boris Ponomarenko, who was in charge of foreign Communist parties, said in 1967, "Comrades, I can understand your view of Australia as a country of little importance to your concerns; I must tell you that you are wrong in this and that you have an important part to play in our operations against this country. You must understand that if we wish to control Asia we must first control Australia."[738]

General Šejna writes that he grasped the details when he could see the Strategic Plan: "According to the Plan, the neutralization of Australia and New Zealand will follow the neutralization of Western Europe. Like Europe, Australia will advance to Socialism and 'neutralism' step by step, and it will only be in the final stage that a revolutionary government will be established."[739]

It is important to remember that the Soviet meaning of Socialism did not resemble our idea of democratic socialism. Soviet Socialism meant the strict militaristic and dictatorial application of all Soviet methods, including nationalization of factories, shops, and services, collectivization of farms, and a police state, as practiced in the Soviet Union and all other Communist states.

In Australia, according to the plan, infiltration and deception had to be exploited. Political parties' established leadership had to be replaced by the methods suggested for Britain and used in all Communist countries. In 1982, when General Šejna's book was published in Great Britain, "The 'liberation' of Australia was to be accomplished by the 1990s. Undoubtedly this timing will have to be revised."[740]

Had Manning Clark been more interested in facts and the real world than in his hopeful fantasies about a new and better Leninist

---

738 Ibid., p. 150.
739 Ibid.
740 Ibid., p. 151.

civilization, he would have studied the methods of modern totalitarian dictators and understood what real values were at stake. But as his writing often demonstrates, like some other bookish intellectuals, he was powerless to resist the appeal the "strong leaders" Communism provided.

3

Manning Clark's "Christlike" And "Compassionate" Hero Lenin Was In Fact A Merciless Mass Murderer

The degree of discrepancy that can exist between a political delusion and reality is exemplified by Professor Manning Clark's perception of Lenin's "Christlike compassion" and the Bolshevik conspirator's extreme lack thereof. Since Clark believed that a new and better civilization would come about based on Leninism, it is very important to realize what that new "ism" really meant and what kind of a person Lenin actually was.

Lenin: A New Biography[741] was published a few years ago. Its author, Dmitri Volkogonov, cannot be dismissed as a bourgeois Western historian prejudiced against Communism, because until his death in 1995, he occupied important positions in the Soviet Union as a member of the party and served as director of the Institute of Military History. What is even more notable, he was a Leninist— until he was allowed access to the secret archives of his idol. When he published *Stalin: Triumph and Tragedy* in 1991,[742] he still was, as he himself readily admitted, a Leninist. Until a few years ago, secret Soviet archives were closed. He was the first one to gain entry. What he discovered shocked him enormously. He decided to expose "the ideological myths of Leninism.... The sickness in the system was in its very foundations."[743]

---

741 New York: Free Press, 1994.
742 New York: Grove Heidenfeld, 1991.
743 Volkogonov, *Lenin*, pp. 458 and 463.

However, Lenin revealed his intentions even before the seizure of power in 1917. Both Volkogonov and Clark could have better understood their idol had they taken his pronouncements seriously. The Russian author recalled some of them: "In 1906, Lenin stated the doctrinal position from which he never departed: 'Dictatorship is nothing other than power which is totally unlimited by any laws, totally unrestrained by absolutely no rules, and based directly on force!'"[744] Volkogonov also recalled that, "During the 1905 revolution ... he [Lenin] urged the revolutionaries to adopt tactics which most people would regard as abnormal and terrible: to fight against the Cossacks, he urged the use of knives, knuckle-dusters, sticks, paraffin-soaked rags, stones and acid 'to throw over the police.'"[745] Before further quoting a few examples of Lenin's merciless treatment of his opponents, here is a sample of the March 31, 1993 Moscow paper *Nezavisimaya Gazeta*: "In 1917 Lenin issued the order of campaigns of mass 'secret terror' in Latvia and Estonia, with a reward of 100,000 rubles for every 'kulak, priest, and landowner who is hanged.' He added that 'we'll make the hangings look like the work of the 'Greens,' and then afterwards we'll put the blame on them.'"

When tens of thousands of farmers rebelled against the Bolshevik misuse of power, similar methods of mass terror were suggested by Lenin in a letter to the Bolsheviks in Penza, not far from Simbirsk:

> Comrades! The Kulak uprising must be crushed without pity.... An example must be made. 1. Hang (and I mean hang so that the people can see) no less than 100 known kulaks, rich men, blood-suckers. 2. Publish their names. 3. Take <u>all</u> grain away from them. 4. Identify the hostages as we described in our telegram yesterday. Do this so that hundreds of miles around the people can see, tremble, know and cry: they are killing and will be killing the bloodsucking kulaks.... P. S. Find tougher people.

The Russian author of Lenin's biography explains the widely accepted Bolshevik lie about the kulaks: "Who were these condemned

744   Ibid., p. 448.
745   Ibid., p. 411.

individuals? Today we know them to have been the hardest-working, most capable of the peasantry."[746]

After the February 1917 genuine people's revolution, the provisional government in Russia abolished the Tsarist secret police and released all political prisoners. A few weeks after the seizure of power, Lenin resurrected it under the name of CHEKA, made it much more horrific, and commented, "Unrestrained, lawless power, based on force in the simplest sense of the word, is precisely what the dictatorship is about."[747] Volkogonov wrote, "Tens of thousands of people were shot without trial in the cellars of the Cheka" (238) and "The Cheka quickly became virtually the chief element of the state." (240) On Lenin's suggestion, "the 'proletarian poet' Demyan Bedny was invited to watch the execution [of Fanya Kaplan], for the sake of revolutionary inspiration."[748] Lenin's speech to the Young Communists in 1919 is quoted: "We do not believe in eternal morality, and we're exposing the deception of all the fairy-tales about morality."[749] Volkogonov comments, "The true father of the Bolshevik concentration camps, the executions, the mass terror and the 'organs' which stood above the state, was Lenin."[750]

The Bolshevik leader, admired by Manning Clark and other Leftist sympathizers in Australia, was a systematic terrorist. "Speaking to the Communist Trade Union faction on 2 January 1920," Lenin said, "We shall not hesitate to shoot thousands of people!"[751] "In the autumn 1920 he wrote to Krestinsky [secretary-general of the Communist Party]: „The preparation of terror in secret is necessary and urgent."[752]

The Russian writer, Maxim Gorky, Lenin's favored chess partner, received a letter from him written on the fifteenth of September 1922. All the Leninist intellectuals should read it: "The intellectuals, the lackeys of capital, who think they're the brains of the nation. In fact,

---

746   Ibid., p. 7.
747   Ibid., p. 237.
748   Ibid., pp. 238, 240, and 227.
749   Ibid., p. 228.
750   Ibid., p. 235.
751   Ibid., p. 438.
752   Ibid., p. 82.

they're not its brains, they're its shit!... We shall cleanse Russia for a long time to come! Cleanse it, that is, of intellectual conscience."[753]

Manning Clark's compassionate Lenin was a figment of his imagination. The real Lenin did not show any compassion, even during the horrible famine that his regime provoked four years after it came to power; *after* the end of the civil war that was caused by Lenin's unwillingness to share power with democratic socialists. Returning now to the Leninist Volkogonov's account: "According to incomplete data, in 1921-22 there were about 25 million people   starving in Russia. During this time the Party leadership was sending vast sums of money and a large quantity of gold and treasure, to foreign Communist Parties to help ignite world revolution. Again according to incomplete data, in the course of 1922 gold and treasure, much of it of Church origin, to the value of more than 19 million of gold roubles were thus transmitted."[754]

Volkogonov continues: "Lenin wrote a (secret) letter on 19 March 1922: 'There is a 99% chance of smashing the enemy on the head with complete success and guaranteeing positions essential for us for many decades to come. With the starving in the localities eating people and the roads littered with hundreds if not thousands of dead bodies, it is now and only now that we can (and therefore must) carry out the removal of church valuables with furious and pitiless energy." Volkogonov adds: "According to a variety of data, between 14 and 20 thousand clergy and active laymen were shot. In his letter he demanded that 'the greater the number of reactionary clergy and reactionary bourgeoisie shot over this issue, the better.'"[755]

That was followed by a typical Leninist touch, alluded to previously: "The journal *Bezbozhnik* (Atheist) catalogued the dark deeds committed by the Church, which it practically accused of having caused the famine."[756]

A Russian presidential commission announced—and it was published in the *West Australian* on November 29, 1995—that two hundred thousand clergy were systematically murdered under the

753 Ibid., pp. 361–63.
754 Ibid., p. 375.
755 Ibid., pp. 378–79.
756 Ibid., p. 384.

Soviet rule in a horrible cycle of crucifixions, scalpings, and tortures. The commission's report was presented by its chairman Alexander Yakovlev who said, "Documents relate how clergymen, monks, nuns were crucified on royal gates and shot in the basements of the Cheka (secret police), scalded, strangled, drowned and submitted to other bestial tortures." Yakovlev added that five hundred thousand religious figures suffered persecution in the decades after Vladimir Lenin's Bolsheviks seized power.

A few years later, the historian Harvard Professor Richard Pipes was allowed to peruse Lenin's documents. In his book *The Unknown Lenin: From the Secret Archive,* he confirmed Volkogonov's findings and added other fascinating documentation to the story.

He reproduced Lenin's birth certificate as Document 1, confirming that "Lenin was a hereditary noble."[757] Document 28 was a letter from the beginning of September 1918 addressed to Comrade Krestinsky (secretary-general of the Communist Party): "It is necessary secretly— and urgently to prepare the terror."[758] In his "Political Report to the Central Committee ... of the Communist Party from 20 September 1920," Lenin proposed a way to deal with his opponents: "We will be shifting from a defensive to an offensive policy over and over again until we finish all of them for good."[759]

During its retreat from Poland, "the Red Army carried out numerous pogroms against the Jewish population. Local Jewish Communists urged Lenin to intercede, but ... he refused to do so."[760]

In his introduction, Pipes wrote that the documents "cast fresh light on Lenin's motives, attitudes, and expectations." Pipes's conclusion? "Those who still idealize Lenin and contrast him favorably with Stalin will find little comfort in the Lenin documents which are now coming to light.... Lenin is revealed in these documents as a thoroughgoing misanthrope."[761]

Pipes commented on documents that prove that after invading Poland in 1920, Lenin planned to export the revolution on the bayonets further, into Czechoslovakia, Hungary, Romania, England, and Italy:

---

757   New Haven: Yale University Press, 1996, p. 19.
758   Ibid., p. 56.
759   Ibid., p. 114.
760   Ibid., p. 116.
761   Ibid., pp. 6 and 11.

His remarks leave no doubt that in the summer of 1920 Lenin believed western Europe to be on the brink of social revolution; this revolution he was determined to promote and consummate with the help of the Red Army.... The purpose of invading ethnic Poland, it now transpires, was not merely to Sovietize the country but to use it as a springboard for the invasion of Germany and England.... Lenin grotesquely overrated the revolutionary ardor of the English workers—indeed, he compared the England of 1920 with the Russia of 1917!—and conceived in his imagination phantom armies of hundreds of thousands of German Communists marching to join the Red Army.[762]

Commenting on documents 91 and 102, reproduced in the book, Pipes wrote: "As far as Lenin's personality is concerned, we note, first and foremost, his utter disregard for human life, except where his own family and closest associates were concerned.... They were his soldiers—but only as long as they obeyed him."[763]

For mankind at large Lenin had nothing but scorn. The documents confirm Gorky's assertion that individual human beings held for Lenin "almost no interest" and he treated the working class much as a metalworker treated iron ore. Calls for the burning of cities and the extermination of their inhabitants are reminiscent of the age of Genghis Khan and Tamerlane.[764]

Introducing several documents on Lenin's wasting large amounts of money on the support of foreign revolutions, Pipes wrote:

The one sentiment Lenin never appealed to was idealism: apparently he had no faith in it. Lenin scattered money around but he also showed no compunction about taking it.... We now learn that as late as August 1918, three months before Germany's surrender, he badgered Berlin for money to carry

---

762   Ibid., p. 7.
763   Ibid., p. 8.
764   Ibid., p. 10.

out anti-French and anti-British—that is, pro-German—propaganda in western Europe through his representative in neutral Switzerland (Document 25). This surely qualified him as a German agent in the strict meaning or the word.[765]

And two final quotations from Pipes's Lenin revelations: "He ordered the GPU to prepare a roster of 'several hundred [intellectuals] who must be deported abroad without mercy' (Document 107)."[766] In another document Lenin praised Machiavelli as "one wise writer on matters of statecraft" who "rightly said that if it is necessary to resort to certain brutalities for the sake of realizing a certain political goal, they must be carried out in the most energetic fashion and in the briefest possible time because the masses will not tolerate prolonged application of brutality."[767]

Volkogonov and Pipes should be able to show to stubborn Leninists their revered guru in his true colors. Some of them might, of course, agree with Lenin that you have to kill if it serves your ideology.

In his 1963 book *A Short History of Australia*, Manning Clark wrote: "While Australia was torn in two by sectarian and provincial rivalries, the Bolshevite party stormed the Winter Palace in Petrograd. On 7 November Lenin told his followers in the Smolny building in that city: 'Today has begun a new era in the history of mankind.'"[768]

Again, the historian did not know the facts. The party stormed the Winter Palace only in a Soviet propaganda film. Actually, a few Red Guards entered the palace through a side door, declared the session of the cabinet over, arrested all, and opened the gates from the inside. In the chapter entitled "The Age of the Optimists," Clark again compares the two worlds: "The news of the successful revolution in Russia, and the Bolshevik slogans of peace, bread and land contrasted sharply with the imperialist slogans of a war to the finish."[769] Yes, the slogans contrasted, but what is more important, the slogans or the nature of

---

765 Ibid., p. 12.
766 Ibid.
767 Ibid., p. 153.
768 New York: New American Library, p. 197.
769 Ibid., p. 197.

the entities behind them? Clark is using a true statement to make a false impression.

A closeminded Leninist and defender of Manning Clark at any cost might object that the Australian historian could not have known what was in the secret files. However, there were hundreds of thousands of refugees who told their stories. There were Lenin's pamphlets available to read.

Not everybody was so easily fooled as Manning Clark. The English philosopher Bertrand Russell went to see Lenin and came back with dire warnings about the cruel dictator, as he wrote in *Bolshevism: Practice and Theory*. After five weeks spent in Bolshevik Russia in May and June 1921, and after his studies of Marxist and Leninist literature, he came to these conclusions:

> I am compelled to reject Bolshevism for two reasons: First, because the price mankind must pay to achieve Communism by Bolshevik methods is too terrible; and secondly because, even after paying the price, I do not believe the result would be what the Bolsheviks profess to desire.... The ultimate source of the whole train of evils lies in the Bolshevik loutlook on life: in its dogmatism of hatred and in its belief that human nature can be completely transformed by force.[770]

The Czech philosopher and historian who later became president of Czechoslovakia, T. G. Masaryk, spent months in Russia in 1917 and wrote about the terror he witnessed. He also warned of the new barbarism coming from Lenin's Russia. Western trade unionists, especially delegations coming from Great Britain, returned from Russia without any illusions about the horrific Red rule. As Russian historian Volkogonov said, "Since the time of Lenin, falsehood had become one of the Party's chief political assets."[771] But those willing to see and think clearly were not fooled.

Had Manning Clark, or any other Communist and fellow-traveller, been interested in facts and truth, he could have discovered the true Lenin in his published works. When Clark came back from his first

770 Bertrand Russell, *Bolshevism: Practice and Theory*, pp. 160 and 180.
771 Volkogonov, *Lenin*, p. 321.

trip to the Soviet Union in 1958, he decided to improve his knowledge of the Russian language. Then he could have—should have—read in the original what Lenin wrote and published. Much was available even before the secret Soviet archives began to be opened in the nineties. Lenin's collected works were not published in full, but thirty volumes of his selected *Sochinenia* were issued in Moscow in 1935–37. A large collection of Leniniana came out in fifty-eight volumes between 1958 and 1966 entitled *Plnoe sobranie sochinenii*. In spite of limitations caused by Stalinist censorship, a serious historian would have looked into these volumes and found the real Lenin.

Many books available while Clark was writing contained quotations from Lenin's writings and speeches in English. Maxim Gorky's *Untimely Thoughts: Essays on Revolution, Culture and the Bolsheviks, 1917–1918* were published in London in 1970. G. H. Leggett picked up many quotations from Lenin's writings and made them accessible in 1975 in a study called "Lenin, Terror, and the Political Police" in the British monthly *Survey* in 1975[772] and in 1981 in a book *The Cheka: Lenin's Political Police.*[773]

If Clark had not had a prejudice against bourgeois authors, he could have read some surprising statements from the great leader in *Cheka*. Proving that "We have never rejected terror on principle, nor can we ever do so,"[774] on November 28, 1917, Lenin urged "revolutionary terror" against the state employees who went on strike protesting his putsch. The same day he signed a decree denouncing them as "enemies of the people." On November 21, 1917, he declared: "The state is an instrument for coercion.... We want to organize violence in the name of the interests of the workers!"[775] „In the name of" is a revealing turn of phrase.

On January 14, 1918, Lenin declared, "Until we apply terror to speculators—shooting on the spot—we won't get anywhere." And in February 1918, "Surely you do not imagine that we shall be victorious without applying the most cruel revolutionary terror."[776] When the second conference of Soviets abolished the death penalty on the military

---

772 Vol. 21, No. 4, pp. 158–87.
773 Oxford: Clarendon Press, 1981.
774 Ibid., p. xxxiii.
775 Ibid., pp. 54.
776 Ibid., pp. 55 and 57.

front in November of 1917, Lenin exploded in rage: "How can one make a revolution without firing squads?" On June 8, 1918, he advised, "We must increase the capture of hostages." When his commissar of justice, I. Z. Steinberg, upset about the consequences of mass terror, protested, "Then why do we bother with a Commissariat of Justice? Let's call it frankly the Commissariat for Social Extermination, and be done with it!" Lenin's face brightened. "Well put ... that's exactly what it should be ... but we can't say that."[777]

The terror did not diminish in 1920 at the end of the civil war which was provoked by the Bolsheviks, because they insisted on ruling without any other party's participation. On July 5, 1921, Lenin said: "Dictatorship is a state of intensified war.... Until the final issue is decided, the state of terrible war will continue. And we say war is war, we do not promise any freedom, nor any democracy."[778]

On December 22, 1921, he advocated "merciless, swift, instant repression." On February 20, 1922, he spoke in favor of "intensifying repression." On May 17, 1922, he said "The law should not abolish terror ... it should be substantiated and legalized."[779]

Contrary to popular opinion, the campaign of terror was not limited to the "exploiting class." Soon after the November coup détat (so-called "October Revolution") the terror was extended to all sections of the population, including workers. In April 1918, Lenin wrote about the need for "the most decisive and draconic measures for raising the workers' and peasants' discipline and self-discipline."[780] In February 1920, Lenin told an audience of Chekists, "Revolutionary violence cannot be withheld from use against wavering and irresolute elements among the working masses themselves."[781] Soon thousands of them were massacred and hundreds of thousands of workers and peasants were imprisoned and sent to labor or concentration camps.

---

777 Ibid., pp. 62 and 56, quoting from I. Z. Steinberg, *In the Workshop of the Revolution* (London, 1955), p. 145. About Lenin's advice of mass detention and execution of hostages. See. pp. 148–49 of Leggett's book.

778 Leggett, *The CHEKA*, p. 349.

779 Ibid., pp. 343, 347.

780 Ibid., p. 172.

781 Ibid., p. 313.

Dzerzhinsky's order of January 8, 1921 said, "The prisons are packed chiefly with workers and peasants instead of the bourgeoisie."[782]

G. H. Leggett, whose book *The Cheka: Lenin's Political Police* (1981) provided all the above quotations, rightly concluded, "The key to understanding the Red Terror and the Cheka system lies essentially in Lenin's doctrine and Lenin's character."[783]

Maxim Gorky criticized his friend and chess partner Lenin for his "lack of morality ... an utterly pitiless attitude ... toward the lives of common people."[784]

For Lenin, terror became a governing instrument, useful for its efficacy. The murderous efficiency of his terror machine is obvious when we compare some fourteen thousand executions during the last fifty years of the Czarist rule, with at least two hundred thousand executions under Lenin from November 1917 to the end of 1923.[785] (In his Appendix 6, George Leggett collected information on "Deaths Attributable to the Chekas" and concluded with this comparison based on Robert Conquest's "The Human Cost of Soviet Communism" in *Document No. 92-36 (92nd Congress, 1st Session) of the United States Senate, Committee on Judiciary, Sub-Committee to Investigate the Administration of the Internal Security Act and Other Internal Security Laws*, July 16, 1971, pp. 5–33.) The Czarist yearly quota of killings was on average 280; Lenin's was more than a hundred times more: 33,333 people executed on average every year. Yet UNESCO did not mind organizing a seminar on "Lenin-the Humanist," instead of the more appropriate "Lenin-the Mass Murderer." Lenin's minority and terrorist government established the first criminal state in modern history, waging a bloody war on its own people. As a Russian newspaper expressed in 1921, "The whole of Russia has been turned into an immense penal servitude prison."[786]

---

782 Ibid., p. 329.
783 *Survey,* op. cit., p. 174.
784 *Untimely Thoughts*, p. 88.
785 Leggett, *CHEKA*, op cit., p. 468.
786 *Izvestia VRK Kronstadt*, 12 March 1921; quoted by Leggett, 1981, p. 338.

4

"Australia Between Two Worlds:" Manning Clark Versus The Refugees

In "Between Two Worlds, 1941–1963," the twelfth chapter of his book *A Short History of Australia*, Clark wrote about the "success of Communism in eastern Europe and China," about "the defeat of reaction and obscurantism in Eastern Europe," and about "the division of the world into Communist and anti-Communists camps."[787] He denounced "reactionary, capitalist America" and reviled "anxious if not strident voices of alarm and prophesy [that] began to be raised again in Australia about the threat of Communism to western civilisation."[788]

On the last page of his book, Manning Clark was obviously siding with these Australians who, as he said, "argued" about "the spiritual sickness of bourgeois civilisation" and who believed that "only the destruction of bourgeois society could liberate the creative spirit of the people and restore to their literature and their art the hope and confidence of men who knew the way forward for humanity." He obviously "knew the way."[789]

The defeat of democratic and humanist forces in Czechoslovakia in February 1948 by the seizure of total power by the Communist Party of Czechoslovakia [CPCZ], according to Manning Clark, was part of "the defeat of reaction and obscurantism."

---

787 New York: Mentor Book, 1963, pp. 224, 236, 231, and 237.
788 Ibid., pp. 240 and 228.
789 Ibid., p. 244.

A few young Australians who settled in Prague at that time also admired "the young revolution" and established a "colony" there, as it was called by one of the enthused "colonists," later to become a disillusioned Communist, Stephen Murray-Smith.[790] Many Australian intellectuals were inspired by Manning Clark to attempt to convince Left-wing dreamers that a new, better world was being created on the ruins of the decadent and moribund bourgeois capitalism by the brave Soviet, Chinese, and East European Communists.

I.

During twenty years of the Communist regime in Czechoslovakia, some 255,000 Czechs and Slovaks left the country illegally, mostly without passports. Sixty thousand of these refugees crossed the heavily guarded frontiers, going west, soon after the coup d'état. Another 245,000 left between 1968 and 1989. A quarter of a million people were imprisoned or sent to concentration camps in the Communist Czechoslovakia. Out of ten thousand political prisoners, 240 were executed or beaten to death.[791]

In the first wave after the coup d'état in 1948, some twelve thousand Czech and Slovak refugees migrated to Australia, fleeing the horrors of Communism. They joined tens of thousands of migrants from other Stalinized countries. There was a chance to learn from them about the true nature of Communist rule. This chance was almost completely missed by intellectuals such as Manning Clark. Their mind was set and closed. They preferred to implicate the immigrants in the larger capitalist conspiracy.

On October 13, 1950, John McIsaac, editor of *Labor News*, sent a four-page letter to Jan Kabourek, International Secretary of ÚRO in Prague, in which he explained the Australian government's policy concerning anti-Communist political refugees. Its alleged aim was to foist US war policy on Australian unionism. "The reactionary national Government" of "Menzies and the monopolists who back

790 Patrick O'Brien's "Transcription of Taped Interview," p. 11.
791 Information provided at "Týden zahraničních čechů" [Week of External Czechs] Conference in Prague on the occasion of 650 anniversary of the foundation of Charles University, 28.6. – 4.7. 1998.

him," according to John McIsaac, wanted to "virtually end the right to strike" and under the pretext of fighting Communism attack "any and all unionists." McIsaac described one of their methods as "A stream of immigrants trained in Nazi principles ultimately to be used as a strikebreaking force.... The Communist paper *Tribune* this week called on the people to fight against the 'conspiracy.'"[792]

For many Australian workers, however, refugees' revelations of Communist methods represented the first truthful information on the dictatorships installed in east central Europe. Former member of the CPA, Geoff McDonald, wrote:

> When many thousands of refugees entered this country decrying life in the Communist countries, the Communists regarded them as fascists, counter-revolutionaries, ex-members of the dethroned bourgeoisie, ex-moneylords and non-cultivating landowners. But the Australian worker on the job knew better. ... It was not long after the waves of migration commencing in 1948 that almost every building job in Melbourne employed a number of workers who had lived under Communist rule. The other workers believed their picture of life in the countries from whence they came, so that when union officials organised delegations to these countries and the delegates came back with one-sided and uncritical reports to the workers, they simply made themselves look ridiculous.[793]

The common man proves more intelligent than his supposed intellectual superiors. The Czechoslovak consulate general in Sydney, of course, refused to help refugee compatriots and, on the contrary, began to spy on them. The Czech Ministry of Foreign Affairs preserved in its archive documents it received from its representatives in Australia. On the basis of one such report, the ministry related to Comrade Michailov (a Russian name) of the CPCZ Central Committee, that immigrant Miroslav Horn\u00e1k was trying to organize Czechoslovak refugees in

---

792 ÚRO [Central Union Council] Archive, 152057/31.10.1950.
793 *Australia at Stake* (Melbourne: Peelprint, 1977), pp. 110–111.

Sydney to join a society called *Pravda vítězí!* ("Truth Will Prevail!").
That was hardly a reactionary slogan learned from the Nazis. It came
from the Hussite religious revolution of the fifteenth century. It was the
motto of the humanist president of the pre-WWII democratic state,
T. G. Masaryk, and was retained until 1948. Václav Havel restored it
as the presidential maxim in the anti-Communist revolution of 1989.
The consul mentioned that Hornák was employed by the Australian
Admiralty in Sydney as a janitor.

Written in Slovak, Hornák's document makes it clear that the
organization aimed to concentrate on social and cultural activities,
including entertainment and sport. Courses in English language played
a prominent role. The major task, however, was to organize financial
and immigration help for tens of thousands Czechs and Slovaks living
in German and Austrian refugee camps.[794]

Few industrialists or wealthy people were in the first wave of refugees
migrating to Australia; most of them were intellectuals, students, middle
class people, workers. In later waves of refugees, the majority would be
farmers, artisans, and miners. The middle-class professionals were not
used to hard manual work—especially when sent for the obligatory
two contracted years of employment (as repayment for the transfer to
Australia by boat) to such locales as the bush, full of flies, poisonous
snakes, spiders, and stifling humidity. It did not create ideal conditions
for fast acclimatization.

Culture shock made matters worse. Heavy drinkers themselves,
Czechs and Slovaks were amazed by the regular drinking bouts of the
locals. They missed their favorite sports, such as soccer and ice hockey,
and did not understand or like Australian football, cricket, and hockey.
Constant betting on horse and dog races seemed silly to them.

So the consul could report to the Ministry of Foreign Affairs on the
situation quite truthfully, using, of course, its own biased vocabulary:

> For a few months now, the Australian press stopped
> publishing tendentious and inimical news about
> Czechoslovakia, by which it has been saturated by
> newly arrived Czechoslovak refugees into Australia.
> One of the reasons for this change is the fact that
> dissatisfaction and unwillingness to work on assigned

---

794 CzMFA Archive, 100/3/21/25, f. 26.

workplaces is spreading among the deportees to Australia on the basis of a two-year working contract.

The consul also reported a growth of criminality and conflicts.[795] Although some criminal acts occurred, it could not have been too bad since the police commander in NSW revealed that in comparison with other immigrant nationalities, the criminality of those originating in the Czechoslovak Republic was relatively low.[796]
The first two years of refugees' and immigrants' lives in any new country are usually the worst. Nostalgia for lost homes, relatives, and friends, together with the shock of the strange new environment, both natural and manmade, are depressing, yet, Czech and Slovak future Australians settled rather fast. On February 20, 1951, the Czechoslovak Foreign Institute, in charge of supervising compatriots abroad, communicated a much more positive picture:

> The largest part of refugees stationed in refugee camps in Western Germany migrates to Australia. On the 17th and 18th November 1950, in Melbourne took place a convention of representatives of the so-called Czechoslovak organisations in Australia and New Zealand. Every organisation sent three delegates. They created a Centre of Czechoslovak Democratic Organisations in Australia and New Zealand. Former Deputy Jindřich Nermuť, now living in Tasmania, was elected as chairman. It was agreed to publish a paper *Hlas domova* ["*Fatherland's Voice*;" for years it represented the best weekly in the whole Czechoslovak exile!] with a sub-title *Australské listy* ["*Australian News*"]. The Czechoslovak Society with its secretariat in Canberra will be a very active part of the Centre. It works socially, helping immigration.… It organises

---

795 Ibid.
796 5 June 1963.

courses of English ... and appeals for donations of
blood for the Australian army fighting in Korea.

The report, without any criticism, also listed established Sokol
gymnastic clubs in nine Australian cities. However, it called for a
systematic propagandistic effort in the distant continent:

> It is certain that this large stream of refugees will try to
> influence previously settled countrymen. Therefore,
> Australia is becoming for us an important field of
> activity. It is certain that the group of compatriots
> in Melbourne cooperates with the refugees, as well
> as former employees of the consulate, General Sakh,
> Tokoly and Hála. Hence it will be necessary to support
> the only positive Czechoslovak circle in Sydney.... It
> is vital to ascertain if the society is financially strong
> to cope with the tasks that face them.... Among its
> members are good workers as can be testified by the
> fact that two delegates, compatriots J. Tříska and Vl.
> Klobušiak, took part in the peace congress in the state
> of NSW.

On November 6, 1951, the Czechoslovak Foreign Institute
submitted another report on the situation in Australia. It disclosed that
the Czechoslovak Society in Sydney had approximately ninety members,
mostly industrial workers or artisans: "[Its] activity is limited by the
political situation, provoked by the reactionary Australian regime....
The financial situation is relatively good and the moral position was
improved by a purge voluntarily undertaken after the February events
in the ČSR."[797]
The report listed the three most activist functionaries: chairman
Václav Mládek, mercenary joiner; Vladislav Klobušiak, a worker; and
Josef Tříska, chairman of the cultural and entertainment committee.
The last two were again praised for having taken part in the Sydney

---

797 As if in preparation for the purge to coincide with the putsch in
Prague, Mládek, Klubušiak and Tříska joined the Club in 1947/48.
See the report by a member of the originally non-political Club, AA,
A61119/90, 2465, Kafka 4, f. 100.

peace congress and for their campaign to win many compatriots in Australia for the signing of a peace resolution.

The report expressed similar ideas as Manning Clark when describing the "opposite of the Czechoslovak Society in Sydney," namely the "reactionary Czechoslovak Organisation in Australia." Regrettably, from the point of view of Czech secret service agents, "Australian offices have addresses of all immigrants, but for security reasons refuse to divulge them."

The brief also discussed some of Clark's suspected "reactionary and obscurantist" ideas of the new settlers: "Units of Sokol founded in 1950 in Australia exist and educate their members in Masarykian and republican ideals.... Fellow countrymen consider themselves as homeless exulants and according to chairman L. Mládek and secretary Václav Pavelka, 'live in faith in a liberated state and by faith that all that is violent and barbaric is only temporary.'"[798]

One year later, on October 23, 1952, a document addressed to the Czechoslovak Ministry of Foreign Affairs revealed that two shipments of books were sent from Prague to the Sydney pro-Communist compatriots' society. According to a former employee of the consulate in Sydney, Comrade Jakš, "in Australia now live approximately 12,000 refugees who have recently showed a great discontent. Their majority is employed in most demanding working conditions for which no local workers can be found.... The Australian Communist Party is active among the refugees."[799]

The Prague regime for years actively supported the only Czech and Slovak pro-Communist club in Sydney, especially its chairman Václav Mládek. Often he was treated to a meal by the Sydney consul general. However, much more was involved, as a secret report from September 18, 1958 specified. It was sent by the Czechoslovak Foreign Institute to the Ministry of Foreign Affairs. Václav Mládek was provided with a Sydney–Prague flight and stayed for three months in his old country, all expenses paid. He spent two weeks in a recreation resort, one week in Slovakia, and was treated to a free trip to the Soviet Union, primarily Moscow and Leningrad. In order to obtain this very unusual benefit, he must have been trusted and highly valued by Soviet secret services.

---

798 CzMFA, ČÚZ [československý ústav zahraniční – Czechoslovak Foreign Institute], III-269.6/5529/51-Ch1.

799 Ibid., III-21161.2/6403/52.Ad.

Even most of the Czech and Slovak Communists were not allowed to travel to the supposed workers' paradise. The report is silent about the remaining two-thirds of Mládek's stay in Czechoslovakia. Was some specialized training involved? The report stressed that "all possible care and solicitude" was taken in order to satisfy the valued guest. It was expected that upon his return he would continue his active support of Communism among Australian citizens, mainly workers. He was provided with "all necessary material." Various gifts would be sent to his group in Sydney for a Christmas bazaar to be sold and thus help the group financially. Mládek promised to send reports on Australia at least once a month and to contact a travel agency in Sydney to organize trips of compatriots to the ČSR. Mládek and his wife were employed by the consulate.[800]

Mládek must have flown to Prague again the next year, because consul general Kafka in his review of activities reported that all members of his staff went to the airport on September 6, 1959 to welcome Mládek back from his visit to Czechoslovakia.[801] In 1962, it became known that Mládek wanted to return to the ČSR at the club's expense.[802]

It might be of some interest that on July 15, 1960, when the Czechoslovak consulate in Melbourne was closed down, "Comrade E. Bílek returned to Comrade J. Kafka his official pistol CZ 50, caliber 7.65."[803]

On March 8, 1966, the Sydney consul general sent its "Plan of Activities among Compatriots in Australia for the year 1966" to Prague

---

800 Ibid., III-010.328/58-Ni. See also AA, A.442/111952/14/5001, a file devoted to Mládek. According to a coded airmail letter from the Sydney consulate general, during her visit to Prague, Mrs. Mládek met former commercial attaché in Sydney, Comrade Jakš. She told him that before her departure she received a personal letter from prime minister Menzies addressed to the British embassy in Prague offering help in case she experienced any trouble in Prague. Her two sons worked for the Australian government. She and her companion, member of the CPA, Jakub Schwarz, were surprised by the quality of life in the ČSR "in spite of the fact that they did not believe Western inflammatory propaganda." CzMFA, 420.091/55-ABO/3.

801 Report by the Sydney consul general.

802 AA, A6119/90/2467, Kafka 6, f. 138.

803 Report by the Sydney consul general.

via special courier. It expressed hope to influence both the pre-1948
settlers in Australia and the refugees with a bulletin to be published
regularly in Sydney. It planned to pay for two study trips and four
compatriots' medical services in the old country. Books and propaganda
material would be sent as usual. The consulate would be forwarding
"more in-depth reports on post-February emigration for an intended
infiltration" of its ranks. Individual refugees would be followed and
reported on. (Practically all refugee organizations suspected that agents
were hidden and active in their midst, but did not know them.) It was
proposed that Czechoslovak coaches working in Australian sporting
clubs should be used for political propaganda.[804] Some members of the
Czech Social Club regularly reported to the consulate on others in the
community.[805]

Finally, it was suggested in the 1966 plan that every year the Sydney
consul general should select a functionary of Czechoslovak associations
for an all expenses paid ten- to twelve-day trip to Czechoslovakia. He
should then work among fellow countrymen in Australia.[806] (That was
the last document that I was able to photocopy at the Prague Ministry
of Foreign Affairs concerning their care of Czech and Slovak refugees
who migrated to Australia. A thirty year statute of secrecy obviously
applied.)

Intriguingly, in thousands of documents retrieved from both
Canberra and Prague archives, only two instances were documented of
the consular care of compatriots that should be the proper business of
their representation in foreign countries, that is excluding the politically
expedient favoritism of Czech and Slovak naturalized Australians used
for information and spying.

In the first case, on October 31, 1961, Stanley James Moran
"informed Joe (Joseph) Tříska (Secretary of the Czech Consulate) that
a Czech national was in a Sydney jail after being caught as a stowaway
on the Wanganella, and asked if he could be given any assistance."
According to the press, his name was Mike Urych. After consultation
with Kafka, Tříska announced that the consul refused to intervene

804   CzMFA, CUZ-S-II, 191.249/66-Ht-Mi.
805   AA, A6119/90/2465, Kafka 4, f. 100.
806   CzMFA, Annex to fn. 18.

"because the stowaway had committed an illegal act and for this reason must take the consequences."[807] Kafka did not want to be bothered.

In the second case, the attitude of another consul was a little more positive. The initiative came from consul general Kraus and his deputy Nekolný. On July 16, 1964, they called on G. Hartley, Department of External Affairs, requesting funds for repatriation of their former citizens who ended up in mental institutions in Australia. Their families would prefer to care of them at home. The department had no funds to spare.[808]

II.

For many years, Australian officials exhibited much more concern about the plight of Czechoslovak refugees than their Czech counterparts. Although from the start self-interest in obtaining a cheap labour force and new citizens went hand in hand with the altruistic tendency to help people in distress, gradually a genuine concern resulted in a systematic campaign called Operation Reunion, begun in 1956. But right from the beginning of the Czechoslovak refugee problem there were instances of wholehearted and effective help given not only to the consular officials who resigned from their positions and requested asylum as described previously.

Here is an example worthy of citing. Major Julius Vaca and Lieutenant Otto Klein, officers of the Czechoslovak army, were among the first to apply for immigration to Australia. They wrote, "For the second time we had to leave our dear country to escape dictatorship and terror, to fight for the four liberties if necessary again." Major-General A. G. Salisbury-Jones, military attaché at the British embassy in Paris, on May 31, 1948, supported their application in his letter to the Commonwealth Migration Officer in Sydney:

> The above-mentioned Czechoslovakian officers, together with their families, have very recently left their own country for reasons which demand the sympathy of all members of democratic nations. These

---

807   AA, A6119/90/2465, Kafka 5, f. 139.
808   AA, A1838/2/1531/17, PT1.

officers during the last war fought with distinction in the cause of freedom and rendered valuable service to Great Britain and the Allies. Major Vaca and Lieutenant Klein have expressed their desire to immigrate with their families to Australia. In view of the past records of these two officers and their services to the British Commonwealth of Nations, it would be greatly appreciated if you could grant them every assistance in achieving their object.[809]

On June 22, 1948, E. Roland Walker, chargé d'affaires at the Australian embassy in Paris, sent a memorandum to the secretary of the Department of External Affairs in Canberra informing him that the day before, the former Czechoslovak ambassador, M. Nosek, "who resigned following the Communist coup in his country," called on him to appeal to the Australian Government "to provide facilities for immigration for some of the political refugees who have left Czechoslovakia since the Communist (sic) seized power." About ten thousand of them were in German refugee camps in the American zone of occupation. He hoped that Czech ex-servicemen like Vaca and Klein could be included in the Allied Ex-Servicemen Immigration Scheme.[810]

The answer sent by the Department of Immigration on May 11, 1949, was negative but said "Australian Selection Teams were operating throughout Germany." However, T. H. E. Heyes, secretary, forwarded a copy of the embassy's memorandum to the head of the Australian Military Mission in Germany.[811]

Exiled Czechoslovak politicians concentrated their efforts on mobilizing support for assistance to their compatriots in refugee camps. In Washington, DC, Dr. Juraj Slávik, former Czechoslovak ambassador, called on the Australian ambassador regarding immigration and presented a review of the refugee situation toward the end of 1949, prepared by the Council of Free Czechoslovakia. There were some twenty-eight thousand refugees, and thousands of them were already being admitted to Australia as immigrants, yet five hundred to six hundred "displaced persons" were "debarred from the care and

---

809   Ibid., folios not numbered.
810   Ibid.
811   Ibid.

maintenance administered by the International Refugee Organization," because they frankly admitted that they took part in the struggle against the Communist regime. The Council of Free Czechoslovakia appealed for help to these opponents of Communism and appointed Karel M. Sakh, former consul general in Sydney, as its representative in Australia.[812]

I understand this tricky legalistic determination from my own experience. In Paris, where many Czech and Slovak students were being generously aided by French authorities, I was expressly refused any help with my studies since I was an *opponent* of Communism and not just its *victim*. The head of the Entre-Aide Committee invited me to dinner but refused any help. He was a member of the French Communist Party.

Some refugees, in order to avoid arrest for being active in non-Communist parties during WWII, fought with British or American armed forces, left in a hurry, and their children or relatives stayed behind; once in Australia they attempted to reunify their families. Often it took years, if ever. According to a message by W. G. A. Landale of the fourth of August, 1959, "Mr. McEwen did in fact make representations in 1956 to the Czech Government on behalf of residents of Australia with relatives in Czechoslovakia."[813]

In the Australian Department of External Affairs, the pile of requests for help grew. In January 1959, Mrs. M. Chvátal pleaded the case of her two daughters. They were born in London in 1941 and 1945 when she was living there. After the war, she took them back to Czechoslovakia, but in 1947, she was sent to work for the embassy of her country in India. When her three-year assignment lapsed, she did not return to the ČSR dominated by the Soviet Union and came to Australia. Since then she had been trying to bring her daughters over through the Red Cross without success. Naturalized in 1957, she begged for help.[814]

Karel Kostelník pleaded the case of his parents (seventy-one and sixty-seven years old). Previous appeals to the United Nations and international Red Cross did not lead to any success, although the

---

812 Ibid.

813 Ibid.

814 Ibid.

elderly couple donated all their possessions to the state hoping that they would then get an exit visa.[815]

A series of documents in the Canberra archives testifies to the plight of Mrs. Helen Vickers (Vorlíček) who had been trying to bring her daughter and mother to Australia. In the first letter written in March 1959, she complained about the "cruel play, punishing us for leaving the country," and ended, "Don't you think, Sir, that to unite the world in peace is not possible without uniting the families first." She and her husband sent a cable to the Soviet deputy premier, Mikoyan, when he was in the USA, asking for help. No reply was received. They appealed to the Czechoslovak president, Antonín Novotný. In reply they were told that her mother had not applied for a passport which was a cruel joke since she was not allowed to obtain the necessary application forms. In May 1959, Mrs. Vickers was informed by the Department of External Affairs that it was consulting the British embassy in Prague. In August 1960, the External Affairs officer in London was advised that "it appears that the refusal in both cases was based upon the fact that Mrs. Vickers had left the country illegally."[816]

In September 1959, Parliamentary Deputy M. G. Haworth, as a member of an Australian delegation (mentioned in another chapter), discussed with the head of the Commonwealth Department of the Czechoslovak Foreign Ministry five cases of "Operation Reunion" that originated in 1956. Mrs. Vickers and Mr. Kostelník were on the list. "The Czech officials showed considerable hostility to the idea of letting people go, on the ground that when they reached foreign countries, they told lies about conditions in Czechoslovakia. Nevertheless, Deputy Haworth was promised that all on his list would be permitted to leave in three months. Only one of them arrived in Australia fifteen months later."[817] The Czechs claimed that they only promised to examine the list.

The review of the "Operation Reunion" prepared by the Department of Immigration in September 1961, quoted above, contained a fascinating instance of Communist refugee policies. Australian endeavors to reunite exiled families were more successful

815   Ibid.
816   Ibid.
817   Ibid. Six pages on "Operation Reunion" were prepared on the 22nd September 1961, pp. 1 and 4.

with the Soviet Union, especially after 1959 when hundreds of people were allowed to leave. The Czechs were not only much more stubborn, but also preferred to give exit visas to their Greek rather than Czech citizens. "From May to October, 1956, twenty people, more than half of them Greek refugees ... were granted permission to come to Australia." The review continued: "Then in the next two years ... the Czechoslovak authorities allowed only 22 Czechs to emigrate to Australia—and in the same period just as many Greeks. In 1959 the numbers were eight Czechs, five Greeks, two Germans and one Austrian. Since the beginning of 1960, only 30, among them 15 Czechs, have received exit visas for Australia."[818]

In the introduction to this book, I called attention to the fate of Greek children kidnapped during the civil war and brought to Communist countries to be educated, that is, indoctrinated in Communism. The controversial study published by the Ministry for Education in Western Australia, "The Soviet Society," was analyzed for its shockingly biased pro-Stalinist propaganda. It was written by one of those Greek involuntary guests of Czechoslovakia who grew up thankful to the Communists. Since it is well known that Soviet secret services and other Eastern European operatives regularly sent their agents out of the country together with genuine political refugees,[819] I wonder how many of those Greeks allowed to migrate to Australia only wanted to find a new home—and not in their native Greece once the civil war was over. How many of them were Soviet agents?

Czechoslovak consul general in Sydney, Jaroslav Kafka, repeatedly showed interest in Greek contacts. For instance, in August 1952, he inquired through Eileen Fitzpatrick of the International Social Club

---

818 Ibid.
819 E.g., Former chief of counterintelligence and major general, KGB, Oleg Kalugin, wrote that a 1968 Czech immigrant to the USA had "taken a job as a contract employee of the CIA, and had access to internal CIA communications as well as messages intercepted by the agency around the world. The Czechs made contact with the man [their agent] in Washingon and he agreed to resume working for them." He helped the Soviets to uncover one of their diplomats, named Ogorodnik, who was a double agent working for the CIA. He poisoned himself when questioned in Moscow. See *Spy Master* (London: Smith Gryphon, 1994), pp. 186–88.

for a list of Greeks waiting in Czechoslovakia to come to Australia.[820] Later, before his return to Prague, his successor, Consul General Miloslav Jandík, supplied the editor of a Greek newspaper in Australia, Thomas Nocolaidis, with a great deal of propaganda literature.[821]

When Kafka returned to Sydney for his second term of duty, his family stayed in contact with the family of the secretary of the Greek consulate, Maria Guma.[822] Of course, such contacts can be completely innocent, but in Kafka's double duty assignment and with his extremely close contact with Soviet diplomats and TASS correspondents, all working for Soviet Intelligence, any relationship warrants suspicion. Also, Czechs might have wanted to be rid of their Greek guests, but having invested much money and training in preparation for their adult life, it would be very surprising had they shown only compassion without further designs. That would have been extraordinarily unselfish and completely uncharacteristic behavior for unrepentant conspirators.

Although Australian officials who tried helping to reunite Czech and Slovak families were getting 50 percent new Greek immigrants for their efforts, they persisted in presenting Prague Communist representatives with various lists of families hoping to be reunited after many years of separation. Many documents testified to their attempts to use the offices of the British embassy in Prague, Australian officials in London and Paris, as well as the Department of External Affairs in Canberra.

On July 18, 1961, A. L. Nutt, acting secretary, Department of Immigration, Commonwealth of Australia, in a list prepared for presentation to the Czechoslovak government, as schedule Nos. 4 and 5, enumerated 218 relatives of naturalized Australian citizens who waited for their exit visas to travel to Australia. From May 1956 to the end of August 1961, only 114 were issued exit visas from the ČSSR out of 472 people nominated. Numbers for Hungary, Poland, and Yugoslavia were much better in comparison.[823]

The very competent translator of Joseph Hašek's *Good Soldier Švejk*, Cecil C. Parrott, acting as British ambassador in Prague, steadily strove to

---

820   AA, A6119/90/2468, Kafka 7, f. 22 and 42.
821   AA, A6119/90/2470, Jandík 2, f. 81.
822   AA, A6119/90/2468, Kafka 7, f. 22 and 42.
823   Ibid.

achieve a breakthrough by getting a Czech invitation for the Australian ambassador in Paris, Dr. E. E. Walker, to intervene on behalf of the separated families. However, he had to face discourteous treatment by Communist officials who insisted that the exiles were traitors, criminals who did not merit any legal help. Canberra confidentially suggested to the British ambassador in Prague that a note accompanying the lists of requests for exit visas should stress the "humanitarian aspects:" "The Australian government wishes to emphasize that it regards the future of these people as a humanitarian, not a legal, problem. It is a problem involving the happiness of several hundred people. The desire of the Australian Government is to reunite the families after many years and see an end put to much unhappiness."[824]

A partial weakening of the grip Stalinism had in Czechoslovakia, in the latter part of 1963, improved the chances of "Operation Reunion" in 1964. According to a confidential report by R. S. Laurie, External Affairs, in a "new stage in the Czechoslovakian retreat from isolation," the country opened itself to tourism and "thereby gained valuable foreign currency deposits."[825]

So at the beginning of 1964, after fifteen years of separation from her daughter Marie, Mrs. Vickers (Vorlíček) was finally able to welcome her sixteen-year-old child to Sydney. Her twelve year old brother John, born in Australia, had never seen his sister. Like many other naturalized Australians, Mrs. Anny Ritter read about it in the *Sydney Morning Herald* and again appealed to Australian authorities to help her get back her daughter Yvonne: "We have been trying unsuccessfully for a great many years."[826] She was just one out of hundreds.

---

824 Ibid. Note No. 13, January 12, 1962.
825 Ibid. File No. 13, January 15/2/1531/17 written 4 March 1964.
826 AA, A1838/2/1531/17 PT1, 8 March 1964.

III

Why had so many Czechs and Slovaks tried to run away or emigrate from a people's democracy that, according to witnesses such as Manning Clark and Wilfred Burchett, was successfully practicing a socialism preferable to bourgeois capitalism? Passport and visa officer, Australia House, L. W. Nelson, visited Prague from the second to the fourth of September 1964 in order to discuss "Operation Reunion" with the British embassy staff. In his report to the secretary, Department of External Affairs in Canberra, he proved to be a much more acute observer than the two biased dreamers mentioned above. His ten page report contains these remarks:

> I have been both astonished and depressed at seeing, at first hand, the complete and utter subjugation of the Czechoslovak people by Communism.... Before a Czechoslovak is able to move in any direction he must first obtain approval from the local "Street Committee" of the Communist Party, e.g., if a couple wish to marry ... if a person wishes to obtain a passport ... if a person wishes to move to an alternative place in Czechoslovakia, approval of the Street Committee must be obtained, and so on.... At the present time Prague is but a shadow of its former self, it is dirty, dreary and dilapidated.... Everywhere there is a general run down appearance.... All first class restaurants and hotels are reserved for foreigners, the Czech proletariat are just not allowed in them.... In many instances the shops are shut as they have nothing to sell. I would estimate that at least 30% shops in the Prague suburbs were closed and at any green grocers shop where vegetables were available people were queuing to buy them.... State toilet paper for which queues form ... Altogether a 'cheap and nasty' atmosphere ... The housing position is so bad that what we regard as normal three bedroomed house is occupied by at least four families, all sharing the same toilet and washing facilities.... The blocks

of flats which are being built and to which I have just referred are box like and unimaginative in design and after a few months of occupation walls bulge, handles fall from doors and electric light switches come away from the walls. It is ironical to report that rents are cheap.

L. W. Nelson found the diagnostic medical facilities good. However, due to a "great shortage of nurses," wives have to go and "look after their husbands and children in hospital." Because of all that penury, "it is not surprising that the local population walk about the streets of Prague looking very miserable, and drab." The observer liked the theater, and the beer was excellent. There was almost no foreign press: "The only British newspaper available in Prague is the Daily Worker and even this is an embarrassment to the Czechoslovak Government at times as it prints news items which would normally be suppressed in that country."

Nelson reported on signs of more lenient attitude to emigration but "only elderly people obtain permission to leave the country for good," and "persons leaving Czechoslovakia are only permitted to export two pounds sterling worth of foreign currency."

Moreover, it was not uncommon for a migrant to have his hand baggage emptied on the floor of the Customs Hall at the Airport and trampled on by the Customs Official as a last indignity before leaving the country. Czechoslovak citizens visiting the State often have their passports confiscated. There is, however, a strong feeling at the Embassy that the Australian passports impounded in this type of case are used to infiltrate Communist Agents into West Germany which is a bogey to Czechoslovakia at the present time.

The last of sixty-nine paragraphs of Nelson's report completed the picture: "Apart from ... the experience of seeing elderly people call at

326   Dangerous Dreamers

the British Embassy in Prague for interview full of excitement, in the knowledge that they will soon be leaving this soul destroying existence in Czechoslovakia to join their relatives in Australia forcibly brought home to me the humanitarian side of Operation Re-union."[827]

It is regrettable that such an excellent review of the terrible living conditions in the most prosperous of the Communist states remained filed away and was not published. Another archival document from the sixties revealed another part of the sad story. It was based on an unnamed Australian businessman's observations. He apparently traded in parcels being sent to Czechoslovakia by relatives or in dollars that could buy so-called Tuzex bonds for which people in the "old country" could shop in special stores selling only for hard currencies. The government allowed its lucky citizens with generous relatives abroad to enjoy luxuries (such as toilet paper, soap, washing powder, food, or even radios, TV, etc.) not available otherwise. That way the government received its share of the bargain, namely hard currency. The businessman reported:

> The business has increased considerably during the past few months, and he attributes this to the fact that conditions in Czechoslovakia are very bad, and the ordinary people find it difficult to buy essential items of food. He said that he has received letters from Czechoslovakia indicating that the people queue up for food at 5am in the morning, and again return to the queues after completing their day's work. This state of affairs, he believes, has been brought about by the reduced output of the collective farms, and the filling of export quotas to the U.S.S.R. As a result of this, local Czechoslovakians are helping relatives at home as much as possible. He also said that he was doing business directly with people in Czechoslovakia, and as in many other instances, his customers avoided the so-called commercial attachés at the Sydney Consulate.[828]

---

827   Ibid. 14 September 1964.
828   AA, A6119/90/2468, Kafka 7, f. 69.

IV

If life was gloomy for ordinary Czech citizens, it was hellish for many thousands of concentration camp inmates and state prisoners. Very often they were victims of provocations staged by police agents in order to eliminate imagined class enemies. Slowly, very slowly, some of the hidden criminal acts of the regime were being put on trial.

It is well known that the Communist Party in power organized several campaigns to get rid of priests who refused to denounce their allegiance to the Vatican. At one point, a Catholic priest named Josef Toufar was tortured to death. The incident became famous when it was included in the novel *A Miracle* written in exile by a well-known Czech writer, Joseph Škvorecký. The police wanted to stage a trial to prove that he arranged a miracle in his church that the police agents actually installed themselves. In 1997, the secret police interrogator Jaroslav Daniel was sent to prison for five years, and in 1998 his colleague Ladislav Mácha received the same penalty for his participation.[829] Thousands of Catholic priests fell victim to the campaigns.

I knew one of them. One year before the end of WWII, friends in Prague introduced me to a monastery priest who was probably the most gifted and remarkable person I have ever met. Several of us youngsters used to meet with him. Dr. Pavel Křivský was a born teacher and wise mentor. After the war, he left the monastery and priesthood, married, and secretly tried to create a boy scout organization *Junák* which was forbidden as an imperialist tool. He also entered the Communist Party together with a few friends because he believed that the party could be changed only from the inside. He was arrested and condemned to life in prison. He was paroled after over thirteen years. He died in 1989.

A few years ago, I went to a lecture at the University of Western Australia given by Adolf Bečvář who had spent four years in Nazi prisons and fifteen years in Communist prisons and concentration camps. I heard him talking about this imprisoned former priest's course in the history of philosophy presented to inmates in Leopoldov prison, an old Austrian-Hungarian fortress turned into a most horrible jail functioning as an extermination prison. He allowed me to duplicate his copy of a secret, sixty-two page document issued on November 7, 1968

---

829 *Klokan* [WA], Vol. 4, No. 12 (December 1998), p. 3.

by the fifth department of the Czechoslovak Ministry of the Interior (police), entitled "Final Account about the Activity of the Commission which Examined the Situation in the Institution Leopoldov on the 31st October 1968."

What is remarkable about this report that my new friend obtained from the secret police archives is not only its frankness, but also that it was prepared during the Prague Spring of 1968, in the Dubček year, and internally issued six weeks after the Soviet invasion and under the Red Army's occupation. It was based on a detailed study of the prison Leopoldov between 1949 and 1960. Several of the prison guards were interviewed.

The document is a horror story about Communist extermination of political opponents or of people the regime considered potential future enemies. Here are a few examples of Manning Clark's "successes of Communism." The report begins:

> The November [1948] session of the Central Committee of the Communist Party of Czechoslovakia, shortly after the February putsch, decided on a political line stressing limitation and liquidation of capitalist elements. *The goal was to sharpen the fight against reaction, that is against citizens who remained faithful democrats.* This task was given to sections of the state security already established and to those newly created for the purpose. To the state security were added state tribunals, prison guards, border sentries, people's militias and, naturally, Party leading organs. From 1948/9, concentration camps were being established and various "socialist reforming institutions"—more truthfully "Soviet type GULAGS," mainly close to shafts of uranium mines. [The USSR imported very cheaply all the uranium it could get from its satellite, the ČSR.] *The policy of the "sharp course" fast changed into lawlessness, arbitrariness, physical terror and psychic execution* caused by false protocols elaborated by the secret police and sanctified by judgments of "state tribunals" that "legalised" this injustice. STB [state police] and a special contingent of guardians of state

prisoners drafted and used a whole, wide scale of ill-treatment, *torture and brutal slaughtering of prisoners.*

The report was prepared by four majors and one captain of the armed forces of the Communist government, which mellowed during 1968 and no longer considered democrats as reactionary state enemies to be mercilessly humiliated and killed. Tens of pages follow describing tortures and murders that were reported to relatives as heart failures.

In order to apply the ordered "sharper course," the report states, "a Communist clan met at the Ministry of Justice [sic!] led by the commanding officer, Lieutenant-Colonel Dr. Kloss." It was decided that guards would be judged by the cruelty showed to the class enemy, their willingness to give prisoners only half of prescribed meals, and the severity of their punishments: "*The prisoner must not be allowed the impression that he has any rights at all.* No sentimentality is appropriate when we have gangsters in prison."

A favored treatment consisted of ordering three hundred squats, sometimes three times a day:

> Once, on order by Josef Bálent (born 4.10.1920) commander in Leopoldov from 1.1.1952 until 15.5.1953, prisoners had to do 400 squats. On his order admission to the hospital was limited—as a consequence, Lieutenant-Colonel Adam died. There was no diet allowed for prisoners with TB. On the suggestion of a prisoner, a doctor, to be allowed a food package for a sick prisoner, Bálent answered: 'You don't need a package; you will kick the bucket here anyway.'... Because of miserable food and lack of care Nedbal, Sacher and General Pešek died of swelling.

The report is full of incidents reported by witnesses:

> Rudolf Eliáš (born 3.4.1920) forced prisoner Svoboda to load coal by a spade. Doubek told him that his sickness does not allow him to do such hard work. Eliáš forced him to continue and Svoboda died with the spade in his hand.... On 21 December 1957 Alois

Rádl died when the cultural [sic!] commander broke his head with a chair.... Prisoners were losing 1½ kilos a week.... Milotinský, MD says that in the case of prisoner Průša who was shot through his head, he was under pressure to write a different diagnosis.... Seventy-year old General Nosal was forced with his group of prisoners to exercise as the others, walking, squatting, walking, running, squatting, walking in squat position, so-called duck-walking while squatting, hopping, etc. In a while he passed out but was forced to continue. Staff captain Karafiát and the prison's commander Bálent kept watching. Such a regime was applied especially harshly to generals of the democratic army, Kultvašer, Pelich, Mrázek and Nosal revealed the 1968 official report.

These were just a few samples of the "sharper course" against democrats used in Leopoldov and examined by the Communist military commission that studied them in 1968. We could go on and on.[830]

Conditions in Leopoldov were so horrible that several political prisoners committed suicide. Among them was even Dr. Pavel Křivský, who for years tried to encourage the victims of the Communist extermination policy through his lectures on philosophy.[831] He was taken down when he was discovered hanged, and revived. After his release from prison, Dr. Křivský obtained a job in the literary archives and wrote several books on individual philosophers and on the history of the Strahov Monastery.

The Australian campaign "Operation Reunion" was faced with the very difficult problem of how to help a Leopoldov prisoner join his

---

830 Czech Ministry of the Interior, KM-0682/35-68. My own underlining.

831 Large excerpts, proving his humanism and incredible memory with detailed knowledge of major philosophers' life and thought, were published in a book entitled *Filosofie za mřížemi* [*"Philosophy Behind Bars"*]: *Leopoldov, léta padesátá* [*"Leopoldov in the Fifties"*] [Prague: Charles University, 1995.] Adolf Bečvář, while imprisoned in Leopoldov, walled in Křivský's notes written on toilet paper in 1955 and recovered them in 1992. Bečvář himself wrote poetry while in prison and issued the collection as *Poesie za mřížemi* [*"Poetry Behind Bars"*] (Zlín, 1995).

brother, Frank Doslík, in Brisbane. D. J. Killen, MP for Moreton, was contacted by B. M. Snedden, attorney general, Commonwealth Offices, with the suggestion of a petition to the president of Czechoslovakia. Jan Doslík had been a political prisoner for the last eighteen years. He was arrested in 1948. A letter from Frank Doslík's brother indicated that he "was in a state of acute anxiety" in Leopoldov.[832] Several letters were exchanged between various Canberra departments. Paul Hasluck, minister for External Affairs, was reluctant to take action, claiming that "as Mr Jan Doslík is a Czechoslovak citizen, however, the Australian Government would have no standing to intercede with the Government of Czechoslovakia in this matter."[833]

When nothing was done, Kellen directed a question to the minister for External Affairs. On the fourth of May, 1967, he said: "There are Communist countries which are members of the United nations Organisation and which habitually violate their obligations under the United Nations Charter, particularly with respect to political prisoners."

Hasluck again refused Australian intervention and stated that "the United Nations, through its appropriate organs, is responsible for the observance of the Charter."[834] In an undated letter to Killen, Hasluck added that sending a petition to the General Assembly of UNO on behalf of Jan Doslík "would contravene the principles of non-intervention into the affairs of other member states; it could also, of course, expose us to reciprocal actions." Doslík continued to suffer in Leopoldov. No representation to the Czechs on behalf of Jan Doslík was considered, because it "would most likely be rejected," as O. L. Davis, first secretary of Division 4 of the External Affairs indicated to his Minister.[835] Finally, Paul Hasluck wrote the persistent D. J. Killen that "the interests of the Australian citizens" would not be "served by any" Australian "representations." He suggested that relatives of Jan Doslík should "consider a petition to the Human Rights Commission through the secretary general of the United Nations."[836] Paul Hasluck

---

832 AA, A1838/2/1531/17 PT1; 5, 7, 12, 21 December 1966.
833 Ibid., 22.12.1966.
834 Ibid., 4.5. 1967.
835 Ibid., 7.6.1967.
836 Ibid., 23.6. 1967.

is the man who repeatedly helped the Soviet and Czechoslovak spy Ian Milner in his offical career.

As Professor Manning Clark rightly suggested in his 1963 book, Australia was indeed placed "Between Two Worlds." The choice was between a totalitarian system using criminal methods against its own citizens and an imperfect but more or less democratic order whose citizens did not have to be afraid of torture and concentration camps. Unfortunately, we know which one was preferred by dangerous dreamers such as Manning Clark and his followers. Some people could not fathom what kind of a new age of propaganda-cum-terror was inaugurated by Lenin that they themselves hoped to bring to Australia.

5

Criminal Governments Create Criminal Societies[837]

The theses of this chapter are: 1) that political crime has been by far the most prevalent crime of our era; 2) that some states were in the hands of felons; 3) that such criminal governments used normally illegal acts on a mass scale in order to stay in power; 4) that criminal governments create criminal societies by forcing almost everybody to act unlawfully not only for his or her career advancement but also for their own survival; 5) that the trend toward state use of criminal methods was spreading; and 6) that such political and military power in the hands of such criminals and madmen constituted a threat to the entire human race.

An attempt will also be made to briefly explain the history of modern criminal governments and include some of the formative ideas and situations that led to their establishment and tendency toward "exterminating populations at an unprecedented rate in world history."[838]

In Hitler's Germany, Stalin's Russia, and Mao's China theft, beatings, kidnapping, torture, and murder of opponents and innocent people, as well as genocide, were standard features of rule. Occasionally, these regimes or their individual acts were called by some writers criminal,

---

837 This chapter and the latter parts of the previous one are based on my paper of the same name, presented at the Tenth World Congress of Sociology in Mexico, 16–21 August 1982. Fortunately, most of the verbs could be changed from the present to the past tense.

838 Alexander Solzhenitsyn, "The West Will Provide Its Own Hangmen," *Bulletin,* 2 February 1982, p. 93.

but although they should have been universally branded as criminal governments, there seems to be an aversion to such terminology. Even the famous trial of war criminals in Nuremberg has often been considered controversial since victors were sitting as judges over those who lost the war and one party (the Soviet Union) was known to have committed similar crimes against its own population.

Somehow it does not seem to be acceptable in polite society to call a spade a spade and use derogatory terms for governments that merit it. A kind of a Machiavellian assumption prevails in many parts of the world that princes and states can commit no crimes and that they have the right to use any methods in order to attain and keep power and guarantee "law and order." However, even Machiavelli and Hobbes, to name just two of the philosophical pessimists about human nature, have set limitations to nasty behavior in the political arena, if not always for ethical reasons then at least in the interest of self-preservation of the actors and for the success of their politics.

Dictators usually treat courteous behavior with contempt. As already mentioned, Count Ciano recorded Mussolini's disgust with the polite treatment he received from the British in his *Diaries*. It encouraged Mussolini in his brutality toward them. Lenin, Hitler, Stalin, and Mao understood politeness only as weakness and defeatism.

When confronted with radical evil, pussyfooting politicians and intellectuals contributed to the repeated victory of dictators. Large parts of the world were in the hands of those who did not mind using "the combination of high technology and high brutality."[839]

Having no conscience to trouble them, perpetrators of such political crimes only feel worried or regretful when faced with discovery and punishment.[840] Following Radio Free Europe broadcasts to Eastern Europe, torturers and brutal jailers often improved their treatment of prisoners after they were named and warned on the radio. In times of crises these people also look to be shown in a better light by changing

---

839   Samuel Pisar, *Of Blood and Hope* (London: Cassell, 1980), p. 267.

840   "In one fell swoop Stalin was branded a criminal by Khrushchev ... On 12 March 1956, the Polish United Workers' Party lost its own leader. Boleslaw Bierut ... died of heart failure in Moscow shortly after reading the secret speech." L.W. Gluchowski, "Khrushchev's Second Secret Speech," Cold War International History Project *Bulletin*, Issue 10, March 1998, p. 44.

their behavior toward prisoners and by offering them favors. After the Hungarian revolution of 1956, when the outraged population lynched some Communists and secret policemen, Soviet and satellite dictators and their stooges lived in fear of their peoples, as attested to by the former secretary of the Communist Party of Czechoslovakia, Zdeněk Mlynář, who wrote, "At the end of 1956 ... we Communists lived in fear.... There was present a fully concrete image of a crowd lynching the Communists and hanging them on lampposts." At a meeting of Warsaw Pact leaders in 1968, Walter Ulbricht reportedly remarked that if no radical action were taken against Dubček, "we will all be hanging from lampposts."[841]

I believe that such a clear demarcation of systematic political crimes is salutary since it helps in separating the truly horrific politicians from the rest of the fray. People's generally low opinion of politicians makes it all the more necessary to make it clear that there is a difference between criminality and mere dishonesty or ineptitude. People who do not like to be called criminal always have a way to avoid it: they can stop acting as criminals and at least partially repair their reputations. A definition could be formulated: A government that not only denies its citizens basic human rights but also brutally punishes those who are claiming them is a criminal government.

LENIN CREATED THE FIRST SYSTEMIC CRIMINAL GOVERNMENT

Political crime is as old as civilization. The Bible is full of shocking stories of merciless massacres, some of them supposedly sanctified by God. Other religions have their own war stories to tell. The Ancients and Medieval Christians were not stopped but rather encouraged in cruelty by their sets of beliefs and massacred uncounted victims. The slaughter did not end with the Renaissance. Our horror at the bloody barbarism of the twentieth century is due to the Enlightenment of the eighteenth, to the growth of humanitarian sentiments of the nineteenth century, and to the expectation of steady progress, which all seemed to be pointing to a better future. Therefore, I will concentrate here on

---

841   *Mráz přichází z Kremlu* (Cologne: Index, 1978), p. 52.

the origins of our modern political criminality, since now it might be finally recognized as such.

Although immoral acts and questionable methods were used by many states before and during the First World War, the distinction of having founded the first criminal government belongs to Lenin. In politics he had almost no moral scruples. Into the foundations of his movement and his state, he put the conscious and systematic use of lies, false pretenses, theft, kidnapping, mass arrests, torture, labor and concentration camps, as well as premeditated murder on an enormous scale. During the four or five years when he was in charge, millions of people were subjected to his systematic use of terror. Hundreds of thousands died as a consequence of his determination to use extreme and savage measures to stay in power.

It does not matter that he acted out of a belief in himself and his mission to lead a class war. All tyrants find some excuses for their massacres. What matters are the victims and the system of misrule he created. Political crimes were no longer just *exceptions* to the general practice of a government, *in spite* of its professions of religious or democratic values. What makes an enormous qualitative and not only quantitative difference is that Lenin's crimes were perpetrated as part of a premeditated plan of terrorist war led against the whole population and that his cruel principles were frankly revealed. Lenin created the first systemic criminal state. He also began an international campaign founded on principles similar to those he was employing in his own dictatorial regime. For instance, he proposed a system of methods to be used in attempts to infiltrate foreign trade unions: "Communists should be prepared to make every imaginable sacrifice, and even, if necessary, resort to all sorts of schemes and stratagems, employ illegal methods and evasions, conceal the truth, in order to penetrate the trade unions, stay there, and at all costs conduct revolutionary work within."[842]

The strength and successes of Leninism were always based to a large degree on such dishonesty, conspiratorial schemes of infiltration, secret police methods, terror, militarism, and the misuse of the good faith and credibility of people who pursued genuine democratic, national,

---

842 Leggett, *The Cheka*, p. 324. Lenin's statement is from 1920.

social, socialist, or trade unionist goals. "The world has been a poorer and bleaker and more dangerous place because Lenin lived."[843]

Lenin's genius lay in his capacity to establish the first party to abolish all other parties, to use carefully studied militaristic doctrines in order to reach power and build the first state in modern history to lead constant war on its whole population. To do this, he combined the terrorist methods previously employed by violent revolutionary individuals and groups, especially in Czarist Russia but also in France, Italy, and Germany. A cold, calculating mastermind of the first order, he created a lawless system that he began to spread all over the world; like a fatal cancer it spread throughout the twentieth century.

One of the dangerous consequences of such a virulent cancerous growth on the body of humanity has been that the defense against it often took a very similar or even identical form. We cannot imagine the victory of Fascism in Italy without Leninism, and Hitler would not have achieved power in Germany so easily without Stalin, and without the systematic weakening of German democracy by Communist subversion and Leftist attacks on the coalition government and its so-called bourgeois values.

There is no need to describe the criminal features of the Fascist and Nazi states. Enough was written about them. What is, however, surprising is that only occasionally will an author talk about "the 'gangsters in a hurry' who ran the Third Reich"[844] or, an another author identifies Eichmann, "this new type of criminal, who in fact is *hostis generis humani* (enemy of the human race)."[845] The Nazi system is not yet regularly designated by sociologists or political scientists as a criminal state, although it was obviously run by a band of criminals who used all the states' resources to committing some twelve million murders (not counting war casualties).

---

843 Max Beloff, "A Neglected Historical Novel," *Encounter*, Vol. XXXIV, No. 3 (March 1970), p. 56.

844 Colin S. Gray, "The Most Dangerous Decade: Historic Mission, Legitimacy, and Dynamics of the Soviet Empire in the 1980s," *Orbis*, Spring 1981, p. 26.

845 Hannah Arendt, *Eichmann in Jerusalem: A Report on the Banality of Evil* (New York: Penguin, 1976), p. 276.

The same is true of Stalin's Soviet Union (referred to exceptionally as a "criminal regime" by Morton A. Kaplan[846]) and his satellite empire. Again, uncounted millions of victims were imprisoned, mistreated, tortured, and many murdered after being accused falsely or without a trial. Polish economist, Edward Lipinski, celebrating his seventieth year as a socialist, nominated as a meritorious teacher of the People's Republic of Poland, wrote in an open letter: "We remember the Bierut era, a period of errors, even crimes. Over those years, there were tens of thousands of prisoners who suffered torture.... It is a rigid system which destroys its critics, a system not answerable to any form of social control, which has no respect for fundamental civil liberties."[847]

Chinese Charter 08, issued in December last year and signed by 303 prominent writers, philosophers, historians, scientists, lawyers, and central or provincial party leaders—later more than eight thousand more signatures were added—reviewed the tens of millions victims of the Communist rule. It proposed a long list of reforms needed in order for China to join the civilized world of democratic states.

Should there be any excuse, any "alleviating circumstances" allowed for such prodigious and systematic murder? The violent crimes of private individuals often upset journalists and the general public, but the worst of them pale in comparison with the millions murdered by Stalin, Mao Tse-tung, Pol Pot, and their accomplices. It is a strange and sad world in which you can be executed or incarcerated for life for one murder, but are allowed to commit millions of "official" murders without any punishment. Mass murderers have been toasted by other heads of government and admired by writers and social scientists or historians. Our yearning for leaders and heroes is probably one of the root causes of this double standard and lack of moral stamina.

CRIMINAL SOCIETIES

All criminal governments, beginning with Lenin's, created their special forces to keep the population terrorized, obedient, and fearful. These specialized terrorists belonged to the new class of privileged elite and

---

846   *The Many Faces of Communism* (New York: Free Press, 1978), p. 4.
847   "An open Letter to Comrade Edward Gierek," *Survey*, Vol. 22, No. 2 (99), 1976, p. 199.k

were vitally interested in the preservation of a regime that gave them power, prestige, and relatively high living standards. Naturally, these police detachments were often composed of amoral and sadistic persons but also included unfortunate collaborators who were induced into active oppression by various means. They committed crimes for which in any normal society there would be harsh punishment: illegal arrests, beatings, kidnapping, extortion, torture, and murder. These were the policemen, jailers, special investigators, and trained torturers. But there were also collaborating lawyers, judges, propagandists, journalists, and social scientists who were sent to world conferences in order to sustain the governmental system of lies, along with ambassadors, consul generals, secret agents, etc.—a great multitude of people actively willing to support the pretenses of their governments. The knowledge of their part in, or their willingness to close their eyes to, felonious acts of their superiors bound them closely to the regime until they became an essential component of it. Their numbers reached the hundreds of thousands, but more importantly, no one was able to completely escape the clutches of the totalitarian government. Every citizen, willingly or unwillingly, became a collaborator, a cog in the machine.

We know about this sort of tacit public approval from the experience of Fascist or Nazi states where all citizens more or less participated in crimes or at least profited from them and did not oppose them. What is less undertood is the situation under Communist governments where the same fate of shared guilt and collaboration threatened the morality and destroyed the human dignity of almost everybody. According to a previously highly placed Czech Communist official, Jiří Pelikán, each citizen became "an opportunist and prisoner of the system."[848] All had to pretend that they believed the official lies even if their mendacity was apparent. All had to concur with false pretenses, be loyal to criminals, venerate them, but be disloyal to their friends. If they wanted to survive, they had to act as if their governments were properly established, as if they eagerly supported them and could not imagine anything better than their rule.

What is worse, all had to lie, steal, and engage in illegal trade and exchange of services if they wanted to survive and to support their families. The criminal government forced its population into crime.

---

848   *S'ils me tuent … Récit recuelli par Frédéric de Towarnicki* (Paris: Bernard Grasset, 1975), p. 141.

It taught and encouraged immorality, fraud, and lawlessness. Workers had to steal tools from their comrades if they wanted to do their job and be paid for it—as was revealed in a television program from Poland when a worker complained about how the Communist government made criminals out of workers.[849]

Here is another document about Czechoslovakia:

> On 29 May, 1968, BBC-1 Television showed a report by their *24 Hours* team from Czechoslovakia including interviews with ordinary Czech men and women. A woman told the reporter that the Czechs would have to learn again how to be honest because the inefficiency of the previous system was such that everybody had to be ruthless and dishonest to provide for himself and his family. Everybody was on his own, people did not dare to talk to each other. Other interviewees explained how they had been stealing things from their offices or workshops because these things could not be obtained in any other way. Stealing was considered normal.[850]

All this was well known to everybody behind the Iron Curtain. Popular Eastern European jokes expressed the reality of the situation: "The government pretends to pay us and we pretend to work," or "He who does not steal from the state steals from his family." Parents who wanted their children to be accepted for higher learning had to spend years without dignity, without protest to criminal activities seen all around, pretending loyalty to a hated regime in order to give their children a chance to be admitted to schools where they would be subjected to false propaganda, encouraged to denounce their parents, but could also obtain qualifications for better paying jobs.

Although education and health services were free, people usually knew the exact price they had to pay corrupt officials and doctors if they wanted to get any attention. Black markets and a whole color scheme of gray, pink, and other colored markets for goods and services

---

849   "Four Corners," Perth, WA, TV Channel 2, 26 September 1980.
850   Ljubo Sirc, *Economic Devolution in Eastern Europe* (London: Longmans, 1969), p. 63.

were part of the daily existence of all citizens. A society run in a constant state of war against all its citizens and against the rest of the world suffered from decades of war economy. False (and sometimes true) denunciations of neighbors were encouraged and rewarded by the authorities. Almost no one was fully trusted, because everybody knew that almost anybody could be either a willing or unwilling collaborator with the secret police. When police files were opened for inspection in the nineties, it was often revealed that even those who were trusted (e.g., many priests) had sometimes worked for the secret police. Jiří Pelikán, who was in a position to know, wrote: "It is necessary to understand that the apparatus of the secret police in a country as, for example, Czechoslovakia, does not have only thousands of employees and officers, but also hundreds of thousands of informers, engaged by the police. Sometimes they are not paid but simply protected and "pushed" in their professional careers. They live obsessed by fear that a clean up would throw full light on their well-hidden responsibilities."[851]

The whole society was, in Dr. Andrei Sakharov's words, sick. In 1977, he wrote an essay entitled "Alarm and Hope" for the Norwegian Nobel Committee: "The Soviet state's sixty-year history has been filled with horrible violence, hideous crimes at home and abroad, destruction, and the suffering, debasement, and corruption of millions of people…. A deeply cynical caste society has come into being, one which is considered dangerous (to itself as well as to all mankind)—a sick society."[852] Russian writer Vladimir Maximov added: „Nothing and nobody can escape being drawn into it and serving it."[853]

Abnormality became normal. The Czechoslovak society whose socialism lost its "human face" in the invasion of 1968 officially became normalized. Again, all citizens were haunted, this time, even long-standing members of the Communist Party, by the corrupt and corrupting system created by the government from above and reaching down to the lowest level. Almost everybody became a big or

851 *S'ils me tuent,* p. 152.

852 "A Sick Society," excerpts from his essay "Alarm and Hope," *New York Times,* January 23, 1980, p. A 23.

853 "The Russian People and the West," interview with G. R. Urban in his *Communist Reformation: Nationalism, Internationalism and Change in the World Communist Movement* (London: Maurice Temple Smith, 1979), p. 260.

small criminal according to the moral and legal standards of a really normal society. The guilt was shared, intentionally, and the shame was pervasive. Cynics survived best. Sensitive and decent people suffered most. Suicide was common.

Communist regimes succeeded in making the normal human right to private enterprise into a criminal activity, prosecuted but illegally prospering. The whole Soviet system of planned economy, celebrated by people abroad who did not have any idea of the facts, would not have survived long without unplanned and illegal activities. Black, gray, pink, and other markets, colors depending on how much the government suppressed or tolerated them, supplemented the official but disorganized and chaotic economy, as has been well documented in many studies.[854] This Soviet system of corrupted officials and illegal producers and tradesmen was exported wholesale to Eastern and Central European satellites and made hundreds of millions of people into cheaters and black marketers.

For example, Karel Pešta, senior officer in the Czechoslovak General Prosecutor's Office, said in a published interview that speculators did not deal only in "necessities" such as food, textiles, and household utensils, but also in "luxuries" such as cars, television sets, and fashion goods. Digital watches, stylish clothing of foreign provenience, as well as homemade spare parts and components were in great demand. Hundreds of millions of Czechoslovak crowns were involved annually. Pešta quoted several uncovered examples of "very extensive illicit entrepreneureship spread over the entire territory of the country."[855]

Socialist economies of the Soviet empire were corrupted from top to bottom and whole populations, in order to survive as part of this corrupted system, traded illegally, bribed and received bribes. Under the influence of felonious officials, they became criminals themselves. "Far from being a 'survival' of capitalism [as the party leaders liked to allege], corruption and illegal entrepreneurship seem to be an inevitable

---

854   See, for instance, Gregory Grossman, "The 'Second Economy' of the USSR," *Problems of Communism*, Vol. XXVI, No. 5 (September–October 1977), pp. 25–40; or Denis O'Hearn, "The Consumer Second Economy: Size and Effects," *Soviet Studies*, Vol. XXXII, 2 April 1981, pp. 218–34.

855   *Tribuna*, 26 August 1981, p. 4.

response to the Soviet form of political-economic organization," according to two acclaimed economists in 1980.[856]

The effects on the moral and ethical standards of people living in such a state were naturally disastrous. A governmental system based on lies, stealing, terror, and murder contaminated the whole society. Many *samizdat* ("underground") publications in Central and Eastern Europe were expressing worries about the long-term consequences of the forced unethical and often criminal behavior on the enslaved nations.

In normal societies, a teacher who morally corrupts his pupils is not allowed to continue teaching and is usually punished, but in Communist states all teachers were obliged to lie to all their students. Everybody received an early education in hypocrisy, cheating, lying, denouncing others, including his or her parents, to the police (indirectly through the teachers), and in all kinds of unethical activities in order to become socialized into the system.

The systematic demoralization of these countries provoked a desperate search for ethical values to guide at least one's private life and to fight the spreading depravity. Voices have been heard from all countries under Soviet domination calling for a life without lies, a return to liberal, democratic, Christian, or other values. They were dismissed by the Leninists with contempt as supposed bourgeois prejudices. Some Communists and Marxists began to study religions and attempted to fill the void of ethical principles in Marxism. In the Polish case, it could be observed that the failure of Marxism-Leninism and of Soviet socialism was primarily moral. The people's return to the values of Catholicism was obvious. Economic failures were to a large degree caused by ethical faults built into the system of lies and terror. The nations tried to defend themselves, but until the revolutions of 1989–1991, the well organized evil again and again proved to be stronger than the good intentions and hopes of millions.

---

856 J. M. Montias and Susan Rose-Ackerman, "Corruption in a Soviet-Type Economy: Theoretical Considerations," paper presented to the conference on "The Second Economy of the USSR," at the Kennan Instituete ofr Advanced Russian Studies, January 24–25, 1980; first delivered at a Workshop in New Haven on 12–13 October 1979.

INTERNATIONAL TERRORISM

The Soviet empire was threatened by its numerous internal crises and weaknesses, but its network of well-organized and trained terrorists all over the world attempted to destabilize the West in order to bring about its collapse. Lenin's strategy of turning an imperialist war into a civil war which helped to bring the Bolsheviks to power in Russia was expanded into a strategy led by an imperialist socialist bloc of states by which an intentional civil war would destroy all the capitalist states. Lenin's use of militarist doctrines in the creation of his party and of his state led to the elaboration of a coherent strategy of gradual destruction of democratic and not-so-democratic countries.

According to a well-documented study, the Soviet Union, through its political and military secret police (KGB and GRU) controlled and manipulated "over 140 terrorist bands from nearly fifty countries or disputed territories."[857] It used "contract killers borrowed from the criminal underworld."[858] Tens of thousands of guerrilla fighters were trained in terrorist camps in Algeria, Bulgaria, Czechoslovakia, East Germany, Hungary, Lebanon, Libya, Cuba, North Korea, Syria, South Yemen, and the Soviet Union. They were sent to Spain, Italy, West Germany, France, Turkey, Nicaragua, El Salvador, and many other countries in order to disrupt and, if possible, take over local governments. One of the organizers of such a "one thousand percent" increase in Soviet spending on terrorism abroad in 1964 was General Jan Šejna. He left Czechoslovakia in 1968 and revealed the existence of these "special guerrilla training schools ... in Czechoslovakia, East Germany and Cuba for 'selected terrorists from all over the world.'"[859] Other camps were added later when global revolutionary strategy involved agents, military forces, and volunteers from Cuba and Libya, along with Palestinians and others. During the 1960s and especially the 1970s, this international organization of a multinational secret army, well provided with armaments by the Soviet Union and its satellites, managed to stage spectacular bombing raids, multiple assassinations,

---

857   Claire Sterling, *The Terror Network: The Secret War of International Terrorism* (New York: Holt, Rinehart and Winston, 1981), p. 10.

858   Ibidem, pp. 10–11.

859   Ibid., p. 14.

kidnappings, and bank robberies all over the non-Communist world.[860]

Claire Sterling wrote: "There was nothing spontaneous about armed revolutions in the seventies. It became a matter of machine-turned, computer calculated urban guerrilla warfare."[861]

Cuban armed forces led liberation wars in several African countries and East German officers achieved power in Africa that Hitler never could have dreamed of. Several terrorists of the Italian Red Brigades admitted that their contacts with Soviet and other Eastern European agents were important for their successful disturbance of Italian democracy. Basque freedom fighters and IRA terrorists, together with dozens of guerrillas around the world, obtained money, armaments, training, and other important help from states ruled by Communist parties or from countries whose rulers decided to participate in this international war against established democracies. Although Soviet spokesmen, following a well formulated policy in place since Lenin, would always refuse to acknowledge their part in such activities, their denials had no value at all when weighed against the accumulating evidence. "The terrorists' primary value to the Kremlin lay in their resolute efforts to weaken and demoralize, confuse, humiliate, frighten, paralyze, and if possible dismantle the West's democratic societies."[862]

Lenin's state terrorism and later international terrorism were based on the same nihilism that was provided in Czarist Russia by Ishutin, Nechayev, Tkachev, and Bakunin. Thanks to Lenin, this anti-humanist cancer spread in the Soviet Union and around the world. The last vestiges are still alive in China and North Korea. (Murderous fanatics basing their organized terrorist acts on the Moslem faith later renewed these tactics.) Trying to defend their countries against this well-organized conspiracy, many politicians and military or police officers used similar or identical inhuman methods and thus were multiplying the murderous effect. It was no longer just a vicious circle; it was a vicious maelstrom that threatened to engulf us all. A French writer's characterization of the times from over forty years ago remained

---

860 According to one estimate, the USSR was spending some $200 million a year on the training of intenational terrorists (*Bulletin*, 25 November 1980, p. 94).

861 op.cit., p. 252.

862 Ibid., p. 295.

current: "We are living in the era of premeditation and perfect crimes. Our criminals are no longer those helpless children who pleaded love as their excuse. On the contrary, they are adults and they have perfect alibi: philosophy, which can be used for anything, even for transforming murderers into judges."[863]

---

863   Albert Camus, *The Rebel* (Harmondsworth: Penguin Books, 1967), p. 11.

Epilogue: The CPA's Probability of Success and Its Character

○ ○

By the time we invaded Czechoslovakia in 1968 only the most fervid ideologue could hold any illusions that the Soviet Union was striving to build a Socialist utopia.

Oleg Kalugin, Spy Master: My 32 Years in Intelligence and Espionage Against the West (1994), p. 123

A few times in their long history, members of the Communist Party of Australia felt that they had come close to the revolutionary seizure of power. Before we consider the real chances of Communism in Australia, let us review the philosophical and political framework of its self-imposed messianic mission, the strengths and weaknesses of the new type of party and its leaders.

In the first volume of his history of the CPA, *The Reds*, Professor Stuart Macintire, himself a former Communist who joined the CPA in 1970 (sic!), identified some basic faults in the premises of the movement and some reasons for its failure. Mentioning "nearly 200 books wholly or partly concerned with Australian Communism," he noted "a growing realisation that the Communist project had failed."[864] Macintire cited several causes of its collapse. Communists remained defiant rather than insurrectionary, incurably majoritarian even though they constituted a tiny minority, convinced that capitalism was doomed

---

864 Stuart Macintire, *The Reds: The Communist Party of Australia from Origins to Illegality* (St Leonards: Allen & Unwin, 1998), p. 6.

and that their own resolution in its death throes would win the support of the working class.[865]

Establishing "labour history as a scholarly discipline, they were convinced historical determinists who enlisted Comrade History as one of their most valuable recruits."[866] Given that he wrote, "The history of Communism up to the Second World War is on an upward trajectory, that afterwards is one of protracted decline." We can assume that in the forthcoming second volume of *The Reds*, the author intended to include more factors in the failure of world and Australian Communism. However, in the first volume he already found the fly in the ointment: "The Communist project itself was deeply flawed ... it nurtured tyranny within its emancipatory scheme."[867] Macintire also pointed out that the supposedly revolutionary proletarian class lacked proper "class consciousness" since the Communists had to "promote" it and that "the party press continued to publish clever articles that dwelt on the backwardness of the masses."[868] That problem already existed in the twenties, but as was documented in other chapters, e.g., the complaints of Humphrey McQueen, the working class continued to prove unsatisfactory to Communist revolutionary intellectuals.

Karl Marx's historical and dialectical materialism misled its followers into believing that history, as some kind of a non-theological God, was on their side. Based on Friedrich Hegel's Christian belief in history's progress toward final salvation, Marx's prophesy proved itself to be a fantasy of irrational determinism. The more capitalism evolved, the more complicated its social situation had became, and the division of the world into two opposed classes, believable around 1850, seemed increasingly preposterous. The workers never accepted their assigned mission as the revolutionary executioners of bourgeois capitalism and were willing to fight only for their own economic and social improvement. Hardly manual laborers themselves, professional revolutionaries whipped the horses to speed them on in a race they were unwilling to run. The Chinese Communists proved that the will to seize power was much more important than the cooperation of the supposed saviours' class of the workers. They used the peasants, a class

---

865   Ibid., p. 210.
866   Ibid., p. 5.
867   Ibid., p. 413.
868   Ibid., pp. 87 and 88.

very much disliked and distrusted by Marx and Engels, as saviours. However, the emotional appeal to intellectuals of finally reaching the blissful goal of ideal Communism was undergirded by the archetypal myth of regaining a lost paradise.

With the substantial help of Trotsky, Lenin came to power using the disruptions caused by the lost war, on the back of the disgruntled workers and peasant soldiers with decisive German financial support, promising to build socialism on the basis of state capitalism. Much more important for the history of the twentieth century, however, was his creation of a new type of political party: militaristic, conspiratorial, merciless, and dictatorial. With that he fatally split the Left-wing socialist movement that was winning majorities in Germany, Russia, and elsewhere. By his violent attacks on reformist socialism and democracy as well as by threatening the property rights of so-called bourgeois capitalists, he disastrously weakened the democratic center and provoked extreme Right-wing reactionaries. Stalin strengthened this catastrophic development by his theory of social fascism. Democratic socialism was doomed and the gates to the Second World War were opened.

Such a conspiratorial, internationalized party led from Moscow naturally attracted dictatorially minded, power-hungry individuals from all classes. They then manipulated sincere and idealistic party members who followed the tempting promise of a just, brotherly future without wars and exploitation. The dichotomy is reflected in Professor Macintire's history. He wrote: "The party's hierarchical structure and subordination to Moscow, its rules of democratic centralism and intolerance of dissent, the authoritarian practices and personality cult that developed around prominent cadres, all undoubtedly disfigured Australian Communism."[869]

In the introduction to *The Reds*, he stated, "Communism collapsed under the weight of its failures. Its refusals of freedom created a barren tyranny."[870] Quoting one of the founders of the Australian Communist movement, he wrote: "'The business of the Communist Party', as Jock Garden perhaps tactlessly put it, 'is to get Communists in control of all positions, and to do anything, and everything, to get them there.'"[871]

---

869 Ibid., p. 414.
870 Ibid., p. 2.
871 Ibid., p. 56.

And elsewhere, "Communism was omnivorous, subordinating every aspect of society to the control of the party." The falsely understood situation led to self-defeating activism: "Their insistence on the forcible overthrow of capitalism fell on deaf ears as impractical, indeed unimaginable, in a country that prided itself on its progressive traditions and democratic opportunities."[872]

From their Soviet masters who helped to train them in special schools and supplied them with funds,[873] Australian Communist leaders learned the Stalinist "manipulativeness, mendacity, suspicion, intolerance, ruthlessness."[874] Macintire cites "the perennial question of how to reconcile revolution and reform" or unionists' genuine interests and the party's misuse of them for its revolutionary aims.[875] There are many instances in his book of Communist cheating, infiltration of Labor Party ranks, rigging of elections, and other unsavory tactics. There is hardly anything positive about CPA leaders: "Kavanagh was pugnacious, dogmatic, egotistical;" "the wavering Lance Sharkey, a scruffy, glum, unsociable man," "a man of limited education," "he was awkward, uncouth, slow in thought and hesitant in speech," "his binges in Moscow were notorious."[876] Bert Moxon, "this shameless adventurer," "this blustering conman," and J. B. Miles, "a demanding patriarch," did not come off much better. "Miles was always loath to concede errors." His "reputation for annihilating comrades who criticise the line of the Party" was "well known."[877]

The CPA was a revolutionary party, a foreign entity, a basically contraband intruder into a system of democratic parties. It fraudulently pretended to be non-violent, not at all bent on revolution, just reformist and democratic, but it was unable to give up the goal of revolution

---

872 Ibid., p. 45.
873 Soviet archival documents prove that between 1953 and 1966, the CPA received from Moscow seven payments totalling US $805,000. The CPA breakaway Socialist Party of Australia obtained another US $40,000 in 1973. See Brian Woodley, "Files reveal 'Moscow gold' paper trail led Down Under," *Weekend Australian*, 10–11 January 1998, p. 5. "The CPA received the 1997 equivalent of $6.06 milion", according to *Courier-Mail*, January 10, 1998, pp. 1 and 4.
874 *Te Reds.*, p. 364.
875 Ibid., p. 338.
876 Ibid., pp. 141–42, 152, 176, and 361.
877 Ibid., pp. 142, 177, 250, and 344.

that was the justification of its existence. The chief spokesman for the CPA between 1930 and 1965 was Lance L. Sharkey. In a collection of his speeches and writings one can read about "revolutionary forces" facilitating "the movement of workers away from reformism to revolutionary socialism," and "the objective must be to politically revolutionise the unions." Defending his "seditious" statement that "Australian workers would welcome Soviet forces pursuing aggressors" he said: "The job of Communists is to struggle to prevent war and to educate the mass of people against the idea of war. The Communist Party also wants to bring the working class to power, but if fascists in Australia use force to prevent the workers gaining that power, Communists will advise the workers to meet force by force.

When we remember that any democrat could be and often was called a Fascist by the Communists, Prime Minister Menzies for example, the threat of force loses its legalistic disguise.

Unfortunately, for its visionary goal of a salutary revolution, the CPA attracted many good men and women in search of a more democratic and socially healthy society. They went on to gradually lose their faith in the Communist Party and leave it, but their youthful enthusiasm and energy would be irretrievably squandered. One of these disappointed enthusiasts, John Sandy, contemplating his comrade, Ralph Gibson, wrote:

> Very often the most idealistic activists devoted their life—or at least a large part of their life – to working for Communism. Naturally, it weakened democratic efforts in two ways: first, it lost support by often the most active part of politically minded public, and, second, another large part of the same population, again the most politically interested people had to devote their energies to fighting the Communists rightly perceived as representing the major threat to democracy. Even more than that: Communist conspiracy provoked similarly dogmatic right-wing activists to exaggerate their conflict with a party that was threatening their interests (capitalist, religious, nationalist). Such a division into three camps was to a large degree occasioned by Lenin's

program of speeded-up Marxism. His conspiratorial aggressivity and dogmatic hate provoked a fatal split between democratic socialism and anti-democratic Communism. Liberal and left oriented socially minded people had then to fight on two fronts: against Leninism, Trotskyism, Stalinism and Maoism on one side and against Fascism and Nazism and minor dictators on the other side. For some eight decades the democratic centre was terribly weakened by the desertion of activists who could have used their energy for improving the political, economic and social lot of their populations.[878]

Some Communists and their sympathizers sometimes claimed that their revolution in Australia would be democratic and non-violent. However, many Russians, Ukrainians, Poles, Czechs, Slovaks, Hungarians, Rumanians, and French entertained the same hopes and illusions. Soviet specialists always proceeded the only proved and approved Leninist/Stalinist way, including murders, tortures, lies, and concentrations camps, liquidating all real or imagined potential opponents. The Stalinization of the CPA in 1930 set the stage for such a seizure of power.

A few Communists or ex-Communists admitted that in the ranks of the party there were members who would have enacted terror and bloody reprisals. For instance, Eric Aarons revealed that "had we been in power, we too could have executed people we considered to be objectively, even if not subjectively (that is, by intention), helping our enemies."[879]

Another Communist activist, Geoff McDonald, warned in 1977–78 that a Communist revolution accompanied by the usual terror could have happened in Australia. The number of Communists dedicated to a violent overthrow of democracy was proportionately much higher in Australia than in Russia in 1917. McDonald was expelled from the CPA in 1962 for reasons that in an established Soviet state would have

---

878 John Sandy, *Ralph Gibson. An Extraordinary Communist* (Melbourne: Ralph Gibson Biography Committee, 1988).

879 *What's Left? Memoirs of an Australian Communist* (Penguin Books, 1993), p. 118.

led to his execution. After thirteen years in the Communist Party, he wrote, "They know that the political crimes with which I was charged met with the death penalty in countries under Communist rule." Using his own case he demonstrated what kind of system would have been created in Australia had the Communists succeeded in their plans for a revolution:

> At a Christmas break-up party I attended in 1962 … I was violently kicked, scratched and dragged along the floor, whilst they heaped on me for my political corruption, and but for a number of Labor Party members who came to my aid I do not know what would have happened. According to witnesses my opponents had continued to punch and kick me while I was unconscious on the ground…. As I was led away from the building by friends I pondered that this was the way these people would run Australia if they ever got the chance.[880]

From the history of Communist regimes in other countries such as the Soviet Union, Hungary, and Czechoslovakia, it is obvious that no deviation, however minor or temporary, from the party line was forgotten, and such deviation could be used as grounds for the murder of otherwise devoted party members. Any criticism of Stalin, his henchmen or their decisions was recorded in cadre records and became handy during party purges. Obedience and discipline were achieved at the price of supreme terror. Every Communist Party was both a fraternal brotherhood and a criminal organization. McDonald also recorded that CPA leader Ted Hill, who "had virtually supreme power in the Victorian Party organisation," considered the execution of Hungarian Communist Laszlo Rajk and Bulgarian Traicho Kostov justified even after their Communist rehabilitation and that he defended Stalin's executions during the thirties.[881] Communist leaders were not known for their gentility.

---

880 *Australia at Stake* (North Melbourne: Peelprint, 1977), pp. 1 and 219–21. In 1978 the book was reprinted by Melbourne's McDonald.
881 Ibid., pp. 152, 145, and 146.

The French editor of *The Black Book of Communism* (1997), Stephane Courtois, calculated that Communists have killed between eighty-five million and one hundred million people. In his review of the book, Ron Brunton wrote, "Communism was criminal in its nature from the start, rejecting the rule of law and committed to achieving its aim through mass terror and violence."[882]

THE LIKELIHOOD OF REVOLUTION 1948–50

The Communist Party of Australia came out of World War II strengthened; the Soviet Union was very popular as victor over Hitler's Nazism, and the CPA enjoyed the benefit of a successful KGB penetration of Australia's Department of Foreign Affairs, opposition Labor Party, and police. Large scale domination of trade unions and lack of understanding of Communist subversive methods facilitated whatever opportunity the CPA had to seize power. Very much like what was successful in Czechoslovakia in 1948 and much less successful in France and Italy, large scale strikes in Australia were creating a revolutionary ferment. There is no doubt that these actions were coordinated and planned by Moscow, together with insurrections in Malaysia, the denunciation of Tito, and the Berlin blockade. As China became Red, the Communist offensive seemed to be unstoppable. In June 1950, North Korea, militarily supported by the Soviet Union and China, invaded South Korea. The American policy of containment of Soviet expansion in Europe had to have its Asian and Australian extension.

A series of major strikes promoted by the CPA between 1947 and 1949 threatened to cripple post-war economic recovery and destroy the Labor government led by Prime Minister Ben Chiffley. As CPA leaders Richard Dixon and Lance Sharkey repeatedly divulged to party members, the strikes, culminating in a seven-week coal strike between June and August 1949, were intended "to draw the masses to the side of the Communist Party" and "to liquidate reformism." On February 22, 1948, the party's organizing secretary, J. C. Henry, told the CP

882 "Unrepentant Communists just unwelcome," *Courier-Mail*, 19 September 1998, p. 21.

central committee meeting, "All the conditions are maturing for a ... break with reformism on the part of the workers."[883] According to Communist Party ideology, reformism was not a proper answer to the situation, but revolution was.

The CPA almost always preached revolution against reformism. In his memoirs, Eric Aarons wrote about 1945 expectations: "After all, wasn't the revolution going to come in five, maybe ten, or certainly no more than twenty years?"[884] When Bernie Taft was getting married in 1948, as he recalled later: "We regarded ourselves as soldiers of the revolution."[885] The revolutionary seizure of power was the goal and the coal strike together with other disruptions was the path to it. According to Aarons, "Jack Henry ... of the central secretariat of the Party, actually had a strategy for the revolution in Australia. This plan involved surrounding Sydney with the militant working-class districts of Newcastle, the South Coast and Litgow. I believe that he saw the miners' strike as a step along that road."[886]

Therefore, the CPA rejected Chifley's offer "which conceded all the miners' demands."[887] J. C. Henry even wanted to "dynamite the Hawkesbury railway tunnel to prevent 'scab' coal from reaching Sydney."[888] Former Communist Keith McEwan recalled that during "the tense situation at the time of the coal strike ... some of the gunmen associated with the waterfront were called in."[889]

Australia then came very close to a Communist revolution. Only Chifley's resolute action, based on accurate intelligence reports and use of the army, prevented the worst. As Robert Manne remarked, "Under Mr. Chifley and Dr. Ewatt the Communist Party had almost, during 1949, brought the nation to its knees."[890] Had Ewatt won the elections in 1954, another danger arrived of a possible Communist revolution.

---

883 See a thorough study "Communism, Security and the Cold War," by Philip Deery, *Overland,* pp. 163–64.

884 *What's Left,* op. cit., p. 60.

885 *Crossing the Party Line,* op. cit., pp. 70–71.

886 *What's Left,* op. cit., p. 66.

887 Deery, op. cit., p. 167.

888 Ibid., p. 169.

889 Ibid., p. 174, quoting *Once a Jolly Comrade* (Brisbane, 1966), p. 20.

890 *The Shadow of 1917: Cold War Conflict in Australia* (Melbourne: The Teet Publishing Company, 1994), p. 110. See also Andrew Campbell,

1960s

Although Murray-Smith expected the revolution in 1959, as he told Patrick O'Brien, the beginning of the sixties was a more realistic prediction. "By 1961 over a hundred Australian Communists had attended study courses in China"[891] and hundreds of others went to revolutionary schools in Moscow, Prague, and elsewhere. When Ted Hill returned in November 1961 from Peking, according to Bernie Taft, "he made the bizarre proposal that the party should start preparing for armed struggle, and should commence training people for it."[892] Other leaders of the CPA were not so shocked by this "bizarre proposal" as Taft. As Ralph Gibson reported, "There was a strong pro-Chinese feeling in the leadership of the Communist Party of Australia. At the key international conference in 1957 and 1960 the PCA delegates had supported the Chinese on virtually all issues debated."[893]

Eric Aarons remembered that Hill declared that "the end of imperialism was in sight" and that we had to prepare for that eventuality by supporting belligerent Chinese attitudes…. "He intimated that we had to prepare organisationally for possible military struggle."[894] At that time a very important issue was discussed between Soviet and Chinese leadership. Mao Tse-tung disliked the Kremlin's denunciation of Stalin and its policy of peaceful co-existence. He wanted to push for the final war against the West. Hill brought this conflict over strategy to Australia.

Luckily for Australia, and also for Australian Communists, Hill provoked strong opposition which gradually led him to leave the CPA and create his own Maoist party. In his own book, *Australia's Revolution*, he recalled the clash of the sixties:

"Dr H.V. Evatt—Part One: a Question of Sanity", *National Observe, Australia and World Affairs*, December 22, 2007, 10 pages.

891 Harvey Barnett, *Tale of the Scorpion* (Sydney: Allen Unwin, 1988), p. 73.

892 *Crossing the Party Line*, op. cit., p. 123.

893 John Sandy, *Ralph Gibson*, op. cit., p. 130. See Vladislav M. Zubok, "Deng Yiaoping and the Sino-Soviet Split, 1956–1963, "*Cold War International History Project BULLETIN* (Washington, DC), Issue 10, March 1998, pp. 152–162.

894 *What's Left*, op. cit., p. 130.

It being a law of history that capitalism must give way
to socialism, that law embraced Australia; Australia
is and could be no exception.... The rejection of
revolutionary force and violence is a bourgeois
idea.... The highest form of revolution is the seizure
of political power by armed force.... In 1961 the
faces of so-called hardened revolutionaries who
called themselves Communists turned white when
the perspective of armed struggle was advocated....
Capitalism is in final crisis. It will be overthrown
soon, soon in the historical sense.[895]

Following Hill's call for armed struggle to be led from the hills in
a guerrilla war, hundreds of high school kids received special training
in camps.

Preparations of perhaps a more serious nature for a southeastern
extension of Soviet-style revolution were then happening in Indonesia.
Between 1955 and 1965, Czechoslovakia, with the assistance of the
Soviet Union, sent huge quantities of military hardware to President
Sukarno and his armed forces. During the 1955 Bandung Congress
of the so-called Third World—ostensibly propagating peace and
disarmament—the Czechoslovak commercial delegation proposed
to send small amounts of old weapons to Indonesia. Indonesian
negotiators refused such a deal and requested modern weaponry for an
army of 250,000 men: hundreds of thousands of automatic rifles and
hundreds of thousands of machine guns. When a civil war broke out
in 1958, Indonesian officers Lieutenant Colonel Pringodisurijo and
Colonel Jani came to Prague and repeated the unfulfilled orders. They
turned to Czechoslovakia because they considered it unreasonable to
turn directly to the Soviet Union. The USSR, however, took part in
the supply since Czechoslovakia was not able to deliver all that was
demanded on its own. Indonesian soldiers and airmen were then
trained in the ČSSR. Between 1958 and 1963, 205 Indonesians went
through military preparations in Czechoslovakia. President Sukarno
officially visited Prague in 1956 and 1961.

---

895 E.F. Hill, *Communism and Australia: Reflections and Reminiscenses,*
   Communist Party of Australia (Marxist-Leninist), Fitzroy, Victoria,
   1989.

The Communist militarization of Indonesia was accompanied by a large scale disinformation campaign led by Czech intelligence officers. Started in 1964, the aim of this operation was to provoke mass anti-American hysteria in Indonesia that would facilitate the planned seizure of power by the Communist party of Indonesia. On September 30, 1965, the revolution, supported by President Sukarno, failed due to disagreements between Soviet and Chinese factions of the Communist Party and General Suharto's counter-coup. According to former major of the Czechoslovak First Administration of the Ministry of the Interior, Ladislav Bittman, the Czechoslovak and Soviet scheme to create a powerful military Communist ally in Southeast Asia failed in spite of the fact that the Soviet government "attached extraordinary importance" to the enterprise.[896]

Had the Communist coup succeeded, in two decades Indonesia would have become a militarily dangerous outpost of the Soviet plans for the rest of Southeast Asia and for Australia, which was an acknowledged target of Soviet imperialism. Its phase of peaceful co-existence was just another way to final victory.

1970's

As the 1971 West Australian Ministry for Education booklet *Soviet Society* proved (see the author's introduction), systematic indoctrination of students in revolutionary attitudes was occurring in Australian schools. According to Bernie Taft, "the Aarons forces" did not like the "gradualist perspective" favored by Taft and to a large degree represented by Gough Whitlam. "They saw a revolutionary situation arising" in the seventies. In Taft's view, very much like Ted Hill's, "the Aarons' style was authoritarian, rigid, and intolerant."[897]

The Communists expected much from Dr. Jim Cairns[898] who wanted to become a member of the CPA after the war but allegedly

---

896   Ladislav Bittman, *Špionážní oprátky* ["*Espionage Gallows*"] (Prague: Mladá fronta, 1982.) Bittman also published a book *The KGB and Soviet Disinformation* (Washington, DC: Pergamon-Brassey's, 1983.)

897   *Crossing...*, op. cit., pp. 253–54.

898   According to John Ballantyne, "Dr. James Ford [Jim] Cairns was a high-ranking member of a Communist front organisation [the World Peace Council], co-ordinated and financed by Moscow and was a long-

was rejected because of his previous membership in the police force. In an interview published in the *Australian Left Review* in May 1971, he expressed his opinion about the chances for revolution:

> The ALP left wing has a very good chance of winning Federal Conference and Executive leadership of the ALP. Among the changes in policy that would bring are: 1. *An end* to the principle that the *US alliance* is crucial ... 4. New emphasis would be given to civil rights.... This would mean a curtailment of the powers of security and other *police* engaged in political or cultural intimidation.... [my italics] I regard the ALP as a vehicle for socialist change in Australia ... To establish socialism in Australia a revolution would be necessary, but the belief that socialism can be established in Australia by force is utopian and mistaken. Contemporary Australian society is so acquisitive, violent and uncooperative that the change necessary to establish socialism would be so great that it could not be other than revolutionary. But socialism could not be established quickly by force.

In the same double interview, Bill Hartley supported the idea of a democratic revolution, but as in similar revolutionary programs of Communist parties and their allies, the term democratic was very elastic; according to Lenin, there was no contradiction between democracy and dictatorship.[899] What really mattered was the revolution. After the sacking of the Whitlam government, Manning Clark several times

---

standing Soviet agent of influence.... It is far more probable that he was advised by senior party colleagues that he could be more useful to the Communist cause by joining the more mainstrem Australian Labor Party, which he did the following year. " John Ballantyne, "Australia's Dr Jim Cairns and the Soviet K.G.B.", *National Observer, Australia and World Affairs,* September 22, 2005, pp. 1 and 4 out of 8.

899 Lenin, *Collected Works*, Vol. 30, p. 503, quoted by Romerstein, Herbert and Stanislav Levchenko, *The KGB Against the 'Main Enemy': How the Soviet Intelligence Service Operates against the United States* (Lexington, Mass.: Lexington Books, 1988), p. XI.

expressed the view that only a revolution could help the people's cause.

At the CPA congress in Sydney in March 1974, Laurie Aarons was re-elected as national secretary of the CPA. He called for "ultimately a revolution." Jack Mundy opened the door to what was traditionally considered revolution's prerequisite: "Jack Mundy ... made an unexpected call for a general strike."[900] His appeal clearly struck a chord. He was elected as party president.

Again, the inevitable forthcoming revolution existed more in the minds of hopeful Leftist dreamers than in reality. However, when Jim Cairns became deputy prime minister of Australia on June 10, 1974, "technically privy to every secret of state when he acted as Prime Minister in Whitlam's absence,"[901] danger signals flashed not only in Australia.

Probably only secret documents still hidden in Soviet archives could answer the question of why Australian Communists and their accomplices never actually triggered a revolution in spite of their preparedness for it on several occasions. Was it due to their own restraint and hesitation or did Moscow decide that the timing and situation were not convenient?

There were both domestic and international causes for the gradual decline of a realistic chance for a successful revolution in Australia. Locally, the surveillance and reports by the intelligence services together with B. A. Santamaria's extraordinary effort to limit Communist power in the unions prevented the worst from occurring. At the same time, local enthusiasts for the Communist cause were gradually losing their zeal while myths about Soviet progressivity were replaced by growing understanding of its mass terror and imperialism, the Hungarian, Czechoslovak, and Afghan invasions, the mass exterminations in Cambodia, etc. Even Chinese Communists reined on the Soviet parade when they criticized the Great Helmsman for his blunders and millions of lives wasted.

Interestingly, many Communist politicians were willing to accept the truth faster than intellectual dreamers such as Manning Clark, Wilfred Burchett, Ian Milner, or Humphrey McQueen. Those historians, educators, and communicators caused much longer-lasting

---

900   Taft, op. cit., pp. 269 and 271.
901   McKnight, op.cit., p. 286.

damage than even Communist unionists who deserve credit for some beneficial work done. The pupils of falsified history and mendacious journalism often retain the ideas and images they have absorbed, and hold to their positions. As long as the intellectuals who supported Communism are taken seriously by anyone, they will remain dangerous dreamers.

Selected Bibliography

INTERVIEWS AND CORRESPONDENCE

Murray-Smith, Dr. Stephen, transcript of recorded interview by Professor O'Brien, Patrick (1975)

Škvorecký, Dr. Josef, to Peter Hruby, 27 September 1997

Turner, Dr. Ian, transcript of a recorded interview with Professor Patrick O'Brien (1975)

TELEPHONE CONVERSATIONS

Milner, Linda in Prague on October 8, 1997

Stříbrný, Professor Zdeněk, the same day

TELEVISION

Four Corners on Channel 2, September 26, 1981

THESIS

Miller, Jamie, "Without Raising Problems of Proof or Refutation": Wilfred Burchett and Australian Anti- Communism, The University of Sydney, 2007

E-MAIL

Several messages to Australia from the Office for Documentation and
Investigation of Communist Crimes, Prague, Czech Republic,
between 1998 and 1999

UNPUBLISHED RECORDS

Australian Archives, Canberra
Archives of Charles University in Prague (Karlova Univerzita), Czech
Republic
Archives of the Ministry of Foreign Affairs of the Czech Republic
(Ministerstvo zahraničních věcí), Prague
Archives of the Ministry of the Interior (Ministerstvo vnitra), Prague
Archives of the World Federation of Trade Unions, Prague
Department of the (US) Navy Files
FBI New York and Washington Bureau Files
Hoover Institute, California
State Central Archive (*Státní ústřední archiv*) in Prague
VENONA Historical Monographs

BOOKS

Aarons, Eric, *Philosophy for an Exploding World*, Brolga Books, Sydney,
1972
Aarons, Eric, *What's Left? Memoirs of an Australian Communist*, Penguin,
Harmondsworth, 1973
Andrew, Christopher, *The Defence of the Realm: The Autorized History
of M15*, Allen Lane, London, 2009
Andrew, Christopher, *The Mitrokhin Archive II: The KGB and the
World*, Allen Lane, London, 2005
Andrew, Christopher, and Oleg Gordievsky, *KGB: The Inside Story of Its
Foreign Operations from Lenin* to *Gorbachev*, Hodder & Stoughton,
London, 1990

Andrew, Christopher, and Vasili Mitrokhin, *The Sword and the Shield: The Mitrokhin Archive and the Secret History of the KGB*, Basic Books, New York, 1999

Arendt, Hannah, *The Origins of Totalitarianism: The Burden of Our Time*, Secher & Warburg, London, 1951

Arendt, Hannah, *Eichmann in Jerusalem: A Report on the Banality of Evil*, Penguin, New York, 1976

Aron, Raymond, *The Opium of the Intellectuals*, London, 1957

Ash, Timothy, *The File: A Personal History*, Random House, New York, 1997

Bacon, E. A., *Outline of the Post-War History of the Communist Party of Australia*, Brisbane, 1966

Ball, Desmond, and David Horner, *Breaking the Codes: Australia's KBG Network*, Allen & Unwin, Sydney, 1998

Barnett, Harvey, *Tale of a Scorpion*, Allen & Unwin, Sydney, 1988

Barron, John, *KGB Today: The Hidden Hand*, Readers Digest Press, New York, 1983

Becker, Jasper, *Hungry Ghosts; China's Secret Famine*, Hachette Livre, 1997

Bečvář, Adolf, *Poezie za mřížemi*, Zlín, 1995

Benda, Julien, *La Trahison des Clercs*, Paris 1927

Bennett, Bruce, and Jennifer Strauss, eds., *The Oxford Literary History of Australia*, Oxford University Press, Melbourne, 1998

Bialoguski, Michael, *The Petrov Story*, Mandarin, Melbourne, 1989

Bittman, Ladislav, *The Deception Game*, 1972

Bittman, Ladislav, *The KGB and Soviet Disinformation: an insider view*, Pergamon-Brassey's, 1985

Bittman, Ladislav, ed., *The New Image Makers: Soviet Propaganda and Disinformation Today*, Pergamon- Brassey's Washington, 1988

Bittman, Ladislav, *Špriondžní oprátky*, Mladá fronta, Prague, 1992

Bridge, Carl, ed., *Manning Clark: Essays on His Place in History*, Melbourne University Press, 1994

Brown, W. J., ed., *The Petrov Conspiracy Unmasked*, Current Books, Sydney, 1957

Brzezinski, Zbigniew, *The Grand Failure: The Birth and Death of Communism in the Twentieth Century.* Charles Scribner's Sons, New York, 1989.

Burbess, Pat, *WARCO: Australian Reporters at War*, William Heinemann Australia, Hawthorn, Victoria, 1986

Burchett, Wilfred, *War Mongers Unmasked*, World Unity Publications, Melbourne, 1950

Burchett, Wilfred, *Cold War in Germany*, World Unity Publications, Melbourne, 1950

Burchett, Wilfred, *China's Feet Unbound*, 1952

Burchett, Wilfred, *People's Democracies*, World Unity Publications, Melbourne, 1951

Burchett, Wilfred, *China: Quality of Life*, Penguin, 1976

Burchett, Wilfred, *Passport: An Autobiography*, Nelson, Melbourne, 1969

Burchett, Wilfred, *At the Barricades*, Macmillan, 1981

Burchett, George, and Nick Shimmin, eds., *Rebel Journalism: The Writings of Wilfred Burchett*, Cambridge University Press, 2007

Cain, Frank, *The Origins of Political Surveillance in Australia*, Angus & Robertson, Sydney, 1983

Cain, Frank, *The Australian Security Intelligence organization: an Unfficial History*, Frank Cass Co, Ilford, Essex, 1994

Cain, Frank, *Menzies in War and Peace*, Allen & Unwin, Sydney, 1997

Cairns, James Ford, *The Quiet Revolution*, Widescope, Melbourne, 1972

Camus, Albert, *The Rebel*, Penguin, Harmonworth, 1967

Catley, Roberts, and Bruce McFarlane, *From Tweedledum to Tweedledee*, Australia and New Zealand Book Companies, Sydney, 1974

Clark, C. M. H., A History of Australia. I From The Earliest Times to the Age of Macquarie, University of Melbourne Press, 1971

Clark, C. M. H., *II New South Wales and Van Diemen's Land, 1822–1838, University of Melbourne Press*, 1968

Clark, C. M. H., *III The Beginning of an Australian Civilization, 1824–1851, Melbourne university Press*, 1973

Clark, C. M. H., IV *The Earth Abideth for Ever, 1851–1888*, Melbourne University Press, 1980

Clark, C. M. H., V *The People Make Laws, 1888–1915*, Melbourne University Press, 1981

Clark, C. M. H., VI *The Old Dead Tree and the Young Tree Green*, 1916–1935, Melbourne University Press, 1987

Clark, Manning, *Meeting Soviet Man*, Angust & Robertson, Sydney, 1960 and 1969

Clark, Manning, *A Short History of Australia*, Mentor Books, Melbourne, 1963

Clark, Manning, *A Discovery of Australia*, 1976 Boyer Lectures, ABC

Clark, Manning, *In Search of Henry Lawson*, Macmillian Co of Australia, Melbourne, 1978

Clark, Manning, *Occasional Writings and Speeches*, Fontana/Collins, Melbourne 1980

Clark, Manning, *The Quest for Grace*, Penguin, Richmond, Victoria, 1990

Clark, Manning, *The Puzzles of Childhood*, Viking-Penguin Books Australia, Ringwood, Victoria, 1990

Clark, Manning, *A Historian's Apprenticeship*, Melbourne University Press, 1992

Clark, Manning, *Dear Kathleen, Dear Manning*, ed. Susan Davies, Melbourne University Press, 1996

Clark, Manning, *Speaking out of Turn*. Lectures and Speeches 1940–1991 by Manning Clark, Melbourne University press, 1997

Cohn, Norman, *The Pursuit of the Millenium*, New York, 1957

Conquest, Robert, *The Great Terror: Stalin's Purge of the Thirties*, London, 1968

Conquest, Robert, *The Great Terror: A Reassessment*, Oxford University Press, Oxford, 1990

Dalziel, Allan, *Evatt the Enigma*, Lansdowne Press, Melbourne, 1967

Davidson, Alastair, *The Communist Party of Australia: A Short History*, Hoover Institution Press, Stanford, California, 1969

Duchacek, Ivo, *Nations and Men: An Introduction to International politics*, Dryden Press, Hinsdale, Illinois, 1975

Ebbels, R. N., *The Australian Labor Movement, 1850-1907*, Landowne Press, 1960 and 1965

Endicott, Stephen, and Edward Hagerman, *The United States and Biological Warfare: Secrets from the Early Cold War and Korea*, Indiana University Press, 1999

Engels, Friedrich, *Utopian and Scientific*, 1880

Filipi, Pavel, *Do nejhlubších hlubin: Život, setkávání, teologie. K stému výročí narození J.L. Hromádky*, Kalich, Praha, 1990

Fitzpatrick, Brian, *A Short History of the Australian Labour Movement*, Macmillan, Melbourne, 1968

Frucht, Richard, ed., Encyclopedia of Eastern Europe. Garland Publishing, Inc., New York and London, 2000

Fukuyama, Francis, *The End of History and the Last Man*, Avon Books, New York, 1993

Gaddis, John Lewis, *We Now Know: Rethinking Cold War History*, Oxford, 1997

Gibson, Ralph, *My Years in the Communist Party*, International Bookshop, Melbourne, 1966

Gibson, Ralph, *The Fight Goes On: A Picture of Australia and the World in Two Post-war Decades*, Red Rooster Press, Maryborough, Victoria, 1987

Gillies, W. J., et al., *Soviet Society: A Study in Communism*, Education Department of Western Australia, 1971

Golland, Robin, *Revolutionaries and Reformists: Communism and the Australian Labour Movement*, 1920–1955, ANU Press Canberra, 1975

Gorky, Maxim, *Untimely Thoughts: Essays on Revolution, Culture and the Bolsheviks,*1917-1918

Gould, L. Harry, *The Sharkey Writings*, Quality Press, 1974

Gross, Paul, and Norman Levitt, *Higher Superstition: The Academic Left and Its Quarrels with Science*, Johns Hopkins University Press, Baltimore, 1994

Hall, Richard, *The Rhodes Scholar Spy*, Random House Australia, Sydney, 1991

Hall, Richard, *The Secret State: Australia's Spy Industry*, Cassell, Sydney, 1978

Hardy, Frank, *Journey Into the Future*, Australian Book Society, Melbourne, 1952

Hardy, Frank, *Power Without Glory*, Sphere Books, London, 1968

Hardy, Frank, *But the Dead Are Many*, Bodley Head, London, 1975

Hartmann, Frederick H., *The Relations of Nations,* Macmillan, 1962

Haylen, Leslie, *Chinese Journey*, Angus & Robertson, Sydney, 1959

Haynes, John Earl, Harvey Klehr, and Alexander Vassiliev, *Spies: The Rise and Fall of the KGB in America*, Yale University Press, New Haven,CT, 2009

Heenen, Tom: *From Traveller to Traitor: The Life of Wilfred Burchet*, Melbourne University Publishing, 2006

Hill, E. F., *Communism and Australia: Reflections and Reminiscences, Communist Party of Australia* (Marxist-Leninist), Fitzroy, Victoria, 1989

Holan, Vladimir, *Selcted Poems, Penguin*, Harmondsworth, 1971

Hollander, Paul, *Political Pilgrims: Travels of Western Intellectuals to the Soviet Union,_China, and Cuba 1928–1978*, Oxford University Press, New York

Hollander, Paul, *The End of Commitment: Intellectuals, Revolutionaries and Political Morality*, Ivan R. Dee, Chicago, 2006

Holt, Stephen, *Manning Clark and Australian History, 1915–1963*, Queensland University Press, St Lucia, 1982

Holub, Miroslav, *Notes of a Clay Pigeon*, London, 1977

Hruby, Peter, *Fools and Heroes: The Changing Role of Communist Intellectuals in* Czechoslovakia, Oxford: Pergamon Press, 1980

Hruby, Peter, *Daydreams and Nightmares: Czech Communist and Ex-Communist Literature, 1917–_1987*, Columbia University Press, New York, 1990

Kalugin, Oleg, *Spy Master: My 32 Years in Intelligence and Espionage Against the West*, Smith Gryphon, London, 1994

Kamenka, Eugene, *A World in Revolution?*, ANU, Canberra, 1970

Kaplan, Karel, *Pět kapitol o Únoru*, Doplněk, Brno, 1997

Kaplan, Morton A., *The Many Faces of Communism*, Free Press, New York, 1978

Kennan, George F, *American Diplomacy, 1900–1950*, Mentor Book, New York, 1954

Kennan, George F., *Memoirs 1925–1950*, Little Brown and Company, 1967

Kisch, Egon Erwin, *Landung in Australien*, Berlin, 1973

Kissinger, Henry, *White House Years*, Little, Brown and Company, Boston, 1990

Klehr, Harvey, *The Heyday of American Communism: The Depression Decade*, Basic Books, New York, 1984

Klehr, Harvey, and John Earl Haynes, *The American Communist Movement: Storming Haven Itself*, Twayne Publishers, New York, 1992

Klehr, Harvey, and John Earl Haynes, *Venona: Decoding Soviet Espionage in America*, Yale university Press, New Haven, CT, 2000

Klehr, Harvey, John Earl Haynes, and Fridrikh Igorevich Firsov, *The Secret World of American Communism*, Yale University Press, New Haven, 1995

Klehr, Harvey, John Earl Haynes, and Kyrill M. Anderson, *The Soviet World of American Communism*, Yale University Press, New Haven, 1998

Knight, Amy, *The KGB: Police and Politics in the Soviet Union*, Unwin Hyman, Boston, 1988

Knightley, Phillip, *The Second Oldest Profession: Spies and Spying in the Twentieth Century*, W.W. Norton, New York, 1986

Knightley, Phillip, *Philby: The Life and Views of the K.G.B. Masterspy*, Andre Deutsch, London, 1988

Knopfelmacher, Frank, *Intellectuals and Politics*, Nelson, Melbourne, 1968

Koch, Stephen, *Double Lives: Spies and Writers in the Secret War of Ideas Against the West*, Free Press, New York, 1994

Koestler, Arthur, *The Invisible Writing: The Second Volume of an Autobiography: 1932–40*, Stein and day, New York, 1984

Kohout, Pavel, *Aus dem Tagebuch eines Konter-Revolutionärs*, G. J. Bucher, 1969

Kramer, Hilton, *The Twilight of the Intellectuals: Culture and Politics in the Era of the Cold War.* Ivan R Dee, Chicago, 1999.

Kriegel, Annie, and Stéphane Courtois, *Eugen Field, Le grand secret du PCF,* Seuil, Paris, 1997

Kundera, Milan, *The Farewell Party*, Alfred A. Knopf, New York, 1976

Leggett, G. H., *The Cheka: Lenin's Political Police*, Clarendon, Oxford, 1981

Levchenko, Stanislav, *On the Wrong Side: My Life in the KGB,* Pergamon-Brassey's, Washington, 1988

Li Zhi Sui, Dr., *The private Life of Chairman Mao: the Memoirs of Mao's Personal Physician*, Random House, New York, 1994

Loebl, Eugen, *Sentenced and Tried: The Stalinist Purges in Czechoslovakia*, Elek, London, 1969

Loebl, Eugen, *My Mind on Trial*, Harcourt Brace Jovanovich, New York, 1976

Lukacs, John, *The Great Powers and Eastern Europe*, American Book Company, New York, 1953

McDonald, Geoff, *Australia at Stake*, Peelprint, North Melbourne, 1977

MacFarquar, *The Origins of the Cultural Revolution, 3: The Coming of the Cataclysm 1961–66*, Columbia University Press, New York, 1997

McGillick, Tony, *Comrade No More*, West Perth, McGillick, 1980

Macintire, Stuart, *The Reds: The Communist Party of Australia from Its Origins to Illegality*, Allen & U   nwin, 1998

McEwan, Keith, *Once a Jolly Comrade*, Jacaranda Press, 1966

McKnight, David, *Australia's Spies and Their Secrets*, Allen & Unwin, Sydney, 1994

McQueen, Humphrey, *A New Britannia: An Argument Concerning the Social Origins of Australian Radicalism and Nationalism*, Penguin, Harmondsworth, 1970 and 1975

McQueen, Humphrey, *Australia's Media Monopolies*, Widescope, Camberwell, Victoria, 1977

McQueen, Humphrey, *The Black Swan of Tresspas: The Emergence of Modernist Painting in Australia to 1944*, Alternative Publishing Cooperative Ltd, 1979

McQueen, Humphrey, *Social Sketches of Australia 1888-1975*, Penguin, 1978, reprinted 1986

McQueen, Humphrey, *Gone Tomorrow: Australia in the 80s*, August & Robertson, London, 1982

McQueen, Humphrey, *Gallipoli to Petrov: Arguing with Australian History*, Allen & Unwin, Sydney, 1984

McQueen, Humphrey, *Suburbs of the Sacred*, Penguin, 1988

McQueen, Humphrey, *Japan to the Rescue*, William Heinemann, Port Melbourne 1991

McQueen, Humphrey, *Tom Roberts*, Macmillan, Sydney, 1996

McQueen, Humphrey, *Social Sketches of Australia, 1888-1988*, Penguin, 1993

McQueen, Humphrey, *Suspect History: Manning Clark and the Future of the Past*, Wakefield Press, KentTown, SA, 1997

Mandelstam, Nadezhda, *Hope Against Hope*, London, 1971

Manne, Robert, *The Petrov Affair: Politics and Espionage*, Pergamon Press, Sydney, 1987

Manne, Robert, *Cold War Conflict in Australia*, Text, Melbourne, 1991

Marx, Karl, and Friedrich Engels, *The Communist Manifesto*, International Publishers, New York, 1948

Masaryk, T. G., *The Spirit of Russia: Studies in History, Literature and Philosophy*, London, 1961–1967

Masaryl, T. G., *Rusko a Evropa*, Jan Laichter, Prague, 1913–1920

Mastný, Vojtěch, *The Cold War and Soviet Insecurity: The Stalin Years*, Oxford University Press, New York, 1996

Mayer, Henry, M*arx, Engels and Australia*, Cheshire, Melbourne, 1964

Méray, Tibor, *On Burchett*, Callistemon Publications, Kallista, Victoria, Australia, 2008

Miller, J. D. B., and T. H. Rigby, eds., *The Disintegrating Monolith: Pluralist Trends in the Soviet World*, ANU, Canberra, 1965

Mlynář, Zdeněk, *Mráz přichází z Kremlu*, Index, Cologne, 1978

Moravec, Frantisek, *Master of Spies: The Memoirs of General Frantisek Moravec*, Bodley Head, London, 1975

Murphy, David E., Sergei Kondrashev, and George Bailey, *Battleground Berlin: CIA vs KGB in the Cold War*, Yale University Press, New Haven, 1997

Murray, Robert, *The Split: Australian Labor in the Fifties*, Cheshire, Melbourne, 1970 and 1972

Murray-Smith, Stephen, *There Is No Iron Curtain*, International Bookshop, Melbourne, 1952

O'Brien, Patrick, *The Saviours: An Intellectual History of the Left in Australia*, Drummond, Richmond, Victoria, 1977

O'Sullivan, Vincent, ed., *Intersecting Lines: The memoirs of Ian Milner*, Victoria University Press, Wellington, 1993

Pelikan, Jiri, *The Czechoslovak Political Trials, 1950–1954*, Macdonald, London, 1970

Pelikan, Jiri, *S'ils me tuent...*, Paris, 1975

Petrov, Vladimir, and Evdokina Petrov, *Empire of Fear*, Frederick A. Praeger, New York, 1956

Pipes, Richard, *The Unknown Lenin: From the Secret Archive*, Yale University Press, New Haven, 1996

Pisar, Samuel, *Of Blood and Hope*, Cassell, London, 1980

Pousta, Zdeněk, ed., *Filosofie za mřížemi: Leopoldov, léta padesátá*, Univerzita Karlova, Prague, 1995

Romerstein, Herbert, and Stanislav Levchenko, *The KGB Against the 'Main Enemy'*, Lexington Books Lexington, Mass., 1989

Russell, Bertrand, *The Practice and Theory of Bolshevism*, 1920

Ryan, Peter, *Lines of Fire: Manning Clark and Other Writings*, Clarion Editions, 1997

Sandy, John, *Comrades Come Rally: Recollections of an Australian Communist*, Nelson, Melbourne, 1978

Sandy, John, *Ralph Gibson: An Extraordinary Communist*, Ralph Gibson Biography Committee, 1988

Santamaria, B. A., *Australia at the Crossroads: Reflections of an Outsider*, Melbourne University Press, 1987

Santamaria, B. A., *A Memoir*, Oxford University Press, 1997

Sejna, Jan, *We Will Bury You*, Sidgwick & Jackson, London, 1982

Sheridan, Tom, *Division of Labour: Industrial Relations in the Chifley Years 1945–1949*, Melbourne University Press, 1989

Sirc, Ljubo, *Economic Devolution in Eastern Europe*, Longmans, London, 1969

Smith, Julian, *On the Pacific Front: The Adventures of Egon Kisch in Australia, Sydney, 1936*

Smolik, Josef, *Josef L. Hromádka: Život a dílo*, Ekumenická škola, Prague, 1989

Solzhenitsyn, Alexander, *Cancer Ward*, The Bodley Head, London, 1968

Solzhenitsyn, Alexander, *The Gulag Archipelago, 1918-1956*, Colling/ Harvill, London, 1974

Solzhenitsyn, Alecander, *The Gulag Archipelago, 1918-1956*, III-IV, Harper & Row, New York, 1975

Solzhenitsyn, Alexander, *The Gulag Archipelago, 1918-1956*, V-VII, Harper & Row, New York, 1978

Steinberg, I.N, *In the Workshop of the Revolution*, London, 1959

Sterling, Claire, *The Terror Network: The Secret War of International Terrorism*, Holt, Rinehart and Winston, New York, 1981

Symons, Beverley, et al., *Communism in Australia: A Resource Bibliography*, National Library of Australia, 1994

373

Taft, Bernie, *Crossing the Party Line: Memoirs of Bernie Taft*, Scribe, Newham, Victoria, 1994

Throssell, Ric, *My Father's Son*, Mandarin Australia, Port Melbourne, Victoria, 1990

Throssell, Ric, *A Reliable Source*, Minerva, Port Melbourne, 1991

Throssell, Ric, *In a Wilderness of Mirrors*, Left Book Club, Sydney, 1992

Thwaits, Michael, *Truth Will Out: ASIO and the Petrovs*, Collins, Sydney, 1980

Trojan, J. S., ed., *Nepřeslechnutelná výzva*, Edice Oikúmené, Prague, 1990

Tumarkin, Nina, *Lenin Lives!*, enlarged edition, Harvard University Press, Boston

Ulam, Adam B., *Lenin and the Bolsheviks*, Collins, London, 1965

Ulam, Adam B., *Stalin: The Man and His Era*, Viking Press, New York, 1973

Urban, G. R., *Communist Reformation: Nationalism, Internationalism and Change in the World Communist Movement*, Maurice Temple Smith, London, 1979

Volkogonov, Dmitri, *Stalin*, Grove Heidenfell, New York, 1991

Volkogonov, Dmitri, *Lenin: A New Biography*, 1994

Westerield, H. Bradford, ed., *Inside CIA's World: Declassified Articles from the Agency's Internal Journal, 1955–1992*, Yale University Press, New Haven, 1997 Whitlam, Nicholas and John Stubbs, *A Nest of Traitors*, Jacaranda Press, Brisbane, 1974

Wright, Peter, *Spycatcher*, Viking, New York, 1987

Wright, Peter, *The Spycatcher's Encyclopedia of Espionage*, William Heinemann, Port Melbourne, 1991

Zubok, Vladislav, and Konstantin Pleshakov, *Inside the Kremlin's Cold War*, Harvard University Press, Boston, 1996

JOURNAL AND NEWSPAPER ARTICLES:

Aarons, Mark, "Cut to Size by the Force of History," *The Australian Literary Review*, 4 July, 2008, No. 10/Memoir/Biography.

Adams, Phillip, "Dictatorships of Popes and Proletarians," *Weekend Australian Review*, 21–22 June 1997, p. 1

Adams, Philip, "A Prophet's Dividents," *The Weekend Australian Review,* 6–7 February 1999, p. 32

Ascherson, Neal, "Khrushchev's Secret," *London Review of Books,* 16 October 1997, p. 26

Ballantyne, John, "Australia's Dr. Jim Cairns and the Soviet K.G.B.," *National Observer, Australia and World Affairs,* September 22, 2005, 8 pages.

Beery, Phillip, "Cold War Victim or Rhodes Scholar Spy? Revisiting the Case of Ian Milner," *Overland,* No. 147, Winter 1997, pp. 9–12

Beloff, Max, "A Neglected Historical Novel," *Encounter,* XXXIV, 3, March 1970

Cain, Frank, "The Making of a Cold War Victim," *Overland,* No. 134, 1994

Cairns, Jim, and Bill Hartley, "An Interview," *Australian Left Review,* May 1971

Campbell, Andrew, "Double Lives: Three Australian Fellow-travelers in the Cold War," *Natioanl Observer, Australia and World Affairs,* June 22, 2006, 10 pages.

Campbell, Andrew, "Dr H.V. Evatt – Part One – A Qustion of Sanity," *National Observer, Australia and World Affairs,* December 22, 2007, 10 pages

Carlton, Peter, "Manning Clark's Medal," *Courier-Mail,* 8 February 1997, p. 27

Carlton, Peter, "Clark Preised Lenin as Teacher of Humanity," *Courier-Mail,* 24 June 1997, pp. 1 and 30–31

Charlton, Peter, and Peter Kelly, "Hero of the Left," *Courier-Mail,* 12 September 1998

Clark, Katherina, "Clark Misquoted on Lenin Speech, *The Australian,* 16 September 1997, p. 14

Clark, Manning, "The Years of Unleavened Bread—December 1949 to December 1972," *Meanjin,* Vol. 32, September 1973, pp. 244–50

Clark, Manning, "Whitlam Has the Formula for a Vision," *Sunday Telegraph,* Sydney, 12 May 1974

Clark, Manning, "1954—the Year of Shame," *Overland,* No. 62, Summer 1975

Clark, Manning, "A View from the Underworld," *Arena*, No. 9, Autumn 1966

Clark, Manning, "In Zhivago's Country: Some Impressions of Soviet Culture and Freedom," *Nation*, February 14, 1959, pp. 15–16

Clark, Manning, "From the Kingdom of Nothingness," *The Australian*, 1 February 1974

Clark, Manning, "Violent Change Next Step," *The Australian*, 12 November 1975

Clark, Manning, "History Will Be Kinder," *The Australian*, January 1976

Clark, Manning, "Are We a Nation of Bastards?" *Meanjin*, Vol. 35, No. 2, 1976

Clark, Manning, "He Wanted a Good Life for Everone," *The Australian*, 16 June 1977, p. 11

Clark, Manning, "Our Civilization Is Now a Graveyard," *Sydney Morning Herald*, 31 December, 1977

Clark, Manning, "Wollongong university Graduation Address," draft, 12 May 1978

Clark, Manning, "The Future of Australia," monograph (of the address), No. 3, pp. 1–8

Clark, Manning, "Interview,", "Professor Warns of Civil War under Radical Government", *Weekend News*, May 13, 1978, p. 1

Clark, Manning, "Clark calling for Robespierre," *National Times*, 11–16 October 1978

Colebatch, Hal, "Letters: Frank and Full Disclosure," *Australia/Israel Review*, 1–14 February 1997, p. 2

Colebatch, Hal, "Manning Clark and Judah Watten," *National Observer—Australia and World Affairs*, April 1,2004.

Colebatch, Hal, "Sunk by Stalinism," *Weekend Australian Review*, 9–10 May 1998

Colebatch, Hal, "Stalin's Literati," *Courier-Mail*, 26 August 1998, p. 28

Colebatch, Hal, "Turning from Stalin," *Courier-Mail*, 5 September 1998, p. 28

Colebatch, Hal, "Memento to Moscow," *Weekend Australian Review*, 16–17 January 1999, p. 10

Conquest, Robert, "Terrorists," *New York Review of Books*, 7 March 1997, pp. 6–9

Craven, Peter, "Between the Metropolitan and the Local," *The Australian*, 2 July 1997, p. 42

Fairbairn, Geoffrey, "Prophet not Scapegoat," *Weekend Australian*, 27–28 May 1978, p. 10

Fee, Kenneth, "Burchett in Korea," *Quadrant*, September 1998, pp. 5–6

Gluchovski, L. W., "Khrushchev's Second Secret Speech," *Cold War International History Project Bulletin*, Issue 10, March 1998, pp. 44–60

Gott, Ken, "Student Life: The Forties," That Other R. S. L. *Melbourne University Magazine*, pp. 19–22, 23–27

Gould, Bob, "The sad, conradictory life of Wilfred Burchett," *Ozleft: An Independent Voice on the Left*, June 4, 2008

Gray, Colins, "The Most Dangerous Decade. Historic Mission, Legitimacy and Dynamics of the Soviet Empire in the 1980s," *Orbis*, Spring 1981

Grossman, "The 'Second Economy' of the USSR," *Problems of Communism*, XXVI/5, September-October 1977, pp. 25–40

Haynes, John Earl, and Harvey Klehr, "The Left continues to deny evidence of the KGB's espionage in America," WWW.FRONTPAGEMAG.COM, June 19, 2009

Hope, Deborah, "Life after Manning," *Weekend Australian Review*, 6–7 June 1998, pp. 1, 5–7

Hruby, Peter, "Secret Life of Agent 9006," *Courier-Mail*, 30 November 1996

Hruby, Peter, "Seduced by Lure of Communism," *Courier-Mail*, 5 December 1996

Hruby, Peter, "Czech Archives prove Evatt's Naivety," *News Weekly*, 24 August 1996

Ionesco, Eugene, "Of Utopianism and Intellectuals," *Encounter*, February 1978

Jeffrey, James, "Red between the lines," *Weekend Australian*, 22–23 March, 2008.

Jolidon, Laurence, "Soviet Interrogation of U.S. POWs in the Korean War," *Cold War International History Project Bulletin*, Washington, DC, Nos. 6–7, Winter 1995, pp. 23–24

Kapel, Michael, "Notebook," *Australi/Israel Review*, 15 February 1997, p. 4

Knopfelmacher, Frank, "The Situation at the University of Melbourne," *Twentieth Century*, Vol. 18, Autumn 1964, pp. 196–207

Knopfelmacher, Frank, "My Political Education," *Quadrant*, Vol. 11, July–August 1967

Knopfelmacher, Frank, "Beware the Phoenix of Labor," *Nation Review*, 19 December 1975, p. 246

Kohout, Pavel, "*Co jsem byl ...*," *Literární noviny*, Prague, 21 March 1964, p. 3

Kozák, Jan, "People's Revolution," *Příspěvky k dějinám KSČ*, Vol. 1, No. 1, Autumn 1957; No. 2, March 1958; Committee on Un-American Activities, U.S. Congress, 30 December 1961

Kramer, Mark, "Moldova,Romania and the Soviet Invasion of Czechoslovakia," *Cold War International History Project Bulletin*, Issue 12/13, Fall/Winter 2001, pp. 326–33

Kramer, Mark, "New Evidence from the Ukrainian Archives," *Cold War International History Project*, Issue 14/15, Winter 2003–Spring 2004, pp. 273–368

Krygier, Richard, "Yalta and Its Aftermath," *Quadrant*, September 1985

Lapsley, Joh, "Violent Change the Next Step, Says Historian," *The Australian*, 12 November 1975

Leggett, G. H., "Lenin, Terror, and the Political Police," *Survey*, 1975

Lipinski, Edward, "An Open Letter to Comrade Gierek," *Survey*, 22/2 (99), 1976

Manne, Robert, "Christ and Lenin," *Australian Review of Books*, October 1996, pp. 6–8

Manne, Robert, "Battle for History's High Ground, *Weekend Australian*, 7–8 June 1997, p. 23

Manne, Robert, "Keith Windshuttle and the Khmer Rouge, *Quadrant*, 6 May 2006, 4 pages

Manne, Robert, "Agent of Influence: Reassessing Wilfred Burchett," *The Monthly*, No. 35, June 2008, The

Monthly Essays, 12 pages.

Mcguiness, "Variety in the Spies of Life," *Sydney Morning Herald*, 26.6.97

McQueen, Humphrey, "Living of Asia, *Arena*, No. 26, 1971, pp. 13–37

McQueen, Humphrey, "Down Under Bunuel," *Meanjin*, Vol. 35, No. 2, 1976, pp. 219–21

McQueen, Humphrey, "National Independence and Socialism," *Melbourne Journal of Politics*, No. 9, 1977, pp. 68–79

McQueen, Humphrey, "The CIA's Operation Culture," *Nation Review*, 5–11, 19–25 May 1977

McQueen, Humphrey, "The Murdoch Press and the Australia Council," *Australian Book Review*, No. 184, September 1996, p. 25

Maryna, Valentina, "*Od důvěry k podezíravosti: Sovětští a českoslovenští komunisté v letech 1945–48,*" *Soudobé dějiny,* Prague, IV/3-4, 1997

Mitchell, Chris, "Evidence File on Clark Grows," *The Australian*, 11 June 1997, p. 12

Montias, J. M., and Susan Rose-Ackerman, "Corruption in a Soviet-type Economy: Theoretical Considerations," Workshop in New Haven, paper, 12–13 October 1979

Moran, Rod, "Reds Like Us," *West Australian*, Big Weekend, 22 August 1998, p. 3

Morgan, Patrick, "Convenient Legend," *Weekend Australian*, 27–28 May 1978, p. 10

Morrisby, Edwin, "Wilfred Burchett of the KGB?" *Quadrant*, October 1985, pp. 28–32

Murashko, Galina P., "*Únorová politická krize roku 1948 v Československu a 'sovětský faktor': Z materiálů ruských archivů,*" *Soudobé dějiny,* IV, 3-4/97

Newmatilda.com, "Remembering Burchett," Nov. 15, 2005.

O'Brien, Patrick, "The Perils of Falsifying History," *Time*, 30 March 1992, p. 64

O'Brien, Patrick, "Death of a Free Spirit," *Courier-Mail*, 14 September 1996, p. 25

O'Hearn, Denis, "The Consumer Second Economy: Size and Effects," *Soviet Studies*, XXXII, 2 April 1981, pp. 218–34

Pacner, Karel, "Nepovinná cetba: Soudruzi, Austráie je dulezitá!," *Mladá Fronta.* 16 June 2007.

Pech, Stanley Z., "Ferment in Czechoslovak Marxist Historiography," *Canadian Slavonic Papers*, Vol. 10/4, 1968

Pemberton, Gregory, "Spy Mystery that Will Not Die," *Canberra Times*, 19 June 1991, p. 21

Pemberton, Gregory, "A Suspect Spy," *Sydney Morning Herald*, 6 July 1991

Pešta, Karel, Interviewed in *Tribuna*, 26 August 1981, p. 4

Polacek, Josef, "*Zu Egon Erwin Kisch's Sprung nach Australien*," *Exil: Forschung, Erkenntnisse, Ergebnisse*, Frankfurt, Vol. VII, No. 2, 1987, pp. 17–33

Pousta, Zdeněk, "*Pražské ženy jako oběť poúnorových soudních represí*," *Sborník příspěvků konference hlavního města Prahy a Nadace* pro gender studies, October 1993, *Žena* v dějinách Prahy, pp. 349–53

Pousta, Zdenek, "Studenti a únor 1948," *Dějiny a současnost*, 1/98, pp. 42-45

Ryan, Bod, "Is this the Beginning of the End for Manning Clark?" *The Australian*, 18 May 978, p. 9

Sakharov, Andrex, "Alarm and Hopc," *New York Times*, 23 January 1980, p. A 23

Smith Wayne, "Manning Clark and the Courier-Mail," *Quadrant*, September 1998, pp. 40–43

Uninews, "Harvard Chair of Australian Studies to Stuart Macintire," Vol. 15, No. 7, 1–15 May 2006.

Veliz, Claudio, "Bad History," *Quadrant*, May 1982, pp. 21–26

Woodley, Brian, "Files Reveal 'Moscow Gold' paper trail led Down Under," *Weekend Australian*, 10–11 January 1998, p. 5

Index

C

Cain, Frank 23, 24, 25, 28, 91, 366, 375

Cairns, Jim 95, 120, 207, 249, 257, 270, 275, 358, 359, 360, 366, 375

Callaghan, L.V.J. 129

Campbell, Peter 240

Carter, Leo 185, 186

Cato, Raymond H. 178

Cavanaghi, J.L. 275

Chandler, Herbert Bovyll 188, 191, 223, 233

Chidzey, Blanche 164

Chifley, Ben 354

Chiplin, Rex [CHARLIE] 32, 176, 187, 188, 191, 215, 216, 223, 227

Chleboun, Edvin 218

Chou En-lai 26, 69

Christopher, Paul 139

Chváta, M. 319

ávrný, Lumír 159

Clancy, Pat 215, 230, 232, 278

Clark, Dymphna 120

Clark, Manning Hope xiii, xxiv, xxxii, 7, 8, 9, 22, 27, 29, 30, 86, 95, 98, 100, 101, 102, 103, 104, 105, 106, 108, 109, 112, 113, 114, 115, 116, 117, 118, 119, 120, 121, 147, 150, 151, 196, 198, 250, 254, 256, 258, 283, 284, 287, 288, 289, 291, 292, 295, 297, 298, 299, 300, 303, 304, 308, 309, 314, 324, 328, 332, 359, 360, 365, 367, 369, 371, 373, 376, 380

Clausewitz, Karl von, Noel 112

Clayton, Walter Seddon [K/KLOD] 43, 120, 176, 183, 194

Clementis, Vladimir 64

Cockerill, Francis Henry 219

Coleman, Peter xxxi, 194

Conquest, Robert 111, 307, 367, 376

Convery, J. 272

Conway, Izrael 187, 192

Cornford, John 24

Counihan, Noel 27, 153, 154

Coursier, F .R. 154

Courtois, Stephane xxv, 354, 370

Coutts, W.C. 250

Crane, C.J. 169

Crossman, Richard 72, 129

Cusack, Dymphna 194, 196, 197, 198

D

Dalziel, Alan [DENIS] 33, 176, 219, 227, 231, 242, 244, 245, 246, 367

Daniel, Jaroslav 327

Davis, O.L. 331

Dekyvere, Victor 172

Delgado, Roy 154

Dickie, Alt 207

Dimitrov, Giorgi 59

Dixon, Richard. *See* Walker, C.R.; *See* see Walker, C.R.

Doslik, Frank 331

Dozofeev, KGB 225, 234

Dub, Bohuslav 210

Duclos, Jaques 136, 137, 138

Dullas, Allen 60

Durbij, E.F.M. 129

Dutt, Palme 137, 138, 139

E

Easman, Bill xxxi

Ebbels, Robert Noel xxvi, 9, 14, 15, 40, 118, 149, 256, 367

Elias, Rudolf 329

Elliot, Eliot Valens 152, 214, 229, 230, 231, 232, 247, 266, 267, 272

Elliot, George 20, 29

KUCERA. *See* Jandík Miloslav
Kurdiakov, Ivab Fedorovich 223

L

Landale, W.G.A. 229, 319
Lane, William 258
Laski, Harold 126, 127
Lawson, Henry 29, 86, 116, 196, 258, 367
Leggett, G.H. 305, 307
Lenin, Vladmir Ilyich 301
Levchenko, Stanislav 243, 359, 373
Levy, N.I. 214
Lindsey, Bruce 142
Lindsey, Jack 153
Lipinski, Edward 338, 378
Li Sen Cho 67
Lockwood, Rupert 26, 160, 227, 244, 257
Loebl, Eugene 162, 163, 370
Lukacs, John A. 130, 371

M

Machacek, Miloslav 44
Macha, Ladislav 327
Machovec, Milan 285
Macintire, Stuart xxxi, 347, 371, 380
Majskij, Ivan xxviii
Makarov, Semyan Ivanovich [EFIM] 224, 225, 226
Malco, Laurie 223
Manne, Robert 26, 82, 98, 126, 151, 243, 355, 371, 372, 378
Mansfield, Katherine 25
Mao Tse-tung 26, 69, 71, 80, 84, 85, 93, 98, 111, 127, 338, 356
Marshall, Alan 194
Marshall, George C. 132
Maryna, Valentina V. xxviii, 379
Masaryk, Jan xxviii, 184
Masaryk, Tomás Garrigue 36, 115, 285, 304, 311, 372
Maximov, Vladimir 341

McDonald, Geoff 60, 61, 310, 352, 371
McEwan, Keith 142, 355, 371
McGillick, Tony 126, 127, 147, 371
McIsaac, John 309, 310
McNight, David 70, 246, 371
McQueen, Humphrey xxiv, xxxii, 25, 84, 86, 121, 147, 348, 360, 371, 378, 379
Menzies, Sir Robert G. 23, 32
Méray, Tibor 78, 81, 82, 372
Merz, Kurt 164
Michailov, Comrade 31, 310
Mikoyan, Anastas Invanovich 320
Miles, J.B. xxxi, 216, 350
Miller, Gwin 207
Miller, Jamie 76, 78, 363
Miller, J.B. 372
Milner, Ian Frank George [BUR, JAN-SKY] xiii, xiv, xxxii, 3, 5, 8, 10, 17, 22, 31, 34, 37, 39, 42, 44, 45, 46, 48, 99, 119, 121, 126, 147, 153, 216, 288, 291, 292, 332, 360, 372, 375
Milner, Jarmila [HALBICH, JULIE] 14, 22
Milner, John Keith 14
Milner, Linda 8, 14, 22, 46, 363
Milner, Margaret [INES] 43, 44
Milotinsky, MD 330
Mindszenty, József 58
Mlynar, Zdenek 335, 372
Moloney, Valentine 240
Molotov, Vyacheslav Mikhailovich xxviii
Monk, A. 250
Monroe, Marilyn 85
Moravec, Frantisek 100, 132, 372
Morrisby, Edwin 69, 379
Morrow, William Robert 234, 235, 236
Mountbatten, Louis 137
Mountier, Paul Francis 233
Moxon, Bert xxxi, 350